Inequality At Work

INEQUALITY
AT WORK
Hispanics in the U.S. Labor Force

GREGORY DeFREITAS

New York Oxford
OXFORD UNIVERSITY PRESS
1991

Oxford University Press

Oxford New York Toronto
Delhi Bombay Calcutta Madras Karachi
Petaling Jaya Singapore Hong Kong Tokyo
Nairobi Dar es Salaam Cape Town
Melbourne Auckland

and associated companies in
Berlin Ibadan

Copyright © 1991 by Oxford University Press, Inc.

Published by Oxford University Press, Inc.,
200 Madison Avenue, New York, New York 10016

Oxford is a registered trademark of Oxford University Press

Library of Congress Cataloging-in-Publication Data
DeFreitas, Gregory
Inequality at work : Hispanics in the U.S. labor force/
Gregory DeFreitas.
p. cm.
Includes bibliographical references and index.
ISBN 0-19-506421-6
1. Hispanic Americans—Employment.
2. United States—Emigration and immigration—Economic aspects.
I. Title.
HD8081.H7D44 1991 331.6′368073—dc20 91-7283

2 4 6 8 9 7 5 3 1

Printed in the United States of America
on acid-free paper

To my parents,
Carol and Louis DeFreitas

Acknowledgments

In the course of the nearly six years that have elapsed since I first began to work on this subject, I benefited from the ideas, suggestions, and support of so many people that a collective thanks to "those too numerous to mention" seems most appropriate. Preliminary drafts of each chapter were presented at many seminars and conferences, here and abroad, and I am indebted to the helpful comments received from other participants. Most of the research and writing took place during my years on the economics faculties of Barnard College, Columbia University, and Hofstra University, and during a visiting professorship at the University of Toronto. I am grateful to these institutions for their ample computer and library resources, and to the many colleagues and students who provided encouragement and intellectual stimulation. My thanks also to the *Journal of Human Resources; Industrial Relations;* and the Institute for Research on Poverty, University of Wisconsin, for permission to make use of some of my previously published work. Generous financial support was provided at various stages by the Mellon Foundation, the Spencer Foundation, and the U.S. Department of Health and Human Services.

Contents

Tables

Figures

Inequality At Work

1

Introduction

Sometime in the next 25 years, the Hispanic population will surpass blacks as the single largest minority group in the United States. The 22 million persons of Spanish origin in the country by 1990 represented a 53 percent increase since 1980—a growth rate five times the national average. Their higher rates of natural increase and of immigration underlie the Census Bureau's prediction that there will be twice as many Hispanic Americans by the year 2015. As Figure 1.1 shows, from that year on their numbers are expected to exceed the more slowly growing black population by an ever-widening margin.

Even these dramatic national figures cannot fully reflect the local impact on the major urban centers in which much of this population growth is concentrated. In the 10 biggest American cities today, an average of one in every four people is of Spanish origin. In seven of these cities, over 200,000 Hispanics were counted in the 1990 census. Their share of the total city population is 24 percent in New York, 40 percent in Los Angeles, and over 55 percent in both San Antonio and Miami.[1]

Hispanics have an even larger impact on the U.S. labor force than on the overall population. The end of the baby boom in the mid-1960s has resulted in a sharp drop in the youth population, and thus in the potential number of new young workers. The youth component of the labor force is expected to be nearly 3 percentage points lower in the year 2000 than it was in 1988. Over this period the Hispanic labor force is now projected to expand 60 percent. Their share of overall labor force growth will be close to 27 percent. Net immigration, much of it from Spanish-speaking countries, will account for nearly one in every four new labor force participants. Besides youth, the most dynamic factor behind the postwar expansion of the work force has been the rise in female workers. Their numbers will continue to increase through the end of this century. But the phase of most rapid participation growth for white non-Hispanic women has passed. The Census Bureau projects that their share of total labor force growth will decline from 50 percent between 1976 and 1988 to 36 percent between 1988 and 2000.[2] Future increases in the overall female working

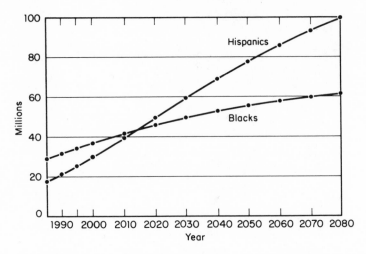

FIGURE 1.1. Hispanics will outnumber Blacks by 2015, if expected fertility, mortality, and immigration trends persist. Sources: U.S. Census Bureau (1986a) and Exter (1987). Projections based on middle-series fertility and mortality and high-series Hispanic immigration assumptions.

population will more and more be driven by the growth in the number of Spanish-origin women.

This book is a study of the employment, unemployment, and economic impacts of Hispanic workers in the United States today. It presents new research findings on how their jobs and earnings have changed over time and relative to non-Hispanics. In attempting to understand these findings, I consider both traditional and alternative economic theories and subject each to various empirical tests with several large data banks.

Five principal themes run throughout the book and serve to unify the diverse strands of the research. First, the postwar employment record of Hispanics appears to divide into two phases: a period of earnings and occupational gains—both in absolute terms and relative to non-Hispanics—through the 1960s, followed by nearly two decades of stagnation and deterioration in their average economic status and rising economic inequality.

The fact that, among Hispanics, the employment experiences of the main national-origin groups have differed markedly represents a second theme. While Cubans approach the white non-Hispanic standard of living, Mexicans and Puerto Ricans remain at a substantial economic disadvantage. One cannot explain the inequality now at work between Hispanics and non-Hispanics without taking into account the continuing inequality among Hispanics.

A third, closely related theme involves the complex but important effects of immigration. For a large part of the nearly one-third of Hispanics born abroad, limited English proficiency appears to significantly hinder their socioeconomic progress. But at the same time, Hispanic immigrants generate long-run economic benefits for the native-born work force large enough to outweigh any short-run costs.

The empirical results of chapter after chapter highlight the fourth theme. While efforts to explain black–white and male–female wage gaps have generally found that educational differences play a significant but relatively modest role, the below average schooling levels of Spanish-origin workers account for a far larger share of their earnings differential with non-Hispanics. Coupled with evidence of continuing high dropout rates and low college enrollment, this strongly suggests that Hispanics will be the group most vulnerable to long-term damage from the ongoing shift in the national wage structure to the detriment of the less skilled.

The last main theme is that the dominant theoretical approach that most economists have relied on to explain inequality is inadequate to the task of understanding the labor market position of Hispanics. Individual workers' job skills and the other supply-side factors stressed by conservative labor economists are clearly of great importance. But the more this research progressed, the more I became convinced that their effects are crucially dependent upon ethnic and class background; changes in the level and composition of labor demand; union coverage and bargaining power; government social, fiscal, and antidiscrimination policies; and other structural forces over which individuals typically have little control. Hence, while I certainly would not claim to have produced a comprehensive study of the Spanish-origin work force, the book is more wide ranging than most in its exploration of those issues selected for analysis.

Few subjects have been as controversial throughout the long history of economics as inequality. Since the early 1970s, a series of hotly contested, overlapping debates have dominated the spotlight. The first of these concerned the income gap between blacks and whites. Some prominent economists contended that a secular narrowing of this gap was underway. Different authors attributed this to either competitive market forces, affirmative action, expanded government transfers, or declines in racial differentials in human capital investment.[3] Critics of this work, while recognizing the advances in combating overt discrimination and in increasing the range of occupations accessible to educated blacks since the mid-1960s, countered that what racial economic progress occurred was a short-term phenomenon. For example, Lazear (1979) held that despite affirmative action's success in lowering racial differentials in entry-level pay, employers systematically channel blacks onto job tracks with few prospects for training, promotions, or rapid earnings growth. Darity and Myers (1980) questioned the observed rise in average black–white wage ratios by emphasizing the sharp increase in the number of blacks without any earnings who dropped out of the labor force from discouragement with their job prospects. After making adjustments to include these individuals, they found that black–white earnings ratios fell between 1968 and 1978. Reich (1981; 1988) disaggregated the national trends into their regional and industrial components. He concluded that most of what improvement there has been in relative earnings is attributable to black migration (from the rural South to higher-wage cities, especially in the North and West) and to the successful political pressures exerted by the civil rights and labor movements, particularly in the early 1940s and the 1960s. Now that the gains from these sources have been largely exhausted, the prospects for future improvements are not bright.

A similar division of opinion has characterized the subsequent debate on the relative economic status of men and women. As the female–male earnings ratio began to increase slowly in the early 1980s for the first time in decades, some cited this as evidence that women had expanded their human capital relative to men and that sex discrimination was falling.[4] But others have argued that this ignores women's consistently slower on-the-job wage growth over the course of their careers as well as chronic occupational sex segregation.[5] Furthermore, most empirical studies find that over one-half of the earnings gap is unexplained by productivity differentials, thereby demonstrating the continuing severity of labor market discrimination.[6]

More recently, both economists and politicians have been arguing over broader national trends toward slower earnings growth and increased earnings inequality since the early 1970s. From 1948 to 1973, real hourly wages rose an average of 3 percent each year. But since then, they have fallen by almost 9 percent. A typical 30-year-old male in 1959 experienced a 49 percent increase in his annual real earnings by 1973. Yet the average 30-year-old in 1973 would experience a 1 percent earnings decline over the next decade. The evidence is strong that skill differentials have been increasing over at least the last decade within major demographic, occupational, and industrial groups, as well as among full-time workers.[7] The largest relative wage losses have hit those already in the bottom half of the earnings distribution.[8] Between 1959 and 1986, the average real wage of young men plummeted 26 percent among high school dropouts and 9 percent among those with no more than a high school degree, but rose 6 percent among college graduates.

The same period has seen a secular rise in the average unemployment rate and a widening gap between skill groups. From 1948 to 1973, the average civilian unemployment rate was only 4.8 percent. It rose to an average of 6.8 percent between 1973 and 1980, and then to 7.8 percent between 1980 and 1987. The double-digit rate reached in late 1982 was the highest recorded since the Great Depression. The less skilled have again been hardest hit: from 1974 to 1988 the unemployment rate of male high school dropouts more than doubled, while the rate for college graduates remained at a constant 1.5 percent.[9]

Controversy has swirled around the causal importance to these trends of demographic changes like the baby boom and rising female labor force participation, structural shifts toward unstable low-paying service jobs, the slowdown in productivity growth, intensified international competition, and the tax and budget changes of the 1980s.[10] However, these debates have long raged with little, if any, reference to the fastest growing low-wage, high unemployment group in the country—Hispanics. Not only is there surprisingly little economic research on the causes and national implications of their current employment problems, but we lack even the most basic historical knowledge of how their economic status has changed relative to non-Hispanics over the postwar period.

One reason for this has no doubt been the government's highly fragmentary data collection on the Hispanic labor force. While detailed wage and employment tabulations by race and sex have been published on a monthly, quarterly, and annual basis for many decades, not until 1974 did similar figures become available on a regular basis for "persons of Spanish origin." Up to that time the sole source of national information on them had been the decennial census. But with every census the criteria used to categorize respondents by ethnicity in published tabulations was substantially altered. As a result, cross-year comparisons of the sort commonly made in economic studies of male–female and black–white differentials seemed infeasible for Hispanics. This problem was compounded further by Hispanics' markedly heterogeneous mixture of national-origin groups and distinctive geographical distribution in the United States. With most Hispanics concentrated in the Southwest, New York, and Florida, any national comparisons of Hispanics' wages and unemployment with those of non-Hispanics risked mistaking regional labor market variations for ethnic group differences.

However, the Census Bureau recently released a large new computer file of raw data from the 1950 census that includes updated information identifying respondents according to the 1980 definition of "persons of Spanish surname." Together with the other information on country of origin and Puerto Rican descent in this and each subsequent census, the new file has made it possible for a researcher to construct from the raw data Hispanic samples defined according to a consistent set of criteria. This book starts by providing, for the first time, income and employment statistics from 1950 through 1980 for the Hispanic population. Applying a consistent definition of Hispanics to the raw data from these four census years enables us to trace the main postwar patterns in their economic status and to contrast them with those of non-Hispanics. In each year, comparisons are made with non-Hispanic men and women living in the same regions in which Hispanics are most concentrated, thereby avoiding the biases otherwise created by their different geographical distributions. In addition to investigating these long-run patterns, I examined year-to-year changes with the annual government data on Hispanics in the Current Population Survey, which has been available since the early 1970s.

Mexicans, Puerto Ricans, Cubans, Central Americans, South Americans, and other Hispanics share important linguistic, cultural, religious, and other features common to most people of Spanish descent. But anyone who, like the author, was raised in southern California and who has lived most of his adult life in Manhattan could not fail to appreciate the rich differentiation among these groups. Intergroup variations extend from their accents and food preferences to sociopolitical and economic characteristics. For example, the very term "Hispanic" is far less common among Mexicans in the West, where "Latino" is more often heard, than in the Northeast. In the interest of consistency with standard official terminology, I use the former term throughout this book. "Spanish origin" is used specifically to refer to those so identified by the Census Bureau definition adopted in the 1970s. Obviously, the non-Hispanic population is also highly heterogeneous. In almost all stages of the empirical work, I present separate empirical results for non-Hispanic blacks and whites (sometimes referred to as "Anglos" for the sake of brevity, though it is understood that non-Anglos are increasingly numerous among whites). But the substantial ethnic and class distinctions within each of these reference groups must be kept in mind when interpreting the findings presented here.

The book is organized as follows. Chapter 2 opens with a historical overview of the evolution of each of the main Hispanic subgroups in the United States. Beginning with the Mexican settlements of the nineteenth century, the key migratory

movements are traced up to the present and the latest research findings on the
demographic and economic characteristics of the most recent immigrant groups are
reviewed.

The following chapter presents a detailed statistical analysis of the principal
trends in Hispanic incomes, unemployment, and poverty from the 1940s through
the 1980s. The findings from census microdata demonstrate that a marked improvement occurred in the relative earnings levels of Hispanics during the 1960s. Since
then, however, most Hispanics have seen a widening gap between themselves and
non-Hispanics. By the late seventies, Hispanic men had an average earnings level
over one-third lower than that of non-Hispanic whites, and the ratio continued to fall
in the 1980s. These reversals have involved not only a drop in the relative economic
status of Hispanic families, but a decline in their standard of living as well. Between
1973 and 1987, their median family income fell (by 9.8 percent, after adjustment
for inflation). The percentage with middle-class incomes ($25,000–50,000 per
year) decreased (by 20 percent) and the percentage below the poverty line increased
(from 19.8 to 25.5 percent). Two out of every five Hispanic children now live in
poverty. The chapter concludes with a lengthy evaluation of a number of possible
explanations for these trends, including deficiencies in schooling and language
skills, migrant adjustment problems, shifts in labor demand and supply, the decline
in unionization, and discrimination.

The next two chapters investigate the factors underlying Hispanics' above average unemployment. Chapter 4 begins by exploring the implications of recent debates in the economic literature on unemployment for an understanding of minority
joblessness. The traditional neoclassical position and the Keynesian critique are
considered, as well as the dual labor market, rational expectations, neo-Keynesia,
human capital, efficiency-wage, and structural models. The next section is an econometric study of cyclical fluctuations in unemployment and labor force participation. The quarterly data on Hispanic workers contained in the Current Population
Survey since 1973 is exploited here to produce the first time-series analysis comparing the impact of recessions and expansions on the employment of white, black, and
Hispanic youth and adults.

Chapter 5 is a cross-sectional study of the differences in unemployment among
the major national-origin groups, and between them and non-Hispanic whites. A
special nationwide government survey (the Survey of Income and Education) made
possible detailed comparisons of intergroup differentials in the incidence and duration of all spells of joblessness experienced during a one-year period.

A growing number of social scientists, impressed by the self-employment experiences of earlier immigrants, have come to view small business formation as a
promising means for disadvantaged groups to create more jobs and to accelerate
their income growth. The sheer numbers of Hispanic consumers today would seem
to offer especially strong market opportunities for new entrepreneurs. Chapter 6
explores the changes in the self-employment patterns of whites, blacks, and Hispanics since 1970 and then evaluates the factors that explain differences in the
likelihood of individuals setting up their own business.

One factor shown to be consistently important to Hispanics' income and employment in chapters 3 through 6 is their below average educational attainment.

Hispanic youth have the highest school dropout rate in the country, twice that of blacks and three times the white rate. Chapter 7 investigates the changes in relative schooling levels in recent years and uses a large 1980 census data set to examine the principal determinants of ethnic differences in enrollment and graduation rates.

Finally, the impact of Hispanic immigration on the U.S. population is the subject of chapter 8. Recent changes in the magnitudes of both legal and illegal entry are examined, as well as research on the first few years of the 1986 employer sanctions and amnesty program. The empirical analysis then addresses two central issues. First, what are the effects of the foreign born on income transfers and other government programs? And second, do immigrants lower the wages or employment of native-born workers?

NOTES

1. U.S. Bureau of the Census, unpublished preliminary tabulations from 1990 Census.

2. All estimates from U.S. Bureau of Labor Statistics' projections in Fullerton (1989). Note that the increase in legal immigration authorized by the 1990 overhaul of the U.S. immigration system could produce even faster growth in the Hispanic American population.

3. See in particular the studies by Butler and Heckman (1977); Freeman (1973); and Smith and Welch (1977, 1986, 1989).

4. See, for example, Beller (1979) and O'Neill (1985).

5. See, for example, Brown and Pechman (1987) and England (1982).

6. See the surveys by Lloyd and Niemi (1979) and Blau and Ferber (1987).

7. See, for example, Bell and Freeman (1987) and Dooley and Gottschalk (1984).

8. Levy and Michel (1986).

9. See Freeman (1989) and Howe (1988).

10. See, for example, Blackburn, et al. (1989); Burtless (1989); and Juhn, et al. (1989).

2

The Emergence of the Hispanic American Labor Force

By almost every measure of socioeconomic well-being, the Spanish-origin population of the United States is today at a considerable disadvantage relative to non-Hispanic whites. The statistical overview in Table 2.1 shows that in the late 1980s, the average Hispanic family had an income ($20,306) over one-third lower than non-Hispanic whites. One in every four Hispanic families was below the official government poverty line, compared with only 8.2 percent of whites. Despite a nearly identical labor force participation rate, Spanish-origin workers were less than half as likely as non-Hispanic whites to hold managerial or professional jobs and nearly twice as likely to be unemployed.

Among the factors often thought to underly such disparities are differences in age, schooling, family composition, migration, and language ability. Hispanics, with a median age of 25, are younger than non-Hispanic whites and blacks by an average of eight years and two years, respectively. Among adults ages 25 and older, 77 percent of non-Hispanic whites and 63 percent of blacks have completed high school, but only one-half of Hispanics. The latter are also the least likely to be college graduates. Families headed by a person of Spanish origin are twice as likely as whites to be stretching their incomes over five or more members, and nearly twice as likely to be female-headed. Finally, nearly three-tenths of Hispanics were born outside the continental United States, and 31 percent of these have only been in the country five years or less (Table 2.2). This is reflected in the fact that, in response to a 1980 census question, only one in five Hispanics said English was their sole language and only three in five were very fluent in English.

Among Hispanics, there are marked differences among the various national-origin groups. Mexicans are by far the most numerous, accounting for 62.6 percent of the total. Puerto Ricans represent another 12.2 percent, followed by Central and South Americans (11.4 percent), the other Hispanic category (8.4 percent), and

Cubans (5.4 percent).[1] Despite gradual geographic dispersion over time, Mexicans, Central Americans, and other Hispanics remain largely concentrated in the Southwest, Puerto Ricans and most South Americans in New York and a few other northeastern cities, and Cubans in south Florida.

The two largest groups are also the most disadvantaged: they have lower median incomes and higher unemployment and poverty rates than all others of Spanish origin. At $15,185, Puerto Ricans' median family income is less than half that of non-Hispanic whites and almost $3,000 below the black average. Some 38 percent of Puerto Rican families live under the poverty line, a rate over four and one-half times that of whites and 8 percentage points higher than that of blacks.

At the other extreme, Cubans have an average family income that is one-third above the all-Hispanic median and less than $3,000 short of the non-Hispanic white level. Cuban workers' average earnings are also well above the average, as is the percentage employed in professional or managerial occupations. Their poverty rate is by far the lowest of all Hispanic ethnic groups and the fraction unemployed is almost identical to the non-Hispanic white rate.

This chapter aims to provide the historical perspective necessary to an understanding of these current patterns. It briefly traces the historical emergence of the principal ethnic subgroups of the Spanish-origin work force. Each section ends with a review of the latest research findings on the economic characteristics of each group's recent immigrants.

Mexican Americans

The origins of the Mexican American population are woven inextricably into the political and economic history of the American Southwest. Until the middle of the nineteenth century, this region was the northern tier of Mexico, a newly independent nation sharing the same continent with the United States but little else. Both began as European colonies, but the early American economy was shaped by England, when it was the most advanced industrial and commercial power of the age, while Spain was still a backward mercantilist colonizer stressing resource and labor exploitation at the expense of local economic development. Mexico was further disadvantaged by the fact that it did not gain independence from Spain until nearly a half century after U.S. independence, and at far greater human cost (500,000 deaths, an estimated one-tenth of its population). In the century following independence, 1821–1920, Mexico was repeatedly the victim of military invasion, at an average rate of about once every decade. The most costly of these came from the United States. First, a series of armed expeditions, often encouraged by Washington, led to the secession of Texas from Mexico in 1836. Then in 1846, one year after annexing Texas, President James Polk exploited a minor incident as a pretext to start a full-scale war. The Mexican War ended with the Treaty of Guadalupe Hidalgo (known to generations of Mexican historians as "the amputation of 1848"), which stripped the country of nearly one-half of its national territory: the area that would become Arizona, California, New Mexico, and large parts of Colorado, Nevada, and Utah. Although the treaty included guarantees from the victor to protect the civil, cultural, language, and property rights of the 80,000 to 100,000 Mexicans who stayed on in

TABLE 2.1. Selected Social and Economic Characteristics of Whites, Blacks, and Hispanics,[a] March 1988

	White	Black	All Hispanic	Mexican	Puerto Rican	Cuban	Other Latin American	Other Hispanic
POPULATION (000's)	205,233	29,847	19,431	12,110	2,471	1,035	2,242	1,573
AGE								
Median	33.0	27.2	25.5	23.9	24.9	38.7	27.6	29.7
16–24 (%)	13.9	15.6	17.0	17.8	16.7	12.9	18.4	13.4
YEARS OF SCHOOLING COMPLETED[b]								
Median	12.7	12.4	12.0	10.8	12.0	12.4	12.4	12.4
12 or more (%)	78.4	64.6	50.9	44.6	50.7	60.5	63.8	65.2
16 or more (%)	20.5	10.7	10.0	7.1	9.6	17.2	16.5	14.0
LABOR FORCE STATUS[c]								
In civilian labor force (%)	65.5	62.8	65.5	67.0	53.2	65.3	72.4	62.6
Unemployed (%)	5.0	12.8	8.5	9.8	9.2	3.1	4.8	9.2
Profsnl. or Manager (%)	26.6	16.0	14.1	11.2	17.4	25.2	13.0	23.4
MEDIAN EARNINGS[d]								
Males	$21,348	14,344	13,599	11,791	15,672	16,634	13,105	15,574
Females	$11,105	10,984	9,188	7,912	11,327	11,364	8,056	11,239
FAMILY INCOME[e]								
Median	$32,274	18,098	20,306	19,968	15,185	27,294	22,939	21,196
Below Poverty Level (%)	8.2	29.9	25.8	25.5	37.9	13.8	18.9	26.1
FAMILY TYPE								
5 or more persons (%)	12.9	19.6	25.7	31.6	16.4	34.4	25.5	13.7
Female head, no husband present (%)	12.9	42.8	23.4	18.5	44.0	16.1	24.4	26.1

[a]Persons of Spanish origin may be of any race.

[b]Persons 25 years old and over.

[c]Civilian population 16 years old and over. Managerial and professional employees expressed as percentage of employed persons.

[d]Annual wages and salaries of civilian workers 15 and over in 1987.

[e]Income and poverty figures for the calendar year 1987.

SOURCE: U.S. Bureau of the Census (1989a; 1989b).

TABLE 2.2. Migration and Language Characteristics of Persons by Race
and Type of Spanish Origin, 1980

	White	*Black*	*All Hispanic*	*Mexican*	*Puerto Rican*	*Cuban*	*Other Hispanic*
ALL PERSONS							
Foreign Born (%)[a]	3.8	2.8	28.6	26.0	48.6	77.9	39.4
Living Abroad in 1975 (%)	1.0	1.1	8.8	7.4	10.2	5.6	12.5
PERSONS 16 YEARS OLD AND OVER							
Fluency in English (%)							
Speak only English	93.1	96.1	19.7	19.5	11.4	7.3	29.3
Speak very well	5.0	2.6	38.0	39.6	41.0	41.4	30.9
Speak well	1.3	0.9	21.1	20.8	27.0	22.7	17.9
Speak poorly or not at all	0.5	0.3	21.2	20.1	20.7	28.6	22.0

[a]Note: In the case of Puerto Ricans those born on the island are here listed as "foreign born" (though they are U.S. citizens).

SOURCE: U.S. Bureau of the Census (1984b: U.S. Summary Vol.) and 1980 Public Use Microdata.

the region, there is ample historical evidence of widespread, often brutal violations of these little-enforced provisions in the years that followed.[2]

If one looked solely at official immigration statistics, it would appear that significant Mexican migration into the Southwest began only in the 1920s. But that simply reflects the fact that port-of-entry stations were not established until 1894 and that the only Mexicans officially counted as "immigrants" before 1908 were the small numbers arriving at U.S. seaports. The actual growth of the region's Mexican–origin population can perhaps be most clearly understood by distinguishing five main phases: the "open door" period (1848–1916); the selective screening period (1917–1929); the "Great Repatriation" (1930–1941); the *bracero* program (1942–1964); and the modern period, years of quotas and economic crisis (1965–1990).

1848–1916

The same year that Mexico lost its northern states also saw the beginning of migration to the United States by Mexican workers. The California Gold Rush of 1848 drew some 20,000 northward in the next two years, most from the silver regions of Sonora and Zacatecas.[3] After 1850, Mexican miners also found work in the mines of Nevada, southern Arizona, and Colorado.

Following the Civil War, a number of developments occurred with fundamental importance for the emergence of mass migration. In Mexico, the land policies of the Porfirio Diaz dictatorship (1876–1911) opened the way for speculators and foreign interests to acquire millions of hectares of farm and pastoral lands, including communal peasant holdings. By the turn of the century, about 90 percent of the land was controlled by only 5 percent of the families, and the large landless population thereby created was forced to find new means of survival.[4]

The size of the population grew at an unprecedented rate in these same years, jumping from 9 million in 1876 to 15 million by 1910. However, it was concentrated far from the northern border; while the population density in 1890 averaged about 90 persons per square mile in the central region, it was below 3 in the big semidesert border state of Sonora.[5] But in the 1880s, American companies began developing mines in Sonora and paid high wages to attract a labor force. Both Mexicans from the interior and Americans from Arizona responded, and a two-way population movement emerged between Arizona towns like Tucson, Tombstone, and Douglas and Sonoran towns and rancherias. This movement was greatly accelerated by completion of the U.S. campaign to forcibly evict the last Native American Indian tribes active in the Southwest and by construction of the first cross-border railroads. In 1884, Mexico City was linked to El Paso, and through that rail hub to Los Angeles and the Midwest. By the end of the decade, American labor agents were active in such recruiting centers as El Paso and Laredo organizing migrant work forces needed to pick cotton, clear land for farms and pastures, and build and maintain the new railroads. Seasonal labor was thus already quite common throughout the region when the first systematic study of Mexican migration was made for the U.S. Department of Labor in 1908. As the report observed:

> The Mexicans who cross the border to work are either making their first trip to the United States or are making a second or third seasonal visit from the interior of Mexico or are of that big class of American-Mexican frontier residents who reside intermittently in either country. These last are apt to travel widely or work regularly, except during cotton-picking time in Texas and in Oklahoma; their migratory habits are not of recent origin and they are not vacating old industries in Mexico to enter new occupations in the United States.[6]

The growth of the Mexican migrant population was made possible by the "open door" immigration policy of the federal government throughout the nineteenth century. Aside from the Alien and Sedition Acts of 1798 (repealed in 1800), immigration into the United States was unrestricted for most of the nation's first century.[7] Selective screening began only in 1875 with a statute banning immigration by convicts and prostitutes. In 1882 the first general immigration law was enacted. It imposed a head tax (50 cents) on each immigrant and added to the list of proscribed entrants the insane and others likely to become public charges. In the spring of that year, Congress approved the Chinese Exclusion Acts, culminating years of increasingly violent nativist hostility and discrimination against Chinese immigrants in California. Besides prejudice against their non-European customs and religions, this legislation reflected the fact that, after their early period of employment largely in mining and railroad construction, the Chinese tended to settle in towns and cities where natives came to see them as competitors for jobs. Also, like the later Japanese immigrants (whose entry would be curtailed by a 1907–08 bilateral "gentlemen's agreement"), their efforts to buy property and become self-employed put them in competition with powerful business interests. Although Mexicans were also victimized by discrimination and were resented by some native workers, they remained far more rural, short-term migrants, and demand for them rose as employers in agriculture lost their Asian work forces.

1990

d of the *bracero* program coincided with the beginning of a new American
ation system. In 1965, Congress, under pressure from the Civil Rights
ent and the booming economy's demand for labor, abolished the racist
l-origins quotas in favor of a new set of criteria stressing family reunifica-
nce the system went fully into effect in 1968, permanent residence status has
anted according to a set of seven preference categories so designed that about
f 10 places have gone to relatives of U.S. residents, the residual divided
n refugees and the small number admitted on occupational grounds. Annual
were established for the Eastern (170,000) and Western (120,000) Hemi-
, as well as annual numeric quotas of 20,000 per country from the Eastern
here. But the exemption of immediate relatives of U.S. citizens and of many
l refugees from these limits has enabled annual inflows to far exceed the
290,000 ceiling. The result has been not only an additional 100,000 or
gal entrants per year but also a dramatic compositional change: as Table 2.3
the proportion from Europe declined from 59 percent of those arriving in the
o only 18 percent of entrants in the 1970s, while the Asian share leapt from
cent to 36 percent and the Latin American percentage from 22 to 40.
all the countries in the world, Mexico has consistently sent the largest
of immigrants here since 1965. Over 443,000 were admitted legally in the
another 637,000 in the 1970s, and more have entered from that one country
980s than from all the European nations combined (Table 2.3). This was for
hought to reflect the exemption of Western Hemisphere nations from the
per-country maximum. But new legislation extended this same quota to the
Hemisphere in 1977. The immediate result was a drop in the number of
trants from Mexico of 24 percent from the year before. Nevertheless, 44,600
immigrants were admitted in 1977 and the following year over 90,000
ted—the highest number of any postwar year. The principal reason for this
is that, while many workers from Mexico return home after only a few
nployment in the United States, enough settled here over the long history of
ration to have created a large resident population by the 1960s. The 1960
ounted 575,902 U.S. residents who were born in Mexico and over twice as
hers (1,160,090) with one or both parents born there. Ten years later, these
had risen to 759,711 and 1,579,440.[17] The 1965 legal changes thus made
the entry of large numbers on the nonquota visas set aside for reunification
diate family members.
the supply of visas fell far short of the demand and thousands continued to
thout legal documents. A large number were former participants in the
program denied readmission after the program ended. In the course of the
's more than two decades, involving 4.5 million participants, information
pportunities in the United States and on the easiest methods to enter and find
been widely disseminated in Mexico, stimulating increased illegal migra-
rder apprehensions rose from 55,349 in 1965 to over a million per year in
1970s.
the recent patterns of legal and illegal immigration cannot be explained

Two legislative changes that had the potential to begin limiting entry from
Mexico occurred in 1885 and 1891. The former year saw passage of the Alien
Contract Labor Law, banning direct contracting of alien workers by American
employers. While congressional advocates claimed it would assuage the rising fears
of some indigenous workers that immigrants were taking jobs from them and
driving down wage levels, it was enforced with great discretion and with negligible
effect on Mexicans. Part of the reason for this was a loophole in the law: a violation
was said to occur only when a migrant arrived at the border with a prearranged U.S.
employment contract. American employers simply instructed their labor agents to
wait until migrants had stepped over the border before signing them up for work.
Also, until 1891, enforcement of immigration law was left to individual states. That
year the federal government assigned this responsibility to a new Bureau of Immigration (initially set up within the Treasury Department). The enabling legislation
also provided for regulation of overland immigration from Mexico and Canada. It
was not, however, Mexicans that were to be kept out but rather any Chinese or other
proscribed groups trying to circumvent the tighter inspections at seaports. The
1,945-mile border with Mexico remained largely unguarded until 1924, when the
small mounted patrol (never more than 75 men) active since 1904 was replaced by a
new U.S. Border Patrol (initially 450 men, their numbers doubled by 1930).[8]

1917–1929

At the beginning of this century, the Rio Grande was still an open border for the
Mexican workers moving back and forth across it regularly. In 1908, the first year in
which border posts were authorized to make full counts of overland migration,
6,067 Mexican immigrants were recorded.[9] But by 1917 three times as many
migrants were arriving and the 1920s saw an average of over 72,000 per year. One
reason for this growth was no doubt the increased refugee outflows caused by the
turmoil of the Mexican Revolution of 1910–1917. But the dominant forces were
those on the demand side. This period saw especially rapid economic growth in the
Southwest with the completion of huge irrigation systems. The need for large
numbers of laborers to work the millions of acres of new farmland was made all the
more urgent by the onset of World War I. The United States' entry into the war in
1917 drew millions of rural workers into uniform or into the generally more skilled,
higher-paying jobs in defense plants. The resulting labor shortage seemed likely to
worsen due to a law passed that same year requiring prospective immigrants to pass
a literacy test and pay an eight-dollar entry tax before admission could be granted.
However, President Wilson not only had this waived for Mexican immigrants but
authorized an "Emergency Labor Program" in which the U.S. Employment Service
itself acted as a labor contractor to recruit more such workers.

Mexico was also exempted (along with other Western Hemisphere nations) from
the ethnocentric national origins quota system created by the immigration acts of
1921 and 1924. This system, which was to remain in place for the next 40 years,
was designed to cut the high volume of Southern and Eastern European entrants.
Migration of workers from Mexico was thus able to fill many of the new unskilled
jobs in the Southwest generated by the 1920s boom.[10] Mexican migration jumped

from just over 91,000 in 1915–1919 to 255,774 in the first half of the twenties, and another 498,945 entrants were recorded between 1925 and 1929.[11]

This period marked the beginning of two trends that were to become increasingly important in later years. First, the wartime labor shortage opened a wider spectrum of jobs for Mexican workers (as for women and blacks). Significant numbers were for the first time in demand by such manufacturing industries as auto, food-processing, iron, and steel. Such jobs both introduced them to new sectors of the American labor market and began to disperse the Mexican population beyond the rural border areas into other states and cities.[12] The higher earnings offered farther inland, especially in industry, were of course a key motivating factor behind this transition. In 1920, real hourly wages (valued in 1967 U.S. dollars) in Mexico averaged only about 20 to 25 cents in agriculture and 50 to 75 cents in industry (factories, mines, railroads), while the average industrial wage in the United States was three to four dollars.[13]

In addition, the distinction between "legal" and "illegal" immigration only began to gain currency at this time. The tightening of immigration restrictions in 1917–1924 made the formerly straightforward act of immigration a cumbersome process demanding birth certificates, evidence of good mental and physical health, proof that one would not become a public charge, visa fees, and entry taxes. For the poor, illiterate peasants long accustomed to free movement into the territories of the Mexican Cession, these new requirements might well have seemed unnecessary administrative interference. Up to this time the border was little more than an imaginary line through a unified Mexican–Anglo economy in which the migrant work force had become incorporated as a vital component. The repeated ad hoc exemptions of Mexicans in past immigration policy no doubt stemmed from an awareness of their importance. After its enormous investment, both military and economic (particularly the massive federal land grants to the new railroads), in the region, Washington viewed business access to a low-wage labor reserve as crucial to profitable business expansion in the Southwest.[14] The government was also certainly not unaware of the fact that, in the 1920s, nearly all American foreign investments were in either Mexico, Canada, or Cuba. Good relations were especially important with revolutionary Mexico because it posed the greatest potential danger of nationalization of American-owned oil fields, mines, and ranches.

1929–1941

With the onset of the Great Depression, the border gates swung shut. Rather than seek a legislative quota for Mexican admissions, the State Department simply used its administrative powers to tighten visa standards. In addition, in 1929 the Registry Act was passed, which for the first time made illegal immigration by an individual a misdemeanor, punishable by up to one year in prison and a maximum fine of $1,000.

As the unemployment rate continued surging upward, both federal and local officials sought to slash the number of immigrants still in the United States. What followed was the controversial "Mexican Repatriation" of the early 1930s. This appears to have occurred in two main phases. Late 1929 to mid-1931 was a period

of largely voluntary return migration by about 200,000 re[...]
work, of whom three-fourths relied entirely on their own r[...]
by Mexican mutual-aid societies and Mexico's consular fo[...]
1931 on, the deepening depression led overburdened state[...]
significant relief aid from the government of President H[...]
various subsidies (e.g., small cash grants, rail tickets, foo[...]
home) to aliens who would return to Mexico. The fed[...]
contribution was to announce a stepped-up deportation [...]
ported relatively few but probably frightened many thous[...]
own. An estimated one-half million returned to Mexico in[...]
138,519 leaving at the peak in 1931.[15]

1942–1964

United States entry into the Second World War at the e[...]
process with remarkable speed. Another labor shortage o[...]
reasons as in 1917–18, but was intensified by the govern[...]
force 100,000 Japanese and Japanese Americans into co[...]
mounting pressure from southwestern business, Preside[...]
August, 1942, signed a bilateral agreement with Mexi[...]
wartime program of importing labor. This was known as [...]
the Spanish for "working hand"). It recruited 52,000 w[...]
for crop harvesting and the rest for railway maintenance[...]
stipulated that those in the program were to be given [...]
ployment protections as Americans in comparable jo[...]
relied largely on "self-policing"; abuses appear to have b[...]
less, and despite mounting opposition by organized labor[...]
after the war. As the economy began its extraordinary [...]
was to produce a doubling of real GNP between 1946 [...]
lobbied hard for a continued supply of low-wage mig[...]
market tightened after the war (the annual civilian unen[...]
percent from 1943 to 1948) and employers sought to [...]
braceros as long as possible. One avenue many follo[...]
Immigration and Naturalization Service adjust their m[...]
temporary braceros to permanent resident immigrants. [...]
nent migrants become in a receiving country the more [...]
families join them. In this way the bracero program e[...]
entry from Mexico. It stimulated increased illegal en[...]
granted legal status for themselves or their relatives b[...]
Naturalization Service (INS) were often encouraged [...]
surreptitiously. In addition, since many more job-seek[...]
recruitment stations (concentrated near the border) than[...]
candidates often joined the illegal influx. Before its den[...]
program was importing over 400,000 per year at its pea[...]
its 23 years the number of persons apprehended fo[...]
exceeded the number of legal bracero entrants.[16]

1965–

The e[...]
immig[...]
move[...]
nation[...]
tion. [...]
been g[...]
9 out [...]
betwe[...]
limits [...]
sphere[...]
Hemis[...]
politic[...]
nomin[...]
more [...]
shows [...]
1950s [...]
6.2 pe[...]
Of [...]
numbe[...]
1960s, [...]
in the [...]
a time [...]
20,000[...]
Wester[...]
legal e[...]
Mexica[...]
immig[...]
increas[...]
years e[...]
this mi[...]
census[...]
many [...]
numbe[...]
possibl[...]
of imm[...]
Sti[...]
enter v[...]
bracer[...]
progra[...]
on job[...]
work h[...]
tion. B[...]
the late[...]
But [...]

TABLE 2.3. Immigrants Admitted to the U.S.,
1961–88, by Region and Country of Origin
(in thousands)

Place of Origin	1961–70	1971–80	1981–88
All Countries	3,321.7	4,493.3	4,710.6
Europe	1,238.6	801.3	510.3
Asia	445.3	1,633.8	2,166.7
Central America	97.7	132.4	211.5
El Salvador	15.0	34.4	76.6
Guatemala	15.4	25.6	36.5
Panama	18.4	22.7	22.2
Nicaragua	10.1	13.0	23.7
South America	228.3	284.4	311.3
Colombia	70.3	77.6	85.0
Ecuador	37.0	50.2	36.1
Peru	18.6	29.1	38.5
Argentina	42.1	25.1	16.9
Cuba	256.8	276.8	138.5
Dominican Republic	94.1	148.0	182.8
Mexico	443.3	637.2	569.1

SOURCE: U.S. Immigration and Naturalization Service (1988; 1989a).

independently of labor supply conditions in Mexico. Like the United States, Mexico experienced a remarkable period of economic growth between World War II and the mid-sixties. The rate of growth in real Gross Domestic Product (GDP) averaged an impressive 6 percent annually in the 1940s. During the years of "stabilizing development" from 1954 to 1971, average annual real GDP growth was 6 to 8 percent and inflation was held to an average rate below 5 percent. Industrial output jumped fivefold between 1940 and 1965. Significant progress was also recorded in education and health. The percentage of the population (ages six and over) who were illiterate fell from 58.3 percent in 1940 to 28.3 percent in 1970. Average life expectancy at birth rose from only 38.9 years to 60.2 between 1940 and 1970. And the falling mortality rate helped the population more than double in size, from 19.6 million in 1940 to 42 million just a quarter century later.[18]

However, the postwar development strategy also produced severe structural problems and greater income inequality, as was to become painfully evident in the spiraling economic crises of the 1970s and 1980s. Successive governments relied heavily on attracting foreign investment, which nearly doubled in volume (in U.S. dollars) in the course of the 1950s and then nearly tripled in the sixties. Over 70 percent of the investment was from a single country, the United States, and U.S.-based companies had by 1970 acquired control of over 50 percent of such key industries as aluminum, automobiles, computers, electrical machinery, industrial chemicals, mining, and pharmaceuticals.[19] Of the country's biggest 100 industrial firms, 47 were foreign owned. From the revenue earned in their Mexican operations, the outflow of their payments to foreign investors was, on average, three to four times larger than the profits reinvested in Mexico.[20] The strong preference of these firms for importing new capital for their plants accounted for an estimated one-third of the country's widening trade deficit in the 1970s. The concentration of agricultural investments in export-oriented crops at the expense of corn and other mass subsistence crops led to sharply rising agricultural imports, which actually exceeded the value of agricultural exports by the early 1980s.[21] The nation's trade deficit in 1980 was four times its 1970 level and growing.

Since much of the postwar investment boom was directed at capital-intensive rather than labor-intensive industries, employment and wage benefits were relatively slim for the bulk of the population. This was especially dramatic in agriculture, where employment dropped by 900,000 in the 1960s, despite the continuing increase in the rural population. Among those with jobs, the all-industry real wage was cut in half between 1939 and 1946 and rose so slowly thereafter that it did not reach the 1939 level again until 1968. The far more rapid increases in returns to capital had the effect of worsening the already severe inequality of income. In 1950 the richest 10 percent of families received 49 percent of all family income, the poorest 10 percent only 2.7 percent.[22] But by 1969 the top decile had increased its share still more to 51 percent as that of the bottom decile shrank to 2 percent. In fact, the richest 5 percent captured a share (36 percent) of income that year that was more than twice as large as the shares of the bottom 50 percent of families combined. The expanded stock of educational and health care services were also distributed in a sharply skewed manner, both regionally and socioeconomically, greatly favoring urban middle- and upper-class families.[23]

The impetus for emigration provided by these trends was greatly intensified by the U.S. recession of 1973–75. It was to be expected that Mexico, by now tightly integrated with the American economy, would be adversely affected. But this proved to be the beginning of a crisis of startling depth and duration. A massive wage of bankruptcies and capital flight forced the Mexican government to seek foreign financial aid. Under pressure from the International Monetary Fund, it adopted an austerity program and devalued the peso by almost 100 percent late in 1976. This in turn nearly doubled import costs and the real value of the foreign debt, as well as slashing the purchasing power of personal incomes. Salaried workers watched their real earnings plummet 36 percent between 1978 and 1980, and the mass of nonunionized private sector laborers unprotected by wage indexation programs suffered even more.[24] The underemployment rate climbed to an estimated 50.3 percent of the labor force.[25] According to the World Bank measure of poverty-level income, more than one out of every three Mexican families were poor in 1977.

Despite some recovery in GDP growth rates from expanded oil production in the late seventies, the "economic crisis" had, by the early eighties, deteriorated into a "national emergency." The onset of a steep fall in world oil prices, rising interest rates, and a severe American recession in 1982 pushed Mexico into its worst depression since the 1930s. Nearly 1 million lost their jobs and the inflation rate topped 100 percent. When, in August 1982, the Lopez Portillo administration revealed that it was unable to meet payments due on the $66 billion public debt for at least three months, a worldwide financial crisis was threatened. The $10 billion international bailout that followed saved the banking industry but still left the nation deeply in debt, its export earnings mortgaged long into the future. The three peso devaluations that year completed a 10-fold decline in its exchange value with the dollar since 1976. What this meant for workers and the unemployed was that the purchasing power of their peso incomes was dropping at the same time that the relative value of the dollars that could be earned north of the border increased.

In the United States, the public concern about undocumented immigration that had been growing since the mid-seventies was intensified by reports by the U.S. Immigration and Naturalization Service of a surge in illegal entrants from Mexico during the 1982 crisis. With the unemployment rate at a postwar high, the argument (heard in every recession of at least the last century) that new immigrants were depressing natives' wages and job opportunities won new popularity. A lengthy congressional drive (starting in the late 1970s) to punish firms employing undocumented workers culminated in November of 1986 when President Reagan signed the Immigration Reform and Control Act (IRCA).

IRCA's two main components are (1) a requirement that all nonfarm employers hiring new workers (after November 1986) obtain at least two documents from each of them verifying that they are citizens or aliens with legal authorization to work. For each worker, a new form (called I-9) must be signed by the employer verifying that the required documents have been examined. Employers are obligated to keep this form for at least three years and may not dispose of it until one year after the relevant employee has stopped working for the firm. Firms violating the law were made subject to fines of from $250 to $10,000 and those engaging in a "pattern and practice" of violations could be sentenced to up to six months in prison. Aliens found to use false documents to get a job can be fined up to $2,000 and imprisoned for up to two years. (2) A general amnesty program was established for a one-year period during which legal status as a Temporary Resident Alien (TRA) was to be granted those undocumented migrants who provided evidence of continuous residence in the United States since January 1, 1982. After 18 months in TRA status, aliens would then be allowed to apply for permanent residence alien status. Applications for amnesty were only accepted through May 4, 1988 and full enforcement of employer sanctions began the following month.

Of the 1.75 million undocumented TRA applicants who filed by the deadline, about three out of four were from Mexico. Another 1.3 million sought the Special Agricultural Worker (SAW) amnesty before its deadline date of November 30, 1988. The SAW amnesty could be obtained by producing evidence that an alien had worked in perishable agriculture in the United States for at least 90 days in the 12 months ended May 1, 1986. Although the INS identified nearly 400,000 of these as potentially fraudulent claims, it investigated only a tiny fraction, citing inadequate staff after three years of budget cuts. Nine out of 10 amnesty applications in both programs were approved in 1989.[26]

The Mexican-origin population in the United States had grown to 12.1 million by 1988. Our knowledge of its demographic and socioeconomic characteristics has improved considerably over the past decade, thanks both to expanded government data collection and to a new wave of social science research on immigration and ethnic minorities. The component of this population about which we know the least is, of course, the undocumented. Nevertheless, a body of generally consistent findings has emerged in the literature on their number and their salient features. First, contrary to the high speculative figures cited throughout the public debates of the 1970s and early eighties, Census Bureau demographers estimated that there were probably no more than about 3.5 million undocumented aliens in the United States in 1980, of whom about half came from Mexico.[27] The number of new illegal entrants from Mexico in the early 1980s each year was estimated by Passel and Woodrow (1987) to have averaged about 140,000 per year. In light of the 3 million who actually surfaced to take advantage of the amnesty program in 1987–89, the Census Bureau's figures do not appear to have been nearly as far off the mark as many critics long thought. This long-running "numbers controversy" is discussed in more detail in chapter 8.

Research in the 1930s and 1940s suggested that the majority of the undocumented originated in only four Mexican states—Guanajuato, Jalisco, Michoacan, and Nuevo Leon—only the last of which bordered the United States. Since then there has been increasing evidence of a widening distribution of migrants across the country. Samora's (1971) study of a sample of 493 Mexicans apprehended for illegal entry in 1969 found that only 30 percent had been born in these four states. The largest number (representing 18.5 percent of the total) were from the northern border state of Chihuahua, and four other border states together accounted for 14.2 percent. Likewise, in a study of 481 undocumented Mexicans apprehended in 1975, North and Houston (1976) found that only one-third were from the four states that had supplied most prewar emigrants.[28] Chihuahua accounted for 11.2 percent of the sample, and four other border states for another 16.4 percent. Unlike the Samora data, North and Houston had information on the state of residence before emigration, not the state of birth. Their findings thus reflect the growing internal movement of the Mexican population toward the northern centers of rapid industrialization and urbanization.

The undocumented population from Mexico has long had a larger fraction with rural backgrounds than any other major sending country. In the North–Houston sample, most hailed from small- or medium-sized towns and nearly half worked in agriculture before emigrating. Two-thirds were from hometowns with populations of 2,500 or more and 9 percent were from cities of over 1 million. In contrast, over half of those interviewed who were from other Western Hemisphere nations (85 percent of whom were from other Spanish-speaking countries) originated in cities of over a million inhabitants.

The Mexican migrants interviewed were also largely young and male. Nearly 47 percent were between 16 and 24 years old. The mean age (27.6) was far below the U.S. average that year (39). The fact that 9 out of 10 were male doubtless reflects the way in which the sample was collected. Only those aliens already on U.S. soil and apprehended by the INS were included. Migrants denied admission at a port of entry are not counted as apprehensions by the INS. Since the INS estimates that a sizable portion of those denied admission are women, reliance on apprehension data entails a sampling bias toward males.

Over 43 percent of the Mexicans interviewed had completed fewer than five years of schooling, and another 42 percent had only between five and eight years. Fewer than 1 percent had received any higher, postsecondary education, compared with over 27 percent of the American labor force in 1973. The mean number of years of educational attainment was 4.9 among the undocumented, 7.5 years lower than the U.S. average. The lower the schooling level, the weaker the knowledge of English. Three out of four said they spoke it "very badly" or "not at all" and another 15.3 percent "not very well." Only 1.5 percent spoke English "very well."

Despite the average undocumented Mexican's relatively young age, limited schooling, and unfamiliarity with English, other characteristics could count in his favor with American employers. First, most are experienced workers, with a mean of nine and one-half years of paid employment behind them in Mexico. Almost 7 percent had white-collar occupations and a substantial number had industrial experience. Nearly 13 percent were formerly machine operatives, another 11.8 percent nonfarm laborers, and 15 percent skilled craftsmen. They also tended to have considerable familiarity with the U.S. labor market and a support network of friends, relatives, and other migrants. Nearly 58 percent said they knew other undocumented migrants in their hometown and 54 percent had lived with other migrants while in the United States. Almost one in every three had relatives living north of the border. Of all migrants of all nationalities interviewed, 45 percent had found their most recent U.S. job through friends or relatives and over half of the respondents had undocumented coworkers. Mexicans were three times more likely than others to work alongside fellow migrants. Finally, most had ample cause to be highly motivated job-seekers and workers. The trek into the United States is risky and costly, usually demanding the investment of much of one's own meager funds together with loans from relatives and others. The debts and other obligations incurred by the typical migrant were such that 9 out of 10 Mexicans reported they sent money home and the average monthly remittance ($169) was over a third of mean monthly earnings. At home were an average of over five dependents per migrant, most relying on these remittances for over half their needs.

In the United States, most of the undocumented succeeded not only in earning far higher wages than were available in Mexico but in working nearly continuously throughout their stay. The average duration of residence before apprehension by the INS of those in the North–Houston study was 2.4 years, of which an estimated 2.1 years were occupied by paid employment. More than one in five had the same job for two years or more. And for most the new jobs represented upward occupational mobility. The proportion doing farm labor (27 percent) was cut to nearly half that in their premigration job distribution, an identical fraction found manufacturing jobs, and one-fifth went into construction. They were still eight times more likely than Americans to be farm workers. But the longer an individual's residence in the United States, the less likely he or she was still a farm laborer: of those who stayed two years or more, only 11 percent were still in agriculture, while 39 percent worked in manufacturing.

Still, only 1.2 percent were hired into white-collar jobs, and the mean hourly wage was $2.34, only about half that of the average male production worker in the United States at the time. Nearly one of every four was paid below the legal minimum wage. The fact that an equal fraction was regularly paid in cash probably reflects the intention of many American employers to avoid leaving any documented proof of exploitative wages. Below-minimum pay was most common in agriculture and in nonunion workplaces. But only 1 in 10 of the undocumented had been represented by an American labor union.

Despite the impression one might get from all the attention given the undocumented, the clear majority of Mexican-born residents of the United States are legal aliens or naturalized citizens. Compared with the undocumented, they are far more likely to come from urban areas of Mexico, have more schooling, and higher average skill levels. This has been confirmed by a unique longitudinal data set that tracks a large sample of individuals admitted to the United States with legal immigrant status between 1973 and 1974. As reported by Portes and Bach (1985), the sample consisted of 822 Mexican immigrants first interviewed in El Paso and Laredo, as well as 590 Cubans interviewed in Miami. Their study sample was restricted to males who were between the ages of 18 and 60 and household heads (i.e., not dependent on others for their livelihood). In addition to the 1973–74 interviews, the same individuals were reinterviewed in 1976 and again in 1979.[29]

Like the undocumented in the North–Houston survey, the legal migrant sample reflected the northward population shift in Mexico. Although three-tenths of their fathers came from the four states that dominated prewar emigration, only 22.3 percent of the sons lived in these states by their sixteenth birthday and only 11.1 percent still lived there just prior to moving to the United States. Almost three out of four were born in one of the northern states. Over 30 percent lived in Chihuahua alone just before emigrating. Nearly 47 percent of the sample were born in a town or city of 10,000 or more inhabitants and 19.2 percent in large cities of 100,000 or more. Rural–urban migration resulted in one-half reporting residence in a large city by the time of emigration.

The educational attainment of these migrants was certainly low by U.S. standards, but it surpassed that of their parents and that of their undocumented countrymen. Only 2.4 percent had no formal education. Nearly two-thirds completed at least primary school, one-fourth completed secondary school, 9 percent finished postsecondary business or vocational training, and 3.6 percent attended a university. Just as their fathers' had schooling and occupational levels above average for Mexico at the time, so also did their sons. Only 34.4 percent of the fathers and 11.5 percent of their sons were farm laborers. Almost one in four sons held manufacturing jobs and 46.2 percent were skilled workers, artisans, or semiskilled urban laborers before emigrating.

Seven out of 10 in the sample had lived in the United States before their legal entry as immigrants in 1973–74, the majority for between one and three years. The importance of return migration to the volume of legal immigration increased with the 1965 legal reforms in the American admissions criteria. The long tradition of Mexican migration into the Southwest meant that many south of the border had relatives already in the United States who could aid their entry. Others could take advantage of the relatively porous border to live and work in the country illegally for a time so as to acquire the social and economic contacts needed to gain legal admission later. Information about survival in the American labor market was available from the many former migrants who had returned home. Cornelius (1978) found that half of a sample of Mexican immigrants entering the United States since 1969 had fathers who themselves once worked here. Portes and Bach made a valuable effort to distinguish the returnees from the 30 percent of their sample who only entered the country for the first time once they could be admitted legally. They found first-time immigrants tended to be younger and slightly better educated than returnees. Their background was more urban and their fathers held more skilled occupations.

Both first-time migrants and returnees were able to rely on cross-border social networks. Only 2 percent of the 1973–74 cohort had no relatives or friends to meet them when they entered the United States. They arrived remarkably well informed about the work they could expect to do. Nearly 8 in 10 knew where their American employer lived. And comparisons of their occupational expectations, as stated in 1973–74, with their actual occupations in 1976 and 1979 showed a close correspondence emerging in most categories the longer their stay. The most unexpected outcome was the 51.5 percent hired into semiskilled urban jobs by 1976. This was twice the proportion in such jobs in Mexico, but as more moved into skilled and service employment, by 1979 the fraction in semiskilled work fell almost to two-fifths.

Ethnic networks extended into most migrants' workplaces. A majority (54 percent) of those interviewed said they worked primarily among Mexican coworkers. These firms were mainly small- to medium-sized, with those whose work forces consisted of 6–20 employees accounting for one-fifth of the Mexican sample and firms with 21–100 employees accounting for another one-fourth of the sample. Only 15.1 percent worked in firms owned by a Mexican national or a Mexican American. Likewise, the respondents reported that in their community they made consumer purchases overwhelmingly in stores owned by non-Mexicans. Even when buying small items, only 27.7 percent bought primarily from Mexican-run stores. This is unsurprising in light of the low rate of self-employment (5.5 percent in 1979) among the migrants.

Finally, despite the generally weak presence of labor unions in the Southwest, over one-fourth of the Mexican workers surveyed were union members. And, when a local union was present at their workplaces, 9 out of 10 migrants joined. In light of the oft-cited difficulties of organizing immigrants, particularly those isolated on farms or in small businesses, this finding may seem quite surprising. In fact, Mexican immigrants have a long history of participation in southwestern union organizing and strikes stretching back to the early years of this century, when Mexican miners were active in the Industrial Workers of the World (IWW). But their role in the union movement only began to attract public attention in the 1960s as a result of the United Farm Workers (UFW) Organizing Committee's grape boycott. Since that time, while the crisis of the national union movement has deepened, Mexican workers have often been at the forefront of organizing activities among low-wage firms in the region. James Cockcroft (1986) has documented their efforts in restaurants, hotels, garment, auto assembly, shipbuilding, and other industries during the 1970s and early 1980s. The evidence of the recent past, coupled with their steadily growing numeric importance in the work force, suggests that Mexican Americans may play a pivotal role in any future reversal of union fortunes.

Puerto Ricans

The Puerto Rican population on the U.S. mainland is only about one-fifth as numerous as Mexican Americans, with marked political, cultural, and economic differences. Nonetheless, both originate from former Spanish colonies that were invaded by the U.S. military and strongly influenced thereafter by American economic development. From Columbus's landing in 1493 until the end of the eighteenth century, Spain's interest in the island was largely confined to its small gold deposits and strategic location on the main sea lane to Europe. After only 30 years of colonization, the native Indian population (an estimated 30,000 Tainos) had been decimated by forced labor and smallpox, the gold mines were exhausted, and the economy was consigned to two centuries of economic stagnation. Despite the use of low-cost Indian and African slave labor to raise cattle and grow sugarcane, the island remained so poor that the costs of the San Juan military garrison and the colonial administration had to be regularly subsidized by the Viceroyship of Mexico.

As the demands on the Spanish treasury mounted late in the eighteenth century, the Crown sought to stimulate greater Puerto Rican self-financing by liberalizing trade relations, allowing European settlers to buy some of the land long monopolized by the state, and offering incentives to new immigration. The result was a larger increase in population growth (in both absolute and percentage terms) in the last 35 years of the century than in all of the previous 250. Colonial restrictions relaxed even more as increasing amounts of Spain's resources were required to fight Napoleon's invasion in 1809 and the Latin American wars of independence that raged until 1824. The economy began to shift from subsistence production to a stronger export orientation, led by expanding sales of sugar (and its rum and molasses by-products) to the United States. Sugar haciendas acquired a growing share of the island's cultivable land, and their increased labor needs (intensified by the decline of the slave trade) were met by the creation of a large, landless wage-labor force. "Antivagrancy" laws (the *libreta* system) were put into effect to coerce the sizable number of squatters and free peasant small-holders to work on the haciendas. But in the 1870s, increased competition from European beet sugar and from low-cost cane producers using new extraction technologies overwhelmed the backward Puerto Rican industry. The investment funds it needed for modernization were unavailable, thanks to Spain's colonial policy of siphoning off any agricultural surplus and suppressing development of indigenous credit institutions.

Coffee displaced sugar as the leading export crop in the last third of the nineteenth century and in so doing moderated the pace of capitalist agricultural development. While still furthering the growth of a wage-labor force, the coffee industry also created parallel opportunities for small-scale subsistence farming. This resulted from the custom of protecting coffee plants by growing them interspersed with other crops, like bananas and plantains. Coupled with the modest capital requirements for preparing coffee for the market, this enabled many independent peasants to produce both a cash crop and the foods needed for their family's subsistence.

By the end of the nineteenth century, the island's embryonic capitalist economy strained against Spain's continuing commercial, credit, and political restrictions.

Many of the immigrants who had fueled the country's population and economic growth were refugees from other rebellious colonies, and their conservatism long contained the developing nationalist movement. But as the economic power of the merchants and large landowners increased, so did their demands for greater independence. Fearing the loss of one of its last imperial possessions, Spain agreed in 1897 to a Charter of Autonomy, which provided for popular election of a bicameral legislature with extensive powers over taxation, budgeting, trade, tariffs, and commercial treaties.

On July 28, 1898, just eight days after the first meeting of the elected Puerto Rican legislature, 16,000 American troops invaded Puerto Rico. In one of the last acts of the Spanish-American War, the United States expended only 21 days and four American lives to seize the island. With the construction of the Panama Canal already planned, Puerto Rico held great strategic value in addition to its demonstrated economic potential. The new legislature was closed down and for the next two years the island was under direct U.S. military control. In May 1900, military rule was replaced by civilian rule, but the key civilians were all Americans and presidential appointees. The 1900 Foraker Act delineated the exhaustive U.S. control over the new colony (formally called a "non-incorporated territory"): the dollar was to replace the local peso as the sole monetary unit, all tariff setting and treaty making were put in American hands, all goods traded with the mainland had to be carried on American-owned ships, English was made the official language of instruction (though only a handful of local teachers spoke it), and, in perhaps the most insulting decree of all, the island's name was Americanized to "Porto" Rico—the official spelling until 1932.

Puerto Rican protests that Spanish colonialism had simply been replaced by American colonialism found an increasingly sympathetic audience in Washington once the mobilization for World War I began. The island's work force was seen as a means to cope with worsening U.S. labor shortages, and the island's role as a coaling station for American warships assumed new importance with the sighting of German submarines in the Caribbean. In March 1917, one month before the United States entered the war, the Jones Act became law. This expanded Puerto Rican political rights to the extent that it authorized a new elective, bicameral legislature, gave all males (but not females) ages 21 and over voting rights, and granted U.S. citizenship to all Puerto Ricans from this point onward. But the U.S. president and Congress retained final veto power over all bills passed by the island legislature, and all the colonial economic controls defined by the Foraker Act were continued. This remained the legal structure for U.S.–Puerto Rican relations from 1917 to 1947.

The American takeover immediately accelerated the transformation of Puerto Rico into an agrarian capitalist economy. The flourishing coffee industry was singled out for contraction in favor of an extraordinary expansion of sugar production. Two of the biggest markets for Puerto Rican coffee were quickly lost when Cuba and Spain, viewing the island as a foreign possession after 1898, substantially raised their tariffs on its coffee. The United States proved to be no help in compensating for these lost sales. Never an important market for the strong Puerto Rican coffee, it imported weaker South American coffees at lower prices. Washington refused to grant special tariff protection to Puerto Rican coffee, leaving it uncompetitive with its rivals. Coffee's share of total island exports collapsed from 60 percent in 1897 to 19.5 percent in 1901, and kept falling to a mere 2.5 percent in 1928.[30]

In sharp contrast, Puerto Rican sugar was granted protection from foreign competitors behind high tariff walls. The reason was not difficult to discern. The American taste for sugar had, by the turn of the century, made it the world's second biggest consumer (per capita), exceeded only by Great Britain. American investors rushed in to buy up the best Puerto Rican land and quickly dominated the industry. Four giant U.S. corporations controlled 24 percent of all cane land by 1930 and produced over half the local ground sugar. Since the majority of sugar exports had long gone to the mainland, the expansion of sugar rapidly increased the economy's dependence on the American market: only one-fifth of the island's trade was with the United States in 1897, but by 1900 that share had leapt to 68 percent. By 1930, the United States accounted for 96 percent of Puerto Rico's exports and 87 percent of its imports.[31]

In addition to sugar, two other industries, tobacco and needlework, attracted U.S. investment capital, which initiated the development of the island's manufacturing sector. Cigar production was transformed from strictly artisan techniques to mechanized factory-based methods dependent only on wage labor. Needlework followed a similar path from a rural cottage industry to large-scale textile production. But the tobacco boom did not survive the 1920s, owing to the steep decline in cigar sales as American consumption and production of cigarettes grew. Textile production began to thrive only in the years after the Great Depression.

The U.S. authorities could claim credit for important advances in schooling, health care, and basic infrastructural investments. After over 400 years of Spanish colonialism, in 1898 the island had an illiteracy rate of 80 percent and smallpox was rampant. Between the U.S. invasion and 1910, the number of public schools had nearly doubled, the illiteracy rate was cut to 66.5 percent, and a smallpox vaccination program succeeded in lowering the mortality rate. Spanish neglect of the transportation infrastructure was reflected in the fact that only 159 miles of railroad (in several different segments) had been built by 1897, on an island of 3,435 square miles. The United States had expanded the total track miles to 923 by 1930.[32]

But the rate of improvement slowed sharply after the first three or four years. By 1920, the illiteracy rate was still 61 percent, in part because only about two-fifths of rural children were enrolled in a school, mainly in half-day programs, and only one in six stayed beyond the third grade. The average mortality rate fell so slowly, that in 1920 it was still twice the U.S. level. And most of the additional railroads built were owned and largely used for freight haulage by the major sugar corporations. Likewise, non-Puerto Rican absentee owners controlled shipping, banking, and public utilities.[33]

This dependent status made it inevitable that the onset of the Great Depression in the United States would quickly inflict severe damage on the island's export-oriented economy. Between 1929 and 1933, Puerto Rico's nominal GNP fell by one-fourth and per capita income tumbled 30 percent. U.S. Secretary of the Interior Harold Ickes, whose office oversaw American policy toward the island, wrote in 1935:

Puerto Rico . . . has been the victim of the *laissez-faire* economy which has developed the rapid growth of great absentee owned sugar corporations, which have absorbed much land formerly belonging to small independent growers and who in consequence have been reduced to virtual economic serfdom. While the inclusion of Puerto Rico within our tariff walls has been highly beneficial to the stockholders of those corporations, the benefits have not been passed down to the mass of Puerto Ricans. These on the contrary have seen the lands on which they formerly raised subsistence crops, given over to sugar production while they have been gradually driven to import all their food staples, paying for them the high prices brought about by the tariff. There is today more widespread misery and destitution and far more unemployment in Puerto Rico than at any previous time in its history.[34]

With the standard of living reduced to the level prevailing at the turn of the century and foreign economic domination as complete as it had been under Spanish rule, the depression ignited nationalist movements seeking political independence and economic restructuring. Labor organizations won growing support and launched a strike wave against the giant sugar corporations. By the end of the decade, a powerful new labor confederation (the CGT) had been formed, uniting a wide array of trades under the banner of industrial unionism.

The United States' entry into World War II coincided with the start of a sustained period of economic reorganization in Puerto Rico. In 1941, Luis Munoz Marin of the Popular Democratic Party (PPD) began 24 consecutive years as the top elected official and embarked upon an ambitious program of land reform and government-led industrialization. The fact that Washington went along with this policy no doubt stemmed in part from its concern that undermining the reformist PPD would tip the political balance in favor of the more radical parties demanding home rule. The presence of German submarines in the Caribbean early in the war reemphasized the island's strategic value to the United States. At the same time, with most of the government's attention focused on the Pacific and Atlantic theaters, it left Puerto Rico with considerable autonomy throughout the war. Finally, the new American governor appointed in 1941 was Rexford Tugwell, an early New Dealer in the Roosevelt administration who was predisposed to using interventionist government policies to promote economic stability and growth.

The Munoz program proceeded through two overlapping phases. The initial period (1941–47) focused on land reform and government-led development of infrastructure and of state-owned factories. This was replaced by "Operation Bootstrap" (*Operacion Manos a la Obra*), begun in 1947 to attract foreign investment. The land reform program involved government purchases of corporate-owned farms of 500 acres or more. Some were reorganized as large worker-managed enterprises, while others were distributed in small parcels to entitled landless farm laborers. However, the program was ended after less than six years, with two-thirds of the large farms still in corporate hands. It was a victim of scarce funds and the government's decision to allocate more resources to its industrialization program. The latter was an import-substitution strategy based on new government-financed and government-operated corporations. Though limited to only four areas (clay building materials, glass products, paperboard, and shoes), it faced mounting opposition from mainland corporations throughout the 1940s. They starved the state enterprises of needed inputs and boycotted their output. The government retreated from this approach and, from the mid-forties on, concentrated mainly on infrastructural improvements to attract foreign investments.

In May of 1947, the Puerto Rican legislature passed the Industrial Incentive Act, inaugurating "Operation Bootstrap." Under its provisions, qualified foreign investors were granted tax-exempt status for 10 years, and a partial exemption for another 3. They also received valuable government benefits such as free use of buildings, utilities, work-training programs, and low-interest loans. The program was initially viewed as temporary, with all exemptions to end by the early 1960s. But the threat by many firms to relocate as soon as their exemptions expired led to new legislation in 1954 and 1963 extending and liberalizing the tax holidays. For example, from 1963 on, foreign investment in less-developed areas outside the main cities could be exempted from all taxes for up to 17 years. For U.S. corporations this meant that virtually all their Puerto Rican income was tax-free, since IRS regulations had long exempted income from Puerto Rican subsidiaries from any U.S. federal income tax.

The rapid industrialization that followed inspired talk of a new "capitalist showcase" in the Caribbean. Between 1948 and 1963 GDP more than doubled, gross investment and exports nearly quadrupled, the contribution of industry to GDP jumped 50 percent and the agricultural share fell by the same amount.[35] Two-thirds of the new foreign firms located in the four biggest cities, which quickly became population magnets. The percentage of the population in urban areas rose from 30.3 percent in 1940 to 44.2 percent in 1960, then climbed in the sixties to nearly 60 percent by the decade's end.

This transformation imposed some serious long-term costs. Among the most obvious was the increase in the already enormous external control over the economy. By 1963 non-Puerto Rican firms accounted for about three-fifths of all manufacturing sales, value-added, and employment. Only four years later, their share had risen to about 70 percent.[36] Ironically, the island's control of its economy was declining just as its formal political autonomy was increasing. In August 1947, President Truman signed legislation that, for the first time, allowed Puerto Ricans to popularly elect their governor. Two years later Public Law 600 gave them the right to draft their own constitution. And in July 1952, 54 years after the U.S. invasion, the island's official status was changed from territory to "commonwealth." But de facto control has stayed with the U.S. Congress and the president, who retain veto power over all legislation and over any proposed changes in the constitution (which have always been rejected). Though the old Jones Act of 1917 has formally been replaced by Federal Relations Law, most of its restrictive provisions live on.

One of the costliest failures of Operation Bootstrap was in the area of job creation. The program was based on the conviction that, since agriculture could not absorb all the country's surplus workers, it should be ignored in favor of maximum attention to rapid industrialization. The subsequent neglect helped speed agriculture's decline: its contribution to total GNP dropped from 17.5 percent to 3.6 percent between 1950 and 1980, and its share of all employment shrank from 36 percent to only 5.3 percent.[37] Until the early 1960s, most of the new investment attracted by the government incentives was in labor-intensive industries, particularly textiles and apparel. By the end of the decade, apparel alone accounted for nearly one-fifth of all manufacturing firms and the same fraction of total employment. Though such growth was acclaimed as the result of Operation Bootstrap, Taylor (1957) found that the industry's relatively low wage scale represented a larger subsidy to investors than tax exemptions. It also appears that almost half of the added jobs in tax-exempt firms simply replaced jobs lost in the largely local firms, who were placed at a competitive disadvantage by the lowered tax costs of their rivals. Manufacturing employment in tax-exempt firms increased by 37,300 from 1947 to 1957, but fell 16,000 over the same period in nonexempt firms.[38]

Of the new jobs that were created in the postwar years, a disproportionately large number were given to women. As the government figures in Table 2.4 show, women have long had lower rates of unemployment than men on the island. Male discouragement over their inferior job prospects may help explain the remarkable decline in the fraction of Puerto Rican men active in the labor force. In 1950, nearly four out of five males living in Puerto Rico were employed or searching for a job, a labor force participation rate less than 7 percentage points below the American average for all males. As is well known, male participation rates in the United States slowly declined in the postwar period (to 77.4 percent by 1980), largely because of expanded schooling and the Social Security program's work disincentives for the elderly. But the male rate in Puerto Rico fell far more sharply, to only 60.7 percent by 1980. In three decades, the gap between the U.S. and the Puerto Rican rates more than doubled in size. This cannot be blamed on work disincentives tied to federal transfer programs, because most programs, such as food stamps, were extended to the island in only the early 1970s, and all were, of course, also available to men in the United States whose participation rates nevertheless did not fall as rapidly as those of Puerto Ricans. Nor can it be attributed to increased school enrollment, since this expanded far more on the mainland than on the island. In fact, the secular decline in male labor force participation began in Puerto Rico at least as early as 1910. The best available estimates indicate that of males 10 years old and over, an astonishing 94.4 percent were economically active on the island that year.[39] But by 1920, this rate had fallen to 88.3 percent and it kept declining to 82.1 percent 10 years later. By 1940, nearly one in four males (24.2 percent) were no longer active in the labor force. Since the male school enrollment rate rose only from 12.4 percent to 13.5 percent between 1910 and 1940, the most likely source of this trend is instead the structural transformation of the Puerto Rican economy begun by the U.S. takeover, which created far too few new jobs for males to replace those destroyed in agriculture.

The bias toward female employment in new manufacturing jobs has been investigated by Safa (1985) through interviews with a sample of female workers in three plants of an island garment firm in 1980. The oldest plant, in the large western city of Mayaguez, was found to employ mainly older, married, urban women. Production was increasingly being shifted to the other two new plants located in the countryside several miles from the city. These plants were far more likely to hire young, single women from nearby rural areas, for two main reasons. First, the younger the employee the lower the firm's costs incurred in contributions to mater-

TABLE 2.4. Labor Force Status, Income, and Poverty, Mainland U.S.
and Puerto Rico, 1950–80

	1950	1960	1970	1980
LABOR FORCE[a]				
PARTICIPATION RATE (%)				
Males				
US	86.4	83.3	79.7	77.4
Puerto Rico	79.5	72.4	65.6	60.7
Females				
US	33.9	37.7	43.3	51.5
Puerto Rico	27.6	22.5	26.0	27.8
UNEMPLOYMENT RATE (%)				
Males				
US	5.1	5.4	4.4	6.9
Puerto Rico	14.0	13.9	11.0	19.5
Females				
US	5.7	5.9	5.9	7.4
Puerto Rico	9.5	11.2	9.0	12.3
MEDIAN INCOME[b]				
Males				
US	$2434	4103	6444	12192
Puerto Rico	$434	987	2259	4314
Females				
US	$1029	1357	2328	5263
Puerto Rico	$247	471	1321	2775
Families				
US	$3073	5660	9596	20835
Puerto Rico	NA	1268	3063	5923
FAMILIES BELOW POVERTY LEVEL (%)				
US	NA	NA	11.6	9.6
Puerto Rico	NA	NA	59.6	58.0

[a]Civilian population 14 years old and over, 1950–60; ages 16 and over for 1970–80. Annual average participation and unemployment rates from Current Population Survey. On comparability of U.S. and Puerto Rican data collection, see U.S. Department of Commerce (1979), pp. 590–602.

[b]Income and poverty estimates are for the last calendar year before each census.

SOURCE: U.S. Bureau of the Census (1953, 1964, 1973a, 1984b and 1984c) and Puerto Rican Department of Labor and Human Resources, Bureau of Labor Statistics.

nity and retirement benefits. Second, interviews with management revealed a perception of such women as more docile than either older women or men. And this appeared to be confirmed by the young women interviewed, who indicated high degrees of job satisfaction, few complaints about management, and a strong work ethic.

How can this be, in an industry that is the lowest paying on the island, paying an average salary of only $4,885 in 1977?[40] Safa attributes the attitudes of these youth to their vital role in supporting typically large rural households. Four of five surveyed lived in households of four or more persons, of which half had seven or more persons. A large fraction of their fathers were displaced agricultural workers now relying on Social Security, food stamps, and their children's earnings. Ninety percent of the young women said it was easier for a woman to find employment than for a man. But, despite the male's declining status as a wage earner, women accepted the traditional patriarchal hierarchy of the peasant family, both before and after marriage (when dominant authority passed from father to husband). Of all the households Safa sampled with working daughters, three-fourths of these women contributed earnings that accounted for 50 percent or more of total household income. They were able to devote their full energy to their jobs because child care and other household responsibilities were largely assumed by unemployed family members, as well as by other relatives in the close-knit kinship networks in which nearly all live in these rural communities.

Besides reliance on the employment of daughters or wives, supplemented by income transfers, the other principal response of men to the island's declining male employment prospects has been emigration. In the Safa study, over three-fifths of the women surveyed had husbands or brothers who had left the island for the United States.[41]

From the early 1960s, Operation Bootstrap shifted its promotional efforts to attracting capital-intensive firms in industries like petrochemicals, electrical machinery, and pharmaceuticals. This was defended as a means to increase the number of skilled, high-wage jobs available and to moderate the economy's cyclical vulnerability. Not surprisingly, the average employment of firms in the program began falling: from 1947 to 1961 they employed an average of 70 workers each, but by the late sixties the average was only 33.3.[42] It had been hoped that capital-intensive firms would create significant indirect spinoff effects on employment. Local "backward-linked" firms would emerge to provide them raw materials and intermediate inputs, and "forward-linked" firms would profit from marketing and distributing their output. But by the 1970s, it was clear that foreign corporations could remain isolated from the rest of the Puerto Rican economy because they already had well-established relations with suppliers and distributors in their home country.

The oil crisis of 1973–74 and the worldwide recession that followed put an abrupt end to the island's high output and investment growth. Real GNP, which had grown at average annual rates of 6.1 percent from 1947 to 1963 and 6.6 percent from 1963 to 1973, slowed to a mere 1 percent growth rate from 1973 to 1977. Real per capita GNP actually fell 2 percent during the mid-seventies.[43] The official unemployment rate jumped to over 16 percent in 1976 and exceeded 23 percent in 1983. Average family income on the island fell from 32 percent of the U.S. income level to 28.4 percent between 1970 and 1980, and the family poverty rate in 1980 (58 percent) was six times the American level (Table 2.4). With the island's unemployment and poverty reaching levels of the sort not seen in the United States since the Great Depression, Washington resorted to massive issuance of food stamps as its principal relief assistance. The first coupons were introduced on the island in September 1974. In their first full year of distribution, food stamps were issued to more than one-fourth of the population. By 1980, over 58 percent were using the coupons and another 10–20 percent were sufficiently poor to qualify for the program, though they were not then recipients.[44]

The failure of the postwar development strategy to create adequate job growth left many with only one reasonable option besides dependence on government transfers: emigration. Puerto Ricans have been moving to the U.S. mainland since the early nineteenth century, but migration, both within the island and abroad, was greatly accelerated by the American invasion. The vast expansion of coastal sugar production at the expense of the inland coffee industry forced large numbers of rural subsistence and coffee farmers to leave the western and central coffee belt to seek work in the coastal canefields or the tobacco factories of the urban San Juan–Rio Piedras area. As unemployment became a growing problem, many left for jobs on the farms and in the mines of Cuba and Hispaniola. Over 5,000 Puerto Ricans were recruited to work on the sugar plantations of Hawaii in 1900–1901. And these years also saw the first small numbers of craftsmen and tobacco workers migrate to New York City, home of a tiny Puerto Rican community founded by early anticolonial political exiles. But the 1910 census counted only 1,513 Puerto Ricans in the country.

World War I brought some 12,000 to 13,000 to the mainland to help fill wartime labor shortages. Another 18,000 Puerto Ricans were inducted into the U.S. military during the war (though, like blacks, they were forced into segregated units). The 1920 census reported that, of the 11,811 Puerto Ricans in the United States, two-thirds of them were in New York City where they congregated in the Harlem and Brooklyn Navy Yard areas. The granting of U.S. citizenship in 1917 freed Puerto Ricans of the visa and other restrictions hindering other migrants. But they still faced a five-day, 1,600-mile sea voyage to New York, which was beyond the means of many. The Great Depression actually caused net return migration from the mainland in every year from 1931 to 1934. The annual number traveling to the mainland was below 30,000 throughout the 1920s and 1930s and net migration (the difference between departures from the island and arrivals) did not exceed 9,000 per year until 1945.[45]

The Second World War and the postwar economic boom in the United States sparked the first mass migration from the island. Frequent commercial airline flights became available only at that time, making the trip relatively brief and affordable. Even as late as 1970, the one-way fare could be under $50 and a ticket could be had on credit from travel agencies for as little as $5 down payment.[46] The number traveling to the mainland more than doubled between 1945 and 1946 and passed the 100,000 mark for the first time the following year. Net migration, a mere 500 persons in 1941, climbed to 33,086 in 1949. Between 1940 and 1950 the census recorded a fourfold increase in the number of Puerto Rican residents in the United States. But the postwar peak in net migration was not reached until 1953, when 74,603 more arrived on the mainland than departed. For the decade as a whole, net migration totaled 461,000. The outflow from the island slowed to 144,724 in the 1960s, but by the end of the decade the census counted 1,429,369 residents of Puerto Rican origin. During the 1970s, for the first time since the Great Depression, more returned to the island (a net outflow of over 158,000) than stayed. But the 1980s saw a revival of the secular pattern of positive net migration.

As the postwar migration has continued, the island-born component of the Puerto Rican population in the United States has decreased and the geographic dispersion of the population has increased. Three-fourths of Puerto Ricans counted in the 1950 U.S. census were born on the island as were 69.3 percent of the 1960 count. But by 1970 this percentage had fallen to 54.8 percent and it dropped slightly below the 50 percent mark for the first time in 1980. While the arrival point for most migrants still tends to be New York City, Puerto Ricans now live in all of the 50 states. The fraction concentrated in New York State fell from four-fifths of all Puerto Ricans in 1940 and 1950 to 69 percent in 1960. By 1980 about half continued to live in the state, with large contingents in New Jersey, California, Florida, and Illinois.

The sudden influx of large numbers of migrants sparked public controversy about their implications for the New York economy. Some critics claimed they were akin to the "new immigration" of Eastern and Southern Europeans at the turn of the century; like them, it was said, the latest migrants were largely Catholics, from low-skill rural backgrounds, and many were dark skinned. The first major study of the initial postwar influx was organized at Columbia University by C. Wright Mills, Clarence Senior, and Rose Goldsen (1950). Interviews of a large sample of persons living in Spanish Harlem and the Morrisania section of the Bronx in 1947 produced information on about 5,000 Puerto Ricans. Just over one-third of their sample was nonwhite (20 percent blacks and 16 percent "mixed blood"), a slightly higher fraction than on the island. But 91 percent of the total study group had lived in urban areas of the island before migrating, two-thirds in either of the two largest cities, San Juan and Ponce. These were not primarily unstable, transient families: four out of five had lived in the same place in Puerto Rico for at least 10 years prior to emigrating and a higher percentage were married than in the general population. In part this reflects migrants' older average age, 24, four years above the island average.

Mills, Senior, and Goldsen also found evidence that, before emigration, most were better educated and employed in more skilled jobs than the average urban Puerto Rican. The illiteracy rate was 8 percent among migrants, compared with 17 percent in San Juan and 32 percent islandwide in 1940. Only 4 percent had been unemployed just prior to migrating, and nearly three out of four had been employed in an uninterrupted full-year job. About 29 percent of the male migrants and 68 percent of females had worked in manufacturing at home, higher proportions than their nonmigrant countrymen. Most of these were in skilled or semiskilled occupations.

Though these early migrants had superior educational and employment credentials than the average Puerto Rican at the time, many were at a substantial disadvantage in the United States. Their average illiteracy rate was twice that of the overall New York City population. On arrival in New York, the majority experienced downward mobility into semiskilled operative or service occupations.

The Columbia study remains a unique source of information on the earliest years of the postwar migration, though caution must always be exercized when interpreting results from samples, such as this one, derived through the nonrandom "snowball" method (locating additional subjects through relatives and various community networks). However, 1950 census data on the educational attainment of Puerto Ricans on the mainland and on the island seem consistent with the view that the early migrants came from the better-educated strata. The average amount of schooling completed by island-born Puerto Ricans living on the mainland in 1950 was 8.4 years, two years more than the island average.[47]

As with any large-scale migration from a small country, it was to be expected that as it continued there would be regression toward the mean levels of schooling and occupation. Thus, by the late 1950s, there were reports of relatively fewer migrants than before from the largest cities and top skill groups.[48] In the late 1970s, by contrast, it was widely believed on the island that the worsening recession was forcing a "brain drain" of much of the business and academic elite who had resisted emigrating earlier. But research comparing the educational and occupational distributions of migrants with the population of Puerto Rico has found that, after adjusting for age differences, there has been little change in the relative selectivity of migration between the late 1950s and the early eighties.[49]

Cubans

Most of the Cuban population of the United States traces its American roots back less than a generation. On the eve of the 1959 revolution, it numbered little more than 30,000. It had taken over half a century to increase by 19,000 over the 1900 census count (11,081). But from 1959 to 1980 about 1 in every 10 Cubans left the island and the number living in the United States leapt to over 600,000. The migration occurred through a number of distinct periods, each conditioned by the course of the revolution and by the state of U.S.–Cuban relations.

The first phase, from early 1959 to October 1962, was one of rapid socioeconomic transformation in Cuba and of growing American hostility to the Castro government. Throughout 1959 and most of 1960, commercial air travel was readily available and the right to exit was unrestricted. But of the roughly 215,000 who left for the United States from 1959 to 1962, fewer than one-fifth of the departures occurred in the first two years.[50] The pace of emigration began to quicken noticeably in the waning months of 1960 with the announcement of a wide-ranging Urban Reform Law. Emigration took off on a sustained increase in 1961, the year in which diplomatic relations were broken off between Havana and Washington and the U.S.-backed invasion at the Bay of Pigs was defeated. Exit and financial restrictions were tightened that year, but direct flights to Miami were not suspended until the Cuban Missile Crisis in October of 1962.

From November 1962 through August 1965, immigration to the United States was possible only by the indirect approach of first securing approval for travel to a third country, or by surreptitious means. The outflow during this period was only about 69,000.

Fidel Castro's speech of September 28, 1965, inaugurated a lengthy period of freer exit. From September through November about 5,000 relatives of exiles already in the United States were allowed to leave from the port of Camarioca. Then, in December, a "memorandum of understanding" between the United States and Cuba instituted an airlift between Varadero Beach, Cuba and Miami. With two flights each day until the airlift's termination in April 1973, over 340,000 migrated.

The period from May 1973 to April 1980 saw a reimposition of the 1962–65 ban on direct flights. The Cuban government permitted a number of political prisoners to emigrate in both 1978 and 1979. In addition to clandestine exists and travelers coming via third countries (particularly Spain), this produced a total of only about 34,500 migrants in the course of these eight years.

The largest Cuban emigration in a single year took place between April 21 and September 26, 1980, from the port of Mariel. Sparked by the occupation of the Peruvian embassy in Havana, the government opened the port to unlimited emigration. With a recession underway in the United States, the Carter administration reflected widespread misgivings about any large new influx by declaring a ceiling of 3,500 refugee admissions. But this was soon eliminated and special processing camps were quickly set up. Although a U.S. naval blockade was begun on May 14 to dissuade others from joining the boatlift, and though Mariel harbor was closed from September 27 on, some 124,769 left for the United States in this period.

Who were the Cuban migrants? Thanks to a number of research studies conducted at different stages of the migration, a great deal is known about their demographic and socioeconomic features. The richest source of information on the earliest exiles is the study by Fagen, Brody, and O'Leary (1968) on Cubans who arrived from 1959 to the end of 1961 and registered at the Cuban Refugee Center (CRC) in Miami. From samples of the subpopulation of 59,682 registrants who were previously employed or employable, they reported that the refugees were far more likely to be relatively well educated urban professionals than was the average island resident.

While their findings show that the farther down the socioeconomic ladder one looked the larger the fraction of people who stayed in Cuba, Fagen, Brody, and O'Leary were impressed by the presence of migrants from many different strata:

> Although the refugee community contains the majority of living members of the Batistiano establishment, corrupt politicians, profiteers, landowners, and gangsters, most of the exiles come from the inclusive social sectors that were squeezed, pressured, or deprived by the revolution not because their members wholeheartedly supported the old order, but because they stood in the way of the new. The Castro government became so radical and reorganized society so thoroughly that almost all social sectors from blue-collar workers through professionals experienced the impact of some revolutionary program in a negative way. Of course, not all negative experiences with revolutionary programs resulted in self-imposed exile, both because of the counterbalancing effect of positive experiences and because of the psychological, physical, and political barriers to leaving the island.[51]

In fact, their findings understated the dominance of high-income emigres in this first wave because their data included only those who registered with the CRC. Since the center was expressly devoted to aiding those without substantial assets or immediate job prospects, the 23 percent of all 1958–61 migrants from the island who chose not to register were likely (as the authors themselves recognized) to be the rich and well connected who fled during the early days of the Castro government. Restrictions on taking personal funds and property from the island were not made stringent until mid-1961.

Later cohorts, while still characterized by educational and occupational backgrounds well above the average in Cuba, have tended to come from more heterogeneous urban sectors than did earlier waves. This reflects in part the dramatic economic shifts undertaken in Cuba in the late sixties. Real national income and consumption expanded from 1962 to 1965, then began to fall sharply. The government responded in 1966 by inaugurating a new, more radical strategy to contract the scope of the private sector in order to reallocate more resources to the public sector. Urban trade and services were rapidly transformed and the resultant increase in middle-class emigration is reflected in the Portes–Bach survey of Cubans arriving in the United States in 1973 and 1974. One-fourth of the males interviewed had worked in white-collar or minor professional jobs at home and another one-fifth had held intermediate service jobs. The modal occupation was the crafts group, accounting for one-fourth of the total. The average level of educational attainment was 9 years. Over one-fifth (22 percent) had completed 12 or more years of school, about five times the average in Cuba. But this represented a decline from the early 1960s, when over one-third of migrants from Cuba reported 12 or more years of educational attainment.[52]

Despite negative publicity claiming that the 1980 wave of "Marielitos" was drawn disproportionately from the Cuban underclass, a survey of a sample of 5,700 found that most had very similar characteristics to earlier cohorts.[53] This was especially true of the 62,000 who arrived in the first few weeks of the exodus and were processed and released in Miami. A large fraction were families being reunited with relatives in the United States. Few had been unemployed in Cuba, and their occupational distribution was much like that of those leaving the island in the early seventies. The later arrivals who were processed at military camps in the North had a larger proportion of younger, nonwhite, unattached males and about one in six had a prison record in Cuba. But overall the refugees processed at the camps had largely urban backgrounds of steady employment, mainly in skilled crafts jobs in manufacturing or construction. Over 9 percent were professional, technical, or kindred workers, of whom the most common specific occupations were teachers, nurses, entertainers, and accountants.

Compared with Mexicans immigrating at the same time, the 1973–74 Cuban cohort averaged three more years schooling. Professional and proprietary occupations accounted for 11 percent of Cuban's premigration positions but for only 1 percent in the Mexican sample. A mere 2 percent of the Cubans had been farm workers, compared with 12 percent of the Mexicans. The main occupational similarity between the two nationalities was in the proportions from skilled blue-collar backgrounds.

Although 9 out of 10 Cubans arriving in the early seventies had no previous experience in the United States, only 6 of the original 586 surveyed by Portes and Bach had no friends or relatives waiting for them at destination. One in four had over 20 friends or relatives already in the country.[54] This is comparable to the finding from a 1968 survey of the large Cuban population in West New York, New Jersey. Nearly 93 percent of the migrants interviewed reported that some family members were waiting for them when they arrived. Almost two-thirds had found jobs through the help of relatives.[55]

The first few years in the American labor market involved downward occupational mobility for many Cubans with high-status positions back home. The proportion of the 1973–74 cohort in white-collar jobs fell from 25 percent before migration to about 10 percent in the United States in both 1976 and 1979. Only 4.6 percent were in professional positions in the United States by 1976, compared with 8.5 percent who held such jobs before leaving Cuba. But some recovery (to 6.4 percent) was evident three years later. By far the largest change was the fourfold increase (to 34.5 percent in 1979) in the share of Cubans in semiskilled industrial work. The greatest stability was in craft positions: the 22.8 percent of 1979 jobs in crafts fields was almost identical to the premigration level. Occupational mobility does not appear to have come at the price of frequent unemployment. Three out of four of Cuban men reinterviewed in 1979 said they had not been unemployed a single time during the past six years in the United States and another 15 percent had only one jobless spell.[56]

Like Mexican workers, Cubans work primarily in small- to medium-sized firms staffed by large proportions of other Hispanics. In 1979, 59 percent of the 1973–74 Cuban cohort reported that most of their coworkers were Cuban. But a very important distinction is evident in the ownership of the businesses they work for. Nearly two out of five Cubans worked in a Cuban-owned firm in 1976, and by 1979 this was the case for 49 percent of the Cuban sample.[57] This is consistent with the remarkable increase recorded in the rate of self-employment among Cuban migrants, from 7.6 percent to 21.2 percent between 1976 and 1979.[58] Not only are Cubans more likely to work for their countrymen than are Mexican immigrants, but they are also more likely to patronize Hispanic-owned stores for both small items and consumer durables.

Other Latin Americans

The most rapidly growing component of the Hispanic immigrant population in recent years is the influx from Latin American nations other than Cuba and Mexico. Excluding the latter two, the countries of Central America, South America, and the Spanish-speaking Caribbean were the source of 564,800 legal immigrants in the 1970s and another 705,800 from 1981 through 1988 (Table 2.3). The average number entering the United States each year from the region jumped 57 percent between the seventies and the eighties, almost five times faster than the Mexican rate of increase. Despite the recency of this migration, by 1988 Central and South Americans numbered some 2.2 million—one in every nine Hispanic Americans.

Dominicans

More Hispanics have immigrated to the United States from the Dominican Republic since 1960 than from any other foreign country except Mexico and Cuba. The 1980 census counted 169,147 Dominican-born residents on the American mainland, of whom over half had arrived during the seventies. Another 183,000 migrated between 1981 and 1988, representing one-fourth of all migration from Latin America (aside from Mexico and Cuba) in this period.

One reason for the unusually large inflows from this small Caribbean island is a close relationship with its immediate neighbor, Puerto Rico. Barely 15 minutes apart by airplane, the two have long been tied by trade and migration. The fact that the Dominican income per capita ($790 in 1985) has averaged only one-third that of Puerto Rico in recent years has drawn many Dominicans to San Juan and other cities in search of work.[59] While the island's limited employment opportunities lead some to return home, others continue on from Puerto Rico to the United States. Since air flights to the mainland from Puerto Rico are considered "U.S. domestic travel" and Puerto Ricans are not required to show passports before boarding, some Dominicans have attempted to enter by illegally misrepresenting their nationality. Recent estimates by Larson and Sullivan (1987) suggest that contrary to widely quoted claims that there are 300,000 or more undocumented Dominicans, the actual number is more likely a quite small part of the overall Dominican influx.[60] Others who intermarry with Puerto Ricans gain preference in obtaining legal entry status.

The increase in political instability from the early 1960s is another oft-cited factor used to explain the upsurge in emigration. The 1961 assassination of the long-reigning dictator Trujillo was followed by five years of political turmoil and economic stagnation. The democratic election of Juan Bosch as the new leader in 1963 was nullified by his overthrow only seven months later by traditional forces opposed to his populist program. In 1965, widespread fears of a military coup sparked the "April Revolution," which, in turn, prompted the United States to launch a counter-revolutionary invasion on behalf of a conservative faction. The late sixties and early seventies witnessed sizable inflows of foreign investment in mining, sugar, communications, tourism, and other industries. But the period was also one of harsh repression in which an estimated 600 to 700 political activists and their relatives "disappeared" or were found murdered. And a sizable share of the returns from economic expansion were widely reported to have been diverted into luxury imports and military corruption.

Those who have left for the United States appear to be drawn disproportionately from the urban, better-educated, white-collar segment of the republic. This emerges clearly from the analysis by Ugalde, Bean, and Cardenas (1979) of a large national survey of 25,000 island households in 1974. The survey, called *Diagnos,* was conducted by the Ministry of Health and included a series of questions about household members who traveled overseas planning to stay there for over a year. Brief tourist and business trips were thereby excluded. If the migrant had not returned by the time of the survey, other household members were asked to provide information on him or her. Of course, the survey had the limitation that it completely missed those cases where the entire household had migrated and was still out of the country in 1974. But it provided a wealth of information on about 125,000 household members.

The survey results show that, of household heads, only 32 percent of nonmigrants were born in a city, compared with 59 percent of migrants. Another 17 percent of migrants, though not city-born, were urban residents in the period before emigrating. The middle and upper social strata account for the bulk of migrants. In a country with a literacy rate of only 61 percent among nonmigrants, 96 percent of migrants were literate and 31 percent had some university training—10 times the nonmigrant percentage.

When questioned about the main reason for leaving their homeland, most cited economic rather than political reasons. Thirty percent moved because of unemployment and another 30 percent left in search of higher incomes. The study's authors note that political persecution may be more likely to force the migration of entire households, who would not be included in this survey. And they point out the interrelationship between political conditions and economic prospects. Indeed, since such a large fraction of these urban, well-educated individuals cited unemployment as the cause of their emigration, it is likely that they were victims of a "middle-class bottleneck" in the government's development strategy.[61] Their economic frustrations could well have been fused with political frustrations, given the effort so many invested in the 1963 election of Bosch and in the 1965 nationalist rebellion.

The survey also provided the strongest evidence to date that Dominicans, like Mexicans and Puerto Ricans, average high rates of return migration. About 39 percent of migrants had returned home by the time of the survey. The largest fraction of middle- and upper-class returnees were those who had completed studies in the United States. Lower-class migrants were more likely to be target earners who returned to the island after accumulating sufficient savings.[62]

In the United States, Dominicans are among the most geographically concentrated of all immigrant groups. In 1980, New York State was the home of 86.5 percent of them, with most living in the Washington Heights area of upper Manhattan or in the Corona section of Queens. The employment experiences of both legal and undocumented Dominicans in the city have been investigated by Grasmuck (1984). She supervised a 1981 project in which seven Dominican interviewers questioned a sample of 301 of their countrymen, of whom 57 percent were documented and the remainder undocumented immigrants. The survey was designed to try to oversample the undocumented and was collected through the chain or "snowball" procedure of locating subjects through community institutions and kinship networks. This approach has the advantage of often insuring greater access to individuals underrepresented in government surveys, but the disadvantage of lacking the desirable statistical property of random sampling.

Like the *Diagnos* findings, the New York sample came from urban areas of the republic and had educational and occupational backgrounds well above the island norm. Contrary to stereotypes, the undocumented exceeded legal immigrants in all of these background characteristics. While three-fourths of legal Dominican migrants had urban origins and their average educational attainment was 7.9 years, 86 percent of the undocumented came from a city and they averaged 8.4 years of schooling. The fraction of each group in a professional, technical, or kindred occupation at home was 26 percent of undocumented males and 29.2 percent of undocumented females, compared with only 11.1 percent and 17.9 percent of legal males and females, respectively. But the undocumented were considerably more likely to be unemployed prior to migration.

In New York, legal and illegal entrants become similarly concentrated in low-wage manual manufacturing jobs in firms with largely Hispanic work forces. Nearly half of males and three-fifths of females interviewed were in blue-collar jobs as craftsmen, operatives, or laborers. Professional or technical jobs were found by only 10.5 percent of males and 3 percent of females. The majority of both the documented and the undocumented worked in firms in which over half of their coworkers and their supervisors were Dominicans or other Hispanics. However, clear distinctions by immigration status emerge when one's focus narrows to firm-level conditions. The undocumented were substantially more likely to work in the smallest, low-wage firms lacking union protections. Three out of every five were in firms with fewer than 50 employees and the same fraction were nonunion, in contrast to a 69 percent unionization rate among documented Dominicans. The undocumented were clearly in great demand as a casual labor supply by employers trying to avoid payment of employment-related taxes and benefits. This is strongly suggested by the fact that 43 percent of undocumented workers were paid in cash, over twice the percentage among the documented.

South Americans

Colombia is by far the single largest source of immigration from South America to the United States. The 143,508 Colombians counted by the 1980 census represented nearly one-fifth of the foreign-born Latin American population (excluding Mexico and Cuba). Theirs is also a recent migration, beginning in the early 1960s. Many of the first emigrants were fleeing the turmoil wrought by "*la Violencia.*" From 1948 to 1964 the country was caught up in the longest period of internal warfare and banditry in modern South American history. The death toll has been estimated at about 200,000. During the National Front period of 1958–1978, the two main political parties worked cooperatively and the worst of the civil strife ended.

Compared with most other countries in the region during the 1970s, Colombia experienced strong employment growth and some reduction in income inequality. The government offered various concessions to emigres in the hope of luring back skilled manpower, though with little success. The continued emigration of professionals and other skilled workers stems in part from the fact that the benefits of government policies accrued more to the top and bottom extremes of the population. Middle-income groups experienced a fall in their share of national income as well as a steep drop in the purchasing power of their earnings. For example, the monthly pay of salaried technicians and managers in manufacturing shrank 18 percent between 1970 and 1976.[63] The decade ended with a revival of guerrilla actions by underground political groups and the escalation of violence by powerful drug traffickers on a national scale. Coupled with evidence of rising government corruption, the violence no doubt intensified the pressure on many to leave the country.

Most Colombian migration has been to its wealthier neighbor Venezuela and, in smaller numbers, to Ecuador and Panama. Only about one-sixth of all those leaving the country have moved to the United States. Their settlement at destination has been much more geographically dispersed than Dominicans. Of all Colombians resident in the United States in 1980, 12.3 percent lived in Florida and 10.5 percent in California. But the largest single concentration (41.2 percent) is in New York State, and 9 out of 10 of these (i.e., about 36 percent of all Colombians) live in New York City.

While many migrants to nearby Latin American nations come from rural Colombia, those arriving in the United States appear to be heavily urban, with educational and occupational levels well above the Colombian average. This has been confirmed from research on migrants just before leaving Bogota and from data on those already settled in New York.[64] The most recent large-scale survey was undertaken by the Hispanic Research Center at Fordham University between June and October of 1981.[65] The main survey site was Queens, where most of the city's Colombians are concentrated in the Jackson Heights, Jamaica, and Elmhurst sections. Nine out of 10 had only been in the United States 15 years or less and almost 45 percent had been here five years or less. Over three-fifths of those surveyed had been born in an urban area with a population of 100,000 or more. Cali alone accounted for 30 percent of all migrants. By the time of emigration, 90.5 percent were urban residents. Migrants were not only more urban but also younger than the national norm. Half were between the ages of 20 and 40, compared with only 29.7 percent of the Colombian population. While the 1970s cohort had fewer college graduates than those arriving in the sixties, both waves had above average educational backgrounds. Only 26.9 percent of the urban labor force in Colombia had secondary schooling and only 4.8 percent had attended universities, but the proportions among the migrant sample were 67 percent and 9 percent, respectively. Their elite educational background was reflected in the fact that over three-fifths had white-collar occupations at home. Among males employed at home, the proportion who had held managerial and administrative positions (15.6) was nearly twice the national average. And, at a time when the official Colombian unemployment rate averaged 10 percent, none of the migrants who had been labor force participants were unemployed just before emigrating.

By contrast, at the time of the survey, 8.5 percent of the migrants were unemployed in New York. This was almost identical to the citywide rate and well below that of all Hispanics in the city (10.9 percent). But the average masks an unusually large sex differential among Colombian migrants: 13.7 percent of women were unemployed, but only 5.2 percent of men. Compared with all Hispanics in New York, Colombian women's unemployment was slightly above the female average (11.3 percent) while the Colombian male rate was less than half the rate (10.7 percent) of all Hispanic men. The high female rate reflected, in part, the increased job search by persons without employment experience before migration; 39 percent of the women had been housewives or students in Colombia but over three-fifths of them entered the labor force in New York. But a more important reason may be the high concentration of women in cyclically vulnerable industries. Manufacturing accounts for 55 percent of employed Colombian women, but only one-fourth of males.

Only 22.6 percent were in the manufacturing sector at home compared with 36.2 percent in New York. The other principal shift was into service jobs like repair, cleaning, and hotel work: 27.3 percent of men and 16.8 percent of women held U.S. jobs in this sector, a three- to fourfold increase over their premigration levels. In Colombia before emigrating, most of those with service jobs had been in higher status professional and specialized services: nearly two-fifths of men and one-third of women in the Queens sample reported previous jobs in that sector. Those who found employment in New York often experienced downward occupational mobili-

ty, at least initially. Just 3.7 percent of males' first American jobs were in managerial or administrative occupations and the fraction of initial jobs in blue-collar occupations was, for both sexes, twice as large as in their premigration distributions.

Like Dominicans and other immigrant groups, Colombians in New York are
concentrated in smaller firms in manufacturing and services. Nearly 56 percent
worked in small firms with total employment of 50 or less. And there is clear
evidence of an ethnic job network in operation. One of every two workers was
employed in a firm where the majority of coworkers were Colombians or other
Hispanics. A quarter of these firms were owned or managed by Hispanics as well.

Central Americans

Over 211,000 Central Americans immigrated to the United States in the first eight
years of the 1980s. The average number arriving legally each year has leapt by 86
percent since the 1970s, the greatest increase recorded from any major region of the
world. This is all the more remarkable in light of the U.S. government's refusal
throughout the 1980s to grant refugee status to those fleeing the political violence in
El Salvador, Guatemala, and Nicaragua.[66] The number who have resorted to illegal
entry is widely thought to be several times larger than the legal influx. But the
Census Bureau now estimates that in the years 1980 to 1983, only about 66,000
non-Mexican undocumented aliens entered the United States from all of Latin
America.[67]

The six Spanish-speaking countries stretching from the Mexican border south to
Colombia are among the smallest and poorest in all Latin America. Most experienced rapid, export-driven growth in GNP during the 1960s.[68] But by 1970, only
Costa Rica and Panama had per capita incomes over $1,000 per year. The seventies
brought a series of economic and political crises. The oil price shock forced sharp
hikes in the critical prices of insecticides, fertilizers, and industrial chemicals,
which led to enormous current accounts deficits. Heavy foreign borrowing proved
to be a short-lived means to sustain growth, for the oil crisis was followed by
declining world prices for the region's primary products as well as the collapse of
the Central American Common Market. Since 1978, both El Salvador and Nicaragua have been torn by war. Guatemala has also had considerable civil strife,
though with less damage to the economy in recent years. Besides the direct human
and material costs of these armed conflicts, they have discouraged foreign investment and tourism and have encouraged capital flight and emigration.

The growth of Central American immigration to the United States is too recent
for much detailed economic or sociological research on it to have been completed to
date. Empirical analysis is hampered by the fact that, though increasing at a very
high rate, the number of migrants from the region is still of such relatively small
size that standard government population surveys have not produced enough sample
observations for extensive statistical tests. But some local research projects have
begun to help remedy this.

In 1979 a survey was conducted of 573 migrants to the United States from urban
areas of Costa Rica and El Salvador. GDP per capita in the former averages about

twice that of the latter, but by 1980 the rate of urbanization of the population in El Salvador (40 percent) was only 5 percentage points lower than in Costa Rica and both were sending growing numbers of urban migrants to the United States. In his analysis of the survey, Poitras (1983) reports that two-thirds of the migrants were male and most were young: two out of three of the Costa Ricans and three out of four Salvadorans were age 35 or under. Sixty percent of the Costa Ricans and half the Salvadorans were married, but most emigrated without their dependents.

Though relatively young, most were old enough to have accumulated some work experience. Far from being part of the marginal surplus labor pool often thought to dominate migration streams, they were invariably employed at the time of leaving the country, except for those still in school. Educational and occupational backgrounds were quite diverse, though certainly not concentrated at the low end of their national distributions. Total years of schooling completed averaged 10.8 for Costa Rican migrants and just over 10 for Salvadorans. Forty percent of the former and over one-fourth of the latter had some higher, postsecondary education. Occupationally, one in three Costa Ricans and one in four Salvadorans had been professionals, technicians, or other white-collar workers at home.

Four out of five were admitted to the United States with proper entry documents. Only 24.5 percent of the Costa Ricans and 8.1 percent of Salvadorans held the status of permanent resident aliens or temporary workers (H-2), which permitted employment. Over half of those from Costa Rica and two-fifths of Salvadorans came on tourist visas, then took advantage of lax INS enforcement to find jobs. A mere 1 percent of Costa Ricans took the risker route of entering without documents, but 41.7 percent of Salvadorans in the sample did so, mainly by traveling the length of Mexico to slip across the northern border.

However, those surveyed overwhelmingly viewed their visit as temporary. On average, Costa Ricans stayed in the United States only two years and Salvadorans one and one-half years. Though not making a long-term commitment to their new labor market, most took full-time jobs throughout their residence. Downward mobility relative to their job status at home was the norm. Three out of four took blue-collar work like restaurant helpers, clerks, domestics, construction crewmen, and manual laborers. Though low wage by American standards, compared with their average premigration hourly earnings in Costa Rica ($1 per hour) and El Salvador ($0.80 per hour), their wages in the United States averaged a fourfold increase for both nationalities. Higher pay was typically achieved by migrants fluent in English, with more premigration work experience at above average wages, and with previous U.S. employment. Nearly three-fifths of Costa Ricans and over 56 percent of Salvadorans indicated that they would try to return later to work again in an American city.

Rodriguez (1987) has reported some suggestive early findings from a study of undocumented Central American migrants in Houston. Interviews were conducted by a team of Spanish-speaking interviewers in 1985 with 150 such migrants, located through community activities and chain sampling procedures. Just over half of the sample were Salvadorans, 21 percent were from Honduras, 19 percent from Guatemala, and 5 percent from Nicaragua. Nine out of 10 were less than 40 years old, with nearly 55 percent between the ages of 18 and 29. About 65 percent had no more than primary schooling, 28.7 percent had completed secondary school, and 6.7 percent had attended a postsecondary institution.

When questioned about their reasons for emigrating, 61 percent of those from Guatemala and 81 percent of those from Honduras said that "economic factors" were most important to them. But 36.7 percent of the Salvadorans cited "political conflict" as their main motivation for leaving, and the large number indicating "economic" motives were found to be largely referring to war-related factors: for example, former vendors cited the destruction of the town marketplace and factory workers complained of being dismissed because of damages sustained by their factory or problems in transporting raw materials or finished products over dangerous or obstructed roads.

Four out of five were employed at the time of the interview, invariably in low-wage, low-status jobs. The average hourly wage was only $3.35, the legal minimum, and 10.6 percent received less than that. These low earnings are in part attributable to the depressed state of the Houston labor market in 1985, when the unemployment rate was 12.6 percent. They also reflect the weak educational background (relative to Americans) and command of English of most migrants. But among those making just $4 an hour were a number from skilled backgrounds at home (mechanics, welders, and school teachers).

The structure of their work groups bears a striking resemblance to that observed for other recent Hispanic immigrants. Nine out of 10 Salvadorans and 84.6 percent of Honduran workers were employed in crews composed either entirely of undocumented aliens or of a mixture of the undocumented and Mexican Americans.[69] Employer interviews revealed that firms valued undocumented work crews not only for their docility but for their ability to quickly recruit other workers to meet sudden increases in business. For newly arrived migrants speaking little English, such ethnic clustering can dramatically expedite job search and on-the-job socialization and skill training.

These findings are generally consistent with those of North and Houston (1976) based on interviews with 237 apprehended undocumented migrants from Western Hemisphere nations other than Mexico. The largest component of this subsample (41.8 percent) originated in Central America and another 40 percent came from South America. Over half had lived in cities of 1 million or more inhabitants at home and a mere 10 percent had been farm workers. Nearly 17 percent had held professional or managerial occupations at origin. Compared with the Rodriguez study group, these migrants were somewhat better educated: 47.8 percent had completed more than eight years of schooling and 14 percent had some postsecondary education. Nearly half spoke some English, though only 18.8 percent felt they spoke "very well."

With an average age of 30 these migrants were younger than the American average by nine years. But they came to the United States with a mean of 12.8 years of work experience. A substantial fraction had relatives or other migrants they could ask for assistance in finding housing and employment. More than one-fourth reported a parent or sibling already in the country. The work they found involved considerable downward occupational mobility for many as well as a sectoral shift

into manufacturing. The proportion with professional or managerial jobs dropped sharply to only 3.4 percent, while the proportion in service work jumped from only 6.9 percent at origin to 24.9 percent and the share of operatives and nonfarm laborers from 31.2 to 48.6 percent. A threefold increase (to 52 percent) occurred in the proportion employed in manufacturing. This no doubt accounts for the tripling of the percentage in labor unions, from 9 percent at home to 29 percent after migration. Despite the cyclicity of much of manufacturing, most appear to have secured relatively continuous employment. On average they worked 2.2 years out of the 2.5 of residence in the country. More than one in three worked on the same job for two or more years. The mean wage on their most recent job was, at $3.05, higher than that of undocumented Mexicans but one-third lower than the U.S. average in 1975.

INEQUALITY AT WORK

Appendix

TABLE 2A.1. Income Shares of Families in Mexico, 1950–69

Decile	1950		1958		1963		1969	
	By Decile	Cumulative	By Decile	Cumulative	By Decile	Cumulative	By Decile	Cumulative
Poorest								
10%	2.7	2.7	2.2	2.2	2.0	2.0	2.0	2.0
2	3.4	6.1	2.8	5.0	2.2	4.2	2.0	4.0
3	3.8	9.9	3.3	8.3	3.2	7.4	3.0	7.0
4	4.4	14.3	3.9	12.2	3.7	11.1	3.5	10.5
5	4.8	19.1	4.5	16.7	4.6	15.7	4.5	15.0
6	5.5	24.6	5.5	22.2	5.2	20.9	5.0	20.0
7	7.0	31.6	6.3	28.5	6.6	27.5	7.0	27.0
8	8.6	40.2	8.6	37.1	9.9	37.4	9.0	36.0
9	10.8	51.0	13.6	50.7	12.7	50.1	13.0	49.0
Richest								
10%	49.0	100.0	49.3	100.0	49.9	100.0	51.0	100.0

SOURCE: Evans and James (1979).

TABLE 2A.2. Demographic and Socioeconomic Indices, U.S. and Major Source Countries of Hispanic Immigrants

	U.S.	Mexico	Dominican Republic	Colombia	Ecuador	Peru	El Salvador	Guatemala
POPULATION (mlns.)								
1985	239	79	6	28	9	19	5	8
2000	262	110	9	37	14	25	6	12
LIFE EXPECTANCY AT BIRTH, 1985								
Males	72	64	63	63	64	57	60	58
Females	80	69	66	67	68	60	67	63
INFANT MORTALITY RATE, 1985[a]	11	50	70	48	67	94	65	65
NUMBER ENROLLED IN SCHOOL AS % OF AGE GROUP, 1984								
Primary	101	116	112	119	114	116	70	65
Secondary	95	55	45	49	55	61	24	17
Higher Educ.	57	15	12	13	33	22	12	7
% OF POPULATION URBAN, 1985	74	69	56	67	52	68	43	41
% OF 1980 LABOR FORCE IN:								
Agriculture	4	37	43	34	39	40	43	57
Industry	31	29	15	24	20	18	19	17
Services	66	35	39	42	42	42	37	26
INFLATION RATE PER YEAR, 1980–85[b]	5.3	62.2	14.6	22.5	29.7	98.6	11.6	7.4
GNP PER CAPITA 1985[b]	$16,690	$2080	$790	$1320	$1160	$1010	$820	$1250

[a]Measured as number of infant deaths per 1,000 births.

[b]Calculated in U.S. dollars, based on 3-year smoothed exchange rates.

SOURCE: World Bank (1987).

NOTES

1. According to the Census Bureau, "Other Hispanic" origin refers to persons whose origins are from Spain or to persons who identify themselves only as Hispanic, Spanish, Spanish American, Hispano, or Latino.

2. See, for example, Acuna (1981).

3. See the estimates in the valuable history by Corwin (1978).

4. See Corwin and Cardoso (1978).

5. Corwin and Cardoso (1978).

6. Clark (1908): p. 467. Quoted in Corwin (1978).

7. In fact, in 1864 Abraham Lincoln signed into law an Act to Encourage Immigration, to help ease the Civil War labor shortage in the North. It allowed private firms to recruit and pay the transportation expenses of immigrants in return for a contractual agreement that the newcomers work for the sponsoring firm exclusively for a specified period. The postwar recession of 1866 set in motion the repeal of the law two years later. On the history of immigration policies, see Briggs (1984).

8. Corwin (1978).

9. U.S. Bureau of the Census (1975a). The definition of "immigrant" on which government statistics are based has varied over time, so caution is required in comparing year-to-year counts. But the general practice has been to count as immigrants only those intending to reside in the U.S. for a substantial period. Intended stays of a minimum of six months or a year were common criteria in the earliest enumeration procedures, while the possession of permanent residence status has been the key distinction between immigrants and "nonimmigrants" (tourists, border commuters, etc.) in recent years. See the discussion in *Ibid.*, p. 97.

10. The labor needs of the northern industrialized states during the 1920s were met by the large-scale migration of blacks from the rural South as well as by many of the 4.1 million legal immigrants who entered the country during the decade. Though less than half the record volumes of 1901–1910, this still-large number of admissions was made possible by the long delays in assigning all national quotas and fully implementing the new system.

11. U.S. Bureau of the Census (1975a).

12. See, for example, Barrera (1980).

13. Corwin and Cardoso (1978).

14. See Bach (1978).

15. See the contrasting estimates and analyses in Hoffman (1978) and McWilliams (1968).

16. For useful examinations of the *bracero* program see Bustamante (1978) and Galarza (1964).

17. U.S. Bureau of the Census (1975a).

18. Aspe and Beristain (1984).

19. Cockcroft (1983), p. 158.

20. For example, in 1970 the net foreign income earned on new investments in Mexico was $473.6 million (U.S.), but only $154.2 million was reinvested. See Cockcroft (1983), p. 158.

21. Barkin (1987).

22. See Appendix Table 2A.1.

23. Aspe and Beristain (1984).

24. Cockcroft (1983), p. 260.

25. Estimate for 1978 from a study conducted under the auspices of the Ministry of Labor, cited in Evans and James (1979).

26. U.S. Immigration and Naturalization Service (1989b).

27. Warren and Passel (1987).

28. The 481 Mexicans were the largest single national subsample of the total of 793 aliens, ages 16 and over, apprehended for illegal entry in May and June of 1975 at 19 sites across the country. This does not necessarily reflect their true share of the undocumented population because the INS concentrates its enforcement effort in the Southwest and because those arriving illegally from other countries are thought to more often seek entry along the East Coast by means of improper documents. To minimize untruthful answers, the project used bilingual interviewers unaffiliated with the INS, assured the aliens that compliance was voluntary and all answers confidential, made no attempt to identify the respondents, and conducted the interviews after all INS processing was completed. Perhaps due to these assurances and the diversion the interviews offered from their boring wait for transportation back home, the nonresponse rate was only 5 percent. Confidence in the honesty of most responses is heightened by the willingness the aliens showed in giving potentially damaging information on such things as whether they intended to return to the United States (over half admitted they did).

29. Due to geographical dispersal over time, particularly among the Mexicans, 46.6 percent of the original sample was not located for the 1976 reinterviews. But 67 percent of the initial Mexican sample and 82 percent of the Cubans were reinterviewed during either the second or the third waves of the project. Portes and Bach's (1985: p. 102) tests of sample mortality bias found no significant effects on any important socioeconomic variables. But the later waves did include relatively larger proportions of those with more children, relatives, or friends in the U.S., since these members of the original sample were easier to locate.

30. CENEP (1979): Table 4.1.

31. CENEP (1979): pp. 52, 108.

32. Dietz (1986): p. 84.

33. Dietz (1986): pp. 126–129.

34. Quoted in Dietz (1986): p. 132.

35. Weisskoff and Wolff (1975).

36. Dietz (1986): Table 5.10.

37. Dietz (1986): Tables 5.5, 5.7.

38. Dietz (1986): Table 4.3.

39. CENEP (1979): Table 4.5.

40. U.S. Department of Commerce, Vol. II (1979): p. 46.

41. Safa (1985): p. 11.

42. Dietz (1986): p. 254.

43. U.S. Department of Commerce, Vol. I (1979): p. 5.

44. Weisskoff (1986): ch. 8.

45. The source of these and subsequent migration figures for Puerto Rico is the Puerto Rico Planning Board.

46. Fitzpatrick (1971): p. 15.

47. U.S. Bureau of the Census (1953): Table 4.

48. See Gray (1975).

49. See Ortiz (1986).

50. This and the following estimates of the inflows in each period are drawn from Azicri (1981); Fagen, Brody, and O'Leary (1968); and Portes and Bach (1985).

51. Fagen, Brody, and O'Leary (1968): p. 23.

52. Portes and Bach (1985): Table 62 and pp. 148–149.

53. Bach, Bach, and Triplett (1981).

54. Portes and Bach (1985): Table 39.

55. Rogg (1974): p. 28.

56. Portes and Bach (1985): Table 62 and p. 193.

57. Portes and Bach (1985): Table 64.

58. Portes and Bach (1985): Table 63.

59. For this and other selected economic and demographic data on the principal source countries, see Appendix Table 2A.2.

60. Their study traces the 300,000 figure back to an early inaccurate tabulation and interpretation of the 1981 Dominican census.

61. There is still relatively little research and many unresolved questions about the role of intermediate sectors in developing economies. See D. L. Johnson (1983).

62. Bray (1985, 1987) reports that a survey of one Dominican town indicated that 84 percent of those in the highest socioeconomic group were return migrants, compared with only 22 percent of the rural sector. Return visits of one to four months each year appeared quite common.

63. World Bank (1984).

64. See Chaney (1976).

65. For survey details and the results cited, see Urrea (1982). See also Gurak and Kritz (1983 and 1988) for comparisons of Colombian and Dominican migrants.

66. See U.S. General Accounting Office (1984).

67. Passell and Woodrow (1987).

68. On the recent economic history of the region see, for example, Weeks (1985).

69. Given the selection method employed and the small sample size, one suspects that such estimates could be biased upward. But the general finding is consistent with the results discussed earlier for other Hispanic immigrant groups in studies using quite different sampling methods.

3

Growth and Stagnation in Employment and Earnings

This chapter investigates the changes in Hispanics' earnings, employment, and poverty over the postwar period. In order to do so, it has been necessary to construct a new data series for the years 1950 to 1980. Raw census microdata were exploited to calculate total income, labor earnings, poverty rates, and employment ratios for a consistently defined Hispanic population amenable to interyear comparisons. After studying the main patterns revealed by these decennial cross-sections, the analysis turns to annual time-series data to track the trends that have occurred from the 1970s through the late 1980s. In attempting to account for the findings, particular attention is directed to the influences of age, educational attainment, immigration, language attributes, discrimination, unionization, and sectoral shifts in demand.

Data Comparability Problems

A principal reason for the dearth of economic time-series research on Hispanics of the sort long widely available on women and blacks is no doubt the absence of consistent data series prior to the 1970s. In fact, not until 1973 did the Census Bureau adopt the current definition of "persons of Spanish origin" (based on self-identification of survey respondents) and begin publishing regular tabulations on their economic characteristics from the monthly Current Population Survey.

Before that, the only national source of information on them was the decennial census. However, successive censuses used different definitions of Spanish origin or descent in collecting and presenting data. The first such data became available in the 1850 census from questions on respondents' country of birth. In 1890 another question was used on parents' country of birth. Then in 1930 the Census Bureau, reacting to the accelerated in-migration of Mexican workers during the 1920s, tried to identify native-born "Mexicans of Spanish-Colonial descent" from a direct question on race—the first and last time the bureau categorized Hispanics as a racial group. But this was replaced in 1940 by another category, "persons of Spanish mother tongue," based on a question on "language spoken in earliest childhood" asked of a 5 percent sample. Published tabulations were made for this group cross-classified by three nativity and parentage classes: foreign born, native of foreign or mixed parentage, and native of native parentage.

The methodology again changed in 1950, to one based on enumerating "persons of Spanish surname" (from official lists of several thousand names) on the census schedules as part of the general coding operation. The same approach was used in 1960, but in both censuses it was applied only to residents of the five southwestern states. Information on the massive postwar Puerto Rican influx to the Northeast was derived from two questions: one on specific state or outlying area of birth and another on "Puerto Rican stock" (either respondent or parents born on the island).

The 1970 census introduced still another characterization, "Spanish heritage," based on mother tongue, Spanish surname (in the Southwest), and Puerto Rican birth or parentage. Although this was used in most of that year's published census tabulations, one volume of Subject Reports focused on "Spanish origin" persons. This new category was based on self-identification as one of five groups: Mexican, Puerto Rican, Cuban, Central or South American, or other Spanish. An annual supplement to the Current Population Survey (CPS) was initiated in November 1969 to provide more frequent demographic and socioeconomic data on the "Spanish origin" population. But when the CPS began collecting monthly data in 1973, revisions were introduced; in particular, expanding the number of responses categorized as Mexican-origin to include "Mexican," "Mexican-American," or "Chicano." Follow-up studies showed that this had the effect of diminishing markedly the comparability of the 1969–72 figures with those compiled under the definition used from 1973 to the present in both the CPS and the census.

Despite the lack of intercensal comparability in the published figures on these various Hispanic classifications, three pieces of information on ethnic and national identity were contained in every census from 1950 through 1980: (1) the country, or outlying area, of birth; (2) whether the respondent is of Puerto Rican stock; and (3) whether the respondent has a Spanish surname. Although the last of these is limited to the five states of the Southwest, native-born persons of Mexican ancestry have long been overwhelmingly concentrated in that region. The other major components of the Hispanic population—Puerto Ricans and immigrants from Mexico, Cuba, and other Spanish-speaking countries—are identifiable from (1) and (2). Hence, this information provides an opportunity to construct socioeconomic series on Hispanics defined in a consistent manner across four census years.

Income and Earnings Trends: 1949–1979

Data and Study Sample

Does the current ratio of Hispanic to Anglo incomes represent a historical reduction or an increase in inequality? The brief time frame offered by the available CPS data cannot answer this. To produce a consistent data series for the postwar period, I have exploited the raw microdata files of the Public Use Samples of the 1950–1980 Censuses of Population. The 1/1000 samples were used for 1960–80, but a larger sampling ratio (.0055) of the 1950 census was used because of the much smaller number of Hispanics enumerated that year.[1] To construct a consistent definition of the Hispanic population I relied upon the only three relevant pieces of information contained in every one of these censuses: respondent's country or outlying area of birth, Puerto Rican stock, and Spanish surname. The census list of Spanish surnames has been updated over the years, creating the possibility of some noncomparability. However, in producing new 1-in-100 samples of the 1950 census in 1984, the bureau added a new variable to the file that identifies individuals according to the 1980 census definition of Spanish surname. My cross-tabulations showed relatively little difference in the subsamples generated from the old and new versions, but the 1980 definition is used here.

There appears to be substantial comparability between our study sample categories and the "Spanish origin" identifier used increasingly by the Census Bureau since 1970. But, cross-tabulations of 1980 census data by both categorizations indicate that 16.6 percent of persons who self-identify as Spanish origin are not included in the study sample categories.[2] Of these, 49 percent are of Mexican origin and another 38 percent in the residual other Spanish grouping. On the other hand, sole use of the Spanish origin classification results in the exclusion of 7.1 percent of those counted as Hispanic in the study sample based on their Spanish surname, place of birth, or Puerto Rican ancestry. Of those excluded, more than 9 out of 10 are in the residual category of other Spanish surname.

To take into account the high degree of geographic concentration of Hispanics in drawing comparisons with non-Hispanics, the study samples of non-Hispanic whites and blacks and of Hispanics were restricted to seven states: New York, Florida, and the Southwest (Arizona, California, Colorado, New Mexico, and Texas). Though Hispanics are now more dispersed than in years past, these states still account for over three-fourths of the entire Spanish origin population.[3]

Principal Findings

Ratios of Hispanic to non-Hispanic white (Anglo) median incomes and labor earnings are presented separately for males and females, by national-origin group and urban residence, in Table 3.1.[4] Several interesting trends over the postwar period deserve to be highlighted:

1. Among men, the overall Hispanic–Anglo annual income ratio did not change at all in the 1950s, but did rise by over 11 percentage points (from .583 to .694) between 1959 and 1969. However, in the 1970s, the ratio turned downward, dropping to .657 by the end of the decade. The two largest ethnic groups, native-born Mexican-origin men (who dominate the "Other Spanish Surname" category in our tables) and Puerto Ricans, began in 1949 with incomes 55 percent and 76 percent, respectively, of the white non-Hispanic level. Both experienced increases relative to Anglos during the 1960s, but the Puerto Rican–Anglo ratio fell in the 1970s and the native Mexican ratio remained stuck at 69 percent. Immigrants from Mexico and

TABLE 3.1. Hispanic–Anglo Median Income and Earnings Ratios by Sex, Ethnic Group, and Urban Residence, 1949–79[a]

	All Areas	Urban Areas	Foreign Born			Puerto Rican	Other Spanish Surname
			Mexican	Cuban	Other		
INCOME RATIOS							
Males							
1949	.586	.700	.552	.672	1.000	.759	.552
1959	.583	.650	.417	.729	.875	.604	.625
1969	.694	.693	.556	.764	.833	.694	.694
1979	.657	.675	.634	.850	.762	.631	.696
Females							
1949	.600	.750	.467	.733	1.000	.933	.600
1959	.722	.737	.528	.778	.861	1.111	.611
1969	.808	.857	.500	1.000	1.231	1.154	.769
1979	.726	.672	.726	.940	.736	.683	.751
EARNINGS RATIOS							
Males							
1949	.586	.700	.517	.690	.845	.724	.517
1959	.592	.660	.408	.694	.837	.571	.653
1969	.667	.705	.567	.760	.800	.667	.667
1979	.659	.667	.534	.733	.667	.662	.667
Females							
1949	.558	.667	.500	.588	.882	.824	.471
1959	.565	.583	.522	.804	.696	.870	.435
1969	.714	.857	.430	.857	.971	1.086	.629
1979	.786	.833	.714	.900	.714	1.000	.764

[a]Hispanics defined as all persons who have a Spanish surname, are of Puerto Rican stock, or were born in a Spanish-speaking country. Sample restricted to the civilian population 16 years old and over resident in New York, Florida, or the 5 southwestern states.

SOURCE: 1950–80 Public Use Microdata Census Samples.

Cuba also enjoyed relative income increases in the 1960s, though the greatest progress for Cubans occurred in the following decade. The relatively small sample of other Latin American migrants in this country before the 1960s renders statistics for the earlier years relatively volatile, but Latin Americans do appear to have suffered a marked drop in their relative income during the seventies.

2. When we narrow our focus to annual wages and salaries (by far the largest single type of income), it is clear that the average male Hispanic's wage was nearly as far below the white non-Hispanic level in 1959 as it had been 10 years before. But in the sixties the wage ratio registered a steep jump from 59.2 to 66.7 percent. As with overall income, wage progress was halted thereafter. The relative earnings of individual ethnic groups followed the general pattern, rising in the 1960s, then stagnating or falling in the following decade.

3. Among women, Hispanics had individual incomes that were an average of 40 percent lower than white non-Hispanics in 1949. But the gap fell through the next 20 years to 19 percent in 1969, before suffering a widening to over 27 percent by

1979. Cuban women had near-equality with Anglos by that year. By contrast, Puerto Rican women fell from near-equality in the 1960s to an average income level in 1979 some one-third below Anglos.

4. The wages of Hispanic women were unchanged relative to Anglo women throughout the fifties, then rose slowly in the 1960s (from 56.5 percent to 71.4 percent of the Anglo level). They continued to increase in the seventies, though at only half the rate of the previous decade. Cuban and Puerto Rican relative wages were well above the other national-origin groups. The fact that the relative wages of Puerto Rican working women rose at the same time that the average income of all Puerto Rican women was falling is most likely the result of their declining labor force participation in the 1970s and 1980s. Since women with the most marginal, low-paying jobs are the most prone to labor force withdrawal, their exit would tend to inflate the average wage level of those still employed. But the average income level would also be depressed by increased unemployment.

Annual Trends: 1973–1987

This section supplements the decennial census data with information from the annual series on Spanish origin households compiled by the CPS since 1973. These data have the dual advantage of being more up-to-date and of revealing year-to-year fluctuations. But they also have serious limitations for studying Hispanics, particularly the lack of any information on English language ability or country of origin. Moreover, very few published CPS tabulations control for type of Spanish origin or geographic region.

If we look first at the overall real income of Hispanic families, Figure 3.1 shows clearly how far it has remained below the average for white families since the early 1970s. Adjusted for inflation, median Hispanic incomes have fallen in both absolute and relative terms since the early 1970s. Living standards for the average family, regardless of race or ethnicity, have declined in this period, but the three recessions (1975, 1980, and 1982) hit minorities especially hard. While the real income level of whites fell by 9.5 percent from 1979 to 1982, black incomes dropped 11.6 percent and Hispanics 13.9 percent. The subsequent economic recovery pulled up the Hispanic average (from $19,106 to $20,306 in 1987 dollars), but much more slowly than either white or black incomes. Hence, by 1987, Hispanic income was still 8.9 percent lower in real terms than in 1973, and the Hispanic–white ratio was only 62.9 percent, compared with 69.2 percent 15 years earlier. In fact, Hispanics' economic status also declined relative to black families, in terms of both median income and poverty rates. For example, in 1973 the average Hispanic family income was 19.8 percent higher than that of blacks; by 1987 the differential had shrunk by over 7 percentage points.

Of course, comparisons of the total incomes of families are extremely difficult to evaluate, given the often substantial differences in the various sources of income, the number of earners per family, and related factors. To start reducing such complications, let us look only at the income of males. Table 3.2 presents my calcula-

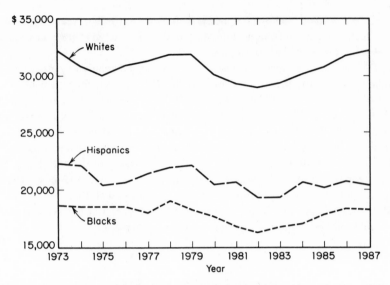

FIGURE 3.1. Median family income, by race and Spanish origin of householder, 1973–1987 (in 1987 dollars). Source: U.S. Bureau of the Census (1988).

TABLE 3.2. Hispanic–White Median Income Ratios, Male Income Recipients, 1973–87

| | | Men 25–64 | |
	Men 15 & Over	All	Year-Round, Full-Time Workers
1973	.734		
1974	.728		
1975	.729	.670	.705
1976	.710	.683	.731
1977	.735	.697	.720
1978	.732	.697	.732
1979	.721	.693	.739
1980	.725	.675	.729
1981	.714	.666	.717
1982	.710	.644	.705
1983	.703	.682	.706
1984	.674	.671	.723
1985	.668	.653	.698
1986	.638	.622	.677
1987	.647	.630	.692

SOURCE: U.S. Bureau of the Census, Current Population Reports, *Money Income of Households, Families and Persons in the US* (Series P-60), various years.

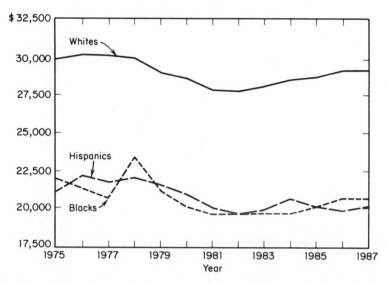

FIGURE 3.2. Median income of males, ages 25–64, year-round, full-time workers, 1975–1987 (in 1987 dollars). Source: U.S. Bureau of the Census (1976–88).

tions of the annual ratios of the median incomes of Hispanic and white male income recipients from 1973 to 1987.[5] With or without controls for age, a clear pattern of decline in Hispanics' relative incomes is evident. Among men 25 to 64 in 1975 (the first year with published incomes for both Hispanics and all whites in this age group), Hispanics received incomes 67 percent of the overall white level. The ratio rose to nearly 70 percent late in the decade, then fell to 64 percent in the 1982 recession. After recovering to the mid-seventies level in 1983, it fell subsequently to only 63 percent in 1987.

Such annual income figures may, of course, be affected by intergroup differences in unemployment. The detailed analysis of unemployment data in the next two chapters reveals a persistent pattern of Hispanic joblessness running half again as high as the white rate. To control for these differences, let us turn to income data on males 25 to 64 who were employed year-round in full-time jobs. Figure 3.2 plots the annual changes in the median income of these workers, expressed in 1987 dollars to adjust for inflation. In 1975, fully employed white workers averaged $29,927 per year, compared with $21,095 for Hispanics. Aside from a spike ($22,006) in 1978, Hispanic income fell throughout the late seventies and early eighties, to a trough of $19,586 in 1982. Though rising slightly (to $20,173) since then, Hispanics in 1987 were still an average of nearly a thousand dollars below their income level over a decade earlier, an overall decline of 4.4 percent. White incomes suffered as well, dropping from a high of $30,277 in 1976 to $27,771 by 1982, before recovering to $29,163 by 1987. But the steeper decline of Hispanic income caused the Hispanic–white ratio to drop from a high of 73.9 percent in 1979 to only 69.2 percent in 1987 (Table 3.2, col. 3).[6]

Poverty: 1949–1987

Even after five years of economic expansion, over 28 percent of Hispanics—five and one-half million people—were poor in 1987. This was over two and one-half times the poverty rate of whites and less than 5 percentage points under the black rate. Two of every five youth of Spanish origin under the age of 18—nearly 3 million children—live in poor families. One in four Hispanic families has an income below the official poverty line. Among Puerto Rican families, the poverty rate is nearly 38 percent (see Table 2.1). This is the worst of any ethnic or racial group in the country, and is more than one-fourth higher than the black rate.

The 1980s witnessed a revival of fierce debates over the nature and causes of poverty. Most focused on the relative importance of changes in family structure, government social programs, and macroeconomic factors in explaining poverty trends over the past two decades. Perhaps the most hotly contested position has been the view that federal antipoverty efforts in the sixties are themselves to blame for the subsequent rise in poverty rates. Murray (1984) presented the most sustained argument for this theory. In his well-known book *Losing Ground,* he contended that poverty was declining rapidly throughout the 1950s and early 1960s, well before the Great Society programs were initiated. Only in the early seventies, when the main expansions in eligibility and benefits in Aid to Families with Dependent Children (AFDC) and food stamps went fully into effect, did the poverty rate end its decline and gradually turn upward. This he largely attributes to the incentives these federal programs created for women to have more out-of-wedlock births and form single-parent households in order to qualify for higher benefits.

This became the philosophical rationale for the Reagan administration's efforts to reduce or eliminate most antipoverty programs. The average growth rates of real federal transfers rose from 7.9 percent per year during the Kennedy and Johnson administrations to 9.7 percent under Nixon and Ford. The inflation of the seventies slashed the purchasing power of benefits without cost-of-living clauses, thereby slowing the annual rate of real social welfare spending to under 4 percent during the Carter years. But the first Reagan administration adopted a conscious policy of cutting antipoverty expenditures, causing their average real growth rate to fall to only 1.5 percent per year.[7] The official poverty rate fell to a low of 11.1 percent of all persons in 1973 and remained close to 12 percent through 1979. But it rose in the 1980s into the 13–15 percent range, the highest since the mid-sixties.

A growing number of empirical studies have tested the relationship between public transfers and poverty on a variety of cross-sectional and time-series data, both at the aggregate and the micro level. For example, Danziger and Gottschalk (1985) tracked increases in the formation of female-headed households against changes in both income and in-kind transfer benefits, adjusted for inflation. They found that the real value of combined AFDC and food stamp benefit guarantees peaked in 1972, then fell 21.8 percent from 1972 to 1984. Even in relatively high-benefit areas like New York City, the AFDC real benefit level dropped by one-third in the 1970s. Darity and Myers (1983) conducted econometric analysis of time-series data on changes in the proportion of black families headed by women since the 1950s. Their results show no significant relationship between trends in transfer payments and female headship patterns. Instead, they found a strong correspondence between higher rates of female headship and declines in the ratio of marriageable men to women in the black population. William Julius Wilson (1987) has also stressed the importance of this factor, which he attributes to black men's relatively marginal employment and high rates of unemployment, incarceration, and premature mortality.

The substantial interstate differences in AFDC benefit levels over time were studied by Bane and Ellwood (1984) to see how they compared to interstate differences in family composition among the poor and nonpoor. They concluded that variations in benefits have had little impact on either divorce or out-of-wedlock birth rates. Danziger, Haveman, and Plotnick (1986) have estimated what poverty rates would have been if all transfers were excluded from money income. They find that the pretransfer incidence of poverty rose from 21.3 percent in 1965 to 24.2 percent in 1983. Since the official, posttransfer poverty rate fell from 17.3 to 15.2 percent over this same period, they interpret this as evidence that public transfers played a positive role in reducing poverty, at least until the mid-seventies. Bane (1986) has studied transitions into and out of poverty with longitudinal data on a large sample of households tracked since 1968 by the Panel Study of Income Dynamics. From the first 15 years of the panel, she found that a surprising amount of poverty results from a reshuffling of poor female-headed families out of the dissolution of already poor two-parent families. Though the proportion of poor blacks who are in female-headed households is far above average, only about 17 percent of black poverty spells start as the result of individuals moving into single-person or female-headed households. Overall, Bane finds that only a quarter to a fifth of poverty has occurred simultaneously with changes in family structure. Instead, she concludes that the bulk of poverty—even that of female-headed households—appears to be explained by changes in jobs or income.

Thus, while demographic changes have clearly put some upward pressure on the overall poverty rate, macroeconomic phenomena are receiving growing emphasis in research efforts to explain the upward trend in poverty in the seventies and eighties. It is clear that poverty rates are strongly correlated with increases in unemployment and decreases in earnings levels. This is to be expected in light of the fact that in recent years about two out of three poor families with a nonelderly household head had at least one wage earner during the previous year. Blank and Blinder (1986) estimate from time-series data that a 1-point rise in the unemployment rate of prime-age males raises the poverty rate by 0.7 percentage points, after controlling for inflation, transfers, and average income. Ellwood and Summers (1986) conducted a time-series analysis of trends in poverty since 1960 among the nonelderly population. They find that once persons over 65 are excluded from the data set, almost all the variation in poverty rates is explained by changes in the ratio of the poverty line to average family income. This close connection suggests to them that the persistence of high poverty rates in the 1970s and 1980s largely reflects the stagnation in real family-income levels. In addition to a decline in the mean of the real wage distribution since the early 1970s, there is now a great deal of evidence that the dispersion of wages (both annual and weekly) around the mean has grown as well. Rising earnings inequality has for over a decade counterbalanced the potentially positive effects of economic growth on the poverty population.[8]

How relevant are these findings to movements in the poverty rate of Hispanic families? Far too little research on the subject exists at present to hazard an answer. Some small progress can be made here by tracing the broad postwar patterns in the incidence of poverty by national-origin group. In order to develop a consistent postwar series for the first time, we once again exploit the raw microdata from the 1950–80 census sample files.

The measure of poverty used in our estimates is based on the official absolute income standard first applied in the mid-sixties. The official government method of calculating the poverty population is based on estimates of an "economy food plan" for different family types. When this method was first developed in the early 1960s, the average family spent about one-third of its income on food. The statisticians at the Social Security Administration defined the poverty line as the cost of the economy food plan multiplied by three. Different income thresholds were calculated to reflect variations in food expenditures by family composition as well as differences in food costs between rural and urban areas. Just as the income threshold was updated in later years via the Consumer Price Index (CPI), so did Orshansky (1974) extend this method backward to derive a 1959 poverty line. We follow this same approach here, using the CPI to project the 1959 line backward to calculate the poverty line income for 1949. For each year 1949–79, we use a series of official poverty lines, which vary by family size, the sex and age of the family head, and residence (farm or nonfarm). Families are categorized as poor or nonpoor according to the total family income as reported by the household head. We rely on information provided by the household head in order to maintain consistency across all three decades. Unlike later censuses, the income information in the 1950 census was collected from a sample of individuals rather than households. The only respondents questioned about the incomes of other household members were household heads. If this method tends to produce different response patterns than direct questioning of each household member, then intercensal comparisons could be misleading. By drawing income responses from only the household head in every census year we avoid this danger, though at the cost of a slight reduction in sample size.[9]

Estimates of the poverty rates of non-Hispanic white and Hispanic families from 1949 through 1979 are presented in Table 3.3. In 1949, 34.2 percent of Hispanic families had incomes below the poverty line, compared with only 10.5 percent of non-Hispanics in the same states. Foreign-born Mexicans averaged the highest rate (41.2 percent) followed by U.S.-born Mexicans and other Spanish surname families. The poverty rate was 29.3 percent among Puerto Ricans and 22.2 percent among Cubans.

Contrary to Murray's (1984) contention that poverty was rapidly declining in the 1950s, the fraction of Hispanic families who were poor was the same in 1959 as in 1949 and there was a 35 percent increase in the poverty rate of non-Hispanics. Poverty fell slightly among Mexican immigrants, but this was offset by growing poverty among Puerto Ricans and other Spanish surname families. The estimated rates for the small Cuban and Central and South American samples were lower at the end of the fifties than in 1949, but these populations were not nearly large

TABLE 3.3. Poverty Rates of Families by Sex and Ethnicity of Family Head, and Proportion of Families Female-Headed, 1949–79[a]

| | Anglo | All Hispanic | Foreign Born | | | Puerto Rican | Other Spanish Surname |
			Mexican	Cuban	Other		
% of All Families Below Poverty Line[b]							
1949	10.5	34.2	41.2	22.2	24.3	29.3	31.6
1959	14.2	34.1	38.6	13.0	3.1	32.2	35.5
1969	11.5	25.2	31.1	14.1	15.1	27.3	25.3
1979	7.2	24.2	26.5	15.2	25.8	31.7	18.9
% of Female-Headed Families Below Poverty Line							
1949	31.3	73.4	76.7	0.0	70.0	75.0	72.4
1959	33.9	54.8	52.6	0.0	0.0	50.0	62.3
1969	28.0	49.1	59.6	30.0	28.6	50.0	50.6
1979	23.1	43.8	50.4	25.6	47.9	55.8	37.2
% of Poor Families with Female Head							
1949	39.1	33.4	30.8	0.0	77.8	54.5	30.4
1959	40.6	24.3	25.0	0.0	0.0	42.5	23.0
1969	51.6	39.5	35.4	40.0	37.5	57.8	35.3
1979	51.5	48.1	35.1	37.0	54.8	72.6	46.2
% of All Families with Female Head							
1949	13.1	15.6	16.5	12.5	27.0	21.3	13.3
1959	17.0	15.1	18.4	17.4	6.2	19.2	13.1
1969	21.3	20.3	18.5	19.2	19.8	31.5	17.6
1979	21.7	24.9	18.4	21.9	29.6	41.3	23.5

[a]Hispanics defined as all persons who have a Spanish surname, are of Puerto Rican stock, or were born in a Spanish-speaking country. Sample restricted to the civilian population 16 years old and over resident in New York, Florida, or the 5 southwestern states.

[b]Poverty-line income defined according to Census Bureau standards, with separate levels for different family sizes and urban/rural residence. 1949 poverty lines estimated by 1959 poverty income levels, adjusted by CPI.

SOURCE: 1950–80 Census Public Use Microdata Samples.

enough at that time to affect the overall figures much. The lower fraction of poor Cubans was probably strongly influenced by the arrival of the initial, high-income wave of exiles in 1958 and 1959.

Only in the 1960s was there a substantial improvement for most Hispanics. The fraction poor declined from over one-third to one-fourth of all families, a percentage-point reduction more than three times that experienced by non-Hispanic whites. The largest reduction in poverty, in both absolute and percentage terms, occurred among other Spanish surname families, followed by immigrants from Mexico. The Puerto Rican rate dropped from 32.2 percent to 27.3 percent.

But the 1970s eroded the gains of the sixties for Puerto Ricans. By the end of the decade, almost as large a proportion were poor as in 1959 and Puerto Ricans had replaced Mexicans as the poorest national-origin group. The now-large population of families from Central and South America also experienced a dramatic increase in the incidence of poverty, from 15.1 to nearly 26 percent. On the other hand, both native- and foreign-born Mexicans continued to achieve lower rates, though at a slower pace than in the previous decade.

Are these decadal trends in poverty related to changes in family structure? Based on the figures in Table 3.3, there appears to be little evidence of any consistent relationship. The fraction of Hispanic families headed by women did rise over the 30-year period, but no faster than was true among white non-Hispanics.[10] By 1979, one in four Hispanic families was female-headed, compared with 21.7 percent of white non-Hispanics. Not only was the difference that year slight, but in 1959 and 1969 such families were more common among non-Hispanics than among Hispanics. And, while the portion of all poor families headed by women rose between 1949 and 1979, it was consistently lower for the pooled Hispanic sample.

Of the largest national-origin groupings, Mexican-born and other Spanish surname families experienced very similar declines in poverty from 1959 to 1979, but very dissimilar changes in family structure. The proportion of families that were female-headed remained constant among Mexican immigrants at about 18.5 percent. But it rose among the residual Spanish surname group from 13.1 to 23.5 percent. Puerto Ricans had both the highest incidence of female headship (41.3 percent) and the highest poverty rate by 1979, but the two only moved in the same direction in the 1970s. In the 1950s, when the fraction of female-headed families was declining among the Puerto Rican population in general, as well as among the poor in particular, their poverty rate was increasing. In the sixties the two rates once again moved sharply in opposite directions.

The relative importance of changes in family structure and in other factors is a complex issue that demands a level of detail in both data and analysis that is beyond the scope of the exploratory discussion intended here. From the findings of other research (reviewed later) it does seem likely that the variables shaping relative income levels are also influencing poverty levels and trends. Of these, the decennial census data provide some indication of the role of industrial and regional distributions in explaining the divergent poverty trends of Mexicans, Puerto Ricans, and other Latin American immigrants in the 1970s. The latter two groups are highly concentrated in the New York metropolitan area, where the overall poverty rate jumped from 9.3 percent in 1969 to 15.4 percent a decade later. In sharp contrast, the southwestern states where most Mexican migrants and natives live enjoyed much stronger economic growth and lower poverty. In California the poverty rate remained below 9 percent in both 1969 and 1979, and in Texas it dropped from 14.6 percent to 11.1 percent.[11]

Year-by-year poverty rates for white, black, and Spanish-origin families across the country have been tabulated by the Census Bureau since 1973. The 1973–87 series in Table 3.4 show that higher proportions of all three groups dropped below the poverty line during the 1980s. In the 1982 recession, the poverty rate was 3 percentage points above its 1973 level for whites, 5 points higher for blacks, and over 7 points higher for Hispanics. The latter have consistently been about three times more likely to be poor than has the overall white population. While blacks continue to have a higher average incidence of poverty than Spanish-origin families,

TABLE 3.4. Poverty Rates of Families
by Race and Spanish Origin of Householder,
1973–87[a]

	Poverty Rate of Families (%)		
Year	*White*	*Black*	*Hispanic*
1973	6.6	28.1	19.8
1974	6.8	26.9	21.2
1975	7.7	27.1	25.1
1976	7.1	27.9	23.1
1977	7.0	28.2	21.4
1978	6.9	27.5	20.4
1979	6.9	27.8	20.3
1980	8.0	28.9	23.2
1981	8.8	30.8	24.0
1982	9.6	33.0	27.2
1983	9.7	32.3	26.0
1984	9.1	30.9	25.2
1985	9.1	28.7	25.5
1986	8.6	28.0	24.7
1987	8.2	29.9	25.8

SOURCE: U.S. Bureau of the Census (1988).

the difference between them was cut in half between 1973 and 1987. Only 4 percentage points separated the black and Hispanic rates by the late 1980s. In some areas poverty has long been more prevalent among Hispanics than blacks. Throughout the 1970s and 1980s in New York City, the poverty rate of families headed by a person of Spanish origin (a high proportion of whom were Puerto Ricans) exceeded that of black families. The Hispanic rate climbed to a peak of 44 percent in 1985.[12]

The annual tabulations also bear out the finding from census data that the higher incidence of Hispanic female-headed households cannot account for the poverty gap. Figure 3.3 plots the poverty rates of married-couple families alone, revealing the striking fact that intact Hispanic families have long had a higher rate of poverty that either whites or blacks and the gaps between them have widened considerably since the early 1970s. Among married-couple families in 1974, 4.6 percent of whites, 13 percent of blacks, and 14.4 percent of Hispanics were poor. The rates for all three fell after the mid-seventies' recession, then rose to their highest levels (6.9 percent, 15.6 percent, and 19 percent, respectively) in the 1982 recession. By 1987, the white rate had declined to 5.1 and the black to 11.9, but 17.4 percent of intact Hispanic families were still poor.

Explanations of the Postwar Patterns

Compositional Shifts

To begin the effort of trying to interpret these patterns, it should first be noted that this period witnessed potentially significant changes in the composition of the

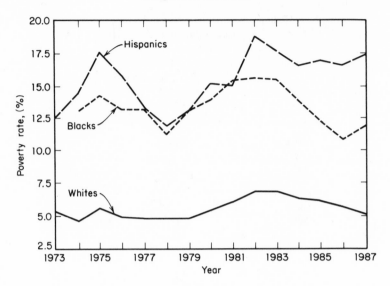

FIGURE 3.3. Percentage of married-couple families below the poverty level, by race and Spanish origin of householder, 1973–1987. Source: U.S. Bureau of the Census (1988).

Hispanic population. First, it was becoming steadily less rural, as Mexicans in particular shifted out of agriculture into jobs in small towns and cities throughout the Southwest. Since urban wage levels typically exceed rural levels, this migration alone could be responsible for some of the observed income progress. And this is in fact suggested by clear differences between overall wage patterns and those evident in urban areas alone (see Table 3.1, col. 2). At the same time that the overall Hispanic–Anglo male wage ratio was increasing, in urban areas it actually fell during the 1950s. The urban ratio did rise in the sixties, but much more slowly than the overall ratio.

Part of the increased urbanization of Hispanics reflects the shifts in ethnic composition brought on by the large Cuban inflow after the 1959 revolution, as well as the expansion of other Latin American immigration from the mid-sixties on. Both groups have concentrated heavily in a few urban areas. They also average educational levels well above Mexicans and Puerto Ricans, which might be expected to exert upward pressure on the overall Hispanic–Anglo wage ratio. To check what effect the increased Cuban and Latin American presence may have had, I recalculated the male earnings ratios for 1969 under the assumption that the ethnic and source-country distribution in that year was the same as in 1959. The results showed that only about 22 percent of the observed improvement in the overall ratio during the sixties is potentially attributable to changes in population composition.

Age and Education

One reason that this figure is not larger may be that improvements in the average educational attainment of Hispanics is not simply a reflection of immigration of

TABLE 3.5. Changes in Educational Attainment of Persons Ages 25
and over by Ethnic Group, 1950–80[a]

			Completed at Least 12 Years of Schooling (%)				
			Foreign Born				*Other*
Year	*Anglos*	*All Hispanics*	*Mexican*	*Cuban*	*Other*	*Puerto Rican*	*Spanish Surname*
1950	42.4	15.5	2.9	39.1	52.4	12.8	17.4
1960	48.8	19.2	6.2	36.7	54.8	19.6	20.2
1970	58.8	30.5	13.4	49.4	50.5	24.5	32.0
1980	77.6	41.9	20.6	56.6	46.7	33.9	50.2

[a]Hispanics defined as all persons who have a Spanish surname, are of Puerto Rican stock, or were born in a Spanish-speaking country. Sample restricted to the civilian population 16 years old and over resident in New York, Florida, or the 5 southwestern states.

SOURCE: 1950–80 Public Use Microdata Census Samples.

better-educated nationalities. In 1950, when 42 percent of all Anglo adults (ages 25 and over) were high school graduates, only 15.5 percent of Hispanics were (Table 3.5). But by 1980, the Hispanic high school completion rate (42 percent) had risen from one-third to more than one-half the Anglo level. The percentage of indigenous Mexicans with at least 12 years of schooling jumped from 17 to 50 percent and it rose among Puerto Ricans from 13 to 34 percent. Clearly, however, these groups remain at a serious educational disadvantage, particularly in light of the far higher rates of college attendance and graduation among Anglos (see Table 2.1).

In order to see what effects adjustments for Hispanic–non-Hispanic education and age differences have on their relative wages, I calculated median annual earnings ratios for males subdivided into five schooling groups and seven birth cohorts in the four census years 1950–80.[13] The use of birth cohort data has well-known advantages over other methods, such as cross-sectional averages of broad age groups. By tracking individual birth cohorts we are able to observe the work experiences of specific groups over the course of their life cycles. This should become clear as we examine the earnings ratios in Table 3.6.

Let us begin by focusing on workers with the lowest level of educational attainment. In 1950, 73.8 percent of male Hispanic workers between the ages of 25 and 64 had completed only eight or fewer years of school, compared with 34 percent of white non-Hispanic men. Among men at this level who were 25–34 (the 1916–1925 birth cohort) that year, the average Hispanic earned only 64 percent as much as whites. This ratio did compare favorably with the 52–63 percent ratios prevalent among older workers that same year. But by 1959, after accumulating another 10 years of work experience, Hispanics of the 1916–1925 cohort were still earning 35 percent less than comparably educated non-Hispanics their age. And in the following two decades the gap widened to 37 percent. That is, by the time they were approaching the end of their careers at ages 55–64 in 1980, the least-educated Hispanics were receiving less relative to otherwise similar non-Hispanics than when they first entered the labor force 40 years earlier.

TABLE 3.6. Hispanic–Anglo Male Median Earnings Ratios
by Birth Cohort and Education, 1949–79[a]

Birth Cohort	1949	1959	1969	1979
Education = 0–8 years				
1946–55				.889
1936–45			.789	.833
1926–35		.675	.806	.675
1916–25	.640	.652	.645	.630
1906–15	.517	.578	.645	
1896–1905	.632	.732		
1886–95	.556			
Education = 9–11 years				
1946–55				.782
1936–45			.914	.820
1926–35		.833	.850	.750
1916–25	.893	.887	.789	.803
1906–15	.833	.764	.797	
1896–1905	1.125	.863		
1886–95	.734			
Education = 12 years				
1946–55				.850
1936–45			.875	.854
1926–35		.800	.889	.909
1916–25	.833	.917	.988	.680
1906–15	.743	.917	.624	
1896–1905	.667	1.002		
1886–95	1.113			
Education = 13–15 years				
1946–55				.781
1936–45			1.067	.800
1926–35		.909	.855	.650
1916–25	.900	.725	.820	.753
1906–15	1.012	.868	.400	
1896–1905	NA	NA		
1886–95	.318			
Education = 16+ years				
1946–55				.844
1936–45			.700	.808
1926–35		.590	.912	.758
1916–25	.817	.788	.812	.397
1906–15	.314	.627	NA	
1896–1905	.761	.917		
1886–95	NA			
All Ages 25–64	.633	.642	.705	.661

[a]Hispanics defined as all persons who have a Spanish surname, are of Puerto Rican stock, or were born in a Spanish-speaking country. Sample restricted to the civilian population ages 25–64 and resident in New York, Florida, or the 5 southwestern states.

NOTE: Ratios are of median annual earnings of Hispanics to white non-Hispanics.
NA = not available, owing to lack of sample observations.

SOURCE: 1950–80 Public Use Microdata Census Samples.

Moving down Table 3.6 to those with 9–11 years of schooling reveals that Hispanics born between 1916 and 1925 were far closer to the non-Hispanic wage level than the less-educated men in their cohort. However, they also saw their relative earnings decline, from 89 percent of the non-Hispanic average to 79–80 percent between 1969 and 1979. Only among the men in this birth cohort who completed high school was there improvement in Hispanics' relative wages through the 1960s. Hispanic high school graduates were earning 83 percent as much as whites their age in 1949, 92 percent in 1959, and had nearly attained earnings parity by 1969. Hispanics with one to three years of college suffered a widening pay gap in the fifties. But the following decade saw their earnings ratio rise from 72.5 to 82 percent. Among college graduates in this same birth cohort the ratio fell in the 1950s but recovered in the sixties, rising from 79 to 81 percent.

Turning to the younger cohort of workers born between 1926 and 1935, we see that Hispanics of most schooling levels made progress in narrowing the wage differential with non-Hispanics in the course of the sixties. The most dramatic improvement seems to have come among college graduates: the wage gap shrank from 41 to only 9 percent.

However, since the 1960s there has been a general pattern of deterioration in Hispanics' relative earnings. For example, the wages of Hispanic college graduates ages 35–44 in 1970 plunged from 91 percent of the non-Hispanic level that year to 76 percent 10 years later.[14] Some cohorts did manage to make progress in the seventies, such as college graduates ages 25–34 in 1970. But of the 15 birth cohorts with earnings in both 1969 and 1979, 11 experienced a decline in Hispanics' relative earnings. The setback was so large for most Hispanic workers between the ages of 45 and 64 that it wiped out the gains of the sixties.

These results demonstrate the importance of schooling and age differences in accounting for Hispanics' lower earnings. This is consistent with the findings of cross-sectional studies of 1970 census and 1976 Survey of Income and Education data.[15] But like these other studies, our results reveal that a substantial portion of the wage gap remains unexplained by these factors alone.

Language and Immigration Problems

The influence of English language ability on Hispanics' earnings has been the subject of a growing number of empirical studies in the last few years. It is generally presumed that individuals with weak command of the language will bear labor market costs that will impede earnings progress. These may be caused by problems in job search as well as on-the-job productivity losses caused by limited communication skills. Reimers (1983; 1984) was among the first to test the wage effects of language problems with data from the Survey of Income and Education (SIE), a special national survey conducted by the Census Bureau in 1976. She estimated separate wage regressions for males of each Spanish-origin group, including in each a dummy variable indicating whether the respondent reports he does not "speak and understand English very well." Poor command of English was found associated with 18 percent lower earnings for Puerto Ricans and from 4 to 14 percent lower earnings for the other main groups (though only the Puerto Rican estimates were statistically significant). Grenier (1984) used SIE information on "language spoken as a child," rather than the respondent's self-assessment of his current speaking abilities, in wage regressions on a pooled sample of Hispanic males. His estimates suggested that language limitations may account for as much as one-third of the wage differential between Hispanic and white non-Hispanic males.

An even larger effect was estimated by McManus, Gould, and Welch (1983). They also worked with the SIE but departed sharply from other studies in constructing their own scalar measure of "English Language Deficiency" (ELD) out of the answers to both questions on comprehension and speaking skills and on types of language usage (e.g., frequency of reading English-language newspapers, usual language spoken with friends). They concluded from their wage regressions that:

> Once ELD [English language deficiency] is taken into account, the differentials in wages which are associated with Hispanic ethnicity, US nativity, schooling abroad and time in the United States are no longer statistically significant. This is not evidence that these factors are unimportant, rather it is evidence that their effects are mediated through measured ELD. (p. 121)

This measure of ELD has been challenged on the grounds that it risks confounding influences of cultural and family life-style with basic communication skills.[16] Further questions could be raised about the techniques used to collapse the 42 "response patterns" they observed into seven levels of ELD. With commendable frankness, they note that this aggregation was done "without hard and fast rules" (p. 126), that wage differentials played the central role in assigning response patterns to their ELD categories (p. 129), and that their main results were "perplexing patterns" that readers would have to decide whether or not to judge as "internally consistent" (p. 122).

More recently, Kossoudji (1988) has found from the same data set that there are large ethnic and occupational variations in the return from fluency in English. Among Hispanic male immigrants holding professional and managerial jobs in the United States, lack of English language ability was not found to have significant negative effects on earnings. But, she argues that focusing only on those actually in such jobs may create biased results, since lack of English language skills tends to restrict Hispanics to service and operative occupations. After taking into account the negative effect that lack of English has on access to high-paying occupations, she found that Hispanics with no knowledge of English averaged 27 percent lower "expected earnings" than those who speak the language fluently. In sharp contrast, non-English-speaking Asian immigrants were found to average 8.6 percent *higher* expected earnings than otherwise similar Asians fluent in the language. Why do Hispanics but not Asians suffer a large language handicap? Kossoudji attributes the difference largely to the far greater tendency of Asians to set up their own businesses or manage those of their countrymen within ethnic enclaves, thereby minimizing the disadvantages of limited English language skills. In a later chapter we will explore self-employment among Hispanics in some detail. Suffice it to say at this point that, aside from Cubans, most Hispanics clearly lack the wealthy, paternalistic support networks that have made such enclaves possible.

All these SIE-based studies are limited to the survey respondent's self-reported assessments of their own abilities to speak English, which may be highly subjective and weakly related to standard measures of language proficiency. Rivera-Batiz (1989) has attempted to obtain more objective evidence from the reading test scores recorded in the 1985 National Assessment of Educational Progress (NAEP) Young Adult Literacy Assessment survey. His results confirm a strong positive association between ability to read in English and wages. Among otherwise similar immigrants from Spanish-speaking and English-speaking countries, differences in reading scores explained 40 (males) to 44 percent (females) of their wage differential. In further investigating the determinants of reading proficiency, he found a high correlation between test scores and individuals' (and their parents') level of educational attainment and length of U.S. residence. However, the study sample was limited to youths 21 to 25 years old and contained a total of only 241 wage earners. And, as in most of the SIE studies (except Reimers), separate estimates were not made for each nationality.

Besides the role that language seems to play in the labor market experiences of the foreign born, migration has been said to affect Hispanic–non-Hispanic income differentials in other ways. According to one theory, the tendency of some Hispanics, particularly Puerto Ricans, to engage in frequent "circular migration" through return visits to their homeland has disruptive effects on their employment. Their close ties to the home country are thought to reduce the incentives to rapidly become fluent in English and to commit themselves to a career with an American firm. Thus, Thomas Sowell (1981) has argued that:

> The progress of Puerto Ricans who have remained permanently in the continental United States for more than a generation is very different from the progress of a changing mixture of people classified under the same label as "Puerto Ricans." There are substantial differences between them in income, occupation, and intermarriage rates. The same is true of Mexican Americans, who also move back and forth in substantial numbers. . . . When compared with people of the same age and education, Puerto Ricans earn comparable incomes.[17]

Sowell has presented no empirical evidence to test this bold assertion. In an effort to do so I have calculated (from the 1980 census microdata) the average 1979 weekly earnings of four subsets of male wage earners 25 to 64 years old: non-Hispanic whites and Mexican-origin workers living in a Standard Metropolitan Statistical Area (SMSA) of California, and non-Hispanic whites and Puerto Rican males living in an SMSA of New York State. To reduce the possible influence of migration and English-language deficiencies as much as possible, the samples were limited to persons born on the American mainland, who resided in an SMSA in 1975 as well as in 1980, and who speak English "well" or "very well." Table 3.7 presents the Hispanic–non-Hispanic earnings ratios for 32 separate age-education cells in each state.[18]

Without taking into account age or schooling differences, English-speaking, United States–born Puerto Ricans earn less than two-thirds (.629) as much as non-Hispanic whites in New York, and Mexican men average three-fourths as much as

TABLE 3.7. Relative Mean Earnings of U.S.–Born, English-Speaking Mexican and Puerto Rican Males by Age, Education, and State, 1979

	Mexicans (California)		Puerto Ricans (New York)	
Years of School Completed	Y^m/Y^a	% of Mexican Sample in Cell	Y^p/Y^a	% of Puerto Rican Sample in Cell
0–8 Years				
All Ages	.649	13.5	.941	6.0
9–11 Years				
All Ages	.922	21.6	.654	21.9
Ages 25–29	1.139	4.2	.588	8.7
Ages 30–34	.917	3.4	.696	5.3
Ages 35–39	.883	2.9	.759	1.9
Ages 40–44	.872	3.0	.847	1.5
Ages 45–49	1.078	2.4	.715	1.9
Ages 50–54	.735	2.9	.944	1.9
Ages 55–59	.819	1.7	.525	0.8
12 Years				
All Ages	.858	30.9	.646	34.0
Ages 25–29	1.014	9.5	.796	15.1
Ages 30–34	.931	6.3	.613	8.3
Ages 35–39	.798	4.8	.736	3.4
Ages 40–44	.937	4.5	.832	2.6
Ages 45–49	.850	2.0	.628	3.0
Ages 50–54	.959	2.0	.895	1.1
Ages 55–59	.771	1.1	.676	0.4
13–15 Years				
All Ages	.846	23.7	.671	24.9
Ages 25–29	.977	6.7	.760	13.6
Ages 30–34	.916	6.0	.994	7.2
Ages 35–39	.837	4.1	.337	0.8
Ages 40–44	.860	2.6	.905	1.5
Ages 45–49	.818	2.2	.634	0.4
Ages 50–54	.658	1.1	.572	1.1
Ages 55–59	.684	0.6	.931	0.4
16 or More Years				
All Ages	.745	10.2	.701	13.2
Ages 25–29	.858	2.9	.778	5.7
Ages 30–34	.951	3.0	.926	4.5
Ages 35–39	.700	1.6	.861	1.1
Ages 40–44	.727	0.8	.955	1.1
Ages 45–49	.751	0.9	.646	0.8
Ages 50–54	.871	0.4	—	0.0
Ages 55–59	.801	0.4	—	0.0
TOTAL	.747	100.0	.626	100.0

NOTE: Y = mean weekly wages and salary in 1979; the superscripts a, p and m represent white non-Hispanic males, Puerto Rican males born in a U.S. state, and U.S.-born Mexican males, respectively. The Puerto Rican and Mexican samples exclude persons who were not fluent in English and who did not live in the same SMSA in 1975 and 1980.

SOURCE: 1980 Public Use Microdata Census Samples.

non-Hispanic Californians. The lower average educational attainment of Hispanics can clearly be seen to affect their relative earnings. Within each of the four levels of schooling, the adjusted earnings ratios are less than the overall, unadjusted values. But, the gap between Hispanics and non-Hispanics remains surprisingly large. For example, among males in New York, the Puerto Rican–Anglo earnings ratio is only .646 for those of all ages who have completed 12 years of schooling (the modal schooling group), and .70 for college graduates. In California, Mexican high school graduates earn an average of 85.8 percent of the Anglo level, and Mexican college graduates earn only 74.5 percent as much as their non-Hispanic counterparts.

Once we control for both age and educational differences, the earnings ratios generally, though not always, increase. This is particularly true for Mexican men in their early thirties who consistently earn over 90 percent of the non-Hispanic level within each schooling group. However, in two-thirds of the age-education cells Mexicans received over 10 percent lower earnings per week than otherwise similar non-Hispanic whites. In the New York samples, Puerto Ricans earned 90 percent of the Anglo level in only 6 of the 26 cells with earnings data. These account for less than one-fifth of the Puerto Ricans sampled. This evidence appears to offer faint support for Sowell's position that differences in migration status, age, and education can alone explain Hispanics' low relative earnings.

Discrimination

What do these research findings indicate about the relative importance of discrimination? The standard approach by economists has long been to first determine the amount of any observed wage gap between a majority and minority group that can be statistically attributed to differences in such individual characteristics as education, years of work experience, and English-language ability. Any residual wage gap left unexplained by these factors is then interpreted as an "upper bound" measure of discrimination. Hence, the gaps of 10 percent or more between non-Hispanics and Hispanics that persist in our comparisons (Table 3.7) even after controlling for age, education, English-language ability, nativity, state, and metropolitan residence can be interpreted as measures of such an upper bound.

Reimers (1983; 1984), using a different data set and methodology, concluded that discrimination may account for as much as 36 percent of the male wage-offer differential between otherwise similar white non-Hispanics and Central and South Americans. The unexplained differential is 18 percent for Puerto Ricans; 12 percent for other Hispanics; and 6 percent for Mexicans.[19]

Grenier (1984) estimated that, among otherwise similar Hispanic and white non-Hispanic men who have spoken English since childhood, the wage differential was 8.1 percent. Of this amount, two-thirds was unexplained by endowment differences and thus potentially attributable to discrimination. However, Grenier, like McManus, et al. (1983) (who found no unexplained residual) did not run separate regressions for each ethnic group as Reimers's work showed is essential to disentangle the very different ethnic group effects. Without such a decomposition it is difficult to know how to interpret these results.

While there is as yet no consensus in this literature, it seems fair to say at this still-early stage in this research that there is evidence of a discrimination component of the adjusted Hispanic–non-Hispanic wage differential. But the studies to date suggest that a far larger share of the observed gap between average Hispanic and non-Hispanic earnings can be accounted for by differences in education, work experience, and other "productivity-related" factors than has been found to be the case in the voluminous research on male–female and black–white differentials.

It is important to recognize that the standard economic criteria for establishing discrimination are quite narrow. Insofar as Hispanics experience "premarket" discrimination in, for example, trying to gain access to additional schooling and better quality schooling this would not be reflected in the economists' measure of wage discrimination. There is, in fact, growing evidence of discriminatory obstacles to improving Hispanic education. Likewise, current estimation techniques and most data sets are poorly suited to discern many forms of labor market discrimination. These could include word-of-mouth recruitment systems, biased employment tests, and discriminatory seniority rules and promotional tracks. Unfortunately, there is such a dearth of research on the impact of civil rights legislation and affirmative action on Hispanics that we can say little about whether or not these forms of discrimination have increased or decreased over time.[20]

Another kind of information generally ignored (or treated with deep suspicion) in studies of economic discrimination is the perceptions of the disadvantaged individuals themselves. According to the classic assimilation model of immigration as newcomers gradually adopt the language, values, and customs of the host society they will be better able to achieve economic mobility and less exposed to discrimination. However, interview surveys of Hispanics' ethnic affiliations and perceptions of anti-Hispanic discrimination have thrown this view into question. In Rogler, et al.'s (1980) survey of Puerto Ricans in New York, the second generation was found to have an equally strong ethnic identity as their first-generation parents. In Portes and Bach's (1985: ch. 8) panel study of newly arrived Cubans, the study sample's perceptions of discrimination steadily increased over time. In 1973 fewer than 5 percent felt subject to discrimination, but by 1979 more than one in four of the same group did. Moreover, surprisingly, it was those with higher educational levels and occupational standing who were most aware of discrimination. Heightened ethnic identity may thus for some be a by-product of years of economic competition with the indigenous majority and greater awareness of discriminatory obstacles to their upward mobility.

Still another form of evidence has emerged recently from government evaluations of the effects of the 1986 immigration law. In a major study mandated by Congress, the U.S. General Accounting Office (1990) concluded that people with "a foreign appearance or accent" experienced job discrimination "across a variety of industries in all areas of the nation and among employers of various sizes." Under the provisions of IRCA, the GAO's negative findings forced Congress to reconsider the merits of extending the employer sanctions.

These findings were based on responses to questionnaires sent to 9,491 employers and on field tests of hiring practices (conducted in Chicago and San Diego). In the latter, the GAO employed college students—half Hispanic, half non-Hispanic—of similar age, education, language ability, and work experience to apply for the same jobs. It was found that non-Hispanic applicants received 52 percent more job offers than the similar Hispanic applicants. The study estimated that 461,000 employers (10 percent of the total) were practicing discrimination based on applicants' national origin and that almost as many had decided to hire only U.S. citizens.

In the months just prior to release of the GAO report, state studies by California and New York had reached similar conclusions. The California Fair Employment and Housing Commission estimated that 53,000 employers throughout the state had a policy of asking only "foreign-looking" job applicants or those with foreign accents to produce work authorization documents. About 73,000 firms in the state appeared to be refusing to hire anyone who was not a U.S. citizen (Bishop, 1990). The following month, the New York State Inter-Agency Task Force on Immigration Affairs concluded that there was a "widespread pattern of discrimination" against the foreign born (M. Howe, 1990). The study was based on a random sample survey of 402 medium-sized companies in New York City, Long Island, and Putnam and Westchester counties. Extrapolating from the survey results, the panel estimated that about one-fifth of the medium-sized firms in the region had policies of denying jobs to anyone born outside the United States.

The Deterioration of Less-Skilled Labor Markets

Since the early 1970s the real earnings of less-skilled male workers have dropped sharply, both in absolute terms and relative to more-skilled labor. This is a development of potentially enormous consequences for Hispanics, since, as we have seen, they continue to have a disproportionately small fraction of high school and college graduates. Likewise, they remain overrepresented on the lowest rungs of the occupational ladder.

The occupational distributions in Table 3.8 show that they have certainly made some progress in moving out of the lowest-paid jobs. The proportion of Hispanic men engaged in farm labor dropped by nearly two-thirds to 5.1 percent. At the same time a growing fraction of Hispanics have succeeded in entering professional and managerial jobs. In the course of 30 years in which the proportion of white non-Hispanic men in these occupations rose from 29.6 to 31.4 percent, the proportion of Hispanic men doubled. However, by 1980, non-Hispanics were still more than two and one-half times more likely to be in the professional/managerial group and, within this broad category, Hispanics were largely concentrated in the lowest-paying positions. Among women, the proportion of Hispanic professionals and managers rose from 8.3 to 10.9 percent over the postwar years. The faster advance of white non-Hispanic women meant that, while they were only 1.5 times more likely than Hispanics to hold such jobs in 1950, they were 2.5 times more likely to in 1980. The sharp decline in the proportion of Hispanic women in semiskilled manual work, from 44.8 percent to 19.2 percent, was matched by a doubling of the fraction in sales and clerical jobs and a nearly fivefold increase in the proportion of low-skill nonfarm laborers.

In order to trace the time-series changes in skill differentials over the life cycle, I computed the ratios of median annual earnings of low-education groups relative to

TABLE 3.8. Occupational Distributions of White Non-Hispanics and Hispanics in New York, Florida, and the Southwest, 1950–80[a]

	Anglos				Hispanics			
	1950	1960	1970	1980	1950	1960	1970	1980
MALES								
Professional & managerial	29.6	24.1	29.3	31.4	6.1	7.0	9.7	12.0
Sales & clerical	19.6	17.6	17.5	18.3	7.4	8.4	9.4	12.8
Crafts	21.4	23.2	20.4	20.9	16.4	15.0	20.3	22.1
Operatives	16.6	19.3	16.0	12.6	27.6	29.1	29.5	21.6
Laborers	3.6	5.8	6.2	6.1	18.6	14.8	9.7	11.2
Service workers	6.7	7.4	8.9	9.5	8.3	10.6	12.5	13.1
Farmers	0.0	0.6	0.3	0.4	1.3	2.1	0.2	2.1
Farm laborers	2.6	2.0	1.4	0.9	14.4	15.0	8.7	5.1
FEMALES								
Professional & managerial	12.5	18.0	20.7	27.8	8.3	4.1	8.1	10.9
Sales & clerical	50.6	50.1	50.4	47.0	16.7	26.9	32.5	35.3
Crafts	2.4	1.1	1.8	2.1	2.1	1.2	2.3	4.3
Operatives	19.5	13.9	9.8	5.4	44.8	39.1	27.6	19.2
Laborers	0.4	0.5	0.7	1.4	1.0	0.7	1.3	4.7
Service workers	13.9	15.9	16.4	15.6	22.9	23.2	22.4	21.7
Farmers	0.0	0.0	0.0	0.3	0.0	0.0	0.2	0.7
Farm laborers	0.7	0.5	0.2	0.3	4.2	4.8	5.6	3.2

[a]Hispanics defined as all persons who have a Spanish surname, are of Puerto Rican stock, or were born in a Spanish-speaking country. Sample restricted to persons 16 years old and over in the experienced civilian labor force resident in New York, Florida, or the 5 southwestern states.

SOURCE: 1950–80 Public Use Microdata Census Samples.

college graduates for four birth cohorts. The calculations in Table 3.9 show that, among Hispanics and non-Hispanics alike, those with less education lost ground in the 1970s. For example, among non-Hispanics ages 25–34 in 1960, high school dropouts earned on average 79 percent as much as college graduates. But by 1969, they earned less than 61 percent as much, and 10 years later the ratio had fallen further to 56.8 percent. Among Hispanics of the same age, the annual wages of high school dropouts averaged 11 percent higher than those of the small number of Hispanic college graduates in 1959. Ten years later these dropouts were receiving some 43 percent less than college graduates and their earnings disadvantage was just as severe in 1979.

Research on national Current Population Survey data by Blackburn, et al. (1989), Juhn, et al. (1989), and others has shown that the most precipitous decline in the relative earnings of less-educated American males began in the early eighties. But no research to date has disaggregated the data to determine whether this has also been the case for Hispanics. I used CPS median annual income tabulations for males in 1979 and 1987 to calculate income ratios by education group for Hispanics and for all whites. The Census Bureau does not publish more detailed earnings break-

TABLE 3.9. Earnings Ratios of Less-Educated Men to College Graduates by Birth Cohort and Ethnicity, 1959–79[a]

	Among Anglo Men			Among Hispanic Men		
Birth Cohort	*1959*	*1969*	*1979*	*1959*	*1969*	*1979*
Ratio of LTHS to CG						
1946–55			.530			.471
1936–45		.570	.462		.649	.476
1926–35	.656	.490	.526	.750	.433	.469
1916–25	.575	.633	.538	.476	.503	NA
Ratio of HSD to CG						
1946–55			.706			.654
1936–45		.700	.600		.914	.609
1926–35	.787	.608	.568	1.111	.567	.562
1916–25	.662	.633	.538	.746	.615	NA

[a]Hispanics defined as all persons who have a Spanish surname, are of Puerto Rican stock, or were born in a Spanish-speaking country. Sample restricted to the civilian population ages 25–64 and resident in New York, Florida, or the 5 southwestern states.

[b]Ratios are of median annual earnings. LTHS = 0–8 years of schooling (less than high school); HSD = 9–11 years of schooling (high school dropout); CG = 16+ years of schooling (college graduate).
NA = not available, owing to lack of sample observations.

SOURCE: 1950–80 Public Use Microdata Census Samples.

downs for Spanish-origin persons by birth cohort or age group, so the data are for all income recipients ages 25 and over.

Table 3.10 demonstrates clearly that the earnings penalty for the less educated has increased among Hispanics as among all whites. In the two columns furthest to the right of the table are the ratios of the average income of low education Hispanics

TABLE 3.10. Income Ratios of Less-Educated Men to College Graduates by Spanish Origin, 1979 and 1987

	Among Whites		Among Hispanics		Less Educated Hispanics Relative to White CG	
	1979	*1987*	*1979*	*1987*	*1979*	*1987*
Ratio of LT8 to CG	.297	.258	.431	.350	.314	.275
Ratio of ESG to CG	.380	.320	.522	.438	.381	.345
Ratio of HSD to CG	.512	.429	.594	.470	.434	.369
Ratio of HSG to CG	.706	.602	.733	.642	.535	.504

NOTE: Ratios are of median annual incomes of all male income recipients, ages 25 and over. LT8 = 0–7 yeras of schooling; ESG = 8 years of schooling (elementary school graduate); HSD = 9–11 years of schooling (high school dropout); HSG = 12 years of schooling (high school graduate); CG = 16+ years of schooling (college graduate).

SOURCES: U.S. Bureau of the Census, Current Population Reports: *Money Income and Poverty Status in the US* (Series P-60), various years; and *Persons of Spanish Origin in the US* (Series P-20), various years.

relative to the average income of white college graduates. In the course of the 1980s the wage gap between Hispanics with no more than a high school degree and white college graduates widened from 46 percent to nearly 50 percent. The gap between Hispanic dropouts and white college graduates increased even more, from 56.6 to 63.1 percent. In light of the fact that nearly half of Hispanic men ages 25 and over still had less than 12 years of education by 1987 and that only 12 percent were college graduates, these figures indicate a severe deterioration in the income prospects of millions of workers.

Shifts in Labor Supply
According to a long-widespread view (which clearly contributed to passage of the 1986 overhaul of immigration law), recent waves of immigrants, particularly the undocumented, harm the wage and employment prospects of native workers by expanding the available supply of less-skilled labor. Low-wage blacks and Hispanics are typically said to be most affected. However, a growing body of empirical research has found little or no statistically significant adverse effects of recent immigration on either the wage or employment levels of indigenous blacks or Hispanics.[21] This appears to reflect both the tendency of a substantial fraction of recent migrants to be concentrated in jobs largely unattractive to natives and the fact that immigration increases total labor demand, both through their expenditures as consumers and the direct job creation by immigrant-owned small businesses.

The supply of less-skilled labor increased from other sources as well. After the enormous expansion of the college-educated population through the 1970s, rates of return to higher education declined and with them the fraction of youth going on to college. The 1980s actually saw an increase in the ratio of the number of males with no more than a high school degree to the number of college graduates. However, most empirical estimates of the impact of such compositional changes have indicated that they play a distinctly minor role relative to other factors.[22]

Shifts in Labor Demand
CYCLICAL EFFECTS   The 1970s and 1980s witnessed the two most serious recessions—in 1975 and 1982—of the entire postwar period. It has long been known that skill differentials tend to widen in business cycle contractions. The unemployment record of Hispanics suggests that they could be particularly affected. The decennial unemployment rates for 1950–80 presented in Table 3.11 show that Hispanics have consistently suffered rates of joblessness over one and one-half times higher than non-Hispanic whites.

Can the income differentials we have observed be accounted for largely by short-run business cycle effects? The annual CPS data enable us to calculate separate estimates of the cyclical fluctuations and the secular trends in the Hispanic–white income ratios since the early seventies. Following Ashenfelter (1970) and Freeman (1973), in their work on racial income ratios, I estimate a simple model of the form:

$$\left(\frac{I_h}{I_w}\right)_t = \beta_0 + \beta_1 DGNP_t + \beta_2 T + \beta_3 \left(\frac{S_h}{S_w}\right)_t + \beta_4 \left(\frac{U_h}{U_w}\right)_t + e_t$$

where, for each year t:

I = median annual income;
$DGNP$ = annual percent change in real GNP;
T = time trend;
S = percent of persons, 25 and over, who have completed 12 or more years of schooling;
U = unemployment rate of males, 20 and over;
e = a disturbance term; and h, w denote Hispanics and whites, respectively.

The $DGNP$ variable captures cyclical influences, while T will pick up any underlying trend. An alternative variable used in other studies as a cycle proxy, the unemployment rate of males ages 35–44, was also tested and yielded similar results. The ratio of high school graduation rates is introduced as a control for changes in relative educational attainment. The ratio of unemployment rates is a proxy for the relative utilization of Hispanic labor each year.

Table 3.12 presents regression results for two samples: all male income recipients 25–64, and year-round, full-time male workers. The principal results are, first, that cyclical fluctuations during this period do not generally appear to significantly alter relative income ratios. Only in the specification including the unemployment ratio is the $DGNP$ coefficient estimate significant. But the time trend is consistently negative and statistically significant. Depending on the specification, the trend coefficients imply an average annual decline in the incomes of Hispanics relative to all whites of 0.6 percent. Even after limiting the sample to full-time workers employed at least 50 weeks of the year and controlling for schooling differences, the results indicate a secular widening of the income gap of 0.4 to 0.5 percent a year.

LONG-RUN DEMAND SHIFTS The changes in the industrial composition of employment since the 1960s have drawn the greatest amount of attention from economists attempting to understand the worsening inequality between low-wage and other workers. This research (discussed further in the next chapter) is ongoing and has not yet produced anything resembling a consensus. Nonetheless, it may be instructive to look at a recent, particularly comprehensive attempt to evaluate the contributions of the key factors at issue. Blackburn, et al. (1989) decomposed the 1979–87 changes in male earnings differentials into three parts: the effect of changes in the allocation of workers of different skill groups across 43 industries; the effect of within-industry changes in wage differentials; and the interaction of the two changes. Their estimates suggested that the largest component of the widening skill differential was associated with growing inequality within industries. But shifts in the industrial composition of employment were also found to independently account for 23–30 percent of the change in the earnings gap between less-skilled and more-skilled workers. This stems in part from the decline in available jobs for all skill groups in industries in which less-skilled workers are relatively well paid. But even more damaging has been the fact that the employment reductions in traditionally high-wage industries have involved the elimination of a disproportionately large portion of the less-skilled positions.

TABLE 3.11. Labor Force Status of White Non-Hispanics and Hispanics
by Sex and Ethnic Group, 1950–80[a]

| | | | Foreign Born | | | | Other |
	Anglos	All Hispanics	Mexican	Cuban	Other	Puerto Rican	Spanish Surname
MALES							
Employment/Population (%)							
1950	80.0	75.0	79.3	92.3	90.6	69.7	73.8
1960	76.7	78.0	78.5	88.0	76.3	79.3	75.1
1970	73.1	73.1	74.1	77.3	74.8	70.9	72.6
1980	72.3	75.7	78.8	80.5	76.7	72.5	74.0
In Labor Force (%)							
1950	84.3	85.2	87.6	92.3	93.8	80.9	83.9
1960	80.2	84.0	83.3	92.0	79.0	84.7	83.7
1970	76.1	77.8	79.8	81.5	78.3	77.3	76.9
1980	75.9	81.4	86.5	82.8	80.0	79.2	80.0
Unemployment Rate							
1950	5.1	12.0	9.5	0.0	3.3	13.9	12.1
1960	4.4	7.2	5.8	4.4	3.3	6.4	8.2
1970	4.0	6.1	7.1	5.2	4.4	8.2	5.6
1980	4.8	7.4	8.9	2.8	4.1	8.4	7.5
FEMALES							
Employment/Population (%)							
1950	29.3	24.7	18.8	40.0	25.0	38.6	23.2
1960	34.2	30.1	21.4	48.3	35.0	37.8	30.2
1970	38.0	33.6	28.7	42.1	43.6	26.9	34.8
1980	46.7	43.7	38.3	49.3	50.2	30.5	47.0
In Labor Force (%)							
1950	30.4	27.2	22.2	40.0	25.0	39.5	25.9
1960	36.1	32.7	24.1	48.3	35.0	41.8	32.4
1970	39.6	36.8	31.4	46.2	46.8	29.8	38.1
1980	49.2	48.7	43.7	52.4	55.0	35.1	52.0
Unemployment Rate							
1950	3.6	8.9	15.1	0.0	0.0	2.2	10.4
1960	5.0	7.5	11.1	0.0	0.0	9.6	6.8
1970	4.1	8.7	8.6	9.0	6.9	9.8	8.7
1980	5.1	10.1	12.9	5.8	8.7	13.1	9.6

[a]Hispanics defined as all persons who have a Spanish surname, are of Puerto Rican stock, or were born in a Spanish-speaking country. Sample restricted to the civilian population 16 years old and over resident in New York, Florida, or the 5 southwestern states.

SOURCE: 1950–80 Public Use Microdata Census Samples.

As Anglo workers increasingly moved out of the most unstable operative and laborer jobs during the fifties and sixties, both Hispanic men and women remained heavily concentrated in these occupations. The fact that much of this employment has been in the same manufacturing industries hardest hit by structural decline in recent years may well help explain why Hispanics have borne a disproportionate share of cyclical spikes in unemployment since 1973 as well as seeing their earnings fall further behind non-Hispanics.[23] In 1950, over a third of Hispanic working

TABLE 3.12. Regression Analysis of Hispanic–White Male Median Income Ratios, 1975–87

| Dependent Variable | Constant | Explanatory Variables | | | | $\bar{R}^2$ |
		Trend	DGNP	S_h/S_w	U_h/U_w	
Male income ratio	.7079 (36.308)	−.0063 (3.052)	.0029 (1.820)			.721
Male income ratio	.7327 (3.870)	−.0062 (2.308)	.0029 (1.550)	−.0404 (.130)		.682
Male income ratio	.8784 (12.281)	−.0064 (3.603)	.0043 (3.065)		−.1065 (2.452)	.828
Male income ratio, year-round, full-time workers	.7463 (51.901)	−.0046 (2.944)	.0014 (.819)			.613
Male income ratio, year-round, full-time workers	.7438 (4.542)	−.0047 (2.256)	.0014 (.706)	.0042 (.016)		.558
Male income ratio, year-round, full-time workers	.8609 (11.281)	−.0043 (3.773)	.0020 (1.155)		−.0733 (1.533)	.655

NOTE: T-statistics in parentheses. DGNP = % change in real GNP since the previous year; S_h/S_w = ratio of the percent of Hispanics who have completed 12 or more years schooling to the percent of whites with at least 12 years completed; and U_h/U_w = ratio of unemployment rates of Hispanic and white adult males. Dependent variables are ratios of median annual incomes of Spanish origin and white male income recipients, 25–64 years old. All regressions corrected for serial correlation with Cochrane-Orcutt iterative procedures.

SOURCE: U.S. Bureau of the Census, Current Population Reports: *Money Income and Poverty Status in the US* (Series P-60), various years; *Persons of Spanish Origin in the US* (Series P-20), various years; and *Educational Attainment of the Population* (Series P-20), various years.

women were in manufacturing but barely one-fifth of their male counterparts.[24] The subsequent decline in female employment as operatives was reflected in a near-equalization of the fractions of Hispanic men and women in the industry by 1980: 26.2 percent of males and 27.2 percent of employed females worked in manufacturing.[25] The same year, only 20.6 percent of white non-Hispanic men and 12.3 percent of white women were in that industry.

The impact of this structural decline has been unusually damaging to the national-origin group with the highest unemployment and the highest poverty rate in the United States today: Puerto Ricans. In 1960, one out of every two Puerto Rican males and three out of four Puerto Rican women working in New York were in manufacturing, compared with only 32 percent by 1980 (Table 3.13). The decline in Puerto Rican representation in the industry might be thought to reflect the gradual reduction in the fraction of the Puerto Rican population from the island. But the table's breakdowns by nativity show that migrants have also experienced a decline in manufacturing jobs.

Much of the deterioration in Puerto Ricans' employment prospects is doubtless a result of the especially sharp contraction of that industry in New York. No other metropolitan area in the country has lost as many jobs in the goods-producing sector over the last four decades. The number of manufacturing jobs in New York City dropped by only 8.9 percent in the 1950s.[26] But during the 1960s, when the city's total employment rose by 5.8 percent, manufacturing jobs fell by 19.1 percent. The

TABLE 3.13. Industrial Distributions of Puerto Ricans in New York
by Sex and Birthplace, 1950–80

	Males				Females			
	1950	1960	1970	1980	1950	1960	1970	1980
ALL PUERTO RICO								
Agriculture	0.0	2.6	0.0	0.6	0.0	0.0	0.0	0.0
Construction	1.6	1.9	4.4	5.7	0.0	0.0	0.0	0.8
Manufacturing	41.3	51.0	31.7	31.5	75.6	77.5	41.8	32.8
Transportation, utilities, & communications	7.9	6.4	15.0	10.1	0.0	0.8	1.5	4.9
Wholesale trade	3.2	2.6	3.3	3.4	0.0	1.7	1.5	6.6
Retail trade	15.9	19.1	16.1	11.2	2.2	8.3	11.2	12.3
Finance, insur. & real estate	7.9	2.6	6.7	10.7	4.4	2.5	10.4	5.7
Services	17.5	14.0	19.4	22.5	15.6	7.5	28.4	27.9
Public administration	4.8	0.0	3.3	4.5	2.2	1.7	5.2	9.0
PERSONS BORN IN PUERTO RICO								
Agriculture	0.0	2.6	0.0	0.6	0.0	0.0	0.0	0.0
Construction	1.6	2.1	2.8	3.8	0.0	0.0	0.0	0.0
Manufacturing	40.3	53.2	33.8	35.6	79.1	80.5	50.5	42.2
Transportation, utilities & communications	8.1	6.4	15.2	9.8	0.0	0.9	2.0	4.4
Wholesale trade	3.2	2.8	2.8	3.8	0.0	0.9	2.0	4.4
Retail trade	16.1	17.7	15.2	12.1	2.3	6.2	12.1	12.2
Finance, insur. & real estate	8.1	2.8	4.8	10.6	4.6	2.6	8.1	3.3
Services	17.7	12.1	23.4	18.9	14.0	7.1	22.2	26.7
Public administration	4.8	0.0	2.1	4.5	0.0	1.8	3.0	6.7

NOTE: Sample restricted to persons 16 and over living in New York State in the census year, who were born in Puerto Rico or report Puerto Rican parentage or ancestry.

SOURCE: 1950–80 Public Use Microdata Census Samples.

rate of decline nearly doubled again in the seventies, to 35.3 percent. Since 1980, there has been a further 23 percent reduction, leaving only 379,000 jobs in manufacturing by 1987.[27]

The employment growth that has occurred in New York has increasingly been confined to skilled, language-intensive positions in finance and in personal and professional services. In common with other low-income residents, most Puerto Ricans have been left unprepared by inner city schools to qualify for such jobs. The resultant discouragement appears to be a primary reason for the city's below average rates of labor force participation among youth and minorities in recent years. As the decadal averages (Table 3.11) show, the participation rate of Puerto Rican men, after climbing to a 1960 level (84.7 percent) higher than any group except Cubans, fell below the rates of all other Hispanics in 1970 and 1980. The patterns for women and young people are far more dramatic. While growing fractions of both Hispanic and white non-Hispanic women and youth have become active in the labor force in the postwar period, the participation rate of Puerto Rican women has declined from the above average level of 42 percent in 1960 to 35 percent in 1980. Likewise, only

TABLE 3.14. Labor Force Status of White Non-Hispanic and Hispanic Youth, Ages 16–24, by Ethnic Group, 1950–80[a]

| | Anglos | All Hispanics | Foreign Born | | | Puerto Rican | Other Spanish Surname |
			Mexican	Cuban	Other		
Employment/Population (%)							
1950	48.2	43.9	56.7	60.0	60.0	46.8	43.0
1960	45.7	48.2	46.4	40.0	55.6	52.8	47.2
1970	50.8	44.4	54.1	55.9	40.4	36.7	47.9
1980	61.5	51.4	55.3	63.5	43.3	38.5	51.7
In Labor Force (%)							
1950	51.6	54.2	56.7	60.0	60.0	56.4	51.9
1960	50.0	53.2	53.6	40.0	55.6	57.6	52.0
1970	55.9	50.4	57.8	61.8	46.2	45.0	54.1
1980	67.2	59.4	65.2	64.9	49.2	46.6	59.5
Unemployment Rate							
1950	7.2	18.9	0.0	0.0	0.0	17.1	17.1
1960	8.6	9.3	13.5	0.0	0.0	8.2	9.2
1970	9.2	11.8	6.4	9.5	12.5	18.4	11.5
1980	8.4	13.4	15.2	2.1	5.8	17.4	13.1

[a]Hispanics defined as all persons who have a Spanish surname, are of Puerto Rican stock, or were born in a Spanish-speaking country. Sample restricted to the civilian population, ages 16–24, resident in New York, Florida, or the 5 southwestern states.

SOURCE: 1950–80 Public Use Microdata Census Samples.

46.6 percent of Puerto Ricans 16–24 years old were employed or looking for work in 1980, down from 57.6 percent 20 years earlier (Table 3.14).

Labor Unions
One of the most heavily researched issues in labor economics is the economic impact of labor unions. Two widely accepted findings from this research are, first, that unions have tended to improve the wages of the less skilled relative to the more skilled and, second, that unions are experiencing a marked decline in both the fraction of employees organized and in wage bargaining power. However, almost no economic research exists on the effects of unions on Hispanics, much less on whether the weakening of unions has played a role in recent trends in Hispanic–non-Hispanic differentials.[28]

Beginning in the early 1980s, the Bureau of Labor Statistics began publishing CPS tabulations of the distribution of employed wage and salary workers by Spanish origin, as well as the average weekly earnings of union and nonunion workers, in the January issue of *Employment and Earnings*.[29] The figures for 1983 and 1988 are reproduced in Table 3.15. In 1983, 24.1 percent of Hispanic working men were union members, a rate well below that of blacks (31.7 percent) but identical with that of whites. Hispanic male union members enjoyed a 42.7 percent relative union–nonunion wage differential, compared with a 49 percent differential among blacks and only a 17.8 percent differential among whites. The large Hispanic union pre-

TABLE 3.15. Union Affiliation and Average Weekly Wages
of Employed Workers by Sex, Race, and Spanish Origin, 1983 and 1988

| | % of Wage/Salary Workers | | Median Weekly Earnings Full-Time Wage/Sal. Workers | |
	Union Members	Represented by Unions	Union Members	Non-Union
MALES				
White				
1983	24.0%	26.9%	$424	$360
1988	19.9	21.8	513	432
Black				
1983	31.7	36.1	366	246
1988	26.1	29.1	458	298
Hispanic				
1983	24.1	27.0	351	246
1988	18.5	20.1	431	283
FEMALES				
White				
1983	13.5	16.7	313	242
1988	11.5	13.7	410	305
Black				
1983	22.7	27.4	291	306
1988	19.8	22.9	374	263
Hispanic				
1983	16.6	20.1	258	203
1988	12.4	14.3	328	249

SOURCE: U.S. Bureau of Labor Statistics, *Employment and Earnings*, January 1984
and 1989.

mium may be a result of the pattern by which unions raise the wage rates of the less
skilled relative to the more skilled. But empirical analysis must be undertaken in the
future to estimate the size of these differentials after controlling for all the various
other factors that can influence wage gaps.

As with white and black women, Hispanic women have a lower rate of union
membership than their male counterparts. Their 16.6 percent rate in 1983 was over
3 percentage points higher than among white workers, but well below the black rate.
In contrast to the situation among males, the relative union–non-union wage differential of Hispanic women (27.1 percent) was less than both the white (29.3 percent)
and the black (41.3 percent) differentials.

Over the brief period 1983 to 1988, the fraction of workers in unions fell among
white, black, and Hispanic men and women. The Hispanic rate fell even faster than
did the others, dropping below the white rate by a full percentage point. As a result,
by 1988 only 18.5 percent of males of Spanish origin were still in unions, compared
with 19.9 percent of whites and 26.1 percent of blacks. A similar pattern held for
female workers: by 1988 less than a percentage point separated the fraction of
Hispanics in unions (12.4 percent) from that of whites. In fact, the absolute numbers

of Hispanic union members increased by 17.1 percent (from 1.042 million to 1.22 million) while the number of white members was dropping 6.1 percent. The decline in the Hispanic membership rate is thus explained by the fact that the size of the total Hispanic work force was growing so much more rapidly—54 percent from 1983 to 1988—and most of it was finding employment in nonunion firms.

The national decline in unionization rates in the 1980s hit less-skilled workers most strongly. Blackburn, et al. (1989) show that from 1980 through 1988 the membership rate of high school dropouts and graduates, ages 25–64, dropped 13 percentage points, compared with a decline of only 4 points among college graduates. They estimated the impact of deunionization on skill differentials by multiplying the decrease in the proportion unionized by the relevant (regression-adjusted) wage premium for each education group. From their results they concluded, "Deunionization in the 1980s substantially widened the earnings gap."

Other Demand Forces

Some little-studied labor market developments in recent years are also likely to have been important to the worsening fortunes of both organized and unorganized workers. First, since the 1970s, employers have increasingly attempted to lower total compensation costs through two-tier wage structures, "bonus" plans, and demands for concessions in wages and benefits. In addition, many have attempted to lower their reliance on full-time employees by increased use of "nonstandard" or "contingent" labor (e.g., part-timers, temporary help, and homeworkers), as well as by subcontracting more elements of the work process to other firms here and abroad.

Government fiscal and regulatory actions have increasingly complemented corporate efforts to weaken labor's wage bargaining power. As more and more firms have moved aggressively to block union organizing or bust existing unions, conservative National Labor Relations Board (NLRB) staffs in the 1980s have proven far less sympathetic to complaints of unfair labor practices by employers and have increased the grounds on which firms can refuse to engage in collective bargaining.[30] Cutbacks in public service employment programs and in nonwage income sources like unemployment insurance and AFDC have increased the potential cost of job loss and thereby further weakened employee bargaining leverage. Several economists have suggested that these developments can best be understood as part of an ongoing process of new "labor force restructuring."[31] Far more research attention needs to be devoted to empirical assessments of their contribution to current wage inequalities.

The Cuban Exception

By nearly every income and employment measure we have examined, Cubans stand much closer to non-Hispanic whites than to their fellow Hispanics. What accounts for their ability to do so much better than other national-origin groups?

One popular explanation in recent years has stressed the implications of the "political" rather than "economic" motivation of most Cuban emigration. Chiswick (1980) argued that the inability of Cuban exiles to return home for political reasons made them necessarily more committed to success in the United States. The fact that migrants from other areas always have the option of return migration was said to dilute the intensity of their investment in U.S.-specific educational and job skills, which, in turn, slows their wage and occupational mobility. However, other studies of migrant surveys that, unlike Chiswick's census data, have direct information on reported reasons for migration show that the weight of political concerns has varied over time. The early Fagen and Brody (1968) study found that only 11 percent of those surveyed in the 1959–62 wave stressed economic losses as their main reason for emigrating. This seemed at first puzzling to the authors, since nearly two out of three refugees had lost income between 1958 and their last 12 months in Cuba. They explained the low reported incidence of economic motivations in three ways. First, these may be the most difficult to admit to others as the justification for abandoning one's homeland. Next, despite wage restraints after the revolution, the reduction in urban rents and the provision of free education and medical care may have enabled many to maintain their earlier living standards. And finally, those displaced from high positions may have been more affected by their lost power and status than any financial losses. This would have applied far more to business owners and landowners than to salaried people, since most of the latter were able to keep their original jobs or were given substitute jobs. Casal and Hernandez (1975) have suggested that genuine political refugees were largely confined to the period between the abortive Bay of Pigs invasion and the 1962 Missile Crisis. They found from a 1970 emigre sample that there was far less mention of concern with personal security or antithetical government policies and far more concern with economic scarcities than in earlier cohorts. And one-third of the 1973–74 cohort admitted that they had planned to leave Cuba even before the revolution.[32]

The above average educational and occupational backgrounds of most Cuban immigrants is widely accepted as an important advantage relative to many other nationalities. However, persons from other less-developed nations often report facing difficulties in transferring their skills and credentials to the job market of a developed economy. The more country-specific their training and the weaker their command of English, the slower the adjustment process is likely to be. The fact that Cubans appear to have experienced unusually rapid occupational and earnings progress, even though a relatively small proportion of recent migrants are fluent in English, has drawn attention to their unique settlement process.

Cuban immigrants benefited enormously from a unique policy of government assistance unavailable to any other Hispanics. Beginning in late 1960, the federal government allocated large sums of money to a coordinated federal, state, and local support effort of unprecedented size and scope. The U.S. Department of Health, Education, and Welfare established a Cuban Refugee Program to fund resettlement, education, retraining, job placement, health services, and surplus food distribution projects. From 1961 to 1974 the program spent an estimated $957 million.[33] Among its main facets was, first, the resettlement of nearly 300,000 refugees in 2,400 communities throughout the 50 states by 1972. This was designed to reduce the refugees' impact on Miami and to help them locate better jobs and higher incomes than seemed available at the time in south Florida.[34]

Next, federal funds were provided for a large-scale bilingual education program, one that was to later serve as a prototype for other school systems. In addition to bilingual instruction for Cuban youth in public schools, the government financed special summer school classes in conversational English, year-long vocational programs, and an English Institute for adults. An average of 20,000 to 30,000 adults attended each year from 1962 to 1972. This education program also created job opportunities for Cubans to work as teachers, teachers' aides, and program administrators. A third major focus was financial aid for college attendance. Almost $34 million was provided refugees in tuition loans between 1962 and 1976.[35]

For those who had already completed their schooling for a profession back home, special efforts were undertaken to expedite the transfer of their credentials to the American labor market. Retraining programs in medicine and teaching at the University of Miami and other schools turned out many thousands of retooled Cuban professionals. The state of Florida acted to ease certification and licensing barriers for them. Since citizenship was one of those barriers in many states, the federal government in 1966 granted Cubans a special exemption from the normally lengthy naturalization process. Cubans alone were permitted to claim up to 30 months in the United States without residence as part of the standard five-year waiting period to obtain citizenship.

In addition to the extraordinary government assistance provided them and the savings, skills, and other resources they brought with them, Cubans' unusually rapid progress has also been shaped by the Spanish-speaking subeconomies in which they have concentrated. The fact that an unusually large proportion of Cubans in Miami work for and patronize Cuban-owned firms has led Portes and Bach (1985: ch. 6) to dub this an "enclave" economy. Enclaves can be advantageous to both employees and employers. Recent immigrants lacking knowledge of English or of the local housing and labor markets can rely on help from their countrymen in finding accommodations and jobs, as well as in social and cultural adjustments. The larger and more prosperous the enclave economy, the more likely it is that many migrants can find work in firms owned and largely staffed by other Hispanics. This reduces the disadvantages lack of English fluency would otherwise create in learning the skills needed to progress in the firm hierarchy. When objective English language comprehension tests were administered to the 1973–74 immigrant cohort in 1979, 38 percent were still unable to correctly answer a single item.[36] Over 75 percent failed to answer at least half the items correctly. Hence, six years after arriving in the United States, only one in four had even a moderate knowledge of the English language. But by that time, most of those whom the Cuban Refugee Program had resettled elsewhere in the country had moved back to Miami. The fact that, 97 percent of the entire immigrant sample lived in the Miami area in 1979 makes their ability to advance economically despite generally weak command of English much more understandable.

Employers gain from ethnic enclaves insofar as they function to lower the costs of locating new employees. Networks of friends and relatives in the workers' community can be an invaluable resource to firms, particularly when unexpected changes in product demand require rapid increases in hiring. High national homogeneity in a firm's work force may also minimize certain production inefficiencies. Workers linked by ethnicity and kinship will be more likely to cooperate on the job, sharing tasks and helping newcomers in improving their performance.

Finally, Cuban family incomes benefit from the fact that Cuban women are more likely than most other Hispanics to be active in the work force. In 1988, the civilian labor force participation rate of Cuban women was 53.6 percent, compared with only 40.9 percent for Puerto Ricans and 52.4 percent for Mexicans. The Cuban rate was exceeded only by Central and South American women, 61.7 percent of whom were in the labor force. The 1950–80 estimates in Table 3.11 show that this has been the consistent postwar pattern.

This is in a way surprising, since one reason for emigration cited by many exiles in past surveys was the revolutionary government's alleged assault on the traditional position of women, moving many from *la casa* (home) to *la calle* (street). A mere 14.2 percent of women were in the island labor force according to the last prerevolutionary census, and this had still only risen to 18.3 percent by 1970.[37] What then accounts for the fact that their counterparts in the United States in 1970 were two and one-half times as likely to be in the labor force?

Prieto (1987) suggests that the middle-class background and aspirations for social mobility of most exiles increased their ability and willingness to find jobs, relative both to the average woman in Cuba and to other Hispanics in the United States. Immigration and the initial retraining period required by many of their husbands imposed strains on family finances. In order to maintain their accustomed standard of living, wives and other family members found jobs.

A complementary reason is that the Miami enclave economy facilitated their incorporation into the local job market. Portes and Bach (1985) found that two-thirds of the wives of the 1973–74 immigrant cohort worked and only 1 percent were unpaid family laborers. They were more occupationally concentrated than men, with two out of three working women in semiskilled jobs. Since a larger proportion of Cuban families are intact with both spouses present than is true of any other Hispanic national-origin group, Cuban families have an above average incidence of multiple earners. Of the four out of five men in the 1973–74 cohort who were married, 90 percent were accompanied by their wives. Of persons in immigrant households other than the husband and wife, 27 percent of Cubans were employed, compared with only 9.6 percent of Mexicans in the same cohort.[38]

Conclusion

Postwar trends in earnings and employment differentials between Hispanics and non-Hispanics were the principal focus of this chapter. Changes in Hispanic poverty rates were also explored. Based on analysis of 1950–80 census data, Hispanics were found to have made impressive progress since the 1950s in educational attainment and occupational mobility. Of the principal national-origin groupings, Cubans have succeeded in reaching near-parity with non-Hispanic whites in most measures of labor market achievement.

However, Mexicans and Puerto Ricans, the largest components of the population, remain at a persistent, substantial disadvantage, which is reflected in the overall Hispanic earnings patterns. After some modest gains relative to non-Hispanic whites during the economic boom of the 1960s, most Hispanics appear to have experienced stagnation in their relative earnings levels in recent years. In fact, regression analysis of annual 1973–87 CPS data showed that the Hispanic–non-Hispanic earnings ratio is in a secular decline: even among full-time, year-round male workers, the ethnic pay gap has been widening at a rate of 0.4 to 0.5 percent per year.

Postwar trends in poverty appear to coincide closely with movements in average incomes. Hispanic families have long suffered rates of poverty two and one-half to three times higher than the white non-Hispanic level. In recent years, the Hispanic poverty rate has increased more rapidly than that of blacks, and the Puerto Rican rate exceeds the black level. Like blacks, Hispanic families are more likely to be female-headed than are white non-Hispanic families. But, while family structure has been much emphasized by some scholars as a principal cause of poverty, trends in female headship do not appear to explain much of the interethnic differences in poverty rates.

Decomposition analysis of decennial earnings ratios found that Hispanics' lower average educational attainment is an important factor contributing to their wage disadvantage. English-language problems also appear to have a strong negative effect. But, in this as in other such research, not all of the gap can be explained by traditional productivity differences. Among the other factors that seem most likely to be important are such secular changes as the decline in unskilled and semiskilled manufacturing jobs and in unionization, as well as various forms of discrimination.

Appendix

TABLE 3A.1. Distribution of Hispanic Study Sample by Spanish-Origin Categories, 1980[a]

	Foreign Born			Puerto Rican	Other Spanish Surname	Not in Study Sample	Total
Origin	Mexican	Cuban	Other				
Mexican	1154	1	12	4	2143	485	3799
Cuban	0	318	0	1	2	64	385
Puerto Rican	0	1	4	501	14	69	589
Other Spanish Origin	44	2	441	16	309	374	1186
Not Spanish Origin	18	0	4	0	359	0	381
TOTAL	1216	322	461	522	2827	992	6340

[a]Hispanics in study sample include all persons who have a Spanish surname, are of Puerto Rican stock, or were born in a Spanish-speaking country. Sample restricted to the civilian population 16 years old and over resident in New York, Florida, or the 5 southwestern states. Spanish origin defined according to 1980 Census Bureau categories.

SOURCE: 1980 Census Public Use Microdata Samples.

TABLE 3A.2. Median Annual Income and Earnings of White Non-Hispanics and Hispanics by Sex and Ethnic Group, 1949–79[a]

			Foreign Born			Puerto Rican	Other Spanish Surname
	Anglo	All Hispanics	Mexican	Cuban	Other		
MEDIAN INCOME ($)							
Males							
1949	2900	1700	1600	1950	2900	2200	1600
1959	4800	2800	2000	3500	4200	2900	3000
1969	7200	5000	4000	5500	6000	5000	5000
1979	14010	9205	8885	11908	10680	8845	9755
Females							
1949	1500	900	700	1100	1500	1400	900
1959	1800	1300	950	1400	1550	2000	1150
1969	2600	2100	1300	2600	3200	3000	2000
1979	7035	5105	5105	6610	5175	4805	5282
MEDIAN EARNINGS ($)							
Males							
1949	2900	1700	1500	2000	2450	2100	1500
1959	4900	2900	2000	3400	4100	2800	3200
1969	7500	5000	4250	5700	6000	5000	5000
1979	15005	9885	8005	11005	10005	9940	10005
Females							
1949	1700	950	850	1000	1500	1400	800
1959	2300	1300	1200	1850	1600	2000	1000
1969	3500	2500	1550	3000	3400	3800	2200
1979	7005	5505	5005	6305	5005	7005	5350

[a]Hispanics defined as all persons who have a Spanish surname, are of Puerto Rican stock, or were born in a Spanish-speaking country. Sample restricted to the civilian population 16 years old and over resident in New York, Florida, or the 5 southwestern states.

SOURCE: 1950–80 Public Use Microdata Census Samples.

TABLE 3A.3. Industrial Distributions of White Non-Hispanics and Hispanics in New York, Florida, and the Southwest, 1950–80[a]

	Anglos				Hispanics			
	1950	1960	1970	1980	1950	1960	1970	1980
MALES								
Agriculture	9.8	6.0	4.0	3.3	24.3	18.1	12.0	6.7
Mining	1.7	1.6	1.2	1.6	1.8	1.7	1.0	1.5
Construction	9.6	10.3	10.2	10.8	10.9	9.8	9.0	13.4
Manufacturing	24.2	26.0	22.0	20.6	19.5	26.4	26.9	26.2
Transportation, utilities,								
& communications	9.5	9.5	9.1	9.9	9.0	6.9	7.1	7.7
Wholesale trade	5.8	4.7	4.8	5.4	4.4	4.4	4.4	5.0
Retail trade	15.2	14.6	15.7	15.6	14.1	13.6	15.8	14.8
Finance, insur. & real estate	4.2	4.9	5.4	5.8	1.9	1.6	2.3	2.6
Services	13.2	16.2	20.5	21.2	9.4	14.0	16.1	17.6
Public administration	6.8	6.0	7.0	5.5	4.8	3.6	5.4	4.7
FEMALES								
Agriculture	2.3	1.6	1.0	1.1	4.4	7.3	6.9	4.1
Mining	0.5	0.3	0.3	0.4	0.0	0.0	0.1	0.4
Construction	0.6	1.0	1.1	1.5	0.0	0.2	0.4	1.1
Manufacturing	22.9	19.4	14.9	12.3	34.4	32.4	29.1	27.2
Transportation, utilities								
& communications	4.4	4.8	4.3	4.7	2.6	2.0	1.6	3.7
Wholesale trade	3.8	3.1	2.8	2.9	3.3	4.4	3.1	3.5
Retail trade	22.2	26.7	23.1	22.6	21.2	18.5	16.6	17.5
Finance, insur. & real estate	8.2	7.8	7.6	9.4	2.9	4.1	5.8	5.5
Services	30.6	31.0	40.7	40.7	28.9	28.4	33.1	33.7
Public administration	4.4	4.8	4.1	4.3	2.2	2.6	3.6	3.9

[a]Hispanics defined as all persons who have a Spanish surname, are of Puerto Rican sotck, or were born in a Spanish-speaking country. Sample restricted to civilian population 16 years old and over resident in New York, Florida, or the 5 southwestern states.

SOURCE: 1950–80 Public Use Microdata Census Samples.

NOTES

1. For detailed information on these data banks, survey design, and questionnaires, see U.S. Bureau of the Census (1972, 1973b, 1983b, and 1984a).

2. See Appendix Table 3A.1.

3. U.S. Bureau of the Census (1984b).

4. The estimated median incomes and earnings with which these ratios were calculated are in Appendix Table 3A.2.

5. Total income is used here rather than wage and salary earnings because of the lack of annual earnings by sex, age group, work experience, and Spanish origin for most of this period in the published CPS tabulations.

6. One possible source of error in using income data to draw comparisons between the early 1970s and later years should be noted. Between the March 1975 and March 1976 Current Population Surveys, the Census Bureau changed its procedures for imputing income to sampled individuals whom it was unable to interview. See Lillard, Smith, and Welch (1986) on the details of this change. Juhn, et al. (1989) investigated the impact of the change in imputation methods on skill differentials from 1963 to 1987 and found that the net effect was to bias downward the estimated increase in inequality in the 1970s. This suggests that our estimates may actually understate to some extent the worsening relative position of Hispanics.

7. All these statistics are from Danziger, Haveman, and Plotnick (1986).

8. See Danziger and Gottschalk (1986).

9. Recent debates on poverty trends have highlighted certain possible sources of bias in the official methodology. The main government poverty series is based on cash incomes from all private and public sources, except capital gains. But it does not include the value of government or private in-kind benefits like food stamps, Medicare, or health insurance. The Census Bureau (1986b) has used several different valuation techniques to measure the contribution of these benefits. Their estimates of incomes including such benefits show that, while the adjusted poverty rate is of course lower (by about 2 percentage points) than the official rate, they both have the same upward trend in the 1980s. Adjustments that would tend to raise the poverty rate above the official government figures include subtraction of taxes from money income, multiplying the "economy food budget" by four to reflect the lower fraction of income now devoted to food expenditures, and replacing the absolute standard with a poverty line defined relative to average income levels. See the analysis of these issues in, for example, Danziger, Haveman, and Plotnick (1986) and Osberg (1984: ch. 4).

10. For a comprehensive analysis of 1960–80 changes in Hispanic fertility and other demographic factors, see the highly informative work of Bean and Tienda (1987).

11. U.S. Bureau of the Census (1973a, state vols.: Table 208; 1984b, state vols.: Table 57).

12. Human Resources Administration, City of New York, 1987.

13. Of course, the ability to speak English is likely to affect the economic value of Hispanics' educations, but the 1950–70 censuses lack any information on language proficiency. Given the strong correlation between schooling level and proficiency in English found in previous research, the effects of educational attainment in our analysis may reflect in part the impact of differential linguistic ability. In the next section, the 1980 information is exploited to compare the earnings of U.S.-born Hispanics fluent in English with those of non-Hispanics.

It is also important to note that such comparisons as these cannot provide information on the role played by the many forms of discrimination that may shape the productivity characteristics that minority workers bring to the labor market. There is certainly considerable research evidence on the significance of family income and educational discrimination for Hispanic youths' high dropout rates and below-average school achievement scores (e.g., Fligstein and Fernandez, 1985; U.S. Department of Education, 1980). This will be discussed further later.

14. The low 1979 ratio estimated for the 1916–25 cohort should be interpreted with caution. Given that college graduates were quite rate among Hispanics of this older age group, the sample size is very small and thus liable to yield statistics of questionable reliability.

15. See, for example, Gwartney and Long's (1978) study of the 1970 census and Reimer's (1983) work on the SIE.

16. Kossoudji (1988).

17. Sowell (1981): pp. 243, 276. See also Tienda and Diaz (1987) on Puerto Rican's circular migration.

18. The calculations for the lowest schooling category (8 years or less) are not shown owing to space limitations in the table. Only 6 percent of the Puerto Ricans and 13 percent of the Mexicans sampled are in this category, and the small sample sizes of individual age-education cells rendered some of the estimates of questionable statistical reliability. Aside from obvious outliers, these results are qualitatively similar to those reported in the table.

19. The fact that this research is based only on large cross-sectional data banks is a result of the inadequate numbers of Hispanics sampled in the relatively small panel data sets available. The exception is the National Longitudinal Survey (NLS) of Youth Labor Market Experience, first conducted in 1979, which purposely oversampled black and Hispanics 14 to 21 years old. Shapiro's (1984) cross-sectional analysis of the first wave found no statistically significant wage gap between whites and Hispanics after controlling for differences in age, schooling levels, job tenure, union membership, employment sector, and other factors. However, as the large research literature on male–female and black–white wage gaps has shown, the typically small differences in youth pay offer relatively little insight into the large wage differentials that emerge among adult workers. If this NLS panel is followed long enough into the future to conduct genuine longitudinal analyses, it could be a unique source of the very information needed to better evaluate Hispanics' relative career mobility.

20. For a rare exception, see Leonard (1984), who concludes from his study of California manufacturing in the 1970s that affirmative action did not significantly affect the employment of Hispanics.

Leibowitz (1982) has argued that, while the EEOC has developed regulations against language discrimination, it has focused its enforcement in the areas of education and politics, to the neglect of employment.

21. See, for example, DeFreitas (1988b) and Chapter 8 and the surveys by Borjas and Tienda (1987), Greenwood and McDowell (1986), and U.S. Dept. of Labor (1989).

22. See, for example, Blackburn, et al. (1989) and Juhn, et al. (1989).

23. See DeFreitas (1986) and the following chapter (this volume).

24. The 1950–80 industrial distributions are in Appendix Table 3A.3.

25. Industrial distributions calculated separately by ethnicity reveal that, despite an over-all decline in the proportion of Hispanic women in manufacturing, one group—women born in Mexico—became increasingly concentrated in the industry. Between 1950 and 1980 their manufacturing share rose from 32.7 percent to 38.4 percent. An even sharper increase was recorded by males from Mexico: by 1980, 33.8 percent were in manufacturing, up from only 14.6 percent 30 years earlier. The same period saw the proportion of these men in agriculture drop from 37.4 percent to 13 percent. These trends were no doubt much influenced by the far stronger performance of manufacturing in California than in the Northeast since the 1960s.

26. U.S. Department of Labor (1984): pp. 574, 579.

27. U.S. Department of Labor (1988b).

28. Leonard's (1985) study of the employment effects of unions on manufacturing employment in California is apparently a unique comparative empirical analysis of Hispanics, whites, and blacks. See the discussion in the following chapter.

29. For details and comparisons with earlier unionization data, see Flaim (1985).

30. See Freeman and Medoff (1984).

31. See Bowles, Gordon, and Weisskopf (1983); Harrison and Bluestone (1988); and Rosenberg (1988).

32. Portes and Bach (1985): p. 159.

33. Pedraza-Bailey (1981/82).

34. Moncarz (1973).

35. Pedraza-Bailey (1981/82).

36. Portes and Bach 91985): Table 54.

37. Cited in Prieto (1987).

38. Portes and Bach (1985): p. 155.

4

Hispanic Unemployment Across the Business Cycle

In addition to workers' earnings levels, the security and stability of employment are crucial indicators of their economic position. In this chapter, we begin with a discussion of the principal theoretical models of unemployment and of their implications for minorities. This is followed by empirical analysis of the question of whether Hispanics experience disproportionately large surges in joblessness in cyclical downturns. The relative impact of business cycle fluctuations on different demographic groups can have important implications for their earnings, as well as being a central issue in cost-benefit evaluations of alternative economic policies. While there have been a number of studies of black–white cyclical differentials, this chapter presents the first such analysis of Hispanic unemployment. Throughout the chapter, findings for Hispanics are contrasted with those for whites and blacks cross-classified by age and sex. I also consider whether changes in the federal minimum wage floor and in transfer benefits have reduced Hispanic participation and/or employment, as some have found to be the case for particular white and black age groups. Finally, where sufficient data are available, national-origin differentials among Hispanics are explored by conducting the empirical analysis separately for Mexicans, Puerto Ricans, and Cubans. A detailed investigation of unemployment differentials among the main Hispanic national-origin groups is left for the following chapter.

Unemployment Theories and Minority Unemployment

Traditional Neoclassical Theory

The basic neoclassical model of the labor market is of a continuous auction between atomistic buyers and sellers of labor. The demand for labor by firms is assumed to be based on workers' marginal productivity and is inversely related to the real wage rate. The supply of labor reflects workers' utility-maximizing behavior in a world in which work is assumed to yield disutility, and is a positive function of the real wage. Competitive forces are said to assure that the real wage moves up or down as needed to equate labor demand and supply at the full employment equilibrium level—at least in the long run. In the short run, Marshall and Pigou, the model's main architects, allowed for the possibility that various "frictional resistances" could impede the instantaneous adjustment of the real wage to maintain the market-clearing equilibrium. But they contended that the resultant unemployment was essentially "voluntary" and subject to remedy by wage reductions. They were confident that competition in labor and product markets would prevail in the long run to eliminate any disequilibria.

Keynes's Critique

In the first sentence of the final chapter of the *General Theory* Keynes wrote:

> The outstanding faults of the economic system in which we live are its failure to provide for full employment and its arbitrary and inequitable distribution of wealth and income.[1]

His dissatisfaction with the neoclassical account of those faults involved a "long struggle of escape" from the theoretical apparatus of Marshall and his other teachers. This is evident in chapter 2 of the *General Theory* where "involuntary unemployment" is said to occur when the real wage exceeds the marginal disutility of labor. This still incorporates the orthodox assumption of a unique inverse correlation between the real wage and the volume of employment, given fixed capital.

However, this chapter was an attempt to expose the orthodoxy's flaws on the basis of its own axioms, and was not integrated into the framework erected in the remainder of the book. Instead, chapter 3 offers a quite different definition of involuntary unemployment as "a situation in which aggregate employment is inelastic in response to an increase in the effective demand for its output."[2] From this point on Keynes departed from the neoclassical practice of focusing on the labor market as the ex ante analytic starting point. In chapter 19 he disputed the possibility of identifying equilibrium output and employment levels from labor demand and supply alone. Working with a two-sector system, he shows that every change in the composition of aggregate demand between wage-goods and non-wage-goods causes a shift in the labor demand curve. And labor supply was unstable as well, since it was likely to be influenced by many other factors besides the real wage. At the very least, workers' utility functions included as arguments not only their individual money wage but also the relative level of comparable workers' pay. Faced with a recession, workers' concern with fairness in pay relativities will lead them to resist money wage cuts if they think other workers will not respond in kind.[3]

Clearly, Keynes's break with the neoclassical model of unemployment was incomplete in the *General Theory*.[4] But thereafter he continued to move still farther away from the chapter 2 definition. In the summer of 1936, he wrote to John Hicks,

"If I were writing again, I should feel disposed to define full employment as being reached at the same moment at which the supply of output in general becomes inelastic."[5] And once the empirical work of Dunlop and Tarshis in 1938–39 found that employment did not tend to move inversely with real wages over the trade cycle, Keynes (1939:p. 401, n. 1) concluded that chapter 2 "was the portion of my book that most needs to be revised." Thus, instead of relying on unstable labor market curves, the sources of unemployment had to be located primarily through aggregate demand and supply analysis.

The Structural Unemployment Controversy

Postwar debates between proponents of the neoclassical model and Keynes's followers were long conducted without much reference to the unemployment problems of specific demographic groups. But the persistence of relatively high rates of joblessness throughout most of the fifties began to change this. The average rate was about 3 percent in the 1951–53 war boom, but climbed to about 4 percent from 1955 to 1957 and to over 5 percent from 1961 to 1964. Among blacks, particularly black youth, it was climbing much faster than for whites. Among 18–19 year olds, the black unemployment rate in 1954 (14.7 percent) was not much higher than the white rate (13 percent). But a decade later, 23.1 percent of black labor force participants in this age group were jobless, a rate 9.7 percentage points above that of white youth.

Economists' disagreements over the causes of this troubling pattern exploded in the early 1960s over the question of whether a new phenomenon, called "structural" unemployment, was to blame.[6] This term was defined as joblessness resulting from a discrepancy between the skill mix demanded by employers and the skills possessed by the unemployed. The existence of some amount of such unemployment was not in question. In a dynamic capitalist economy it is to be expected that new technologies, industries, and occupations will emerge to force the adjustment or abandonment of existing technologies, industries, and occupations. However, some economists argued that the mismatch between jobs and workers had significantly worsened in the 1950s. Charles Killingsworth (1963) attributed this situation to a series of unprecedented structural changes: the sharp decline in agricultural employment; a seemingly permanent shift in consumer buying patterns toward education, health, recreation, and other services; and the rapid automation of production and record keeping, greatly accelerated by the adoption of computers for commercial use from about 1955 on. The resultant "twist" in the demand for labor away from the unskilled and semiskilled toward highly skilled, better-educated workers was viewed as a long-term phenomenon. What was needed from policymakers were substantial increases in funds for education, training, job placement programs, and labor mobility assistance.

President Kennedy's Council of Economic Advisers (CEA), led by Walter Heller, countered that inadequate aggregate demand was the main culprit. While recognizing structural unemployment was substantial, the CEA rejected the notion that it had become much worse in the late fifties.[7]

However, widespread rejection of the structuralist view was the result, not of doctrinal debates or the handful of quantitative studies done at the time, but of the dramatic fall in unemployment after the $13 billion tax cut of 1964. From 5.4 percent in early 1964, the jobless rate dropped to 4.1 percent by the end of 1965 and continued declining, though at a slower pace, through 1969.[8]

Labor Market Segmentation

The Institutional Approach

Although the Heller–CEA position had, by the mid-1960s, been adopted by the overwhelming majority of economists, a number of researchers studying specific urban labor markets proposed an alternative view of unemployment. Drawing on the earlier analysis of internal labor markets by Kerr, Dunlop, and others in the Institutional School of industrial relations, Peter Doeringer and Michael Piore (1971) argued that the labor market is divided into two separate submarkets: the primary and the secondary segments. Jobs in the primary market are characterized by largely firm-specific skills, acquired by means of on-the-job training. The major share of the costs of such training is typically borne by the employer, and the payoff period on his investment is a positive function of the length of tenure of each worker. In consequence, primary sector firms try to minimize quit rates by offering relatively high wages, job security, and promotional opportunities governed by seniority. Because it is in the interests of both employers and employees to maintain a stable employment relationship, unemployment in this sector is of the involuntary sort generated by cyclical contractions.

Jobs in the secondary sector are, in contrast, low paying and unskilled with little seniority or chance for advancement and frequent quits and discharges. The high turnover of the secondary work force is attributed to a complex interaction between jobs and workers. On the one hand, the nature of an employer's product market or of the product's technology may discourage the formation of internal labor markets offering continuous employment. For example, firms subject to high variability of product demand and/or product design, such as in the clothing industry, are unlikely to provide specific training when production periods tend to be so brief and unpredictable that returns cannot be captured sufficient to outweigh training costs. In other cases, such as low-wage menial jobs in hotels, hospitals, and restaurants, relatively stable employment may be available but without the opportunities for training, advancement, or wage increases needed to induce such stability.

However, even if one assumes initially that all workers have similar levels of work commitment and that the instability of secondary jobs reflects employer preferences, eventually workers in unstable, undesirable jobs without rewards for punctuality or regular attendance will themselves develop work traits unacceptable to primary sector employers. Piore (1975, 1979a) has attempted to apply recent findings in developmental psychology to an explanation of the relationship between the lower-class "subculture," secondary employment, and unstable life-styles and work routines. As these behavioral traits become reinforced through working in secondary jobs, subsequent employers are more likely to adapt the structure of work and production to an unskilled, unreliable work force than to risk training workers who might quit well before investment costs have been recouped.

The picture of unemployment that emerges from this analysis is quite at variance with either the structuralist or the Heller–CEA conceptions. Whereas both of these earlier views saw most unemployment as involuntary, if for quite different reasons, Doeringer and Piore argued that this is only true of workers in the primary market. Most unemployment is concentrated in the secondary sector and reflects, not a shortage of vacancies, but the often voluntary turnover of highly mobile workers. The emphasis was thus shifted to frictional employment:

> Because secondary sector jobs tend to be self-terminating or are basically unattractive, they provide little incentive for workers to stick with them, and consequently have high voluntary turnover as well. Unemployment in the secondary sector thus is not associated with workers waiting around to regain an accustomed position, but is part of a shuttling process from one low-paying position to another.[9]

Although sharing some of the qualms about structuralism raised earlier by the Kennedy CEA, Doeringer and Piore charged the proponents of the 1964 tax cut with seriously overestimating the ability of expansionary fiscal policies to improve the employment prospects of secondary workers. While increased demand does cut unemployment in the primary sector by enabling firms to recall temporarily laid-off employees, primary sector firms are unlikely to move far enough down the employment queue to hire the most unstable workers. Rather than incurring the costs and risks of enlarging their training and upgrading activities to include secondary workers, primary employers tend to adjust to tight labor markets through increased reliance on subcontracting, temporary workers, and other short-term expedients. Substantial reductions in unemployment are thus viewed as impossible without interventionist policies by government aimed at improving the quality of secondary employment and accelerating the transition from the secondary to the primary sector.

The Radical Perspective

The view that the bulk of unemployment is frictional, largely reflecting unstable behavior and high turnover in the secondary sector, was shared throughout the 1970s by a number of the most influential young radical labor economists. According to Edwards:

> We find, then, that instability in work behavior pervades the secondary market. Although the statistical evidence is more fragmentary and less persuasive than in the case of primary markets, its direction is nonetheless clear. Employers offer little incentive to workers to stay at one job; workers respond by switching jobs frequently, as they suffer little or no reduction in their wage rate and at least achieve job variety. Job performance tends to be unstable, unreliable, and unpredictable; secondary workers demonstrate high absenteeism, are often not punctual, and typically work with little "discipline." Since they have little reason for long-run commitment to their jobs, these workers are rebellious towards the tyrannical power of their employers, but because of the high turnover, the worker resistance is usually individualistic rather than organized. Finally, job turnover is high, and consequently "frictional unemployment" is also high. In all three areas then, secondary workers exhibit extreme instability.[10]

The notion that unstable work habits of secondary workers make them unsuitable for primary employment may be contrasted with the classic Marxian analysis of the reserve army of labor. A pool of the unemployed readily substitutable for currently employed workers, the reserve army was for Marx the essential mechanism by which employers could counter working-class efforts to raise wages, reduce profits, and thereby slow the rate of capital accumulation. However, insofar as secondary workers account for most unemployment and, at the same time, lack the behavioral traits needed for access to the primary sector, this mechanism becomes inoperative.[11] The question then arises as to what alternative weapons are available to capitalists in combating labor.

Although not explicitly rejecting the reserve army concept, these radical theorists seemed at the time to have, in effect, replaced it with labor market stratification. Whereas Doeringer and Piore presented a time-specific analysis stressing the technological causes of segmentation, radicals incorporated segmentation into a broader historical and political framework in which labor force divisions play a functional role in perpetuating capitalist control of the labor process.[12] The destruction of many skilled crafts and the expansion of factory production in the nineteenth century were associated with the progressive homogenization of the labor force. To combat the resulting increase in class consciousness and worker militancy, employers consciously created segmented internal labor markets as part of a "divide and conquer" strategy. This process began in the 1920s but was not fully consolidated until after World War II. The proliferation of separate job ladders, though accelerated by the growing importance of firm-specific training, was primarily a means to draw artificial distinctions between workers to prevent those in more desirable jobs from making common cause with those at the bottom. As oligopolistic corporations with stable product markets and internal labor markets consolidated their power over small business, the gap between their primary sector work force and secondary sector laborers widened.

More recent empirical studies within the segmentation framework have suggested that the importance of unstable behavioral traits in disqualifying secondary workers from recruitment as a reserve army to the primary sector may have been overstated. Buchele's (1975) research on the National Longitudinal Sample of middle-aged white American men found that, while secondary workers do average less job tenure with the same employer (11.3 years) than either lower tier (13.8 years) or upper tier (15.2 years) primary workers, secondary sector job tenure is far lengthier than one would expect of a supposedly unstable, high turnover labor force. In fact, the tenure rates of secondary workers are quite similar to those of professionals and craftsmen. Likewise, in Rosenberg's (1975) sample of men 21–64 years old in four large cities, secondary workers' job tenure is substantial. It ranges from an average of 4 years for Hispanic workers in San Francisco to 10 years for blacks in Detroit. These relatively stable work histories help explain his finding of a significant degree of upward occupational mobility among these workers, though seldom beyond the lower tier of the primary sector. These results suggest that, though conditioned and constrained by market segmentation, intersectoral labor substitution by firms in the primary market is more extensive than was previously thought.[13] And, of course, they raise fundamental questions about theories of unemployment based on the assumption of high turnover among secondary workers.

Modern Neoclassical Theories

As some segmentation theorists began emphasizing the importance of frictional unemployment in the late 1960s and early seventies, a growing number of more orthodox economists were doing so as well, though for quite different reasons and with markedly different theoretical models. Segmentation research focused on high turnover rates to better understand the problems of poor white and minority workers in low-wage urban labor markets and the "feedback effects" between job characteristics and the behavioral traits of workers. Most concluded that only active government intervention to restructure the primary and secondary sectors could significantly reduce market dualism and the extreme job instability of minority and poor white workers. In contrast, most neoclassical economists have attributed unemployment not to the inadequacy of jobs in one portion of the labor market, but largely to the supply decisions of the workers themselves.

The "Natural" Rate of Unemployment

In a celebrated attack on the Phillips curve relation between inflation and unemployment, Milton Friedman (1968) argued that, in the long run, there is no such relation and a capitalist economy gravitates toward an equilibrium level of unemployment. This so-called natural rate was said to reflect the normal occurrence of frictional market forces. With no long-run tradeoff between unemployment and inflation, countercyclical government policies could only lower unemployment below the natural rate temporarily and would fuel inflation in the process.

The claim that most unemployment is essentially voluntary was rooted in the notion that job search is a form of productive self-investment.[14] Just as utility-maximizing consumers must expend resources to acquire price and quality information on goods to make the optimal purchase, so were job-seekers envisioned as allocating time and money to track down job offers. As a result, frequent entry and reentry into the labor force was to be expected for many workers, and with it a high incidence of relatively brief unemployment in the search period prior to job attainment. In a much-cited empirical analysis of government data on gross flows of workers between jobs and between employment and unemployment, Hall (1970) concluded that the majority of unemployment recorded in 1969 could be attributed to persons out of work four weeks or less. Only 7.4 percent of unemployed males— 70,000 persons—reported unemployment of six months or more. The relatively high jobless rates of minorities, youth, and women were said to largely reflect their preferences for frequent periods to engage in job search and in nonmarket activities (schooling, child rearing, etc.) as well as a certain amount of dissatisfaction with the jobs available to them.[15]

However, a growing number of studies since the mid-seventies have looked at detailed data on the actual process of job search with rather surprising results. For example, Matilla (1974) found that the majority of job changers move directly from old to new jobs without an intervening period of unemployment; that is, most are able to search while on a job through phone calls, want ads, and the help of friends. Rosenfeld's (1977) analysis of the first national survey of job search by the unemployed showed that, of that minority of job-seekers who are unemployed, those jobless four weeks or more search an average of only 17 hours per month. Holzer

(1988) found that, among unemployed nonstudent males 16 to 23 years of age, only one in three received a job offer in the course of a full month and for 64 percent of these individuals that was the sole offer they received all month. And Stephenson (1976) and Jackman (1985) report that, among the unemployed, the vast majority accept the very first job they are offered. These findings from surveys of the unemployed have been confirmed in Barron, Bishop, and Dunkelberg's (1985) research on surveys of employers.

Rational Expectations

The "New Classical" or "Rational Expectations" theory pioneered by Robert Lucas and Thomas Sargent gained considerable influence in the profession in the late 1970s. One of its main elements, the "Lucas supply function," is little more than a restatement of Friedman on the natural rate of unemployment in terms of aggregate output. Production is assumed to hold at a natural output level (consistent with the natural unemployment rate), deviating from it only under the impact of unantici- pated changes in wages and prices. But, contrary to Friedman, expectations of inflation are not simply a weighted average of previous inflation rates. Instead, it is postulated that all available information on a variety of influential factors are used by individuals to form "rational expectations." If most people do so, workers will not repeatedly mistake money wage for real wage changes, since they will not be guided solely by inflation's past history. Natural disasters, wars, and the like are among the rare unanticipated events capable of changing output and employment levels. A short-run inflation-unemployment tradeoff is thus ruled out and with it any hope of an effective demand-management role for government. Finally, if all eco- nomic agents act to maximize expected utility, then all markets will continually be in equilibrium.

True to their neoclassical roots, these authors hold that, given a fixed demand curve for labor, real wage reductions are needed to expand the number of job openings. Blame for unemployment is placed firmly on the supply side. Any excess of measured unemployment over the natural level is attributed to workers' move- ment between jobs and to persons who, though officially counted in the labor force, are not actually willing to work at current wage levels. They subsist instead on unemployment benefits, public assistance transfers, and cash wages for off-the- books employment. Unemployment is thus viewed as completely voluntary, an option chosen by rational individuals operating in competitive markets distorted by government intervention. For Lucas, the "unemployed worker at any time can always find *some* job at once and a firm can always fill a vacancy instan- taneously."[16]

Neo-Keynesianism

The traditional neoclassical model of unemployment has been strongly questioned by empirical research dating back to the late 1930s. The early evidence against countercyclical real wage movements has been reinforced by recent studies using both aggregate statistics and microdata. Thomas Coleman (1984) and Mark Bils (1985) have found that real wages have generally been acyclical in the postwar years. The 1970s stand out as an exceptional period during which declining real wages in recession years resulted in a procyclical pattern.

According to orthodox labor market analysis, a recessionary drop in product demand leads profit-maximizing firms to cut back on demand for labor. The resultant downward shift in the labor demand curve produces increased layoffs, but the lower equilibrium wage established should also cause an increase in quits. But as Zarnowitz (1985) shows, the typical U.S. recession is characterized by no fall in real wages, by a decline rather than an increase in quits, and by increases in unemployment of at least 2–4 percentage points.[17] In their major survey of this and other evidence, Kniesner and Goldsmith (1987: p. 1245) concluded: "The concept of an auction for labor has been *particularly unsatisfactory* in helping economists understand aggregate changes in real wages, employment, and unemployment over time in an economy characterized by cyclic fluctuations in labor demand."

In the neoclassical synthesis that emerged from the early work of Hicks, Modigliani, and Samuelson, Keynes's critique of traditional unemployment theory was reduced to a special case of the basic neoclassical model. The possibility of downward wage rigidity was conceded, but without questioning the underlying model of labor supply and demand. Instead, their efforts went into devising explanations of when and why such rigidity might occur. The two that have drawn the greatest attention are formal legal and institutional constraints and implicit contracts.

Collective bargaining agreements and minimum wage laws were viewed as the main formal constraints on wage movements. A large theoretical and empirical literature has addressed the effects of legal wage floors on employment and labor force participation. While statistically significant negative effects have been found, their magnitudes have been relatively small in most studies and confined to youth.[18] These studies were all based on data for the 1960s and 1970s. Throughout the 1980s, the minimum wage remained unchanged at $3.35 per hour and thus fell sharply relative to the average national wage level (from 48 percent to 37 percent, 1981–86). The fact that unemployment reached a postwar high during this same period cast still more doubt on the importance of the legal minimum as a source of joblessness.

Far less research exists on the possible unemployment effects of labor unions. Freeman and Medoff (1984) have looked at the relationship between interstate variations in unionization and in unemployment rates. Their regression estimates indicated that the unemployment rate in highly unionized states averages 1 percentage point above that of states with a low fraction of workers in unions. But there was no statistically significant relationship between unionization and the proportion of each state's population with jobs. This suggests that unions do not reduce the number of jobs, but rather draw additional job-seekers into the labor force.

In an all-too-rare study of unions, which included separate results for Hispanics, Leonard (1985) explored 1974–80 longitudinal data on a sample of over 1,200 manufacturing firms in California. He found that after statistically controlling for various relevant factors, the employment share of blacks was significantly greater in unionized firms than in nonunion firms. Hispanic men also had greater representation in the union sector in the early seventies. However, their faster employment growth in the nonunion sector left no significant union–nonunion employment difference by 1980. As the American unionization rate continued its secular decline in the 1980s, falling below 17 percent by the end of the decade, the likely importance of unions for national unemployment trends may well have diminished as well.

Recent debates among Western European economists and policymakers have highlighted other institutional factors alleged to impede labor market "flexibility."[19] Legal regulations on hiring and firing practices, mandatory prenotification of layoffs, limitations on fixed-term employment contracts and personnel leasing, high government assistance payments to the unemployed, and housing policies discouraging geographic mobility have been blamed for the failure of real wages to adjust as rapidly as is now required by structural changes in the world economy. This is said to account for the slow job growth and high unemployment in Europe compared with that in the more flexible U.S. economy. But Robert Gordon (1987) has found that intercountry differences in the "wage gap" (excess of real wage over productivity growth) have no statistical correlation with differences in unemployment in OECD nations. Richard Freeman (1988) likewise finds little empirical basis for a clear link between the extent of labor market regulation and international differences in real wage growth. He also stresses a fact often neglected in these debates that American employment growth came at a high cost: extraordinarily slow growth in real wages and productivity. Many of the new jobs created in the 1980s have been needed by other family members to help recover the family living standard lost by the real wage declines suffered by prime-aged male workers.

An alternative explanation of wage rigidity was developed in the 1970s, beginning with the work of Martin Baily (1974) and Azariadis (1975).[20] Workers and firms were said to often have "implicit contracts," a kind of insurance for employees that guaranteed them steady wages regardless of the state of product demand. In the event of a recession, employers respond only by laying off some of the work force with the promise of eventual recall. This image of the layoff component of unemployment as a series of brief, temporary episodes that are part of a voluntary contract is quite complementary with that projected by search theory.

A number of questions have been raised about the contracting model. First, why should workers generally opt for a firm's pledge of stable wages if it comes at the cost of unstable employment? The most common answer from the theory's advocates is that the availability of unemployment benefits during the relatively brief spells of temporary layoffs in effect substitutes the government for the employer in maintaining workers' income level. However, the fraction of the unemployed receiving unemployment compensation has fallen to a minority. Burtless (1983) shows that in 1975, when the national jobless rate was 8.5 percent, about 78 percent of unemployed persons received some benefits during the year. But in 1982, the year that set the post-Depression record for high unemployment, only 45 percent of the unemployed received unemployment benefits. This was largely the result of a tightening of eligibility standards in the early 1980s and an increase in the minimum unemployment rate required before extended benefits can be paid those workers jobless more than 26 weeks. Among the minority who manage to qualify for benefits, only a modest portion of their lost wages are replaced. For example, the average unemployment payment per week in 1984 was $123, only 42 percent of the average weekly wage (before taxes) of private nonfarm production workers. If fringe benefits like health insurance were included, the replacement rate would be even lower.

Furthermore, there is no strong evidence as yet of the hypothesized link between job tenure, wage stability, and implicit contracts. It is true that, at least in the 1960s and 1970s, a sizable portion of the work force had lengthy job tenure. For example, an Organization for Economic Cooperation and Development (OECD) (1984) study of Bureau of Labor Statistics (BLS) data estimated that just over one-fifth of American workers in 1983 had over 10 years on the same job. But the same study found little statistical relationship between job tenure and various measures of cyclical variability in real wages across OECD countries.

Finally, why are the contracts supposedly implicit instead of explicit? There have been many types of explicit wage and employment guarantees in collective agreements, such as minimum wages to be paid in the event of materials shortages or equipment failure, as well as profit sharing and other performance-related benefits. Yet Marsden's (1986: ch. 2) review of British, French, and German collective bargaining agreements and labor legislation produced no references to implicit wage insurance agreements of the sort claimed by the contracting literature.

Human Capital

In the late 1950s, a number of economists at Columbia and the University of Chicago began a sustained effort to apply neoclassical microeconomics to labor market research. Within a decade they had pushed institutional and industrial relations research to the margins of American labor economics. Their guiding assumption was that each individual's decision on the amount of schooling, job training, and other forms of "human capital investments" is based on the discounted stream of net income expected in return. The different volumes of human capital embodied in different workers are then said to generate the distribution of marginal physical productivity on the job, which in turn is the key neoclassical explanation of differences in labor market outcomes.[21]

It was not, however, until the 1970s that some began to move beyond the dominant focus on income differentials to attempt to integrate the theory with neoclassical models of unemployment. For example, occupational choice was taken to be another form of human capital investment decision. In choosing the volume and character of their schooling, vocational training, and other occupational preparation, individuals were said to factor into their estimates of future returns the likely variability of employment in different occupations. Those less risk averse are more likely to opt for more seasonal and cyclical fields like construction, while others will invest in preparation for more secure occupations. Job search was also interpreted as a form of self-investment. The greater one's stock of human capital, the greater the ability and willingness to invest further in information about labor market conditions and job search techniques. If the result is more efficient job search then, holding the reservation wage level constant, the briefer should be any search-related spells of unemployment. Higher-level occupations are also more likely to enjoy a wider range of opportunities in the national and even international labor market. And the presumed link between self-investment and labor productivity implies that employers will more readily hire those they observe to have greater, higher-quality human capital. Finally, the theory has also been used to account for differences in the likelihood that those with jobs will subsequently quit or be laid off. Since on-the-job training is costly to firms providing it, they are more willing to do so the longer the trainee's likely tenure with the firm, during which it will recoup its investment. The more training is firm-specific, the less applicable it is to other firms and thus the less likely workers with such training are to receive other wage offers as high as their current level. Hence, workers with more firm-specific human capital are both less likely to be discharged by their employer and less likely to quit. The tendency for older workers to average lower separation rates is thus attributed to an inverse relationship between length of current job tenure and the probability of separation.[22]

Discrimination Models

The Conservative View

The first systematic treatment of economic discrimination was the pioneering human capital treatise by Gary Becker (1957). Although its focus was largely on wage differentials, the Becker model had clear implications for minority unemployment.[23] Consistent with basic neoclassical price theory, he began by assuming that certain individuals simply have a "taste for discrimination," which can in theory be measured by the cost they are willing to bear to realize it. Blacks and other minorities subject to discrimination will only be hired when the white–minority wage ratio is sufficiently high to compensate discriminatory whites for associating with them. Differential cyclical rigidity is central to explaining differential cyclical unemployment patterns. If discriminatory employers are prevented by various forms of wage rigidity from paying minorities sufficiently lower wages than whites to provide full compensation for the employers' coefficients of discrimination, minorities may be largely restricted to less stable occupations and more seasonal and cyclical industries with higher average layoff rates. If sluggish wage adjustment for minority workers during recessions results in a reduction of the white–minority wage ratio below the level required to compensate discriminatory employers, they may respond by laying off minority employees or using occupational downgrading as an alternative means of compensation.

Statistical Discrimination and Segmentation

As the civil rights movement and the urban unrest of the 1960s attracted increasing attention, more and more economists belatedly began trying to explore the problems of discrimination.[24] The Becker model was soon subjected to sharp criticisms from several different quarters. Perhaps the most frequently questioned aspect was its prediction that market competition would eliminate employer discrimination. Becker claimed that the higher costs incurred by discriminatory employers would weaken their competitiveness and that lower-cost nondiscriminatory firms would drive them out of the market. The implication was that the capitalist marketplace could reduce discrimination more efficiently than explicit government policies.

Arrow (1972) attacked the theory's failure to account for the persistence of substantial discrimination throughout the long history of capitalism. As an alternative he proposed a "statistical discrimination" theory. Given the time and money costs for employers of determining the true productivity of job candidates, it was argued that cost-minimizing firms typically rely on easily observable characteristics like sex, race, or ethnicity. Individual job-seekers are assumed to have the average productivity of their demographic group. Employment discrimination persists because, even if employers do not themselves hold discriminatory attitudes, the practice of using stereotyped beliefs that minorities have lower average productivity results in individual minority group members being routinely ranked lower in the queue of job applicants. The resultant statistical discrimination will follow a countercyclical pattern if tight labor markets encourage employers to revise their stereotyped images and expand minority hiring.

Doeringer and Piore (1971) incorporated some of the statistical discrimination view into their criticisms of the Becker model. But the principal force behind the persistence of discrimination was held to be chronic segmentation of the labor market. Oligopolistic primary-sector firms are insulated from much competition and are able to practice long-term discrimination without the concern over lower-cost rivals that bedevils secondary-sector employers. In slack labor markets, primary firms seek to minimize screening costs and statistical discrimination of job candidates results. Minorities are thus disproportionately blocked at entry ports and left no option but low-wage, dead-end jobs in the secondary sector. Within internal labor markets employer discrimination seldom takes the form of differential treatment of minorities and whites in the same jobs. Rather, it involves the confinement of minorities to less-skilled, more unstable job titles and slower promotional tracks.

Radical Theory

Radical economists have disputed both the Becker and the statistical discrimination models. The former is faulted for assuming that the "tastes" of discriminators are formed independently of economic interests and for its fundamentally incorrect view of the roles played by competition and profit maximization. The latter is said to exaggerate the typical firm's costs in screening job candidates. A great deal of information is usually readily available through schooling and previous job references, job-related tests, and observation of new employees during an initial probationary period with the firm. Less prejudiced personnel officers would be expected to use these inexpensive informational sources to correct any systematic misperceptions about individual job applicants based on racist stereotypes.

Contrary to the view of employer discrimination as imposing costs on the firm, Reich (1981: ch. 4) concludes from empirical tests of both 1960 and 1970 census data that high-income groups tend to benefit from employment discrimination against blacks while most white workers lose. He explains this as reflective of employers' greater ability to hold down wages and forestall unionization efforts when the labor force is weakened by racial divisiveness.

As the radical literature has grown over recent years, the question of whether or not white workers benefit from racial discrimination has been subject to growing debate. For example, Shulman (1990) contends that the frequent periods of white working class resistance to black advancement reflected, among other factors, economic self-interest. He presents some limited empirical support for the notion that higher levels of racial income inequality (his proxy for discrimination) may be associated with preferential white access to steady employment. While considering this a potential source of white unity, he nonetheless views it as a short-term benefit that must be weighed against the long-term harm inflicted on white wage bargaining power by racial divisions.

In general, radical economists agree that such divisions make discrimination primarily beneficial to employers as a means of weakening labor and raising profit rates. Persistent racial and ethnic inequalities are thus expected to overlay the basic class inequalities characteristic of capitalist economies. This does not mean that progress against such inequalities is impossible, as the experiences of the 1940s and 1960s suggest. But these bursts of improvement in blacks' relative economic status were primarily attributable to unprecedented pressure from militant civil rights and labor activists, not to market forces or benign government initiatives. Any hope of further gains is thus largely dependent on efforts to forge new multiracial sociopolitical coalitions in the future.

A New Structural Unemployment?

The persistence of historically high levels of unemployment throughout the 1970s and into the early eighties sparked a revival of interest in the question of whether much of it was "structural" in nature.[25] A powerful new attack on the high turnover/voluntary unemployment view was launched in two widely discussed empirical studies, one by George Akerlof and Brian Main, the other by Kim Clark and Lawrence Summers. Both criticized official government tabulations on the duration of unemployment as misleading. The Department of Labor's main data series has long measured only the length of time those unemployed on the day of their interview have been out of work; that is, they capture "interrupted spells" in progress.

The much-cited figures on average spell duration give a far more misleading indication of the extent of unemployment among that sizable group with multiple periods without work in the course of a year. For them, the sum total of the lengths of all completed spells recorded yearly is a more accurate measure of hardship. Akerlof and Main's estimates of this "unemployment experience" range from an annual average of 18.4 weeks for persons having two jobless spells in 1976, to 20.3 weeks for those having three or more spells.

Despite its superiority over more commonly used measures, however, the duration of "unemployment experience" must itself be taken as only a lower-bound estimate of the length of joblessness suffered by that component of the unemployed who withdraw from the labor force entirely in the course of prolonged periods without work. Clark and Summers (1979) spotlighted the "hidden unemployment" of those persons who react to unsuccessful job search by temporarily suspending their efforts out of discouragement. Regardless of their reasons for doing so, jobless individuals who tell government interviewers they have not actively searched for work in the last four weeks are officially categorized as "not in the labor force" and are thus not counted among the unemployed.

Clark and Summers proposed a new measure to capture the full duration of discouraged worker joblessness. "Nonemployment" was estimated by summing the weeks of officially defined unemployment with the weeks outside the labor force of those whose principal reason for part-year employment was difficulty in finding work. The average length of nonemployment in 1974 was calculated as four and one-half months, nearly a month longer than the official estimate of the mean duration of unemployment. Even using the standard definition of unemployment, they found a high concentration of lengthy jobless spells in a small fraction of the labor force. While only about 2.4 percent of the labor force was officially listed as being unemployed more than six months in 1974, they accounted for 41.8 percent of all weeks of unemployment that year.[26] Turning from Current Population Survey (CPS) cross-section data to the National Longitudinal Survey of men aged 45 to 59, Clark and Summers found that, among that one-fifth of the labor force experiencing some unemployment in the boom years 1965–68, an average of 20.3 weeks were spent looking for work. About 40 percent of all unemployment over this period was concentrated among those jobless for a full year or more.

A U.S. Labor Department study of the seven recessions from the early 1950s to 1982 found that the number of long-term unemployed rose nearly five times faster than the overall increase in unemployment.[27] The largest recent increases have occurred among prime-age males, blacks and Hispanics, and workers in manufacturing and construction industries. Podgursky (1984) also concluded from analysis of 1969–83 aggregate data that the single most important factor in the secular rise in unemployment since the mid-1970s was prime-age men. The declining youth share of the labor force since then has acted to reduce total unemployment, and prime-age women, though an increasing portion of the labor force, do not appear to have contributed to higher unemployment. But prime-age men, while only 36.7 percent of the labor force by 1982, accounted for 56.7 percent of the 1975–82 jump in the national jobless rate. The unemployed have been disproportionately blue-collar workers in goods-producing industries. Likewise, the share of the labor force in manufacturing and construction was down to 25.9 percent by late 1982, but their contribution to the 12-year run-up in unemployment was 37.2 percent. This secular growth in unemployment was clearly not the result of greater frequency of brief spells of voluntary joblessness. Podgursky found that the average length of time out of work jumped 88 percent since 1969. The extended duration of jobless spells accounted statistically for all of the unemployment increase over the period.[28]

If the bulk of the unemployed are mature males, job-losers, and the long-term unemployed, then claims that the natural rate of unemployment has been raised by increased proportions of new young and female job-seekers are discredited.[29] Though the economists who stressed these compositional shifts had correctly noted the increased impact of the expanded youth cohort in the early seventies, they did not fully anticipate the rapid diminution of that impact soon thereafter. They also neglected countervailing compositional changes. The dramatic increase in the fraction of the labor force with some college education should, all else the same, reduce unemployment. The same is true of the increased number of female workers, since a disproportionate number have gone into the service industries with below average unemployment rates.

Thus, quite a large body of empirical research since the late 1970s has thrown sharply into question both the traditional neoclassical belief in cyclical real wage movements and the modern neoclassical claims that most unemployment is short-term and voluntary. But the consistency of these empirical findings has not yet led to much agreement on how best to explain unemployment today. Perhaps the most that can be said is that even many long-time advocates of orthodox theory have begun to appreciate the value of more eclectic approaches. Thus two well-known neo-classical labor economists concluded their recent survey of unemployment research with the admission that: "Perhaps no single model applies to all labor markets. For instance, some employees may be working in jobs involving a long-term association with their employers while other employees work under short contracts."[30]

"Efficiency Wage" Theory

This recognition of labor market heterogeneity has, as we have seen, been most developed in the structuralist and segmented labor market literature, now enjoying a strong revival.[31] A number of the most recent theoretical papers have embarked on an ambitious effort to integrate Keynes's argument about wage relativities with key aspects of structural, segmentation, and "efficiency wage" models.[32] For example, Bulow and Summers (1986) begin with the assumption that the involuntarily unem-ployed are those who cannot find a job at a wage equal to that currently paid other workers with the same qualifications. The persistence of such wage differentials is attributed primarily to labor market segmentation. The more that workers are con-cerned with fair pay relativities, the more likely they are to queue for higher-paying primary-sector jobs. But the question then arises why high-wage employers don't lower their pay level to clear the labor market. Unions are one obvious reason, but sizable interfirm wage differences are known to persist even in nonunion areas. The reason may have to do with efficiency wage considerations. The basic idea of the latter is that employers have an incentive to pay above-market wages because of the positive productivity effects they yield. Higher wages help to raise morale, reduce shirking on the job, and make workers less likely to be absent or quit. If employers have the goal of minimizing labor cost per unit of output (i.e., per "efficiency unit"), then they will adopt a long-term strategy of maintaining the firm's wages above the market-clearing level. This explanation implies that some workers forego low-wage work while waiting for a job paying wages commensurate with their skill level. Summers (1986) suggests that an unemployed worker may be dissuaded from taking work at a low-wage firm because this could be interpreted by potential high-wage employers as signaling that the worker has inferior abilities, and thus damage her chance of being hired. But this part of the model needs further development, since it does not seem fully consonant with the relative inelasticity of labor supply.

"Deindustrialization"

One of the most widely discussed new theories has been that of Bluestone and Harrison (1982). They argue that the increase in long-term unemployment stems from a structural shift of the economy away from primary sector jobs in goods-producing industries.[33] This process has been characterized by accelerated capital mobility across state and national borders, a high volume of permanent layoffs and plant closings in basic industries in the 1970s, downward trends in growth rates of capital formation and research spending, and the dramatic import penetration of American markets for manufactures. New jobs are being created, but largely in lower-wage sectors. If low-wage jobs are defined as those paying below one-half the average 1973 real wage, Bluestone and Harrison (1988) estimate that nearly three-fifths of net new jobs created between 1979 and 1984 were low-wage. This is a dramatic change from the earlier 1963–79 period when under one-fifth of net new employment was low wage. A major reason for this finding is that more than 9 out of 10 of the net new jobs created from 1979 to 1984 were part-time or part-year.[34] But even after restricting their samples to year-round, full-time workers and extending the time span to 1986, the authors still find a sharp increase in wage polarization since the late 1970s.

Critics have attacked Bluestone and Harrison for exaggerating the "deindustrialization" of an economy in which the absolute number of goods-producing jobs has remained close to 30 million throughout the past quarter-century. Although agriculture has continued its secular decline, manufacturing employed about the same number of workers (close to 20 million) in 1984 as in 1959. A Labor Department critique by Kutscher and Personick (1986) was based on the finding that, of 101 goods-producing industries, over three-fourths had positive real output trends between 1959 and 1984. However, their own data show that over 55 percent of these same industries had a declining trend in employment over this period. And 23 especially troubled industries, including steel, tires and rubber, leather, and iron mining, had negative trends in both output and employment.

In January 1984, the Labor Department (1985) undertook a special survey as part of the national CPS to estimate the extent and nature of displacement caused by the back-to-back recessions of 1980 and 1982. It found that, from January 1979 to January 1984, 11.5 million workers aged 20 and over lost their jobs as the result of plant closings or major employment cutbacks. About 5.1 million of these were long-term employees of three years or more. Just over half of the latter were prime-age males, 25–54. Over 600,000 were black and 300,000 Hispanic. Manufacturing alone accounted for 49 percent of the displaced long-term workers.

By the time of the 1984 survey, 25.5 percent of the 5.1 million job-losers were still unemployed job-seekers and another 13.7 percent had dropped out of the labor force entirely. The median duration of unemployment was nearly half a year for the full sample during this period. But those still unemployed when interviewed had been jobless an average of over 32 weeks and those not in the labor force an average of nearly 57 weeks. Yet in the course of the five-year span one-third had never obtained unemployment compensation. Of those who did, one-half had exhausted their allowed benefits by 1984.

Among those with full-time jobs before being displaced who were reemployed by 1984, nearly 13 percent had found only part-time work and about one-half were working in a different industry. Industrial mobility and earnings losses were especially common for those displaced from manufacturing. The three out of five former manufacturing workers reemployed by 1984 reported an average wage on their new jobs of $273 per week, compared with $344 in their lost jobs. If these figures were adjusted for inflation their real earnings loss would be even larger.

Clearly, a massive structural shift is underway, which has sharply reduced the relative importance of goods-producing industries in the economy. These industries accounted for 40 percent of all jobs in 1959 but only 28 percent in 1984. Manufacturing went from 25.1 percent to 18.5 percent of all employment. Meanwhile service employment jumped from 60 to 72 percent of the total. There have, of course, been important regional differences. While New York was suffering unusually severe losses in basic industry, manufacturing employment in southern California was increasing. And it is undeniable that not all of the vanished manufacturing jobs were high-wage and not all of the new service jobs are low-skill and low-wage.

But studies using quite different methodologies than Bluestone and Harrison have also produced evidence of increasing inequality in the overall income distribution. For example, a Labor Department analysis of CPS data on full-time, year-round workers for the period 1973–1982 by McMahon and Tschetter (1986) concluded that while the fraction of employment in traditionally low-pay occupational categories appeared to decline, there was nonetheless increasing income inequality among more narrowly defined jobs *within* the broad occupational groupings. Levy and Michel (1986) investigated real income changes within age cohorts and found a sharp decline in within-cohort wage growth rates in the late seventies and the early 1980s. They point out that even in the late 1940s the service sector accounted for one-half of all full-time jobs and averaged earnings 10–15 percent below manufacturing. But interindustry differences were less important because real wages were growing in all sectors, thus assuring a laid-off worker that he could regain his former living standard after a few years on a new job. However, this prospect vanished with the wage stagnation of the seventies and eighties, and intersectoral wage gaps assumed much greater significance. They project that as the shift to more service employment continues in the future, youth in the large baby boom cohort will be ever more crowded into low-wage sectors and their prospects for lifetime earnings growth will suffer accordingly.

For the many blacks and Hispanics who followed earlier waves of migrants into entry-level jobs in manufacturing, recent industrial restructurings have been especially costly. First, these minorities are far more concentrated than whites in central cities and the northeastern and northcentral states where heavy industry has declined the fastest. They have thus shared less in the business expansions that have occurred in suburbia and in the West. Suburban housing segregation has combined with poverty to limit these minorities' ability to move to where the jobs are. For example, Bluestone and Harrison (1982: p. 55) give an example of a Detroit manufacturing firm that left the city for a facility just across the state line in rural Ohio. Salaried employees, most of whom were white, were given relocation aid by the firm, whereas the largely black production staff was not. Minorities' share of employment dropped from 40 percent before the relocation to 2 percent after. Another disadvantage has been the lower average age of minority groups. Their relative youth, coupled with the relatively short time since racial and ethnic hiring barriers were dismantled in most industries, has meant that a smaller proportion have sufficient job tenure to be protected from dismissal by seniority systems. And their below average incomes make minorities more dependent than the average white family on wages and salaries. Most lack the substantial savings needed after a layoff to relocate or train for a new occupation.

Cyclical Fluctuations in Participation and Employment

If the recent economic literature on unemployment has not yet produced a single, widely accepted theoretical framework for studying white–minority differentials, it has at least spotlighted a number of potentially important factors that need to be taken into account. The relative importance of wage rigidity for Hispanic unemployment depends on the influence of such factors as the minimum wage and trade unions. Unfortunately, despite a vast empirical literature on the effects of changes in the minimum wage and in union membership, their effects on Hispanics have been little studied. Given the large fractions of youth and of low-wage adults in the Spanish-origin population, it could be argued that changes in the legal minimum have a disproportionate impact on their employment.[35] And, with a similar proportion (16 percent by 1988) of white and Hispanic wage and salary workers represented by labor organizations, unions may play at least as important a role in restraining wage declines among Hispanics as they do for other groups.[36] On the other hand, the relatively high proportion of Hispanics (particularly recent immigrants and the undocumented) in marginal firms and casual employment situations are more vulnerable to employer violations of minimum wage and other labor standards.[37] Even those represented by unions, if they are in highly competitive industries like apparel, where many Hispanics work, may be under more intense wage-cutting pressure than the typical white union member.

About 30 percent of the Hispanic population is foreign born. Insofar as immigrants are substitutable for natives at low-skill levels they may alter the structure of labor demand in their favor and weaken the downward wage rigidity of low-paid groups, particularly minorities, women, and youth. But if, as Chiswick argues, recent migrants have high interfirm mobility during the first few years of adjustment and often possess nontransferable skills, employers may find it especially difficult to evaluate their job histories and may screen them out as unreliable.[38]

This presumption might be reinforced by observation of the heavy representation of employed Hispanics in seasonal and cyclically sensitive occupations and industries. Two out of every five are in blue-collar occupations, compared with one-third of blacks and 29 percent of all whites. Agriculture, construction, and durable manufacturing industries account for one-fourth of Hispanic employment, but only 17 percent of blacks' and 22 percent of whites' jobs. This no doubt reflects, in part, below average educational attainment (particularly among Mexicans), but Cubans and the growing influx of immigrants from other South and Central American countries average close to the white non-Hispanic schooling level, yet also have larger concentrations in the most unstable sectors. Thus, other factors, including discriminatory occupational downgrading by employers and labor market segmentation may be responsible.

Whatever the causal pattern, Hispanics' occupational and industrial distributions, high proportion of recent immigrants, and record of above average unemployment make it likely that they will have low job tenure.[39] Briefer tenure with an employer generally implies greater vulnerability to cyclical downturns. From the human capital perspective, more junior employees represent smaller volumes of firm-specific training investments by the employer and are thus less costly to lay off. From the segmentation point of view, newer employees have less claim on seniority protections and are less likely to have attained positions within internal labor markets that are well insulated from external market forces.

Two questions have been central to the analysis of time-series changes in demographic unemployment differentials.[40] First, do recessions have a more adverse impact on minority groups than on whites? Second, if they do, to what extent is this attributable to discriminatory hiring and firing practices and to what extent can it be explained by other factors? From the outset, it is necessary to recognize explicitly that, as a wealth of studies on female labor supply and the youth labor market have by now made clear, the impact of changes in economic variables on unemployment rates depends on their impacts on labor force participation and employment. Otherwise it is always possible that if, for example, one observes little effect of a fall in labor demand on a group's unemployment rate this could be due to a decline in labor force participation by persons discouraged from job search rather than evidence of the group's immunity to economic conditions. Only by a simultaneous examination of these two component parts can the welfare implications of intergroup differentials in cyclical behavior be properly assessed.

In 1973, information on Hispanic labor force activity from the national Current Population Survey first became available on a monthly basis. Twelve years of these data (April 1973 through December 1984) are used here for the first time in a detailed econometric analysis of cyclical changes. Average white, black, and Hispanic unemployment rates at cycle turning points (as designated by the National

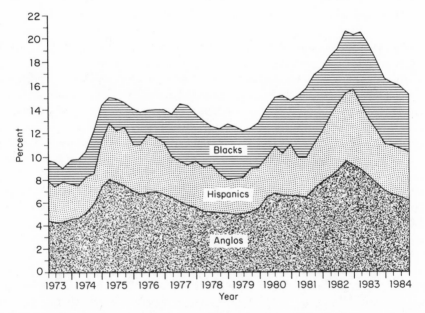

FIGURE 4.1. Unemployment rates by race and Spanish origin, 1973–1984. Source: Quarterly averages for 1973II–1984IV from U.S. Department of Labor, Bureau of Labor Statistics (1974–85). Deseasonalized by author (using X-11 Program of U.S. Bureau of the Census).

TABLE 4.1. Peak-to-Trough Changes in Unemployment Rates[a]
by Age, Sex, Race, and Spanish Origin, 1973–83

	Peak	Trough		Peak	Trough		Peak	Trough	
	Nov 1973	March 1975	IR	Jan 1980	July 1980	IR	July 1981	Nov 1982	IR
Total 16+									
White	4.0	8.3		5.7	6.8		6.3	9.4	
Black	8.5	15.1	1.5	12.6	15.6	2.7	16.4	20.2	1.2
Hispanic[b]	7.4	12.5	1.2	9.5	10.8	2.1	10.3	14.8	1.4
Both Sexes 16–19									
White	12.6	18.1		14.7	16.2		16.0	21.3	
Black	29.7	40.0	1.9	37.7	38.6	0.6	42.3	49.9	1.4
Hispanic	20.8	28.0	1.3	21.2	26.4	3.5	25.5	31.5	1.1
Men 20+									
White	2.5	7.0		4.6	5.5		4.9	8.4	
Black	5.1	13.8	1.9	11.1	13.4	2.6	13.3	19.3	1.7
Hispanic	5.0	10.9	1.4	6.6	8.5	2.1	7.7	12.9	1.5
Women 20+									
White	4.0	7.8		5.1	6.0		5.9	7.7	
Black	8.2	11.9	1.0	10.1	12.4	2.6	14.1	16.1	1.1
Hispanic	7.0	11.8	1.3	10.6	8.9	1.9	10.0	13.7	2.1

[a]Three-month averages centered at cycle turning points. See text for incremental ratio (IR) formula.

[b]Hispanics include all persons of Spanish origin regardless of race.

SOURCE: *Employment and Earnings,* various years, and Bureau of Labor Statistics, unpublished tabulations.

Bureau of Economic Research) were first calculated from monthly CPS data. Three-month averages, centered at the turning point dates, were used to reduce sampling variability and seasonal swings.[41]

Figure 4.1 and the calculations presented in Table 4.1 reveal that among men and women of all ages, Hispanic jobless rates have consistently been at least 50 percent higher than those of whites, though never as high as blacks'. Across the decade's three business cycles the ratio of Hispanic to white rates averaged 1.64.

But to determine whether Hispanics have been more adversely affected by recessions, this "relative unemployment ratio" must be supplemented with the ratio of the absolute change in Hispanic unemployment to the change in white unemployment between each peak and trough.[42] This "incremental ratio" (IR) is computed according to the formula:

$$IR = \left(\frac{U_c^m - U_{c-1}^m}{U_c^w - U_{c-1}^w} \right)$$

where the superscripts m and w denote minorities (alternatively blacks and Hispanics) and whites, respectively, and c denotes cycle turning points. Whenever IR > 1, the minority rate is changing more than is the white rate.

It appears that both Hispanics and blacks generally do experience relatively larger increases in unemployment during business downturns than whites.[43] For

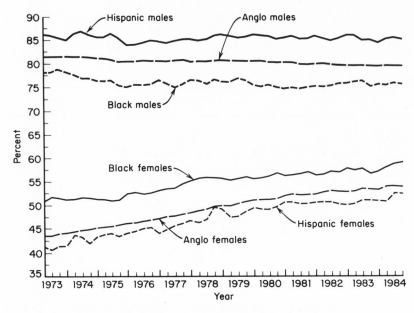

FIGURE 4.2. Labor force participation rates of persons ages 20 and over, by sex, race, and Spanish origin, 1973–1984. Source: Same as Figure 4.1.

example, in the 1981–82 recession, the worst in three decades, joblessness among adult male Hispanics jumped by over 5 percentage points, from 7.7 to 12.9 percent, while the white male rate rose only from 4.9 to 8.4 percent. That is, about 15 Hispanics and 17 blacks became unemployed for every 10 white males.

If workers of Spanish origin bear a disproportionate burden in slack labor markets, it is important to observe that their unemployment situation appears to improve relative to whites during expansions. Incremental ratios measured from trough to peak (not shown) are higher for Hispanic teenagers and men 20 and over than for comparable whites. In the recovery starting in March 1975, the incidence of joblessness among adult males fell from 10.9 to 6.6 percent for Hispanics but declined by only 2.4 percentage points (to 4.6 percent) for whites. The difference is, however, smaller during the 1980–81 upturn, and unemployment actually increases rather than decreases among black teenagers and black and Hispanic women. In contrast to the findings of Gilroy and others for the 1950s and 1960s, blacks appear to have benefited less than whites from the expansions of 1975–1980 and 1980–1981. This is reflected in the gradual increase in the black–white unemployment ratio from 2.1:1 at the November 1973 peak to 2.6:1 at the peak in July 1981.

The participation trends charted in Figure 4.2 show what appears to be a more fluctuating pattern for both Hispanic men and women than for all whites, even in data restricted to the more stable population aged 20 years and over. At the same time, there is a stable secular tendency for Hispanic males to maintain consistently higher activity rates than Anglos, and Hispanic females have steadily increased their

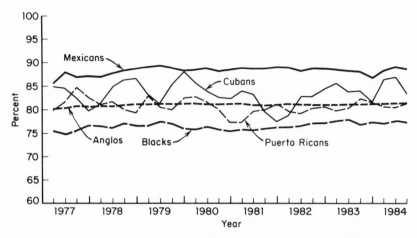

FIGURE 4.3. Labor force participation rates of males, ages 20 and over, by race and type of Spanish origin, 1977–1984. Source: Same as Figure 4.1.

participation, at a faster rate than other women. Furthermore, once these data are disaggregated into the main Spanish-origin subgroups (Figures 4.3 and 4.4) it turns out that Mexicans have the least, not the most, unstable pattern.[44] Among the possible reasons for this are the secular decline in the fraction of employed Mexican Americans in seasonal farm labor, the faster job growth in the Southwest than in the East during this period, and the greater variability of statistical estimates based on the relatively small Puerto Rican and Cuban samples.

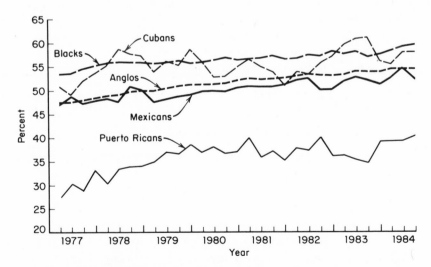

FIGURE 4.4. Labor force participation rates of females, ages 20 and over, by race and type of Spanish origin, 1977–1984. Source: Same as Figure 4.1.

Econometric Findings

To control better for the influence of seasonality and to gauge the relative importance of employment and participation changes in accounting for these results, quarterly data from the CPS spanning the period 1973II–1984IV were exploited to conduct a multivariate regression analysis. Let us begin by noting the identity:

$$\frac{E}{P} = \left(\frac{L}{P}\right)\left(\frac{E}{L}\right)$$
(1)

where E represents the employment of a given age/sex/race/ethnic group, P the size of the group's civilian population, and L the number active in the civilian labor force. Then, expressing this in natural logarithms and differentiating yields:

$$d\ln\left(\frac{E}{P}\right) = d\ln\left(\frac{L}{P}\right) + d\ln\left(\frac{E}{L}\right)$$
(2)

which can alternatively be put in terms of the unemployment rate as:

$$d\ln\left(\frac{E}{P}\right) = d\ln\left(\frac{L}{P}\right) + d\ln\left(1 - \frac{U}{L}\right)$$
(3)

Clark and Summers recently used such a model to conduct a decomposition of cyclical employment movements for whites and nonwhites, by age and sex, over the period 1954–76.[45] We depart from that study not only by extending the analysis to Hispanics and focusing on the more recent 1973–84 period but also in expanding the model to control for other factors widely thought to influence demographic employment and participation differentials.

To operationalize the decomposition of changes in the employment-population ratio, separate participation and "employment rate" $(1 - U/L)$ equations of the following form are estimated for the ith group:

$$\ln\left(\frac{L}{P}\right) = \alpha_0 + \Sigma_{j=0}^{7}\gamma_j(UA)_{t-j} + \alpha_1 S_1 + \alpha_2 S_2 + \alpha_3 S_3$$
$$+ \alpha_4 T + \alpha_5(MW)_{it} + \alpha_6(GB)_t + e_{it}$$
(4)

$$\ln\left(1 - \frac{U}{L}\right) = \beta_0 + \Sigma_{j=0}^{7}\lambda_j(UA)_{t-j} + \beta_1 S_1 + \beta_2 S_2 + \beta_3 S_3$$
$$+ \beta_4 T + \beta_5(MW)_{it} + \beta_6(GB)_t + e_{it}$$
(5)

where UA is a measure of aggregate demand, represented by the unemployment rate of adult males 35–44,[46] $S_1 - S_3$ are quarterly dummy variables,[47] and T is a time trend (included to capture unmeasured socioeconomic forces and the presence of any autocorrelated trends).[48] To take into account expectational uncertainties among employers and employees, UA is estimated as an eight-quarter lag (the same length used in the Clark and Summers study), thereby facilitating comparisons of our results. Experiments with different lag lengths and a polynomial lag structure did not produce qualitatively dissimilar findings.[49]

To test the effect of changes in the minimum wage we calculated a measure of the form first proposed by Kaitz,[50] which has the advantage of summarizing in a single index information on the relation between the minimum level and the prevailing market wage, the degree of coverage, and differences in the legal minimum and in coverage rates of newly covered and other industries. For each major industry the ratio of the legal minimum wage to the average hourly earnings of production workers was weighted by the fraction of covered employment. This figure was, in turn, weighted by the ratio of industry employment to total civilian employment. Separate indexes, based on age-specific industrial distributions, were calculated for individuals 16–19 and for those aged 20 and over.[51]

A major topic of concern in the labor supply literature of the last decade has been the effects of government transfer benefits on the low-wage population. Benefits may reduce the cost of unemployment and thereby influence the level of each worker's reservation wage. This could both contribute to wage rigidity among the employed and make corner solutions on workers' indifference maps more likely, reducing participation rates. But positive participation and/or employment effects could emerge insofar as recipients are subject to work requirements or use higher benefits to expand job search. The government benefits variable (GB) is the sum of average monthly payments per recipient in the Aid to Families with Dependent Children program plus the cash value of average monthly food stamp assistance per recipient deflated by the Consumer Price Index (1967 = 100).[52] Inclusion of this variable as a regressor together with the minimum wage index could create a multicollinearity problem the more that policy decisions on changing the minimum are coordinated with decisions on income maintenance payment levels. The relatively low correlation between the minimum wage (MW) and government benefits in our data series and the insignificant variations in the standard errors of coefficients estimated in alternative specifications suggest that this is not a serious problem here. To take into account the intertemporal correlation of residuals, a maximum likelihood iterative procedure was used (based on a first-order autoregressive error specification).

The empirical results in Tables 4.2 and 4.3 reveal that among the civilian population 16 and over, Hispanic participation and employment rates are significantly more affected by changes in aggregate demand than are those of all whites.[53] Teenage participation is far more cyclically sensitive than that of persons 20 and over (whose coefficients are generally low and insignificant), with economic downturns having the largest negative effects on black and Hispanic youth. In the employment regressions, the estimated Hispanic coefficients are half again as large as those of whites in the full sample, reflecting especially large differentials among male teenagers and adult women. Taken together, the two tables' results imply [by identity (1)] that, on average, a percentage point increase in the prime-age-male jobless rate is associated with a drop in the employment-population ratio by 2.8 percent for all Hispanics and 2.4 percent for blacks, but only 1.6 percent for whites. For all groups except female Hispanic teenagers, movements in this ratio are dominated by changes in employment rather than participation rates.

TABLE 4.2. Regression Analysis of Determinants of Participation Rates
of Whites, Blacks, and Hispanics by Sex and Age, 1973–84

	UA	MW	GB	TREND	R^2	SEE	ρ
		Explanatory Variables					
Total, 16 and over							
White	−.564	.033	.001	.002	.982	.003	.330
	(9.25)	(.74)	(1.55)	(15.74)			
Black	−.953	−.151	.001	.002	.930	.006	.822
	(2.32)	(1.58)	(.94)	(3.34)			
Hispanic	−1.166	.096	−.0001	.002	.891	.009	.070
	(4.48)	(.81)	(.15)	(8.14)			
Men, 16–19							
White	−2.108	.155	.005	.001	.980	.012	.151
	(5.47)	(1.11)	(3.22)	(1.64)			
Black	−5.429	−.791	.003	.002	.852	.055	.346
	(2.70)	(1.20)	(.40)	(.68)			
Hispanic	−3.612	−.829	.019	.006	.642	.064	.501
	(1.31)	(1.08)	(1.88)	(1.47)			
Women, 16–19							
White	−1.612	.548	.003	.003	.839	.030	.198
	(1.60)	(1.55)	(.76)	(1.81)			
Black	−5.613	−.304	.009	.006	.822	.058	.357
	(2.59)	(.44)	(1.03)	(1.73)			
Hispanic	−2.84	−.824	.027	.008	.633	.069	.113
	(1.34)	(1.06)	(3.10)	(2.21)			
Men ≥ 20							
White	−.182	.029	.001	−.0003	.965	.002	−.200
	(1.94)	(.81)	(1.21)	(1.62)			
Black	.009	−.204	.006	.001	.475	.007	.585
	(.01)	(1.14)	(1.35)	(.70)			
Hispanic	.165	.169	.003	.001	.374	.004	−.056
	(.64)	(1.70)	(1.67)	(.94)			
Women ≥ 20							
White	−.674	.156	−.003	.004	.976	.005	.005
	(2.13)	(1.29)	(1.42)	(5.11)			
Black	−.195	−.105	.007	.004	.826	.008	.587
	(.26)	(.51)	(1.84)	(2.64)			
Hispanic	−.598	.510	−.005	.003	.813	.015	.060
	(.59)	(1.42)	(.84)	(1.32)			

NOTE: Dependent variable is ln(L/P). T-statistics in parentheses. UA coefficient above is sum of coefficients from 8-quarter UA lag. Three quarterly dummies also included as controls. Equations estimated by a maximum likelihood iterative procedure, 1973III–1984IV.

A comparison of these findings for 1973–84 with those for 1954–76 in Clark and Summers' study of white–black differentials reveals a substantial increase in the cyclical sensitivity of black teenagers' employment-population ratios. While the two studies' estimates for white teens are quite close, demand swings have almost twice as large an impact on blacks today: a 1 percentage point decline in UA cut the

TABLE 4.3. Regression Analysis of Determinants of Employment Rates
of Whites, Blacks, and Hispanics by Sex and Age, 1973–84

	Explanatory Variables						
	UA	MW	GB	TREND	R^2	SEE	ρ
Total, 16 and over							
White	−1.025	−.024	−.001	.0002	.955	.003	.491
	(7.29)	(.49)	(1.21)	(1.12)			
Black	−1.471	−.027	−.001	−.001	.935	.008	.601
	(3.62)	(.18)	(.72)	(1.50)			
Hispanic	−1.605	.010	−.001	.0003	.896	.007	.515
	(4.01)	(.08)	(.66)	(.77)			
Men, 16–19							
White	−2.666	−.348	.003	.001	.911	.012	.274
	(8.27)	(2.49)	(1.73)	(2.13)			
Black	−5.886	−.700	.004	.001	.853	.040	.408
	(3.62)	(1.44)	(.75)	(.27)			
Hispanic	−4.804	−.342	.005	.003	.765	.032	.250
	(4.47)	(.89)	(1.12)	(1.63)			
Women, 16–19							
White	−1.900	−.245	.002	.001	.876	.008	.520
	(4.91)	(2.37)	(1.27)	(2.75)			
Black	−5.569	−.979	.004	.003	.594	.048	.245
	(2.33)	(1.74)	(.61)	(1.24)			
Hispanic	−1.949	.224	−.004	−.001	.371	.038	−.246
	(2.16)	(.62)	(1.14)	(.33)			
Men ≥ 20							
White	−.949	.055	.002	.001	.969	.003	−.136
	(3.57)	(.76)	(1.84)	(1.92)			
Black	−2.764	−.126	.008	.003	.963	.008	.107
	(5.39)	(.64)	(2.36)	(2.46)			
Hispanic	−1.015	.274	.005	.001	.952	.006	−.297
	(3.34)	(2.27)	(2.34)	(1.64)			
Women ≥ 20							
White	−.818	−.042	.003	.002	.894	.003	.250
	(3.18)	(.57)	(2.08)	(3.18)			
Black	−2.054	−.178	.003	.002	.904	.008	.195
	(1.97)	(.92)	(1.01)	(1.85)			
Hispanic	−1.678	.007	.001	.002	.463	.014	.275
	(1.50)	(.02)	(.14)	(.74)			

NOTE: Dependent variable is ln(1-U/L). T-statistics in parentheses. UA coefficient above is sum of coefficients from 8-quarter UA lag. Three quarterly dummies also included as controls. Equations estimated by a maximum likelihood iterative procedure, 1973III–1984IV.

employment of nonwhite (overwhelmingly black) youth by 6–7 percent in the earlier period, but now produces an 11 percent reduction. This increase reflects greater sensitivity in both their participation and employment rates. In contrast, for persons 20 and over the 1973–84 estimates are only slightly above the earlier ones.

Among Hispanics, substantial national-origin differences in the level of unem-

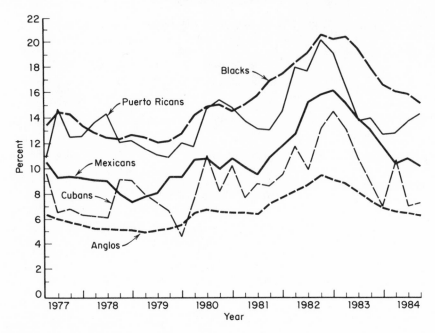

FIGURE 4.5. Unemployment rates of persons ages 16 and over, by race and type of Spanish origin, 1977–1984. Source: Same as Figure 4.1.

ployment seem to have persisted over time, with the relatively low rates of Cubans sharply contrasting with Puerto Rican joblessness nearly as high as that of blacks. The time-series plots in Figure 4.5 suggest that the overall Hispanic pattern in Figure 4.1 may obscure underlying differences in the pace and magnitude of cyclical swings in each group's unemployment. When regression analysis was conducted separately for the three subgroups it was found that the reduced degrees of freedom caused by the shorter time span for which BLS data are available (only starting with the second quarter of 1977), as well as the larger standard errors of statistics derived from the small national-origin samples, produced relatively few statistically significant estimates.[54] That in mind, results in Table 4.4 nonetheless suggest that it is Mexicans and Cubans who tend to have high employment elasticities, while the only subsample whose participation rates were significantly affected by the business cycles of this period were Puerto Ricans.

The age breakdown reveals that the latter finding is largely attributable to the cyclical sensitivity of Puerto Rican women 20 and over. Cooney has shown that the sharp decline in demand for operative and unskilled labor in New York City during the 1970s played a major role in discouraging their labor force attachment.[55] The reasons for the unusually high employment elasticity of adult Cuban women are less well understood, but may in part be due to their similar concentration in the most vulnerable jobs. Of Cuban women workers in Miami, the 1980 census shows that 24 percent are in the lowest-skilled occupations, over twice the proportion among the overall white female work force.[56]

TABLE 4.4. Cyclical Sensitivity of Participation, Employment, and Employment-Population Rates by Age, Sex, and Ethnic Group, 1977–84

	Participation Rate	Employment Rate	Employment-Population Rate
Total, 16 and over			
White	−.266	−.914	−1.80
	(1.44)	(4.51)	(4.19)
Black	.122	−2.581	−2.388
	(.23)	(5.91)	(3.45)
Mexican	−.429	−1.469	−1.898
	(.78)	(1.91)	(2.01)
Puerto Rican	−3.023	−1.071	−4.094
	(4.54)	(.78)	(2.70)
Cuban	2.133	−2.166	−.033
	(.88)	(1.88)	(.01)
Men ≥ 20			
Mexican	.121	−1.292	−1.171
	(.39)	(4.39)	(2.73)
Puerto Rican	.686	−.876	−.190
	(.40)	(.64)	(.09)
Cuban	−.075	.281	.206
	(.03)	(.17)	(.07)
Women ≥ 20			
Mexican	.801	−.508	.293
	(.71)	(.26)	(.13)
Puerto Rican	−8.851	−1.052	−9.903
	(7.74)	(.67)	(5.11)
Cuban	2.591	−4.472	−1.881
	(.72)	(3.15)	(.48)

NOTE: Entries in cols. 1 and 2 are sums of coefficients from 8-quarter UA lag (T-statistics in parens.) from maximum likelihood estimates of equations (4) and (5), respectively, for 1977III–1984IV. For calculation of col. 3 entries, see fn. 49.

Turning to the other variables, the results in Tables 4.2 and 4.3 indicate that the minimum wage effect (evaluated at the variable's mean) on white teenagers' employment-population ratios is negligible. But a 10 percent rise in the MW index is associated with a 5.1–5.9 percent employment decrease among black men and women, and a 2.4–4.6 percent reduction among Hispanic men and women, respectively. While these are above the estimates of the many studies based largely on 1960s data, they are consistent with the higher effects found for nonwhites by Wachter and Kim using data covering the 1970s.[57] However, for no group is the estimated impact on the employment ratio statistically significant. Likewise, we find no evidence from these results of an important explanatory role for increases in transfer benefits in worsening Hispanic participation and employment patterns. In fact, the only significant coefficients are positive, perhaps due to work requirements or the intensified job search made possible by higher benefits.[58]

Finally, the lack of any time-series data on Hispanic unemployment or participation rates by occupation group makes it impossible to compare their experience with whites and blacks in similar jobs. Within-occupation regressions would doubtless yield smaller demographic differentials in cyclical sensitivity than those reported here. Some suggestive evidence can be drawn from available BLS information on unemployment by educational attainment, which is closely correlated with occupational level.[59] When Hispanics ages 35–44 were assigned the same educational distribution as whites in 1981, their estimated unemployment fell, but only from 8.3 to 7.5 percent (compared with a white rate in that age group of 4.9 percent). For the full Hispanic labor force, the jobless rate estimated after such an adjustment differed insignificantly from the actual rate, 11.2 percent. Likewise, when the experiment was repeated for 1978, a year of substantially less unemployment, the predicted and actual rates (8.7 and 9.5 percent, respectively) differed by less than a percentage point.

However, it can be argued that controlling for occupation is improper in research attempting to evaluate the importance of employment discrimination, since occupational downgrading may itself be a common means by which prejudiced employers put minorities at a disadvantage relative to otherwise comparable whites, particularly in the presence of downwardly rigid wages. Thus, Mincer questioned the within-occupation results in Gilman's pioneering 1963 paper on white–nonwhite unemployment differentials and emphasized instead that:

> As the proposition ["last hired, first fired"] refers to layoffs and not to quits, one possibility is that in good times temporary unemployment associated with quits is a larger component of white than of Negro unemployment. If true, equal amplitudes of total unemployment would mean larger amplitudes of involuntary unemployment among nonwhites.[60]

This certainly appears to be the case for Hispanics. Table 4.5 presents age/sex breakdowns of the average shares of unemployment attributable to layoffs, quits, and labor force entry or reentry in the period 1976–80. Regardless of sex or age, Hispanics are less likely than whites to be unemployed due to quitting their last job and considerably more likely to have been indefinitely laid off or fired. For example, among adult unemployed men, the white quit rate was 13.2 percent, the Hispanic only 11.8. The percentage of Hispanic job-losers was, at 69.6 percent, less than 3 points higher than for whites, but whites were far more likely to be on temporary layoffs than were unemployed Hispanic men.[61]

Conclusion

Recent debates over the nature and causes of unemployment have generally been conducted with little consideration of the experiences of Hispanics. This chapter begins with a review of the principal theoretical controversies and discusses their possible implications for a better understanding of the particular problems of minor-

TABLE 4.5. Distribution of Unemployed Whites, Blacks, and Hispanics by Reason for Unemployment, Sex, and Age, 1976–80 (Percent)

	Job-Losers		Job Leavers	Reentrants	New Entrants	Total
	Layoff	Other				
Total, 16 and over						
White	15.6	31.6	13.9	26.9	11.8	100
Black	9.9	33.0	9.4	30.7	17.0	100
Hispanic	11.2	39.5	12.2	23.0	14.1	100
Mexican	10.3	39.9	11.8	23.9	14.0	100
Puerto Rican	12.2	39.0	11.3	22.1	15.7	100
Cuban	15.3	43.5	15.1	14.1	13.3	100
Both Sexes, 16–19						
White	5.9	16.1	11.4	27.9	38.4	100
Hispanic	4.2	19.3	9.4	28.3	38.8	100
Men ≥ 20						
White	22.4	44.6	13.2	17.5	2.2	100
Hispanic	14.1	55.5	11.8	13.9	4.4	100
Women ≥ 20						
White	11.8	27.1	16.8	36.8	5.0	100
Hispanic	12.4	34.2	15.3	30.4	8.3	100

NOTE: Totals may not sum to 100 percent due to rounding.

SOURCE: Averages calculated from unpublished annual BLS data, 1976–80.

ities. Then, for the first time, a time-series analysis is undertaken of the first 12 years of quarterly CPS data on Hispanic unemployment. It reveals that Hispanics have averaged unemployment rates over 1.6 times as high as whites. In the recessions of the seventies and early eighties—two of which were the worst since the Great Depression—Hispanics suffered disproportionately large increases in joblessness. The elasticity of their employment-population ratio with respect to aggregate demand is nearly twice that of the white population.

By statistically decomposing this ratio's fluctuations into the underlying changes in labor force participation and in jobless rates it was determined that both are more cyclically sensitive among Hispanics than for whites. But it is the harsher impact of demand shifts on Hispanic unemployment rates that accounts for the bulk of declines in the fraction holding jobs. And, contrary to oft-heard claims that minimum wage hikes hurt minority employment and expanded public assistance discourages labor force participation, these factors do not appear to play a significant role in Hispanic employment problems.

While Hispanic joblessness clearly increases relatively more than white unemployment in cyclical downturns, it is also reduced disproportionately during expansions. This suggests that stimulative aggregate demand policies, in conjunction with expanded educational and antidiscrimination programs, could be effective means to help alleviate their employment difficulties.

NOTES

1. Keynes (1973a): p. 372.

2. Keynes (1973a): p. 26.

3. See Darrity and Horn (1983); Eatwell (1983); Kregel (1984–85); and Rima (1984).

4. Victoria Chick (1983) has suggested that the *General Theory*'s discussion of the labor market was made less contentious in deference to Harrod's protests, just as Milgate (1983) has argued was the case with the book's criticisms of orthodox interest rate theory.

5. Keynes (1973b): p. 71.

6. For a review of this debate, see Gilpatrick (1966).

7. The CEA's empirical backing can be found in Council of Economic Advisors (1961). For empirical challenges to that work see Lipsey (1965) and Killingsworth and King (1977).

8. Killingsworth and King (1977) have pointed out that part of the fall in unemployment after 1964 is attributable to the government's redefinition of the unemployed in the mid-sixties. Those jobless persons who were enrolled in government training programs were, from 1965 on, counted as "employed" and teenagers 14–15 years old were, from 1967 onward, excluded altogether from labor force counts. Since such youth have above average unemployment, the effect of this was to lower the official unemployment rate thereafter. Further declines from mid-decade on were, of course, much influenced by the expansionary impact of the Vietnam War. Nevertheless, the largest single factor behind the unemployment reduction prior to the wartime buildup appears to be the tax cut.

9. Doeringer and Piore (1975).

10. Richard Edwards (1975): pp. 19–20.

11. See the discussion in Rosenberg (1977).

12. See Reich, Gordon, and Edwards (1973); Richard Edwards (1975, 1979) and Gordon, Edwards, and Reich (1982).

13. See Rosenberg (1977,1979) and Edwards (1979).

14. See Lippman and McCall (1976).

15. The pervasive influence of this "new microeconomic view" in the 1970s is suggested by the approving comments it received from unexpected quarters. For example, Robert Solow, though a self-styled Keynesian, staff member on the Kennedy CEA, and frequent advocate of government intervention in labor markets, wrote in 1973:

> Groups with relatively high unemployment rates have them because they have relatively many short spells of unemployment, not so much because they become unemployed and stay unemployed for long periods of time. . . . Much of the turnover of young and black workers is voluntary, initiated by the worker himself. . . . It is actually easy for them to find jobs. (Solow, 1973)

Likewise, Doeringer and Piore (1975) accepted the findings of Hall (1970) and Feldstein (1973) as supporting their own characterization of unemployment, though they faulted them for neglecting the effects of market dualism and the need for government-initiated upgrading of secondary sector workers and jobs.

16. Lucas (1981): p. 242.

17. See also the study by Altonji and Ashenfelter (1980).

18. See the survey by Brown, Gilroy, and Kohen (1982).

19. See OECD (1986) and Boyer (1987).

20. For a review of the contracting literature see Rosen (1985).

21. Osberg (1984: ch. 9) provides one of the best surveys of the human capital literature.

22. See Mincer and Jovanovic (1981). See also Parsons (1977).

23. See Gilman (1963) and Flanagan (1978).

24. I only intend here to outline some of the salient positions in this vast literature. For an exceptionally comprehensive and up-to-date survey of major conservative, liberal, and radical theories, see Cherry (1989). Other useful, if less wide-ranging surveys are in Cain (1987) and Marshall (1974).

25. On the renewed structural debate in the United States, see Charles Killingsworth (1978). In Europe, most of this research focused on Great Britain (Cripps and Tarling, 1974; Bosanquet, 1979; and Disney, 1979) and the Netherlands (Driehuis, 1976; and Klundert, 1976). See the review by Walsh (1987).

26. According to Summers's (1986) updated estimates, long-term unemployment accounted for 46 percent of all unemployment in 1978 and for 54 percent in 1984.

27. See Rones (1984).

28. Still another type of supportive evidence has come from research on the fragmentary government data available on job vacancies. Abraham (1983) investigated vacancy data collected by BLS pilot projects and by several large industrial states. She estimated that, in the mid-1960s, there were roughly 2.5 unemployed persons for every vacant job. Since then the ratio has worsened. By the early 1970s the average of job-seekers per vacancy had risen to 4.0 and by the late seventies to 5.0. She concluded that, while improvements in skill training and job-matching services were still needed, such supply-side measures are no substitute for more effective aggregate demand stimulation. Even if the labor market could match an unemployed person with every open position instantaneously, when there are five job-seekers per vacancy such matching would only lower the unemployment rate 20 percent.

29. For recent critiques of the natural rate hypothesis, see Gordon (1988); Krashevski (1988); and Blanchard and Summers (1988).

30. Kniesner and Goldsmith (1987): p. 1275.

31. See Dickens and Lang (1988).

32. See Bulow and Summers (1986), Summers (1988), and the papers in Akerlof and Yellen (1986).

33. The goods-producing sector is defined as agriculture, mining, construction, and manufacturing.

34. On the increasing proportion of part-time and part-year jobs, see Nardone (1986); Shank (1986); and Stinson (1986).

35. The proportion of full-time Hispanic workers earning below the minimum (17 percent) is almost twice that for whites (see Mellor and Stamos, 1982).

36. See the discussion of Hispanic union representation in the preceding chapter.

37. Investigators from the U.S. Department of Labor, Employment Standards Administration (1983) estimated that, between September 1979 and April 1980, nearly 1 in every 10 establishments violated the minimum wage. Noncompliance with the law was most common in retail and service industries, which alone accounted for 83 percent of minimum wage underpayments. Given the high proportion of recent migrants in low-wage jobs in these industries, they may be disproportionately victimized by employer noncompliance.

38. Chiswick (1980; 1982).

39. CPS data show this to be the case even within narrow age groupings: among men 35 to 44 in 1981, the median number of years on the current job was 6.7 for all whites and 6.2 for blacks, but only 3.7 for Hispanics (Horvath, 1982).

40. See the articles on the black–white differential by Gilman (1963, 1965) and Flanagan (1978), as well as the studies cited therein.

41. Seasonally adjusted labor force data are unavailable for Hispanic age/sex groups. Monthly observations on whites and blacks were obtained from U.S. Department of Labor (1973–85), while those for Hispanics are from unpublished BLS tabulations.

42. For a detailed comparison of the differences between the two measures, see Gilroy (1974).

43. The sole exception for Hispanics were adult women, whose jobless rates fell rather than rose between January and July of 1980. But this only reflects the fact that their rates began increasing before and subsequently fell earlier than those of white and black women. Nonetheless, the incidence of unemployment in July was still higher among Hispanic than among white women.

44. The 1973–76 unemployment and participation rates of Hispanics cannot be graphed by individual ethnic group, since the BLS only began publishing separate quarterly estimates for Mexicans, Puerto Ricans, and Cubans in the second quarter of 1977.

45. Clark and Summers (1981).

46. An alternative demand proxy, the full-employment GNP gap, was tested in place of UA for the period 1973II–1981IV (quarterly values were drawn from the *Survey of Current Business*) and found to yield qualitatively similar results. The GNP gap series was, however, ended under criticism in 1981 and thus could not be employed in the 1977–84 regressions on specific ethnic groups (see Table 4.4).

47. Use of seasonal dummies permits seasonal variability in the dependent variable independent of any seasonality in the regressors. Wallis (1974) has demonstrated that this approach is preferable to the use of seasonally adjusted data, which can introduce distortions in estimated response patterns.

Among teenagers, seasonal fluctuations reflect in part the differential behavior of school enrollees and dropouts. Unfortunately, the lack of quarterly labor force data by enrollment status for Hispanics makes it impossible to run separate regressions for enrollees and dropouts. Inclusion of enrollment rates as another regressor would be incorrect, since tests indicated them to be a function of the determinants of participation and employment. Insofar as high proportions of enrollees contribute greater variability to an ethnic group's labor force activity this effect should have been weakest for Hispanic youth, whose enrollment rate has fallen relative to the consistently higher white and black rates (see chapter 7).

48. Omission of the time trend was found to result in higher serial correlation coefficients and slightly lower (in absolute value) estimates of the UA coefficients, but no change in demographic differentials in the latter.

49. Given identity (1), the employment-population ratio is related to UA and the other variables by:

$$\ln\left(\frac{E}{P}\right) = \alpha_0 + \beta_0 + \Sigma_{j=0}^{7}(\gamma_j + \lambda_j)UA_{t-j} + (\alpha_1 + \beta_1)S_1$$
$$+ (\alpha_2 + \beta_2)S_2 + (\alpha_3 + \beta_3)S_3 + (\alpha_4 + \beta_4)T$$
$$+ (\alpha_5 + \beta_5)(MW)_{it} + (\alpha_6 + \beta_6)(GB)_t + e_{it}$$

Hence, the cyclical responsiveness of E/P can be measured as the sum of the demand coefficients estimated in the participation and employment regressions:

$$(\gamma_j + \lambda_j)$$

Its standard error is estimated assuming zero covariance of the two components.

50. Kaitz (1970).

51. Mean quarterly wages were calculated from monthly U.S. Department of Labor figures in *Employment and Earnings* (1973–85) and industrial distributions by age group were drawn from unpublished BLS tabulations. For details on construction of the index, relevant data sources on coverage rates and a survey of previous estimates of minimum wage effects, see Brown, Gilroy, and Kohen (1982).

52. Data from U.S. Bureau of the Census (1987) and unpublished Dept. of Health and Human Services estimates.

53. Chow tests indicated that the white, black, and Hispanic coefficients differed significantly across age and sex groups. For all males and females 16 and over, the computed F-statistics were 5.63 from the employment regressions and 5.83 from the participation regressions.

Because the black and Hispanic labor force statistics are derived from relatively small CPS samples they are subject to greater sampling error. To take this into account, the black and Hispanic regressions were reestimated with all observations weighted by the approximate size of each group's CPS sample. Over the years, the Census Bureau has tended to expand the number of households surveyed, thereby reducing the random variability of small sample statistics. While our weighted regressions placed more emphasis on the more recent (and presumably more accurate) observations, they did not yield significantly dissimilar results.

54. This is especially true for the teenage samples of each Hispanic grouping. Their regression results (not shown) exhibited such large standard errors as to render almost all estimates insignificant and the drawing of any firm conclusions hazardous. Full regression results for all age groups are available from the author.

55. Cooney (1979). See also the discussion in the following chapter.

56. U.S. Bureau of the Census (1984c).

57. Wachter and Kim (1982).

58. Betsey and Dunson (1981) found that increased AFDC benefits per recipient had a positive effect on the employment-population ratios of both white and nonwhite teenagers in the 1970s, though only the white estimate was statistically significant.

59. U.S. Bureau of Labor Statistics (1979; 1983).

60. Mincer (1963).

61. This is consistent with the Labor Department (1987) findings from 1984 and 1986 CPS data on displaced workers. Among those workers with at least three years of job tenure before losing their jobs, Hispanics were less likely to have been reemployed and had longer durations of unemployment by the survey week than did all whites. For example, of former long-term jobholders laid off between 1981 and 1986, 27.2 percent of Hispanics were still unemployed by the survey week compared with only 16.2 percent of all whites.

5

Unemployment Differentials Among Spanish-Origin Groups

The unemployment rate of the total Hispanic labor force has consistently exceeded the white rate by at least 50 percent, but there are marked differences among the different national-origin groupings. As the annual figures for 1976–87 in Table 5.1 show, the fraction of the Puerto Rican labor force out of work has remained above that of Mexicans, while Cubans have had the lowest unemployment of the major national-origin groups. The analysis of time-series trends in the last chapter could provide only limited information on the nature of and reasons for these differences, because the relatively small size of the individual national-origin samples in the monthly CPS household survey prevent more detailed breakdowns. In this chapter I exploit an unusually large cross-sectional data bank to more fully investigate the characteristics and determinants of unemployment differentials between non-Hispanics and persons of Mexican, Puerto Rican, Cuban, Central and South American, and other Hispanic origin.

Evidence on Spell Frequency, Length, and Causes

In May and June of 1976, the Census Bureau conducted a special, expanded version of the Current Population Survey that oversampled the Hispanic population. Dubbed the Survey of Income and Education (SIE), it was designed to collect a wealth of otherwise unavailable demographic, immigration, and employment information.[1] From the complete file of 151,170 households, I extracted a subfile of individuals 14 years of age and over that included all persons born outside the United States plus a random sample of the native born. For separate analyses of Hispanics, I also used all native- and foreign-born persons of Spanish origin in the full SIE sample. The study sample was restricted to individuals who reported their national-origin

TABLE 5.1. Civilian Unemployment Rate, Persons 16
and Over by Sex and Type of Spanish Origin, 1976–87

	Mexican	*Puerto Rican*	*Cuban*
Both Sexes			
1976	11.1	15.6	11.4
1977	10.1	13.6	8.9
1978	8.9	13.2	7.2
1979	8.2	11.3	8.2
1980	10.3	13.6	8.4
1981	10.5	13.6	9.0
1982	13.9	17.6	11.2
1983	14.7	15.9	11.9
1984	10.9	13.5	7.9
1985	10.9	13.9	7.3
1986	11.2	14.0	6.4
1987	9.9	10.1	5.2
Males			
1976	9.8	15.9	12.6
1977	8.5	13.9	8.0
1978	7.1	12.5	7.1
1979	6.6	11.5	6.6
1980	9.6	13.1	9.0
1981	10.0	14.2	9.1
1982	13.9	17.3	10.8
1983	14.6	17.0	11.6
1984	10.9	12.5	8.6
1985	10.5	13.0	7.5
1986	11.0	13.4	6.5
1987	9.5	10.4	5.1
Females			
1976	13.3	15.9	10.0
1977	12.8	13.6	10.4
1978	11.9	14.8	7.6
1979	11.1	11.5	9.9
1980	11.5	14.7	6.4
1981	11.3	12.6	9.0
1982	14.1	18.0	11.7
1983	14.9	14.4	12.1
1984	11.1	15.0	6.9
1985	11.6	15.2	7.0
1986	11.7	15.0	6.3
1987	10.4	9.6	5.3

SOURCE: U.S. Bureau of Labor Statistics (1977–88).

group and country of origin, who were not born in an outlying territory of the
United States, and were not full-time students.

Information on various dimensions of the sample, stratified by sex, ethnicity,
and nativity, is presented in Table 5.2. The table entries are sample means. The
calculations in the leftmost column show that Hispanics were substantially more

TABLE 5.2. Selected Characteristics of Unemployment among White Non-Hispanic
and Hispanic Men and Women by Ethnic Group and Nativity[a]

	Unemployed	Weeks Unemployed	Multiple Spells	Quits	Layoffs	Entrants
MEN						
White Non-Hispanic						
Native Born	.1449	17.58	.0466	.0074	.0278	.0146
Foreign Born	.1673	18.78	.0499	.0051	.0345	.0117
Mexican						
Native Born	.2233	17.78	.0832	.0069	.0437	.0208
Foreign Born	.2110	19.04	.0769	.0118	.0552	.0237
Puerto Rican						
Native Born	.1892	16.71	.0676	.0135	.0676	.0676
Foreign Born	.2595	19.25	.0572	.0153	.0534	.0153
Cuban						
Foreign Born	.2166	19.91	.0573	.0000	.0955	.0255
Cen. & So. Amer.						
Foreign Born	.1783	16.39	.0318	.0000	.0446	.0064
Other Hispanic						
Native Born	.1833	16.91	.0774	.0020	.0387	.0285
Foreign Born	.1846	15.00	.0462	.0000	.0154	.0000
WOMEN						
White Non-Hispanic						
Native Born	.1480	15.72	.0375	.0114	.0232	.0222
Foreign Born	.1690	17.02	.0502	.0087	.0243	.0156
Mexican						
Native Born	.1872	16.29	.0536	.0150	.0386	.0433
Foreign Born	.2275	19.40	.0772	.0086	.0214	.0472
Puerto Rican						
Native Born	.3125	19.53	.0417	.0417	.1042	.0625
Foreign Born	.2732	23.34	.0581	.0000	.1163	.0116
Cuban						
Foreign Born	.1931	22.68	.0483	.0276	.0483	.0276
Cen. & So. Amer.						
Foreign Born	.2147	14.82	.0452	.0056	.0452	.0226
Other Hispanic						
Native Born	.1473	15.46	.0036	.0078	.0232	.0362
Foreign Born	.2174	16.80	.0870	.0217	.0435	.0000

[a]Table entries are sample mean values.

SOURCE: Survey of Income and Education.

likely to have been unemployed at some point in the course of the 1975 recession
than non-Hispanic whites. Among males, over one-fifth (21.5 percent) of all Hispanics experienced at least one spell without work during the year compared with
less than 15 percent of white non-Hispanics.[2] The incidence of unemployment was
slightly higher for Hispanic immigrants (21.4 percent) than for natives (20.5 percent) and was higher for non-Hispanic immigrants (16.7 percent) than for non-
Hispanic natives (14.5 percent) as well. But the difference in means was only
statistically significant for non-Hispanics. Among Hispanic males, incidence varies

from 22.8 percent for all Puerto Ricans and Cubans to 21.4 percent for Mexicans to a low of 17–18 percent for other Central and South Americans and the other Hispanic residual. The nativity breakdowns reveal that 26 percent of men born in Puerto Rico suffered some unemployment in 1975, an incidence 7 percentage points above the level of their U.S.-born counterparts and over 3 percentage points above that of the next highest national-origin group. Among Mexicans and other Hispanics there is no significant difference in rates by country of birth.

Looking next at the duration data on males, the length of time out of work during the year before the survey averaged about 18 weeks for all Hispanics as for non-Hispanics. Hence, the higher incidence of Hispanic unemployment must reflect more frequent spells. Indeed, 13.5 percent of all Hispanic men were found to have experienced one spell and 7.3 percent had two or more, while the corresponding frequencies for non-Hispanics were 10.3 and 4.7. Cubans, Puerto Ricans, and Mexicans had the longest mean duration of unemployment, whereas other Latin Americans and other Hispanics were out of work even fewer weeks than non-Hispanic whites. In contrast to the pattern for Mexicans and Cubans, the unemployment of Puerto Ricans appears to be more concentrated in single rather than multiple spells.

Despite a much higher incidence of unemployment, Hispanic men appear to have been no more likely than non-Hispanics to drop out of the labor force in 1975. Although the number of "discouraged workers" doubtless increased in all groups as the recession deepened, the threat it posed to family living standards compelled many to persist in job search. Overall, Puerto Ricans and Central and South Americans averaged one week less spent out of the labor force than non-Hispanics, and Cubans averaged briefer spells of nonparticipation than any other group.

To explore further the determinants of unemployment associated with interjob and inter-labor-force mobility, it would be most desirable to have comparable data on the relative frequencies of quits, layoffs, entrants, and reentrants for each national-origin group in 1975. Unfortunately, the only information in the SIE on specific reason for unemployment is for the survey week of 1976 and it is restricted to those unemployed at that time. However, unemployment remained at historically high levels well into 1976; the annual average for the nation was still 7.7 percent and in New York and Florida it was above 10 percent. This suggests that comparisons across national-origin groups by reason for unemployment in 1976 may give a useful indication of the previous year's pattern.

As one would expect in depressed labor markets, quit rates were low for all groups, with insignificant differences among males between the native and foreign born or between different national-origin groups. The last two columns of Table 5.2, however, reveal a tendency for most Hispanic groups to have higher probabilities of unemployment due to layoff and to labor market entry and reentry than non-Hispanic whites. The layoff rate for all Hispanic men was 4.7 percent, well above the 2.9 percent non-Hispanic level. Surprisingly, the highest male layoff rate in 1975 was that of Cubans (9.6 percent). Although the difference in layoff rates between native- and foreign-born Hispanics is relatively small and only significant at the 10 percent level, other tabulations by immigration cohort revealed that Mexicans, Puerto Ricans, and Cubans moving to the United States since 1965 averaged higher rates than did earlier waves of their countrymen or than non-Hispanics. In contrast, native-born Hispanics have higher unemployment due to labor market entry than the foreign born. In fact, mainland-born Puerto Ricans have three times the unemployment rate of those born on the island.

Throughout most of the postwar period, rates of unemployment among women in the Unites States have exceeded male levels. High female propensities to enter and reenter the labor force and to quit their jobs have long been thought to contribute to this trend. But while women continue to have higher labor turnover than men, recent research has suggested that their turnover has been decreasing, both in the aggregate and within specific age groups, as their labor force participation rates have continued to rise.[3] Studies by Blau and Kahn (1981b) and Viscusi (1980) indicate further that among workers with otherwise similar personal, job, and labor market characteristics, women actually have lower quit rates than men. And with or without controls for such characteristics, women are on average less likely to be laid off than men. This appears to be strongly affected by the female concentration in service industries and low representation in construction and other cyclical industries.[4]

The calculations on the incidence of unemployment reveal a general tendency for both non-Hispanic and most Hispanic women to have a higher fraction of labor force members unemployed at some time that year. Only women from Cuba and natives of Mexican or other Hispanic origins averaged a lower incidence than men of their national-origin group. However, while women had higher incidence figures, they also typically experienced fewer weeks of unemployment and a lower incidence of multiple spells during the year than men. The mean length of time spent looking for work was 16 weeks for white non-Hispanic and 17.6 percent for all Hispanic women, compared with 17.7 weeks and 18.0 weeks for non-Hispanic and all Hispanic men, respectively. The incidence of multiple spells was 4 percent for non-Hispanic women, 5.2 percent for Hispanic women, 4.7 percent for non-Hispanic men, and 7.3 percent for Hispanic men.

Thus we find that the high female unemployment rate reflects a higher incidence of single, rather than multiple spells, during the year. Turning to the reported reasons for unemployment, the averages in the three rightmost columns of Table 5.2 suggest that relatively high labor force entry and reentry rates may be influential factors. For, while women had roughly similar low quit rates and especially low layoff rates, their incidence of unemployment due to labor force entry or reentry in 1976 tended to exceed that among men. Aggregate figures for 1974–75 show that some 63 percent of all labor force entrants were women and that the incidence of unemployment due to entry was twice as high for women as for men.[5]

Among women, as was the case with men, Hispanics experience a higher incidence of unemployment, more weeks out of work, and a greater likelihood of multiple spells than white non-Hispanics. Puerto Rican women are by far the most prone to unemployment. Over 31 percent of Puerto Ricans born on the American mainland and 27.3 percent of those born on the island experienced at least one bout of joblessness in the course of the year. In both incidence and duration these women exceed the levels of Puerto Rican men and of men and women in most other national-origin groups. And with layoff rates of over 10 percent and a quit rate among the native born (though not island born) well above the male rate, they appear to constitute a striking exception to the patterns discussed previously.

Foreign-born women average higher rates of unemployment and more weeks out of work than women of the same national-origin group who were born in the United States. For example, 22.8 percent of Mexican immigrants were out of work one or more times in the past year for an average of over 19 weeks, whereas U.S.-born Mexican-origin women had an incidence of 18.7 percent and mean duration of 16.3 weeks. Immigrants were typically more vulnerable to multiple spells as well. However, given the potentially important differences in age, schooling, fluency in English, and other characteristics between the native- and foreign-born subsamples, multivariate regression analysis is needed to test the independent influence of foreign origins among otherwise similar individuals.

The Relative Importance of Incidence and Duration

The previous chapter reviewed the theoretical and empirical literature on the relative importance of high turnover and long-term joblessness in accounting for the bulk of unemployment. We can address this question with the SIE data by first defining a personal unemployment rate (u_i) for the ith individual during the year as the ratio of weeks unemployed (W_{ui}) to the total number of weeks in the labor force (W_{li}):

$$u_i = \frac{W_{ui}}{W_{li}}$$

It can easily be shown that a weighted average of these rates for a given group can be computed as:[6]

$$\frac{\Sigma W_{ui}}{\Sigma W_{li}} = \left(\frac{U}{L} \right) \left(\frac{W_u}{52} \right) \left(\frac{1}{1 - W_{olf}/52} \right)$$

where

U = number of individuals unemployed during the year,
L = number of individuals in the labor force during the year, and
W_{olf} = number of weeks spent out of the labor force by labor force participants during the year.

Table 5.3 presents calculations of these components for white non-Hispanics and individual Hispanic national-origin groups by nativity. The general pattern revealed in these findings may be simply stated: regardless of sex, ethnicity, or place of birth, the duration component ($W_u/52$) was typically the most important factor behind the unemployment levels experienced in 1975. Although for women the nonparticipation component ($1/[1 - W_{olf}/52]$) plays a relatively greater role than for men, it is nonetheless exceeded in significance by duration. Thus, while it is true that the principal difference between Hispanics and white non-Hispanics observed in Table 5.2's averages is in the incidence of unemployment, for both groups we find that the length of jobless periods is more important than the incidence of spells.

TABLE 5.3. Decomposition of Unemployment Rates
of White Non-Hispanic and Hispanic Men and Women
by Ethnic Group and Nativity, 1975

	U/L	$Wu/52$	$1/(1 - W_{otf}/52)$
MEN			
White Non-Hispanic			
Native Born	.1449	.3381	1.0865
Foreign Born	.1673	.3612	1.0811
Mexican			
Native Born	.2233	.3419	1.1043
Foreign Born	.2110	.3662	1.0998
Puerto Rican			
Native Born	.1892	.3213	1.1255
Foreign Born	.2595	.3702	1.0469
Cuban			
Foreign Born	.2166	.3829	1.0332
Cen. & So. America			
Foreign Born	.1783	.3152	1.0565
Other Hispanic			
Native Born	.1833	.3252	1.0961
Foreign Born	.1846	.2885	1.0509
WOMEN			
White Non-Hispanic			
Native Born	.1480	.3023	1.2343
Foreign Born	.1690	.3273	1.2140
Mexican			
Native Born	.1872	.3133	1.3506
Foreign Born	.2275	.3731	1.2799
Puerto Rican			
Native Born	.3125	.3756	1.2865
Foreign Born	.2732	.4484	1.2155
Cuban			
Foreign Born	.1931	.4362	1.1094
Cen. & So. American			
Foreign Born	.2147	.2850	1.2360
Other Hispanic			
Native Born	.1473	.2973	1.2488
Foreign Born	.2174	.3231	1.1965

SOURCE: Survey of Income and Education.

Unemployment By Labor Market Segment

The research literature on labor market segmentation has contended that minorities
are disproportionately concentrated in those jobs and firms prone to above average
unemployment. Among Hispanics, according to Piore (1979a), recent immigrants
are channeled into the secondary sector where many jobs are so physically taxing
and low-status as to be unacceptable to indigenous workers. To explore the relationship between market structure and Hispanic joblessness, we employ a set of

detailed segmentation criteria developed by David Gordon, which uses both occupational and industrial characteristics to define the secondary and primary sectors. Reich, Gordon, and Edwards (1973) argued for taking into account the complex variety of employment in the primary sector by distinguishing between skilled crafts jobs, "subordinate primary," and "independent primary" jobs. The latter are higher-level jobs involving considerable individual initiative and often professional standards of work. The subordinate primary tier consists of routinized factory and office jobs with little individual responsibility entrusted in the worker. Gordon follows this approach by, first, grouping occupations according to Labor Department information on the length of "specific vocational preparation" (SVP) required and the degree of autonomy in work tasks. Those demanding the most training and permitting the greatest independence are classified as primary independent occupations, followed by primary crafts, primary subordinate, and secondary, in descending order of skill and autonomy. Industries are then categorized according to labor market power, using a factor analytic separation between the noncompetitive "core" and the competitive "peripheral" industries. Finally, all workers in semiskilled and unskilled occupations in core industries are classified as subordinate primary workers, while those in the same skill grades but in peripheral industries were classified as secondary. All other workers are allocated to labor market segments exclusively on the basis of occupational information.

The sectoral distributions of non-Hispanic whites, blacks, and Hispanic national-origin groups in Table 5.4 reveal a clear sectoral division between non-Hispanic whites and the minority groups. Over 30 percent of male white non-Hispanics, natives as well as immigrants, were in the top tier of primary independent jobs in 1975. Less than one-fifth of Hispanics and blacks were in such jobs. At the other extreme, under 30 percent of whites were in the secondary sector, compared with about two-fifths of Hispanics and blacks. Mexicans, Puerto Ricans, and blacks have the lowest representation in the primary independent tier and are also far more concentrated in the secondary sector than white non-Hispanics. In all groups except blacks, immigrants are more likely to be in the secondary sector than the native born. Roughly similar national-origin and racial patterns prevail in the female distributions. But compared with otherwise comparable males, women are far less likely to hold primary independent jobs and far more likely to be in the two lowest tiers.

To examine the nature of joblessness in different labor market segments, Table 5.5 presents calculations of the incidence and duration of unemployment by specific segments for white non-Hispanic and all Hispanic men. Due to the small sample of most of the individual national-origin subsamples when subdivided by market segment, the pooled Hispanic sample was used to ensure statistical reliability. The tabulations indicate that among white non-Hispanics, workers in the secondary sector were the most vulnerable to single and multiple spells without work in 1975. Foreign-born Anglo men in the secondary sector, with an incidence figure of over 29 percent, were more than four times more likely to be unemployed than native- or foreign-born men in the primary independent sector, as well as having an incidence that exceeded that of indigenous whites in secondary jobs by 5 percentage points. Non-Hispanic immigrants in secondary jobs also had over two weeks more unem-

TABLE 5.4. Sectoral Distribution of Workers by Race, Ethnicity, and Nativity (%)

| | Labor Market Segments[a] | | | |
	Primary Independent	Craft	Primary Subordinate	Secondary
MALE				
White Non-Hispanic				
Native Born	30.2	17.0	20.3	24.8
Foreign Born	30.7	12.5	16.7	29.3
Mexican				
Native Born	14.9	15.6	24.7	38.0
Foreign Born	8.5	12.2	28.6	45.4
Puerto Rican				
Native Born	16.2	12.2	23.0	39.2
Foreign Born	13.4	11.1	26.7	43.5
Cuban				
Foreign Born	18.5	16.6	22.3	36.9
Cen. & So. American				
Foreign Born	19.8	12.1	17.2	46.5
Other Hispanic				
Native Born	18.9	18.1	17.9	35.8
Foreign Born	26.2	9.2	15.4	43.1
Black				
Native Born	13.4	10.0	25.9	43.8
Foreign Born	13.2	15.3	22.2	42.4
FEMALE				
White Non-Hispanic				
Native Born	17.4	4.2	43.4	26.9
Foreign Born	18.1	4.1	37.3	35.5
Mexican				
Native Born	9.9	3.3	35.5	45.2
Foreign Born	6.0	4.3	31.8	56.2
Puerto Rican				
Native Born	16.7	2.1	54.2	25.0
Foreign Born	9.3	1.7	31.4	51.2
Cuban				
Foreign Born	11.0	1.4	33.8	42.8
Cen. & So. American				
Foreign Born	4.5	5.1	36.7	44.6
Other Hispanic				
Native Born	16.3	3.6	42.1	30.8
Foreign Born	8.7	2.2	34.8	50.0
Black				
Native Born	12.8	5.9	33.5	42.9
Foreign Born	8.1	0.6	48.8	33.8

[a]Rows may not sum to 100 owing to exclusion of certain industries from the segmentation scheme. See discussion in text.

SOURCE: Survey of Income and Education.

TABLE 5.5. Selected Characteristics of Unemployment of White Non-Hispanic and White Hispanic Men, by Labor Market Segment, 1975

	White Non-Hispanic		White Hispanic	
	Native Born	Foreign Born	Native Born	Foreign Born
Unemployed				
Primary Independent Sector	.0696	.0680	.1352	.1064
Primary Crafts Sector	.1840	.1845	.2100	.1955
Primary Subordinate Sector	.1219	.1161	.1924	.2226
Secondary Sector	.2401	.2908	.2534	.2500
Multiple Spells				
Primary Independent Sector	.0139	.0146	.0472	.0213
Primary Crafts Sector	.0536	.0601	.0972	.0827
Primary Subordinate Sector	.0426	.0223	.0626	.0906
Secondary Sector	.0898	.0918	.1003	.0572
Weeks Unemployed				
Primary Independent Sector	16.33	14.07	16.09	13.00
Primary Crafts Sector	16.73	17.28	15.09	19.54
Primary Subordinate Sector	17.72	18.92	17.73	21.86
Secondary Sector	18.33	20.82	18.48	17.23
Proportion of Unemployed Jobless > 26 Weeks				
Primary Independent Sector	.2467	.1786	.2326	.2667
Primary Crafts Sector	.2915	.3488	.1340	.3462
Primary Subordinate Sector	.2825	.3462	.3023	.3898
Secondary Sector	.3035	.3860	.3422	.2373
All Sectors	.2882	.3460	.2950	.2936
N	6589	1261	1822	1011

SOURCE: Survey of Income and Education.

ployment on average than their native-born counterparts in such jobs, though there was little difference in the incidence of multiple spells. Nine percent of secondary sector whites experienced more than one spell out of work, well above the primary independent rate, though only 3–4 percentage points higher than craftsmen.

The differences by sector are, however, generally less pronounced among Hispanics. While the average incidence and duration of unemployment is clearly greater in the secondary sector than in primary independent jobs, there is considerable similarity between the secondary and lower-tier primary sectors. And, in contrast to the findings for non-Hispanics, Hispanic immigrants in the secondary sector are no more likely than natives in that sector to experience unemployment and are much less likely to have multiple spells. Indeed, among Hispanics, secondary sector immigrants have an incidence of multiple spells below that in any sector other than the primary independent, and below that of white non-Hispanics in secondary and craft jobs.

However, for both Hispanics and non-Hispanics, regardless of nativity or labor market segment, an extraordinarily high proportion of workers went more than half the year without finding work. From 29 to 34.6 percent of immigrants and nonimmigrants were jobless 26 weeks or more, reflecting the overall importance of the duration component depicted in Table 5.5. Interestingly, while 23.7 percent of Hispanic immigrants in the secondary sector experienced long-term unemployment, this was one of the lowest rates for any sector of either Hispanics or non-Hispanics.

Puerto Rican Unemployment and Industrial Decline

Although Puerto Ricans are not alone in being highly concentrated in low-wage secondary-sector jobs, the fact that they have been disproportionately employed in goods-producing industries in northeastern cities has had especially damaging long-term effects. Large-scale immigration from Puerto Rico began just as the manufacturing base of many of these cities fell into a severe secular decline. The steepest drop has been in New York City, home of the single largest mainland concentration of Puerto Ricans. The number of jobs in the industry was slashed from 1.07 million in 1950 to less than 380,000 by 1987.[7] Over one-third of the jobs lost have been in apparel, a principal employer of Puerto Ricans, particularly women, in the postwar period. With Puerto Rican workers overwhelmingly confined to laborer and operative occupations, they have been especially hard hit.

Why have Puerto Ricans displaced from these jobs experienced such difficulty finding stable employment elsewhere? One possible explanatory factor stressed by some economists and politicians has been the upsurge in immigration to the city from Asia and Latin America since the mid-1960s. The seeming paradox of growing in-migration to an area suffering rising unemployment could be interpreted as implying that new immigrants have been competing for jobs with Puerto Ricans, thereby making their employment problems that much worse. However, careful analyses of industry-by-industry data in the late seventies and early 1980s have provided little support for this position. Instead, it appears that the low-wage jobs filled by immigrants have largely been either created by immigrants themselves through new restaurants, food stores, or small service businesses or have been concentrated in what Adriana Marshall (1983, 1984) has dubbed "labor sensitive" activities. These are economic activities in which employers' demand for labor is unusually responsive to labor availability. The abundance of docile, desperate immigrants is exploited by small firms, which are often only able to survive under sweatshop conditions of subminimum wages and substandard working conditions.

The apparel industry is a prime example of this process. As international competition intensified, large numbers of medium-sized, often unionized firms in the mass-production end of the business took advantage of new production technologies to relocate to lower-cost regions or abroad. These were the firms in which Puerto Ricans were most heavily represented. Marketing, design, and the less-mechanized small manufacturers serving the spot market were all that remained in the city by the 1980s. The small-batch contract shops have survived in no small part thanks to their ability to tap immigrant kinship networks as needed to quickly recruit enough workers to fill retailers' last-minute specialty orders or inventory gaps.[8]

One reason for Puerto Ricans' difficulties in finding alternative employment is clearly their poverty and isolation in the central city. The most rapid economic

TABLE 5.6. Access to Personal Transportation
of Central-City Households in 7 Cities by Race
and Spanish Origin of Householder, 1980

City	No Vehicle Available (%)		
	White	Black	Hispanic
Los Angeles	13.6	28.1	23.5
San Diego	11.1	23.0	15.8
San Francisco	33.3	42.8	36.5
Miami	23.2	40.1	26.2
Boston	40.5	51.3	54.9
Philadelphia	31.1	50.9	50.8
New York City	53.0	69.3	71.3
Bronx	54.5	71.1	72.9
Brooklyn	52.3	72.2	73.9
Manhattan	78.4	84.7	83.5
Queens	37.5	43.4	49.4
Staten Island	16.9	54.2	38.6

SOURCE: U.S. Bureau of the Census (1982b).

growth has increasingly been occurring in suburban and exurban areas. Puerto Ricans, the poorest major ethnic group in the country, have faced serious obstacles to acquiring their share of these new jobs. As Table 5.6 reveals, while Hispanics average less access to private transportation than the full white population in major cities, the largest white–Hispanic difference is in New York. In the Bronx, the borough with the highest concentration of Puerto Ricans, 73 percent of Hispanics have no access to a private vehicle compared with 54.5 percent of all whites. Perhaps an even more dramatic indication of their problems in job search is the surprisingly large number who do not even have a telephone. Nearly one in three Puerto Rican households in New York State does not have its own telephone (Table 5.7). In contrast, only 4 percent of non-Hispanic whites and 17.7 percent of blacks in the state lack telephone service.

Access to suburban housing and jobs is also undoubtedly impeded by discrimination against Puerto Ricans. They are not only victimized by anti-Hispanic preju-

TABLE 5.7. Access to Personal Transportation and Telephone Service of Households
by Race and Type of Spanish Origin of Householder, New York State, 1980

Households in New York State	Anglo	Black	All Hispanic	Mexican	Puerto Rican	Cuban	Other Hispanic
No Vehicle Available (%)	24.2	61.2	64.9	53.1	70.2	51.7	58.4
No Telephone (%)	4.0	17.7	25.3	17.2	31.3	9.0	17.8

SOURCE: U.S. Bureau of the Census (1982b).

dice, but often by antiblack prejudice as well. Of all Spanish-origin groups, the Puerto Rican population has the highest proportion of persons who identify them-selves as black or are perceived to be black by white non-Hispanics. The residential proximity of many Puerto Ricans and non-Hispanic blacks in segregated central-city areas like Harlem and the South Bronx appear to strengthen this perception.[9] How-ever, Puerto Ricans have benefited much less than even blacks from anti-discriminatory policies. A major federal study found that Puerto Ricans have tended to be underrepresented in government jobs and in job-training programs. The study concluded, "Official insensitivity, coupled with public and private acts of discrimi-nation, has insured that Puerto Ricans often are last in line for benefits and oppor-tunities made available by the social and civil rights legislation of the last decade."[10]

Within the central cities of the Northeast, the new jobs that have been created tend to require educational and language skills above those of the average Puerto Rican worker. The increasing polarization of the job structure has been illustrated with special clarity in Kasarda's (1985) analysis of employment change in industries classified by their work force's average educational attainment. The findings pre-sented in Table 5.8 reveal that all four East Coast cities studied experienced losses in entry-level jobs and growth in knowledge-intensive jobs during the 1970s. New York suffered the largest relative decline in unskilled and semiskilled positions: a net loss of 472,000 jobs not requiring a high school diploma occurred over the decade, while 92,000 jobs were added in industries in which the average worker had some college training. Not only did the latter growth fall far short of compensating for the contraction in low-skill jobs, but most Puerto Ricans displaced from such jobs lacked the educational and occupational skills to compete for the new vacan-cies. In stark contrast, southwestern cities have enjoyed growth in both knowledge-intensive and entry-level jobs. The latter increased by 73.8 percent in Houston, 19.5 percent in Denver, and 10.2 percent in San Francisco. Puerto Ricans in New York were thus placed at a considerable disadvantage relative to other Hispanics of comparable age and educational levels.

A striking piece of evidence to this effect is provided by comparing the par-ticipation and unemployment rates of Puerto Ricans in New York with those in the more robust labor markets of California and Florida in 1980 (Table 5.9). Published census figures for the year show that the latter two states had lower non-Hispanic and Hispanic unemployment rates than New York, and also had generally higher rates of labor force participation.[11] Puerto Ricans in California and Florida had unemployment rates below 10 percent and three-fourths of Puerto Rican men and one-half of women were active in the labor force. In fact, these participation rates exceeded those of Anglos in the same states and were very close to those of Cubans. In startling contrast, Puerto Ricans in New York that same year suffered double-digit unemployment, which apparently has driven many out of the labor force in discour-agement. Only 66 percent of Puerto Rican men and 35 percent of women were employed or looking for work.

The worrisome long-term consequences for Puerto Ricans and other minorities of the disappearance of entry-level jobs in New York are suggested by the declining share of its youth who are active in the labor market. In 1980, only 30.3 percent of the city's teenagers, ages 16–19, were in the labor force and only 24 percent were

TABLE 5.8. Urban Employment Changes by Average
Educational Requirements of Industry, 1970–80

City and Industrial Categorization[a]	Number of Jobs (thousands)		Change 1970–80 (%)
	1970	1980	
New York			
Entry-level	1,235	763	−38.2
Knowledge-intensive	370	462	24.9
Philadelphia			
Entry-level	310	208	−32.9
Knowledge-intensive	66	91	37.8
Baltimore			
Entry-level	160	108	−32.4
Knowledge-intensive	27	32	20.6
Boston			
Entry-level	149	115	−22.6
Knowledge-intensive	56	75	33.3
Atlanta			
Entry-level	155	136	−12.1
Knowledge-intensive	30	41	35.6
Houston			
Entry-level	263	457	73.8
Knowledge-intensive	69	152	119.4
Denver			
Entry-level	96	110	14.5
Knowledge-intensive	23	44	91.4
San Francisco			
Entry-level	129	142	10.2
Knowledge-intensive	44	65	46.8

[a]Entry-level industries are those in which the mean educational attainment of
employees is less than 12 years; knowledge-intensive industries are those in
which mean educational attainment is more than 14 years.

SOURCE: Kasarda (1985).

employed. These low figures actually overstate the situation of the city's minority
youth. Separate tabulations for black and Hispanic teenagers in New York reveal
that their labor force participation rates were 22.7 percent and 25.9 percent, and
their employment-population rates were a mere 14.9 percent and 19.4 percent,
respectively.[12] Of course, such factors as school enrollment, the availability of
government transfer income, early pregnancies, drug-related problems, and jobs in
the underground economy also affect the willingness and ability of youth to find
work. But youth in other large cities are also influenced by these forces, yet are far
more active in the job market than their New York counterparts. For example, in Los
Angeles, which has an even larger share of the population who are black, Hispanic,
or immigrants, 46.7 percent of teenagers were in the labor force and 40 percent were
employed in 1980.[13] In all urbanized areas of the country that year, the youth

TABLE 5.9. Labor Force Participation and Unemployment Rates in California, Florida, and New York by Race and Ethnicity, 1980

	Non-Hispanic		All Hispanic	Mexican	Puerto Rican	Cuban	Other Spanish
	White	Black					
CALIFORNIA							
Males							
In Labor Force (%)	76.5	68.5	80.8	81.0	78.2	77.1	80.4
Unemployed (%)	5.3	11.2	9.0	9.4	8.1	6.2	7.5
Females							
In Labor Force (%)	51.7	55.0	52.7	51.3	53.9	56.5	57.6
Unemployed (%)	5.4	9.8	10.3	11.2	9.4	6.3	7.5
FLORIDA							
Males							
In Labor Force (%)	65.9	67.5	76.4	74.5	77.7	77.8	73.0
Unemployed (%)	3.9	7.9	4.8	7.0	5.6	4.4	4.7
Females							
In Labor Force (%)	43.5	56.2	52.2	50.1	49.0	54.0	49.3
Unemployed (%)	4.9	8.9	7.0	9.2	9.0	6.6	6.5
NEW YORK							
Males							
In Labor Force (%)	73.8	64.6	70.6	72.1	66.3	74.5	76.8
Unemployed (%)	6.2	12.7	9.7	8.7	11.2	6.6	8.3
Females							
In Labor Force (%)	47.9	52.9	42.5	46.8	35.3	53.0	52.3
Unemployed (%)	6.2	9.9	11.4	9.4	12.7	7.6	10.6

NOTE: Population 16 years of age and over.
SOURCE: U.S. Bureau of the Census (1984b: state volumes).

participation and employment-population rates were 49.1 percent and 42 percent, respectively.[14] In fact, between 1980 and 1987, the rate of youth labor force participation rose to 52.6 percent for the country as a whole, but fell further in New York City to only 22.1 percent. This led the U.S. Department of Labor's regional bureau to warn:

> The data suggest that the New York economy generates fewer job opportunities for younger workers, fewer opportunities for younger workers to gain a foothold in the labor market. When coupled with the city's massive high school dropout rate, the data point to problems in the years ahead in moving significant numbers of younger workers into the mainstream of the economy.[15]

Multivariate Analysis of Incidence and Duration

Methodology

To investigate the independent roles played by personal, job, and labor market characteristics, the following unemployment probability function is estimated for males and females subdivided by ethnicity and national origin:

$$P(UNEMP75 = 1) = f(EDFOR, EDUS, EX, EXSQ, MSP, CHILD5,$$
$$CHILD517, HEALTH, IMM7475, IMM7073,$$
$$IMM6569, IMM6064, IMMPRE60,$$
$$NONWHITE, FLUENT, OTHINC,$$
$$PARTTIME, UNRATE, OCC, IND, HISPROP) \quad (1)$$

where UNEMP75 = 1 if the respondent was unemployed at least one week during 1975, 0 otherwise. All other variables are defined in Appendix Table 5A.1. The effects of the independent variables given above on two other dependent variables— the probability of experiencing more than one spell of unemployment during the year (SPELLGT1) and the total number of weeks of unemployment in 1975 (WKSUN75)—will also be explored. Both UNEMP75 and WKSUN75 were constructed from responses to the SIE question:

"You said (household member) worked about __weeks in 1975. How many of the remaining weeks was (household member) looking for work or on layoff from a job?"

Interviewers were instructed to ask the question only of those persons who worked fewer than 50 weeks that year.

Predicting the signs of all the explanatory variables in equation (1) is particularly difficult because the dependent variable includes both the probability of quitting and the probability of being laid off. But 1975 witnessed the highest national unemployment up to that time in the postwar years and an extremely large share of it was accounted for by layoffs. As a result, the unemployment variable in (1) is no doubt weighted toward the layoff rather than the quit dimension. Once this is recognized, it is possible to focus mainly on predictions from the economic literature on layoffs about the anticipated effects of a number of independent variables.

Most of the handful of empirical studies of Hispanic unemployment have stressed the importance of national-origin differences in age, schooling, immigration patterns, and occupation or industry of employment.[16] Insofar as older workers are more likely to have accumulated longer tenure with an employer, both the human capital and the segmented labor market views predict that age will be inversely related to both layoff and quit probabilities. Since the SIE lacks direct information on job tenure, we adopt the standard approach of using a proxy: potential labor force experience since leaving school (EX), entered as a quadratic. More years of schooling completed is also generally expected to reduce the likelihood of layoffs or quits. From the human capital perspective, those with a demonstrated propensity to invest in more schooling will also probably invest more in the accumulation of specific capital on the job. From the segmentation viewpoint, schooling not only shapes aspirations and work traits but also may be used by employers as a credential for sorting workers. If better-educated workers are more likely to gain access to internal labor markets, then they will average higher tenure and seniority as well as lower layoff and quit rates. Unlike the decennial census and most other data sources, the SIE distinguishes between schooling completed in foreign countries (EDFOR) and that acquired in the United States (EDUS). If employers give less weight to workers' schooling abroad as a credential, then it will have a weaker positive effect on turnover than American schooling. The effects of these same variables on the duration of unemployment are more ambiguous. On the one hand, older and more educated persons may have higher expected returns from devoting a lot of time to job search. If search is not conducted while holding a job, this would tend to lengthen unemployment spells. But foregone earnings from search are also higher for such persons and they may also be more efficient in quickly finding new jobs. In slack labor markets like those of the mid-1970s, the latter considerations would seem more compelling, implying an inverse relationship between schooling, experience, and duration of unemployment.

The implications of migratory differences are even less obvious. Recent immigrants may be at some disadvantage in the American labor market relative to earlier migrants and the native born because of their smaller stock of information about the economy, language problems, the imperfect international mobility of skills, and a variety of legal restrictions on the employment of noncitizens in certain occupations. Chiswick (1982) suggests that their quit rates will be high, at least in the initial period after arrival, as they try out a number of jobs in various industries and locales. Starting from a quite different theoretical position, Piore (1979a) concludes that the channeling of most Hispanic migrants into unstable secondary sector firms will shape their turnover behavior. And Tienda and Diaz (1987) have recently argued that frequent circular migration between the United States and their homeland helps account for Puerto Ricans' high unemployment. All thus predict relatively high rates of turnover and unemployment among recently arrived cohorts.

On the other hand, much of the sociological literature on immigrants has stressed their high motivation to locate jobs quickly in order to end dependence on friends and relatives, to begin accumulating savings for self-support and to remit to their families back home, and to acquire U.S.-specific and firm-specific training. Kinship networks already established at destination play an important role in advising on the optimal timing of the immigration, expediting the legal arrangements with the INS, arranging initial housing accommodations and social contacts, and helping the newcomer find work.[17] Prior migrants thus reduce the economic as well as psychic costs of immigration for new arrivals and accelerate the successful entry of newcomers into the labor market.

The rich detail of the SIE with respect to information about individual respondent's ethnicity, migration history, and unemployment experiences is unfortunately not matched by its information on job characteristics or local labor market conditions. To attempt to control for industry-by-industry variations in employment conditions, the regression equation includes a dichotomous variable (IND) that is set equal to 1 if the respondent's longest recent job was in the durable manufacturing or construction industries. In the course of 1975, durable goods manufacturers, led by auto and related industries, experienced the largest absolute employment reduction of any industrial group, accounting for two-thirds of the overall drop in manufacturing jobs.[18] The highest unemployment rate of any single industry (18.1 percent) was in contract construction, where the work force was cut sharply as housing starts plummeted with the tightening of the money market. Although joblessness in white-collar occupations reached postwar highs, semiskilled and unskilled workers were, as in previous recessions, the most vulnerable to cyclical fluctuations.[19] A dummy variable (OCC) was defined to equal unity if an individual was employed in craft, operative, service, laborer, or farm occupations, 0 otherwise. Another dummy was included for part-time employment (PARTTIME), which is likely to be especially unstable, characterized as it is by few seniority or union protections against layoffs and by employers' perceptions of part-time workers as quit-prone.

Three approaches were adopted in an effort to take into account the markedly different regional distributions of the various national-origin groups. First, the annual unemployment rate (UNRATE) of the SMSA of residence or the nearest SMSA was drawn from published Labor Department (1978) tabulations. The reduced number of vacancies and increased costs of search in slack labor markets are likely to be associated with increased layoffs, lower quit rates, and longer periods of joblessness. Second, as a rough test of the oft-heard view that the "crowding" of Hispanic workers in particular areas may shrink local employment opportunities, the variable HISPROP was defined as the proportion of Hispanics in each state's population. Finally, where sample size permitted, separate regressions were estimated for subsamples living in a few regions of the country with high concentrations of Hispanics.

Though more than 9 out of 10 Hispanics identify themselves as whites, the above average fractions of nonwhites in certain national-origin groups may have employment consequences. Although recent research has indicated that black workers tend to have lower quit rates than whites with similar personal and job characteristics, discriminatory employers will be less likely to provide them with firm-specific training and more likely to confine them to less secure jobs. A dichotomous variable (NONWHITE) is thus included in each regression.

Finally, controls were also included for two types of income: the dollar amount of nonlabor income (OTHINC) and a dummy (UI) set to 1 if an individual reports receipt of unemployment benefits during 1975. To the extent that nonlabor income is tapped to finance extended job search, it may be positively related to the duration of unemployment. Likewise, many studies have contended that the availability of unemployment compensation leads to lengthier spells between jobs.[20]

Regression Estimates

Males

The summary statistics on male labor force participants reveal striking differences between Hispanics and non-Hispanics, as well as among Hispanic national-origin groups, in a number of characteristics.[21] With an average of less than 10 years of schooling, Mexicans and Puerto Ricans were 3 years below the non-Hispanic level and 1 to 2 years below other Hispanic groups. Cubans were, on average, older (mean age: 41), with more years of potential work experience than any other group, but much of that experience was in the Cuban labor market. About 95 percent of the Cubans surveyed were foreign born and nearly 42 percent had been in the United States 10 years or less by 1975. Central and South Americans are even more recent migrants. Nearly two-fifths arrived in the early 1970s and another 24.7 percent in the period 1965–69. Fewer than one in four Puerto Rican men were born on the mainland. In contrast, three out of four persons of Mexican origin and 87 percent of other Hispanics were native born. In light of the high proportions of Puerto Ricans, Cubans, and Central and South Americans born abroad, it is unsurprising to find that the majority of their schooling took place in their countries of origin and that many are not fluent in English. In fact, only 42 percent of Cubans and somewhat more than one-half of Puerto Ricans and Central and South Americans could speak and understand English very well.

These three groups tend to reside in labor markets that had average 1975 unemployment levels well above those prevailing in Mexican and other Hispanic areas of settlement. Whereas most of the latter two national-origin groupings lived in the Southwest and over two-fifths were outside metropolitan areas, four-fifths of Cubans, Puerto Ricans, and Central and South Americans lived in SMSAs, most in the East. One-third of Puerto Rican men and 31 percent of Central and South Americans were employed in the most cyclical industries, compared with 26–28 percent of other national-origin groups. And more than four-fifths of Puerto Ricans and Mexicans worked at low-wage occupations, compared with only 58 percent of non-Hispanic whites and just over 70 percent of the other Hispanic groups.

Regression estimates of the model of unemployment incidence are presented in Table 5.10. As expected, more highly educated individuals have a lower probability of unemployment in all national-origin groups, although the coefficient estimates are not statistically significant for Puerto Ricans and Cubans. The extremely small size of the Cuban sample no doubt accounts for their relatively few significant parameter estimates. To the extent that schooling undertaken in the United States provides language training and useful country-specific credentials and labor market information, one would expect that the impact of EDUS would be larger (in absolute value) than that of EDFOR. The estimates support this presumption for the full Hispanic sample and the Mexican and other Hispanic subsamples. But there does not appear to be a consistent pattern across national-origin groups, as the incidence of unemployment among non-Hispanics, Puerto Ricans, and Cubans is more influenced by the amount of premigration schooling.

The anticipated inverse relationship between years of work experience and the probability of unemployment is confirmed for all groups except Cubans. Likewise, marriage and additional dependents seem to be typically associated with more stable employment, though the coefficients are only significant for non-Hispanics. Among otherwise similar Hispanic men, health limitations and race do not appear to exert a significant influence. Puerto Ricans able to speak and understand English very well have a significant advantage over other Puerto Rican men. The estimated effect of fluency in English is weak for the other subsamples. But its impact may be captured in part by other variables in the equations, in particular schooling and years since immigration.

Despite the adjustment difficulties recent immigrants may face in a new labor market, our results for individual cohorts indicate that most had a probability of unemployment during 1975 that was either insignificantly different from or significantly lower than their native-born counterparts. Among all Spanish-origin men, those in the United States only since 1974 were about 5 percent less likely to be out of work than otherwise similar indigenous Hispanics. The differential is larger (12–15 percent) for those who arrived between 1965 and 1973, and the estimate is highly significant. After about 25 years in the United States, however, foreign-born Hispanics appear to be as susceptible to unemployment as are natives.

Among white non-Hispanics the results are less consistent and more difficult to interpret. Immigrants arriving since 1970 have a likelihood of being unemployed that is insignificantly different from that of natives. But the coefficients change sign and are significantly positive for two earlier cohorts (1965–69 and pre-1960). One must bear in mind that non-Hispanic immigrants are a very heterogeneous group of widely varying ethnic and national origins about whom it is difficult to generalize.

The pattern observed for the pooled Spanish-origin sample is much influenced by the tendency among the numerically dominant Mexican subsample for immigrants to have unemployment probabilities 13.5 to 18 percent lower than native-born Mexicans during the first decade in the United States. The other Hispanic grouping, also concentrated in the southwestern states, exhibits a similar pattern and has differentials even larger than those among Mexicans.

Puerto Ricans are the sole national-origin group in which the most recent cohort of males arriving from the island had a significantly higher probability of at least one spell of unemployment in 1975 than those of Puerto Rican origin born on the mainland. However, while all the other migrant cohort coefficients have positive signs, they decline in magnitude and none attain conventional levels of statistical significance. The coefficient on the 1965–69 cohort only approaches significance at about the 10 percent level. Men born in Puerto Rico who came to the United States in the period 1970–73 had the same likelihood of unemployment as mainland-born Puerto Ricans, and this also appears to be the case for migration streams prior to 1965.

Residents of high-unemployment labor markets, part-time workers, and those in unskilled or semiskilled occupations, whether Hispanic or non-Hispanic, face higher probabilities of job loss. Part-time employment and low-skill occupations have more consistently positive and large impacts among Cubans, raising their unemployment probabilities by 35 and 25 percent, respectively. Likewise, workers in the durable manufacturing and construction industries are, as expected, more vulnerable to unemployment than those in other industries: the likelihood of job loss is increased by about 9 percent for non-Hispanics and by over 11 percent for the full Hispanic subset. Of individual national-origin groups, workers in cyclical industries are about 11 percent more prone to unemployment among Mexicans and other Hispanics, and about 6 percent more among Puerto Ricans.

Although some economists have claimed that geographic concentrations of Hispanics may "crowd out" other job-seekers, the regression estimates do not indicate any higher unemployment probabilities among white non-Hispanics living in states with relatively large Hispanic populations. What is more, Hispanics in states with higher proportions of Hispanics have significantly lower likelihoods of being out of work during the year. This may reflect certain regional labor market differences, as well as the advantages job-hunters may enjoy in areas with already settled populations of one's own national-origin group.[22]

In regressions on the pooled Spanish-origin sample, dummy variables were included for the major national-origin groups, with Puerto Ricans as the excluded benchmark. The results imply that once measurable differences in personal, job, and

TABLE 5.10. Logit Estimates of Probability of Unemployment Equations, White Non-Hispanic and Hispanic Men by Ethnic Group (Dependent Variable: UNEMP75)

Variables	White Non-Hispanic	All Hispanic	Mexican	Puerto Rican	Cuban	Other Hispanic
EDFOR	-.1202***	-.0782***	-.1245**	-.0922	-.0418	.0927
	(.0195)	(.0223)	(.0374)	(.0595)	(.0738)	(.0711)
EDUS	-.0977***	-.1202***	-.1561***	-.0687	-.0529	-.1060*
	(.0146)	(.0200)	(.0254)	(.0656)	(.1014)	(.0543)
EX	-.0414***	-.0599***	-.0518***	-.1436***	-.0350	-.0690**
	(.0081)	(.0118)	(.0153)	(.0450)	(.0671)	(.0293)
EXSQ	.0002	.0004**	.0000	.0022***	.0004	.0007
	(.0002)	(.0002)	(.0003)	(.0008)	(.0011)	(.0005)
MSP	-.3353***	-.1656	-.0612	.0785	-.0739	-.4251
	(.0908)	(.1264)	(.1654)	(.4172)	(.5617)	(.3301)
CHILD5	.0028	-.0187	-.0476	-.0540	-.7598	.1464
	(.0664)	(.0740)	(.0874)	(.2569)	(.6839)	(.2392)
CHILD517	-.0802***	-.0093	-.0487	.1050	.0270	.0814
	(.0280)	(.0316)	(.0386)	(.1106)	(.1810)	(.0859)
HEALTH	.3414***	.2512	.1256	.5221	1.0420	.3299
	(.1115)	(.1718)	(.2196)	(.5163)	(.8132)	(.4299)
IMM7475	.3644	-.2091	-.7755*	2.0244**	-.3642	-.2451
	(.4158)	(.2954)	(.4012)	(.8768)	(1.4205)	(1.5913)
IMM7073	.3322	-.6887***	-.7931**	.2278	-1.7648	-2.5295**
	(.3173)	(.2549)	(.3594)	(.6996)	(1.2121)	(1.1331)
IMM6569	.4992**	-.8829***	-1.0339***	1.2083*	-1.6736	-2.3950**
	(.2408)	(.2534)	(.3729)	(.6763)	(1.1220)	(1.0799)
IMM6064	-.0921	-.5087**	-.2198	.6685	-1.0052	-2.1170*
	(.2946)	(.2594)	(.3862)	(.6706)	(1.0823)	(1.1002)
IMMPRE60	.4136***	-.2515	-.1414	.5690	-.9295	-.5876

	(1)	(2)	(3)	(4)	(5)	(6)
NONWHITE	— (.1399)	.2843 (.2220)	.4818 (.3559)	.4405 (.5042)	-.0938 (1.2272)	-.0908 (.5534)
FLUENT	.1320 (.1184)	-.1794 (.1117)	-.1270 (.1441)	-.7495*** (.3495)	-.8613 (.5645)	-.0610 (.2991)
OTHINC	-.0016*** (.0004)	-.0011 (.0009)	-.0002 (.0012)	-.0006 (.0035)	-.0026 (.0046)	-.0610 (.2991)
PARTTIME	.1418 (.1112)	.3889** (.1648)	.4327** (.1996)	.5346 (.5561)	1.4891 (1.0714)	.4121 (.4734)
UNRATE	.0854*** (.0145)	.0568*** (.0200)	.0720*** (.0230)	-.0947 (.0873)	.0017 (.1221)	-.0227 (.0699)
OCC	.6812*** (.0835)	.5276*** (.1447)	.5186*** (.1916)	.0939 (.4610)	1.4478** (.6499)	.4483 (.3548)
IND	.6834*** (.0677)	.6050*** (.0982)	.5796*** (.1275)	.3951 (.3040)	.4080 (.4700)	.9405*** (.2480)
HISPROP	-.0105 (.0070)	-.0186*** (.0052)	-.0193*** (.0066)	.0115 (.0467)	.0194 (.0793)	-.0123 (.0109)
Mexican	.0018 (.1691)					
Cuban	.3718 (.2509)					
Cen. & So. America	-.1858 (.2639)					
Other Hispanic	.0145 (.1998)					
Constant	-1.0423*** (.2896)	.1410 (.4006)	.3950 (.4565)	1.2472 (1.4045)	-.0706 (2.5110)	.4498 (.9729)
-2x Log Likelihood	6597.03	3039.18	1872.27	324.31	151.72	479.30
N	8480	3164	1937	328	163	566

NOTE: *p < .10; **p < .05; ***p < .01. Standard errors in parentheses.

labor market characteristics are controlled for, there were not highly significant differences among national-origin groups in the incidence of unemployment in 1975. The only group whose estimated coefficient approached significance at the 10 percent level were Cubans. In addition to reflecting the above average statewide joblessness in Florida that year, this finding could also be influenced by our exclusion of self-employed persons from the study sample. A relatively large fraction of Cubans operate their own businesses and the self-employed average lower reported unemployment rates.

Another set of regressions were run on an expanded sample of all labor force participants, adding a dichotomous variable for self-employment status to the full set of other regressors in equation (1). The coefficient estimates and standard errors (in parentheses) were: $-.1144$ (.214) for the self-employment dummy, and .4455 (.228) for the Cuban dummy. Self-employment is thus associated with an insignificantly lower unemployment probability, and the Cuban differential moves to the edge of significance at the 5 percent level. This lends more credence to the notion that Cubans were indeed relatively hard hit by the deep recession of 1975.

Turning to the determinants of multiple spells of male joblessness, Table 5.11 reports logit estimates of regressions in which the dependent variable (SPELLGT1) in equation (1) is set equal to 1 if the respondent had two or more spells of unemployment during 1975, 0 otherwise. The relatively small numbers with values of 1 for the dependent variable defeated efforts to derive separate logit estimates for individual national-origin groups. As in the UNEMP75 equations, education, work experience, and marital status all appear to be stabilizing influences that significantly reduce the likelihood of multiple jobless spells for both non-Hispanic and Hispanic men. Hispanic immigrants are generally less susceptible to multiple spells than the native born within each group, but the coefficient estimates are only significant at the 5 percent level for one cohort. The non-Hispanic migrant cohort estimates are insignificant except for 1970–73 and pre-1960 entrants, which are significantly positive. Both Hispanic and non-Hispanic employees in unskilled and semiskilled occupations and in cyclical industries were found to have significantly higher probabilities of multiple spells, as were Hispanics in part-time jobs. And once again the only indication of any national-origin differentials among otherwise similar Hispanics is given by the positive Cuban coefficient, whose estimate is on the borderline of statistical significance at the 10 percent level.

Having focused thus far on the incidence of single or multiple spells, we now move on to consider the duration of time spent looking for work as reported by men who experienced some unemployment during 1975. The dependent variable is WKSUN75 (total number of weeks unemployed) and the regression specification differs from equation (1) only in the inclusion of another dummy variable (UI) set equal to 1 if the individual reported receiving any unemployment insurance during the year, 0 otherwise. By restricting the sample here to men with some unemployment, the sample size for individual national-origin groups became too small to run separate regressions for each group.

The estimates in the rightmost columns of Table 5.11 indicate that better-educated persons who experience some unemployment are out of work for a shorter amount of time than are the rest of the unemployed. For all Hispanics, an additional

TABLE 5.11. Logit Estimates of Multiple Spells Equations and OLS Estimates
of Unemployment Duration Equations, Non-Hispanic White and Hispanic Men, 1975

| | Depndt. Var.: SPELLGT1 | | Depndt. Var.: WKSUN75 | |
Variables	Non-Hispanic	Hispanic	Non-Hispanic	Hispanic
EDFOR	−.151***	−.112***	−.376*	−.204
	(.035)	(.039)	(.219)	(.229)
EDUS	−.093***	−.112***	−.180	−.646***
	(.024)	(.031)	(.219)	(.229)
EX	−.026*	−.058***	.078	−.106
	(.014)	(.018)	(.090)	(.136)
EXSQ	.000	.001*	.000	.003
	(.000)	(.000)	(.002)	(.003)
MSP	−.531***	−.430***	−2.276**	−3.761***
	(.148)	(.192)	(.965)	(1.308)
CHILD5	.046	.187*	.519	.539
	(.110)	(.110)	(.771)	(.759)
CHILD517	.063	−.049	−.051	−.702**
	(.042)	(.048)	(.299)	(.316)
HEALTH	.411***	.342	.925	1.328
	(.173)	(.252)	(1.175)	(1.772)
IMM7475	.273	−.318	4.584	−1.079
	(.788)	(.455)	(4.668)	(3.051)
IMM7073	1.185**	−.854**	4.414	−2.652
	(.466)	(.422)	(3.393)	(2.735)
IMM6569	.166	−.471	−1.833	−.743
	(.439)	(.392)	(2.424)	(2.786)
IMM6064	.093	−.930*	4.056	−2.406
	(.506)	(.476)	(3.208)	(2.680)
IMMPRE60	.665***	−.115	−.047	−2.819
	(.218)	(.288)	(1.512)	(1.976)
NONWHITE		−.925*		1.224
		(.526)		(2.223)
FLUENT	.478*	−.122	−.604	1.154
	(.213)	(.174)	(1.303)	(1.186)
OTHINC	−.002***	−.001	.005	.007
	(.001)	(.001)	(.005)	(.010)
PARTTIME	.235	.437**	2.190**	1.872
	(.171)	(.223)	(1.106)	(1.543)
UNRATE	.070***	.036	.586***	.595***
	(.024)	(.030)	(.164)	(.213)
OCC	.959***	.706***	−.125	−1.279
	(.154)	(.252)	(.968)	(1.652)
IND	.678***	.629***	.249	1.286
	(.109)	(.147)	(.761)	(1.033)

(*continued*)

TABLE 5.11. (*Continued*)

Variables	Depndt. Var.: SPELLGT1		Depndt. Var.: WKSUN75	
	Non-Hispanic	Hispanic	Non-Hispanic	Hispanic
HISPROP	.006	−.011	.038	.002
	(.010)	(.008)	(.078)	(.055)
Mexican		.156		.126
		(.285)		(1.726)
Cuban		.768*		−.978
		(.412)		(2.581)
Cen. & S. America		−.123		−4.524
		(.501)		(2.840)
Other Hispanic		.265		−1.514
		(.328)		(2.068)
UI			3.529***	4.026***
			(.771)	(1.055)
Constant	−3.044***	−1.388***	12.731***	19.854***
	(.486)	(.628)	(3.202)	(4.183)
−2 X Log Likelihood	3019	1560		
R²			.053	.092
N	8480	3164	1305	678

NOTE: *p < .10; **p < .05; ***p < .01. Standard errors in parentheses.

year of U.S. schooling is associated with some two-thirds of a week less of job-hunting. The coefficient estimate is highly significant at the 1 percent level. Additional work experience has a very weak effect for all groups. But married Hispanic males have nearly four fewer weeks without work during the year than single Hispanics and the estimate is highly significant.

Just as most Hispanic immigrants have probabilities of unemployment lower than or insignificantly different from their native-born counterparts, so also do they appear to have briefer spells out of work, though the differentials are uniformly insignificant. The same is true of the positive cohort estimates in the non-Hispanic equation. Although, as expected, a higher local unemployment rate contributes significantly to the length of residents' joblessness (by over one-half week for both Hispanics and non-Hispanics), differences by occupational and industrial sectors appear to be insignificant. Receipt of unemployment insurance in 1975 was associated with longer periods between jobs. Although such findings have often been interpreted as evidence of voluntary unemployment, this seems especially suspect in a severe recession like 1975 when aggregate demand and job vacancies contracted sharply. The longer average duration of insured unemployment may simply reflect the fact that in order to qualify for continued benefits, these individuals waited longer than the uninsured unemployed to drop out of the labor force from discouragement with the bleak employment picture. Finally, the estimated coefficients of the national-origin group dummies imply that among otherwise similar Hispanics who were out of work sometime in 1975, there were not significant interethnic variations in the duration of time lost.

Females

Both Hispanic and white non-Hispanic women average about the same educational attainment but fewer years of potential work experience than men of their national-origin group.[23] The fact that only about three-fifths of women with some labor force background are married compared with close to three-fourths of men reflects the stronger child care and other household pressures on married women that still keep a larger fraction out of the work force than is the case for married men. These same pressures also help explain why the proportion of women with part-time jobs is three times or more that of males of the same ethnicity. While the smaller fractions of women than men who are married, have long experience, and full-time employment may increase their vulnerability to unemployment, the smaller fractions in cyclical occupations and industries count as advantages relative to males. Among Hispanic women, Puerto Ricans are more concentrated in cyclical occupations and industries than any other group, while Cubans are the least concentrated in such industries. Cubans also have the advantage of being the least likely to hold part-time jobs (only 11.6 percent, half the Hispanic average), but in 1975 they faced the disadvantage of residing in areas with the highest unemployment rate (11.2 percent).

Maximum likelihood logit estimates of selected variable coefficients in the probability of unemployment equations for Hispanic and non-Hispanic women are presented in Table 5.12. Most of the results are quite similar to those found for males. More schooling and years of work experience generally lowered the likelihood of being unemployed significantly, whereas health limitations and higher local joblessness raised it. The estimated effects of marital status, children, non-white race, part-time employment, and the fraction of Hispanics in the local population were all negative but statistically insignificant. Immigrant cohort coefficients were mostly positive, but typically far smaller than their standard errors. Nor do there appear to be significant differences between Puerto Ricans (the benchmark in the regression in the second column of the table) and otherwise comparable Spanish-origin women, though the dummy variables all have negative coefficients.

The general tendency for female immigration coefficients to be statistically insignificant is evident once again when we turn to the multiple spells and duration regressions in Table 5.13. While more schooling and marriage are both associated with lower probabilities of more than one spell of joblessness for Hispanics and non-Hispanics alike, little else appears to exert a significant impact on Hispanics' susceptibility to multiple spells. The immigrant cohort coefficients are generally positive but nearly all are smaller than their standard errors. The same is true in the OLS regressions with duration of unemployment (WKSUN75) as the dependent variable. Indeed, the only statistically significant finding for Hispanics is that Central and South American women experienced nearly seven fewer weeks out of work than did the benchmark group, Puerto Ricans.

TABLE 5.12. Logit Estimates of Probability of Unemployment,
Non-Hispanic White and Hispanic Women, 1975

Variables	Non-Hispanic	Hispanic	Mexican	Puerto Rican
IMM7475	.587	.272	−.256	.311
	(.385)	(.402)	(.653)	(1.146)
IMM7073	.109	.078	−.561	−1.112
	(.333)	(.314)	(.526)	(.942)
IMM6569	.271	.294	−.061	1.001
	(.267)	(.287)	(.474)	(.795)
IMM6064	.046	.163	.242	.982
	(.268)	(.296)	(.422)	(.773)
IMMPRE60	.198	.074	.202	.401
	(.155)	(.235)	(.351)	(.562)
Mexican		−.331		
		(.207)		
Cuban		−.141		
		(.282)		
Cen. & S. American		−.256		
		(.255)		
Other Hispanic		−.386		
		(.239)		
−2 X Log Likelihood	5384	2159	1355	222
Mean of Dependent Variable	.152	.197	.194	.292
N	6624	2287	1436	212

NOTE: Standard errors in parentheses. Regressions include full set of variables in equation (1) of chapter 5.

Decomposition of the Unemployment Gap

To what extent are the sizable differences in the average incidences of unemployment of white non-Hispanics and the major Hispanic national-origin groups attributable to their differences in schooling, job, and other characteristics? In an effort to answer this important question, each national-origin group's estimated coefficient vector from its UNEMP75 regression is employed together with their mean values of all variables to calculate predicted probabilities of unemployment.

Looking first at the male results, differences in predicted probabilities between white non-Hispanics and the various national-origin groups are presented in the first row of Table 5.14. The predicted difference between all Hispanics and non-Hispanics turns out to be identical to the actual average difference of .0662 (= .2146 − .1484). Our model was especially successful in predicting the Mexican and Puerto Rican probabilities, but underestimated the actual Cuban–non-Hispanic differential by about one-third.

Next, the average characteristics of each Hispanic group were substituted into

TABLE 5.13. Logit Estimates of Multiple Spells Equations and OLS Estimates of Unemployment Duration Equations, Non-Hispanic White and Hispanic Women, 1975

Variables	Depndt. Var.: SPELLGT1		Depndt. Var.: WKSUN75	
	Non-Hispanic	Hispanic	Non-Hispanic	Hispanic
EDFOR	−.101***	−.151***	.059	−.382
	(.035)	(.049)	(.230)	(.342)
EDUS	−.118***	−.116***	.068	−.409
	(.031)	(.043)	(.191)	(.293)
EX	−.044***	−.029	.012	−.094
	(.016)	(.025)	(.101)	(.196)
EXSQ	.000	.000	.001	.001
	(.000)	(.001)	(.002)	(.004)
MSP	−.258*	−.346*	−.379	.616
	(.143)	(.208)	(.884)	(1.464)
CHILD5	.030	.071	.717	−1.470
	(.134)	(.178)	(.871)	(1.383)
CHILD517	−.022	−.099	1.144***	.116
	(.059)	(.072)	(.358)	(.470)
HEALTH	.073	.332	1.327	2.593
	(.250)	(.360)	(1.519)	(2.290)
IMM7475	−.056	.371	−.872	2.583
	(.705)	(.632)	(4.178)	(4.679)
IMM7073	.370	.334	−1.540	.230
	(.496)	(.508)	(3.588)	(3.824)
IMM6569	.273	−.054	2.176	2.142
	(.436)	(.519)	(3.028)	(3.442)
IMM6064	.189	.095	2.940	.850
	(.437)	(.508)	(2.856)	(3.780)
IMMPRE60	−.016	.428	−.811	3.347
	(.293)	(.392)	(1.748)	(2.991)
NONWHITE		.646		1.222
		(.409)		(3.189)
FLUENT	−.067	−.372	−.668	−.332
	(.225)	(.240)	(1.505)	(1.882)
OTHINC	−.003***	.000	−.012***	.009
	(.001)	(.002)	(.005)	(.012)
PARTTIME	.031	−.142	1.204	.828
	(.144)	(.237)	(.899)	(1.630)
UNRATE	.080***	.062	.462	.326
	(.029)	(.044)	(.185)	(.328)
OCC	.680***	.351	2.077***	−.331
	(.145)	(.244)	(.903)	(1.661)
IND	−.104	−.109	2.240***	.302
	(.109)	(.338)	(1.267)	(2.246)

(continued)

TABLE 5.13. (Continued)

Variables	Depndt. Var.: SPELLGT1		Depndt. Var.: WKSUN75	
	Non-Hispanic	Hispanic	Non-Hispanic	Hispanic
HISPROP	.015	−.014	−.105	.081
	(.012)	(.011)	(.091)	(.080)
Mexican		.442		−3.173
		(.382)		(2.407)
Cuban		.461		−.987
		(.509)		(3.382)
Cen. & So. America		−.085		−6.831**
		(.502)		(3.132)
Other Hispanic		.322		−3.881
		(.443)		(2.925)
UI			4.764***	4.558***
			(.872)	(1.585)
Constant	−1.822***	−1.709**	7.930**	19.746***
	(.562)	(.808)	(3.484)	(5.244)
−2 X Log Likelihood	2086	890		
R^2			.098	.082
N	6624	2287	1005	450

NOTE: *p < .10; **p < .05; ***p < .01. Standard errors in parentheses.

TABLE 5.14. Decomposition of Differences in Unemployment Probabilities Between White Non-Hispanic and Hispanic Men by National-Origin Group

Assumptions	Hispanic/Anglo Differential	Mexican/Anglo Differential	Puerto Rican/ Anglo Differential	Cuban/Anglo Differential
Group's Own Characteristics & Coefficients	.0662	.0681	.0845	.0569
Group's Own Characteristics, Anglo Coefficients	.0418	.0466	.0839	.0247
Group's Own Coefficients, Anglo Schooling Characteristics	.0191	.0050	.0696	.0370
Group's Own Coefficients, Anglo Job & Labor Market[a] Characteristics	.0727	.0832	.0951	.0507
Group's Own Coefficients, All Anglo Characteristics	.0242	.0130	−.0146	.1075

[a]Average white non-Hispanic (Anglo) values for PARTTIME, UNRATE, OCC, IND, and HISPROP were assigned to each Hispanic group.

the white non-Hispanic logit function to evaluate the role of differential treatment. If Hispanic characteristics were treated in the same manner as those of non-Hispanics, the findings in row 2 reveal that the difference in their unemployment probabilities would fall from an unadjusted .0662 down to .0418, a reduction of over 36 percent. The reductions by national-origin group range from 31.6 percent for Mexicans to 56.6 percent for Cubans. Only Puerto Ricans would be unaffected by such a change, largely due to the greater impact of occupation and industry in the non-Hispanic equation. Overall, it appears that relatively unfavorable treatment of Hispanic characteristics in the labor market accounts for a substantial fraction of the unemployment differential.

To examine the relative importance of particular characteristics, I first assumed that each national-origin group kept its own coefficient vector and its own values of all characteristics except educational attainment (EDFOR and EDUS). The large "schooling gap" (over three years in our sample) between Hispanics and non-Hispanics has often been cited as one of the most serious disadvantages hindering Hispanic earnings and employment progress. Its singular importance for unemployment is confirmed by the results reported in row 3: over 70 percent of the difference in unemployment probabilities between Hispanic and non-Hispanic men would be eliminated solely by equalizing educational attainment levels. For Puerto Ricans, the differential falls by only 18 percent and for Cubans by one-third; these smaller impacts result from their lower EDUS coefficients relative to EDFOR and other groups' schooling coefficients. But assigning Mexican men the same average schooling level as non-Hispanics lowers the gap between their unemployment and that of non-Hispanic whites by 85 percent.

When non-Hispanic job and labor market characteristics alone are substituted into the Hispanic equations, the difference in the incidence of unemployment between all Hispanics and non-Hispanics increases. This reflects the fact that, for example, Mexicans are less likely than non-Hispanic whites to be part-time workers, to live in SMSAs with high rates of joblessness, or to be in the durable manufacturing or construction industries. Only the Cuban–non-Hispanic differential is reduced (by 10.9 percent), due primarily to non-Hispanics' lower local unemployment rates and smaller proportion of workers employed in unskilled and semiskilled occupations, as well as to the unusually large estimated impact of local unemployment conditions in the Cuban incidence equation. Again, it should be noted that the SIE data bank lacks the detailed information on job and labor market characteristics needed for a full assessment of their influence.

In the last row of Table 5.14 are the results from substitution of the full set of non-Hispanic personal and labor market characteristics into the male Hispanic equations. They suggest that, with the same average values of all characteristics as white non-Hispanics, Mexican men would have nearly the same probability of unemployment and Puerto Ricans a slightly lower probability than non-Hispanics. The Cuban–non-Hispanic differential is the only one to rise, nearly doubling as a result of non-Hispanics' smaller proportion of schooling abroad and smaller fraction foreign born, both variables that are given considerable weight in the Cuban function. However, the overall difference between all Hispanics and white non-Hispanics in

TABLE 5.15. Decomposition of Differences in Unemployment Probabilities
between White Non-Hispanic and Hispanic Women by National-Origin Group

Assumptions	Hispanic/Anglo Differential	Mexican/Anglo Differential	Puerto Rican/ Anglo Differential
Group's Own Characteristics & Coefficients	.0475	.0448	.1182
Group's Own Characteristics, Anglo Coefficients	.0482	.0593	.0927
Group's Own Coefficients, Anglo Schooling Characteristics	.0239	.0134	.0606
Group's Own Coefficients, Anglo Job & Labor Market[a] Characteristics	.0456	.0543	.1055
Group's Own Coefficients, All Anglo Characteristics	.0478	.0012	.0736

[a]Average white non-Hispanic (Anglo) values for PARTTIME, UNRATE, OCC, IND, and HISPROP were assigned to each Hispanic group.

the likelihood of unemployment would have been reduced by 63.4 percent if they shared the same measured characteristics.

The results of a similar decomposition of differentials in unemployment probabilities among the female sample are presented in Table 5.15. As in the case of males, schooling differences appear to be of particular importance: bringing all Hispanic women up to the white non-Hispanic level of educational attainment would reduce the unemployment gap between them by nearly one-half (49.7 percent). Again, the effect is especially pronounced for Mexicans, for whom the differential would be slashed by over 70 percent, from .0448 to .0134. For Puerto Rican women, equalizing schooling levels with non-Hispanics would cut the unemployment differential by a projected 48.7 percent. Education thus appears to play a more substantial role for Puerto Rican women than for Puerto Rican men, who would experience only an 18 percent reduction in their unemployment gap from attaining the non-Hispanic level of schooling. Overall, with the mean values of non-Hispanic personal, job, and labor market characteristics but keeping their own coefficients, Mexican women would have about the same incidence of unemployment as white non-Hispanic women but the non-Hispanic–Puerto Rican gap would be reduced by only 37 percent.

Conclusion

This chapter has exploited a special nationwide Census Bureau survey containing detailed information on the incidence and duration of unemployment to draw comparisons between non-Hispanics and Hispanics, as well as among Hispanics by national-origin group. On average, Hispanics experienced a far higher incidence of single or multiple spells of unemployment in 1975 than white non-Hispanics and had more weeks without work in the course of the year. The finding that the average duration per spell of unemployment was slightly lower for persons of Spanish origin than for non-Hispanics implies that Hispanics' longer yearly duration of joblessness is the result of their greater frequency of unemployment. Still, for Hispanics and non-Hispanics alike, the length of time out of work was determined to be the dominant component of unemployment. The importance of long-term joblessness is suggested by the fact that nearly one-third of those unemployed in 1975 were out of a job for six months or more. Coupled with our findings in both this chapter and chapter 4 that layoffs have been by far the main cause of unemployment, these results are roughly consistent with those of recent studies on the growth of structural joblessness discussed in the previous chapter.

While all the main Spanish-origin groups experienced a higher incidence of unemployment during the year than white non-Hispanics, there were marked differences among them. The historical pattern of above average unemployment among Puerto Ricans and Mexicans was evident in 1975. The main departure from that pattern was the finding that Cubans were especially hard hit by the deep 1974–75 recession. Their geographic concentration in Florida, where statewide unemployment exceeded the national average during the recession, seems to have been one of the reasons for this. But the extremely small size of the Cuban subsample, particularly its native-born component, made a more detailed investigation impractical.

Nevertheless, Cubans' above average schooling and accumulated work experience clearly help give them a long-term employment advantage over other national-origin groups. For schooling and experience were found to reduce consistently the incidence of unemployment significantly, for both males and females. A decomposition of the Hispanic–non-Hispanic unemployment gap revealed that of the factors taken into account in our regression analysis, schooling differences were the most important of all the personal characteristics. For Mexicans, their low educational attainment dominated all other factors in accounting for higher unemployment. Statistically assigning them the same average schooling level as otherwise similar non-Hispanics resulted in a dramatic narrowing of the difference in the two groups' jobless rates.

However, a substantial role also appears to be played by employer's differential treatment of Hispanic work traits, no doubt reflecting the persistence of ethnic stereotypes and discrimination. And, particularly in the case of Puerto Ricans, long the highest unemployment group, still other factors also seem to be most important. Some have claimed that their history of migration from and frequent remigration to the island has had a uniquely destabilizing effect on their employment. But our findings showed that their unemployment was dominated by layoffs, not quits or labor force entry, and that they did not have an above average frequency of multiple jobless spells. Regression tests of the unemployment impact of migration from Puerto Rico did not yield consistent or significant findings of more frequent or longer spells among those from the island compared to otherwise similar persons born on the U.S. mainland. A more compelling case can be made for the view that

Puerto Ricans have suffered disproportionately from postwar industrial restructuring as a result of their concentration in declining manufacturing industries in the Northeast. Their below average schooling and fluency in English, as well as their limited ability to afford job search and retraining, have left many ill equipped to compete for new jobs in more stable, expanding industries.

Appendix

TABLE 5A.1. Definitions of Variables, Unemployment Regressions

UNEMP75	1 if out of work and looking for a job or on layoff for 1 or more weeks in 1975; 0 otherwise
SPELLGT1	1 if more than 1 period of time spent unemployed during 1975; 0 otherwise
WKSUN75	Number of weeks spent looking for work or on layoff during 1975
EDFOR	Years of schooling completed abroad
EDUS	Years of schooling completed after moving to the U.S. (Total years of schooling—EDFOR)
EX	Years of estimated postschool work experience (Age in 1975—Age at completion of schooling)
MSP	1 if married, spouse present; 0 otherwise
CHILD5	Number of children in family under age 5
CHILD517	Number of children in family ages 5–17
HEALTH	1 if have a disability that limits work; 0 otherwise
IMM7475	1 if born outside U.S. and migrated 1974–present; 0 otherwise
IMM7073	1 if born outside U.S. and migrated 1970–73; 0 otherwise
IMM6569	1 if born outside U.S. and migrated 1965–69; 0 otherwise
IMM6064	1 if born outside U.S. and migrated 1960–64; 0 otherwise
IMMPRE60	1 if born outside U.S. and migrated before 1960; 0 otherwise
NONWHITE	1 if nonwhite; 0 otherwise
FLUENT	1 if speak and understand English very well; 0 otherwise
OTHINC	Other family income, excluding labor earnings and unemployment benefits of respondent or spouse and earnings-related transfers
PARTTIME	1 if worked fewer than 35 hours/week when employed in 1975; 0 otherwise
UNRATE	Unemployment rate for respondent's SMSA in 1975
OCC	1 if employed as craftsman, operative, laborer, or service worker on longest job in 1975; 0 otherwise
IND	1 if employed in durable manufacturing or construction industries in 1975; 0 otherwise
HISPROP	Percentage of state population of Spanish origin
UI	1 if received any unemployment compensation in 1975; 0 otherwise

TABLE 5A.2. Means of Explanatory Variables for Unemployment Analysis,
Males by Type of Spanish Origin, 1976

Variables[a]	White Non-Hispanic	Mexican	Puerto Rican	Cuban	Cen. & South American	Other Hispanic
EDFOR	1.137	1.237	5.019	8.764	9.572	1.146
EDUS	11.350	8.360	4.729	2.717	2.497	10.049
EX	20.960	18.770	20.222	23.696	18.868	21.401
EXSQ	687.065	575.990	607.220	774.699	483.414	703.576
MSP	.745	.700	.771	.739	.687	.728
CHILD5	.221	.457	.356	.180	.380	.254
CHILD517	.889	1.385	1.111	.919	.795	1.103
HEALTH	.079	.078	.070	.062	.042	.075
IMM7475	.007	.029	.041	.037	.102	.004
IMM7073	.012	.054	.092	.124	.289	.025
IMM6569	.021	.048	.086	.255	.247	.037
IMM6064	.015	.028	.102	.342	.139	.025
IMMPRE60	.103	.096	.448	.186	.151	.043
NONWHITE	—	.022	.086	.037	.133	.050
FLUENT	.911	.671	.540	.422	.506	.792
OTHINC (00's)	45.887	30.607	22.100	34.399	24.341	34.473
PARTTIME	.094	.088	.060	.042	.053	.072
UNRATE	8.322	8.144	9.486	10.947	9.635	8.780
OCC	.576	.808	.806	.702	.729	.742
IND	.276	.268	.329	.258	.306	.258
HISPROP	3.080	12.741	4.299	5.533	5.628	15.284
N	8,480	1,937	328	163	170	566

[a]NOTE: Variable definitions in Table 5A.1.

SOURCE: Survey of Income and Education.

TABLE 5A.3. Means of Explanatory Variables for Unemployment Analysis, Females by Type of Spanish Origin, 1976

Variables[a]	White Non-Hispanic	Mexican	Puerto Rican	Cuban
EDFOR	1.312	.856	4.821	8.596
EDUS	11.057	9.163	5.288	3.014
EX	19.918	16.157	16.363	22.527
EXSQ	644.635	445.821	440.033	707.705
MSP	.622	.603	.580	.630
CHILD5	.164	.343	.255	.075
CHILD517	.782	1.445	1.057	.753
HEALTH	.068	.068	.085	.027
IMM7475	.008	.013	.033	.027
IMM7073	.012	.030	.104	.144
IMM6569	.021	.033	.085	.240
IMM6064	.022	.032	.094	.322
IMMPRE60	.112	.062	.485	.212
NONWHITE	—	.020	.094	.048
FLUENT	.890	.666	.495	.418
OTHINC (00's)	51.705	35.539	29.514	43.493
PARTTIME	.311	.256	.198	.116
UNRATE	8.241	8.073	9.543	11.152
OCC	.361	.596	.618	.493
IND	.089	.080	.198	.075
HISPROP	3.007	12.459	4.090	5.743
N	6,624	1,436	212	153

[a]NOTE: Variable definitions in Table 5A.1.

SOURCE: Survey of Income and Education.

NOTES

1. For a full description of the data bank, see U.S. Bureau of the Census (1977a). Individual record weights were also included in the raw survey data, to permit inflation of the sample in approximations of the full national population. No such attempt is made in the current study; instead we followed the conventional approach of most researchers and employed the unweighted sample.

2. Sample values for the overall Hispanic sample are not shown.

3. See the research reviewed in Lloyd and Niemi (1979).

4. See Blau and Kahn (1981a).

5. Lloyd and Niemi (1979): Table 4.3.

6. See Mincer and Leighton (1982).

7. U.S. Department of Labor, Bureau of Labor Statistics (1988b).

8. See Marshall (1983, 1984) and Waldinger (1986).

9. See Massey and Bitterman (1985) and Safa (1988).

10. U.S. Commission on Civil Rights (1976): p. 144.

11. For a comparison of structural changes in the New York and Los Angeles labor markets, see Sassen-Koob (1984). The low labor force participation rate among non-Hispanic whites in Florida is strongly affected by the relatively large fraction of retired persons in the population. The rates for blacks and Hispanics are much higher and conform to the interstate pattern of high labor force participation in low unemployment areas.

12. U.S. Bureau of the Census (1984b: New York volume): Tables 120, 134, 152.

13. U.S. Bureau of the Census (1984b: California volume): Table 120.

14. U.S. Bureau of the Census (1984b: U.S. Summary): Table 103. The youth enrollment rates for New York City were quite similar to the average rate for all urbanized areas of the country. See Table 102 in the above census volume and U.S. Bureau of the Census (1984b: New York volume): Table 119.

15. U.S. Department of Labor, Bureau of Labor Statistics (1988b): p. 19.

16. See, for example, the following and the other work cited therein: National Commission for Employment Policy (1982), Newman (1978), and Tienda, et al. (1981): ch. 9.

17. See, for example, Levy and Wadycki (1973) and Bach and Portes (1985).

18. See the survey of 1975 labor market conditions in St. Marie and Bednarzik (1976).

19. Cohen and Gruber (1970).

20. See the review of this literature in Hamermesh (1977).

21. See Appendix Table 5A.2.

22. Separate regression estimates of two regional subsamples of Hispanics (in the Northeast and in the Southwest) yielded qualitatively similar results. See DeFreitas (1985).

23. Summary statistics for the female sample are in Appendix Table 5A.3. Separate statistical analyses of Central and South American and other Hispanic women were unfeasible because of the small size of their samples with labor force information.

6

Hispanic Capitalism: Dimensions and Prospects

At the turn of the century in the United States one of every three workers was self-employed. While the majority were farm owners, the self-employment rate in nonagricultural industries was over 24 percent. But from 1900 to 1960 the aggregate rate plummeted to 13.8 percent and the nonfarm figure to 10.4.[1] This statistical free-fall was matched by a steep drop in economic research on self-employment. Throughout the 1960s and 1970s, economists routinely excised all but wage-earning employees from their data samples, usually on the grounds (if any were mentioned) that the self-employed were a marginal, secularly declining group whose income included returns to physical capital that rendered them noncomparable with wage earners.

Recently there has been a striking revival of interest in small business and its effects on the employment and incomes of women, youth, and minorities as well as on macroeconomic performance. Beginning in the mid-seventies, a series of Labor Department studies suggested that the long-term decline had ended and that self-employment was now rapidly increasing, especially among women.[2] Rising concern over lagging U.S. productivity growth focused attention on the contributions of small firms to technical innovation.[3] At least one influential observer felt this contribution to be so disproportionately large as to signal the emergence of a new "entrepreneurial economy."[4] Much-publicized research on the relationship between firm size and job creation by David Birch (1979) claimed that two-thirds of the net new jobs generated between 1969 and 1976 were attributable to firms with 20 or fewer employees. As immigration has increased since 1965, particularly from Latin America and Asia, the historic role assigned to small business ownership as an avenue for the occupational and income mobility of successive waves of the foreign born has been reemphasized by both economists and sociologists. Some have drawn the implication from the immigrant experience that increased self-employment of

Hispanic men and women might be an effective means to accelerate their upward mobility, as well as to avoid the career obstacles often posed by discriminatory employers or fellow employees.

This chapter explores the key economic determinants and consequences of contemporary self-employment among both Hispanics and non-Hispanics. First we consider some of the principal theoretical expectations in the literature regarding racial, ethnic, and sex differences in self-employment. Then logit regression techniques are applied to a 1980 census microdata set to evaluate the relative importance of a variety of personal, job, and labor market variables. The income consequences of self-employment are then estimated on the same census data, supplemented by firm performance information drawn from the Surveys of Minority-Owned and Women-Owned Businesses.

Changes in Self-Employment, 1970–1980

Most recent discussions of trends in self-employment rely on published Labor Department data, drawn from the monthly Current Population Survey (CPS). These figures point to a turnaround in the secular pattern in about 1970. Before that, the postwar drop in aggregate self-employment had mainly reflected a steep fall in farm ownership, which dominated the more moderate declines in nonfarm business. The latter did drop sharply in 1967, but this was due to that year's major revision in the Labor Department definition of "self-employment": from that point on, the self-employed have included only those persons working in their own *unincorporated* business, profession, or trade. The reclassification of the owner-operators of incorporated businesses as "employees of their own corporation" largely deflated the nonagricultural sector, where the vast majority were.[5] But CPS figures for unincorporated nonfarm self-employment began showing increases by the early 1970s, which have increasingly come to outweigh the continued but far slower declines in farm ownership. The result was a gradual rise in aggregate self-employment throughout the 1970s.

The widely distributed CPS findings are, however, of limited value, since the low national incidence of self-employment results in minute survey subsamples vulnerable to extreme sampling variability and too small to conduct reliable statistical tests by sex, race, or ethnicity. Hence, we present in Table 6.1 census of population figures for 1970 and 1980 on aggregate and nonfarm self-employment of white, black, Hispanic, and Asian men and women. The total number self-employed had fallen to 5.9 million by 1970. But a 21 percent increase in non-agricultural self-employment was more than sufficient to outweigh contractions in farm ownership and push the aggregate figure to 6.7 million by 1980. Among women, nonfarm self-employment jumped by nearly 42 percent, almost three times faster than the male figure. The increases were especially dramatic for Hispanic and Asian women.

But these increases appear to largely represent increases in the numbers of labor force participants rather than a change in propensities to engage in self-employment. In the aggregate, women experienced a 43.7 percent increase in nonfarm employment during the 1970s, outweighing the numerical rise in self-employment. This is evident in the calculations in Table 6.1 of the fraction of the nonfarm work force owning unincorporated businesses: less than 4 percent of all working women were self-employed in both 1970 and 1980, regardless of race or ethnic group. Among men the rate actually fell slightly, for all groups except Asians. The figures also show that if the pre-1967 definition including owners of incorporated businesses was still in use, the rate would increase to 10.5 percent for men but result in a trivial change for women.

Table 6.2 breaks down the 1970–80 changes by major industry. Perhaps the most dramatic changes are in two areas: business services and finance, insurance, and real estate (FIRE). Male self-employment rose by 47 percent in the former and 42 percent in the latter, while the female figure in both more than doubled. The fact that, for black men, these two sectors grew while business ownership was falling in most other industries has been cited by Bates (1978) as signaling a shift away from traditional, low-skilled retail businesses toward more capital- and skill-intensive growth industries like computer and data processing services. These firms have indeed grown, although the business services category is still dominated by auto repair and building services.

These figures bear testimony to the fundamental importance of secular interindustry shifts in explaining changes in self-employment. In the aggregate, increased self-employment in services alone accounted for 43.6 percent of the net 1970–80 increase. But this was mainly due to the expansion of the service sector: the self-employment rate in that industry actually fell (from 8.9 to 7.9 percent). In fact, had the 1970 rate prevailed through 1980, the intercensal growth in service jobs would have generated an increase in the number self-employed equivalent to 74 percent of the actual observed change.

Determinants of Self-Employment

Theoretical Framework

Despite the proliferation of research on labor supply and occupational choice over the past two decades, there are few guidelines in the literature for modeling the self-employment decision.[6] Clearly, unlike wage employment, establishing a business requires an initial stock of financial resources and management skills. Since young workers are less likely to have accumulated sufficient savings or to qualify for bank loans, one would expect the probability of self-employment to rise with age. Marriage may also be related to greater self-employment, insofar as dual-earner families produce a larger pool of savings and older children may be available to help with business operations. Likewise, better-educated persons may be more inclined to set up a business to the extent that schooling provides: (1) quantitative and other business-related skills; (2) information about the local economy and consumption habits; (3) lower subjective discount rates; and (4) higher savings, made possible by the higher incomes obtained, on average, by more-educated workers.

Of course, the higher average earnings of older, married, and better-educated

TABLE 6.1. Changes in the Components of Self-Employment by Sex, Race, and Ethnicity, 1970–80

	All	Whites	Blacks	Hispanics	Asians
MALES					
All Industries					
Self-employed, un-incorporated					
1970	4,849,994	4,618,663	182,263	108,858	49,068
1980	5,148,681	4,844,385	165,909	159,720	71,663
Self-employed, inc. & uninc.					
1970	5,820,964	5,564,759	199,715	120,250	56,940
1980	6,821,020	6,476,605	200,028	207,699	103,461
Nonagriculture					
Self-employed, un-incorporated					
1970	3,474,274	3,303,459	137,070	89,018	23,745
1980	3,999,961	3,739,443	143,787	139,692	60,552
% of All Empld.					
1970	7.69	8.09	3.57	5.06	4.74
1980	7.44	7.89	3.16	4.54	6.90
Self-employed, inc. & uninc.					
1970	4,407,176	4,212,462	153,716	104,673	31,005
1980	5,656,975	5,317,157	177,648	187,369	91,998
% of All Empld.					
1970	9.75	10.31	4.00	5.95	6.20
1980	10.53	11.35	3.91	6.09	10.48
FEMALES					
All Industries					
Self-employed, un-incorporated					
1970	1,061,210	985,146	61,197	24,651	14,867
1980	1,529,190	1,420,135	57,899	46,275	31,252
Self-employed, inc. & uninc.					
1970	1,230,125	1,145,718	67,543	28,461	16,864
1980	1,886,515	1,752,917	68,987	58,146	40,856
Nonagriculture					
Self-employed, un-incorporated					
1970	984,154	915,078	55,905	23,765	13,171
1980	1,393,261	1,288,274	56,190	44,643	29,967
% of All Empld.					
1970	3.44	3.66	1.71	2.39	3.65
1980	3.39	3.71	1.21	2.10	3.87
Self-employed, inc. & uninc.					
1970	1,149,672	1,072,421	62,152	27,532	15,099
1980	1,740,487	1,611,092	67,232	56,444	39,517

(*continued*)

TABLE 6.1. (*Continued*)

	All	Whites	Blacks	Hispanics	Asians
% of All Empld.					
1970	4.02	4.29	1.90	2.77	4.19
1980	4.23	4.64	1.45	2.66	5.10

NOTE: Hispanics include all Spanish-origin persons regardless of race.

SOURCES: U.S. Bureau of the Census (1973c: Table 44); (1973d: Table 47); (1984b: Tables 144, 154); (1984c: Table 288).

workers could also induce them to forego the risks of a new business start-up in favor of wage work. So, for any given age, marital status or educational attainment level, we need to determine what other considerations would tip the balance toward self-employment.

Many of the explanatory factors proposed in recent years can be usefully grouped into two broad categories, which I will call the *mobility motive* and the *escape motive*. The first has received its most extensive discussion in the historical and sociological literature on immigrants, for whom small retail proprietorships, particularly those serving the special consumption needs of the migrants' ethnic group, are said to have accelerated their socioeconomic adaptation and progress. Most such work has long focused on the major Asian nationalities, for whom various types of "rotating credit associations" have been viewed as an important source of start-up funds.[7] More recently, the Cuban refugee community in Miami has been identified as a new "ethnic enclave" in which a high concentration of migrant-owned businesses has been nurtured by and, in turn, has itself strengthened a network of close kinship and ethnic bonds.[8] About two-thirds of all construction firms and one-fifth of Miami's commercial banks appear to be controlled by Cubans. These firms have served to provide entry-level jobs to new arrivals, as well as training and financial support to selected employees aiming to one day establish their own businesses. Sowell (1978) has argued that much the same has been true of black West Indian immigrants, who: "have long had higher incomes, more education, higher occupational status, and proportionately far more business ownership than American Negroes."

From another perspective, self-employment is less a positive career decision on the optimal route to upward mobility than a means of escape from unemployment, low wages, and blocked promotional paths. The early seventies' optimism of some observers that much-expanded educational opportunities together with civil rights legislation would translate into a substantial narrowing of male–female and white–minority employment differentials has been the target of increasing criticism of late.[9] Faced with higher layoff rates and lower earnings growth on the job, women and minorities may opt more and more to foresake their position as employees in favor of self-employment.[10]

The implications of sex, race, or ethnic discrimination for self-employment

TABLE 6.2. Nonfarm Employment and Self-Employment by Selected Industry,
Sex, Race, and Ethnicity, 1970–80

	All Races		Blacks		Hispanics	
	1970	1980	1970	1980	1970	1980
MALES ('000s)						
All Nonfarm Industries						
Total	45,182	53,738	3,841	4,550	1,760	3,077
Self-employment	3,474	4,000	137	144	89	140
Construction						
Total	4,364	5,260	387	378	170	330
Self-employment	627	826	36	33	15	31
Manufacturing						
Total	14,185	14,919	1,270	1,353	579	926
Self-employment	232	253	10	9	5	8
Trans. & Utilities						
Total	4,086	5,334	405	587	148	268
Self-employment	149	187	14	15	5	8
Wholesale Trade						
Total	2,374	3,083	164	192	92	166
Self-employment	164	189	4	4	4	6
Retail Trade						
Total	6,637	7,712	446	515	270	487
Self-employment	881	762	24	24	23	31
Finance, Insur., etc.						
Total	1,930	2,476	104	163	58	108
Self-employment	187	265	3	5	2	5
Business Services						
Total	1,735	2,702	140	210	75	173
Self-employment	349	514	16	22	10	21
Other Services						
Total	6,377	8,177	615	782	226	411
Self-employment	903	948	34	31	18	28
Government Sector	6,712	8,118	764	1,069	225	421
FEMALES ('000s)						
All Nonfarm Industries						
Total	28,622	41,113	3,263	4,632	993	2,124
Self-employment	984	1,393	56	56	24	45
Construction						
Total	270	480	13	26	7	18
Self-employment	15	26	0.4	0.6	0.2	0.7
Manufacturing						
Total	5,633	6,996	512	810	291	553
Self-employment	39	64	1	2	1	3
Trans. & Utilities						
Total	1,122	1,753	100	240	32	83
Self-employment	11	17	1.0	0.9	0.3	0.7
Wholesale Trade						
Total	726	1,134	43	68	31	66
Self-employment	16	29	0.5	0.5	0.4	1

(*continued*)

TABLE 6.2. (*Continued*)

	All Races		Blacks		Hispanics	
	1970	1980	1970	1980	1970	1980
Retail Trade						
Total	5,629	8,004	366	521	171	359
Self-employment	340	419	14	12	9	15
Finance, Insur., etc.						
Total	1,922	3,422	116	287	59	152
Self-employment	41	92	1	1	0.6	2
Business Services						
Total	692	1,380	56	130	23	68
Self-employment	53	132	2	6	1	4
Other Services						
Total	11,357	15,717	1,874	2,166	341	714
Self-employment	492	610	38	33	11	19
Government Sector	5,635	8,543	814	1,463	140	402

SOURCE: U.S. Bureau of the Census (1973d): Table 38; and (1984c): Table 288. Govt. overlaps inds.

propensities are not unambiguous. For example, Gary Becker's (1957) well-known model would seem to predict that insofar as discrimination mainly takes the form of white male employers or fellow employees expressing their distaste for physical proximity with a particular group, self-employment will be a relatively attractive refuge for group members. A similar prediction could be derived from the later "statistical discrimination" models of the sort developed by Arrow (1972), which emphasize employers' adverse perceptions of a group's average productivity level. Since the informational costs of determining an individual's actual productivity are lowest for that individual herself, persons in groups stereotyped as less able should have all the more incentive to "hire themselves" through self-employment.

But discrimination is clearly not confined to employers and fellow employees. Women, blacks, and Hispanics thinking of establishing viable businesses must also consider the possibility of prejudiced customers and lending institutions. Perceptual discrimination by the latter in assessing credit worthiness could result from the same societal stereotypes about average productivity levels that are thought to impede female and minority wages and employment progress.[11] This has been disputed by several scholars like Sowell (1981) and Glazer and Moynihan (1970) who argue that Asians, Cubans, and West Indians prove by their high rates of business ownership that sufficient funds can be generated within the ethnic/racial community without recourse to high-cost bank loans. Others have attacked these claims as exaggerated, pointing instead to the relatively high premigration occupational status and accumulated savings of these groups, without which their pooled loan arrangements would be inadequate.[12]

The foregoing considerations suggest a model of the following sort to evaluate the independent contributions of these various factors:

$$\ln \frac{P}{1 - P} = \beta_0 + \beta_1 A_{25} + \beta_2 A_{45} + \beta_3 A_{55} + \beta_4 S + \beta_5 M + \beta_6 I_{75}$$
$$+ \beta_7 I_{70} + \beta_8 I_{65} + \beta_9 I_p + \beta_{10} F + \beta_{11} G + \beta_{12} U$$
$$+ \beta_{13} E + \beta_{14} D + \beta_{15} R_1 + \beta_{16} R_2 + \beta_{17} R_3 + e_{ij} \qquad (1)$$

where:

P = probability of self-employment;
A_{25} = 1 if individual age 25–34, 0 otherwise;
A_{45} = 1 if individual age 45–54, 0 otherwise;
A_{55} = 1 if individual age 55–64, 0 otherwise;
S = individual's years of schooling completed;
M = 1 if individual married, spouse present, 0 otherwise;
I_{75} = 1 if immigrated to U.S. 1975–79, 0 otherwise;
I_{70} = 1 if immigrated 1970–74, 0 otherwise;
I_{65} = 1 if immigrated 1965–69, 0 otherwise;
I_p = 1 if immigrated prior to 1965, 0 otherwise;
F = 1 if fluent in English, 0 otherwise;
G = growth rate of real retail sales receipts in individual's SMSA, 1972–77 (local product-demand proxy);
U = number of weeks individual unemployed last year;
E = percentage of SMSA population black (in blacks' regressions)/Hispanic (in Hispanics' regressions);
D = ratio of median annual earnings of black/Hispanic/women high school graduates ages 35–44 to white male high school graduates ages 35–44, in same SMSA;
R_1 = 1 if SMSA in Northeast, 0 otherwise
R_2 = 1 if SMSA in South, 0 otherwise;
R_3 = 1 if SMSA in West, 0 otherwise.

Aside from the standard human capital variables, the model includes variables for immigrant cohort, English fluency, and population share of each group in the individual (of that group's) SMSA to provide a test of the "mobility motive." The weeks unemployed (U) and inverse measure of income inequality in the SMSA (D) may be interpreted as reflective of the "escape motive."

Empirical Findings

The principal data source is the Public Use Microdata Sample of the 1980 Census of Population. The sampling proportions for Hispanics, non-Hispanic blacks, and non-Hispanic whites were 1/100, 1/200, and 1/1000 respectively. The study sample was restricted to residents of the 79 SMSAs with populations over 500,000. It was further limited to nonstudents in the 25–64 age group who reported all relevant personal and employment information.

These selection criteria appear to have generated a sample of persons strongly attached to the work force, reducing the likelihood of sample selection bias. Tests of the regression equations using Heckman's (1979) selection correction indicated little change in the coefficients. Evans and Leighton (1989) report similar results in their analysis of self-employment among whites, using a different data set.

Looking first at the summary statistics on selected characteristics in Table 6.3, it is clear that there are large differences in the average probabilities of self-employment by group. White non-Hispanic men are more than twice as likely to own businesses full-time and more than six times as likely to engage in self-employment as part of multiple jobholding than any other subset. Black men and women have by far the lowest incidence. By industry, male Anglos are self-employed in the FIRE sector at twice the rate of others, but have a similar rate to others in business services. Within that category, however, disaggregated statistics show them more concentrated in higher skill sectors. Women have far more of their self-employment in the generally low-income retail trade and personal service industries.

The figures on immigrants may be surprising: only male Anglo immigrants have, on average, a greater fraction self-employed (16 percent compared with the

TABLE 6.3. Means of Selected Employment Characteristics, Males and Females by Self-employment, Race, and Ethnicity, 1980

	Males			*Females*		
	Anglo	*Black*	*Hispanic*	*Anglo*	*Black*	*Hispanic*
Self-employed on Main Job	.124	.048	.071	.051	.017	.032
Self-employed & Part-time Employee	.039	.001	.003	.002	.0003	.001
Employee & Part-time Self-employed	.024	.011	.015	.010	.005	.005
Self-employment among Immigrants	.161	.047	.078	.042	.016	.036
Age 25–34:						
All Workers	.347	.390	.426	.384	.414	.444
Self-employed	.231	.236	.291	.301	.233	.320
Years of Schooling:						
All Workers	13.40	11.72	10.27	12.93	12.06	10.38
Self-employed	13.90	11.91	11.42	13.25	11.89	11.06
Industrial Distrbtn. of Self-employed:						
Manufacturing	.074	.030	.074	.060	.038	.084
Construction	.167	.224	.167	.027	.000	.030
Trans. & Utilities	.089	.154	.126	.045	.044	.056
Wholesale Trade	.069	.024	.054	.031	.006	.041
Retail Trade	.172	.165	.224	.282	.241	.292
Finance, Ins., etc.	.074	.046	.030	.072	.038	.034
Business Services	.115	.136	.128	.114	.103	.112
Entertainment	.024	.036	.022	.033	.026	.009
Personal Services	.031	.076	.061	.145	.326	.234
Professnl. Services	.179	.110	.111	.190	.179	.109

NOTE: Sample restricted to nonstudent workers, ages 25–64, in SMSAs with populations ≥ 500,000. The Anglo and black subsamples include only non-Hispanics; the Hispanic grouping includes all persons of Spanish origin regardless of race.

SOURCE: 1980 Census of Population, Public Use Microdata Samples.

group average of 12.4). Under 5 percent of black men and 2 percent of female black immigrants own businesses. This clearly raises some doubt about the claims of Sowell and other on West Indians' progress in the United States.

But these descriptive statistics could be nothing more than the result of other factors. Anglo men are, on average, older (only 35 percent are in the youngest age set, 25–34), with more schooling, traits that could largely account for their higher mean self-employment.

To control for such differences, we next estimate equation (1), using a maximum likelihood logit approach. This enables us to avoid the well-known problem that in regressions with dichotomous dependent variables, OLS produces heteroscedasticity and biased predicted values.

The regression results reported in Table 6.4 confirm our prior expectation that younger, less-educated, and unmarried workers are typically less likely to undertake the expense and risks of running a business. The age differences are strongest for Anglo and black men. Fuchs (1982) has shown that for older men self-employment has become a valuable income supplement to retirement funds.

Immigrants in the United States under 10 years are generally less likely than the native born (the reference group) to be self-employed. This may reflect the need for an adjustment period to learn American business practices and customer preferences, as well as the need to demonstrate one's ability to potential creditors. For all except blacks, older migrants settled here before 1965 are significantly more prone to own businesses. The coefficients are, however, quite small. The findings for blacks are, in fact, consistent with those of Smith (1977) for West Indians in Great Britain in the mid-seventies and of Borjas (1986) for males based on a different methodology.

The evidence is mixed for the escape motive: higher recent unemployment generally lowers the probability of self-employment (perhaps mainly through depressing the family income available to finance a start-up), but the higher the female–Anglo male (in the women's regressions), the black–Anglo (for male blacks), or the Hispanic–Anglo (for male Hispanics) full-time earnings ratios in one's SMSA, the lower the attractiveness of self-employment for most groups. But the coefficients are again quite small.

Finally, among Hispanics, Cuban, other Latin American, and other Hispanic men have significantly higher rates than do Mexican or Puerto Rican men (the reference group). This may reflect the higher initial family incomes of these groups, as well as the low educational attainment and above average unemployment rates of the Mexican and Puerto Rican populations.

Consequences of Self-Employment

Analysis of Earnings Differentials

Despite creating a new academic industry in estimation of earnings functions in the 1970s, labor economists have yet to turn their attention to such an analysis for the self-employed. The standard excuse has been that self-employment income is under-

TABLE 6.4. Logit Regressions of Probability of Self-Employment by Sex, Race, and Ethnicity

Independent Variables	Males			Females		
	Anglo	Black	Hispanic	Anglo	Black	Hispanic
Age 25–34	−.061 (10.09)	−.030 (6.61)	−.034 (7.77)	−.017 (3.86)	−.009 (5.06)	−.010 (2.77)
Age 45–54	.015 (2.46)	.003 (.66)	−.002 (.51)	.000 (.01)	.006 (3.68)	.010 (2.79)
Age 55–64	.014 (2.25)	.016 (3.27)	−.008 (1.40)	.005 (1.08)	−.005 (2.48)	−.008 (1.73)
Schooling	.008 (11.09)	.002 (4.32)	.003 (6.37)	.003 (4.24)	.000 (.16)	−.001 (3.58)
Married	.015 (2.65)	.005 (1.51)	.012 (2.84)	.016 (4.13)	.004 (2.66)	.013 (4.15)
Immigrated, 1975–79	.009 (.34)	−.022 (1.14)	−.008 (.97)	−.010 (.39)	−.006 (.67)	.007 (1.18)
Immigrated, 1970–74	.045 (1.56)	.004 (.31)	−.002 (.21)	−.028 (.87)	.000 (.00)	−.004 (.66)
Immigrated, 1965–69	.068 (2.89)	.017 (1.30)	.007 (1.12)	−.008 (.41)	.003 (.66)	.005 (.99)
Immigrated, Pre-1965	.037 (3.55)	.009 (.59)	.016 (3.05)	.018 (2.48)	.001 (.15)	.011 (2.63)
English Fluency	.036 (1.18)	−.013 (.51)	.013 (2.60)	.037 (1.11)	−.009 (1.00)	−.001 (.34)
Unemployment Last Year	.0001 (.36)	.0003 (1.83)	−.001 (1.90)	−.001 (2.64)	−.0001 (1.08)	−.001 (2.41)
Retail Sales Growth Rate	.0002 (1.93)	.00001 (.08)	.0001 (1.73)	.00003 (.49)	.00003 (1.01)	.0001 (1.89)

(continued)

TABLE 6.4. (*Continued*)

Independent Variables	Males			Females		
	Anglo	Black	Hispanic	Anglo	Black	Hispanic
Ethnic/Racial Concentration	—	-.009	.038	—	-.011	.019
		(.29)	(1.88)		(.86)	(1.24)
Earnings Inequality	—	-.034	-.018	.024	-.007	-.028
		(.29)	(1.88)	(1.36)	(.93)	(1.69)
Constant	-.366	-.119	-.206	-.236	-.044	.109
	(11.35)	(3.82)	(11.57)	(6.58)	(3.92)	(7.76)
Log Lklhd.	-7787.4	-2738.5	-4505.9	-3268.4	-2491.6	-1989.7
N	21,348	14,066	18,470	16,514	15,099	14,330

NOTE: Table entries are partial derivatives, calculated as products of the logit regression coefficients, β_1, and $P(1 - P)$, where P is the probability the individual is self-employed. In addition to the variables above, four ethnic group dummies are included in the Hispanic regression (coefficient estimates reported below), and three regional dummies in all regressions. Asymptotic t-ratios are in parentheses.

SOURCE: 1980 Census of Population, Pulbic Use Microdata Samples.

reported and contains returns to capital. But Lillard, Smith, and Welch (1986) have now shown that wages and salaries recorded in the principal data banks are far more underreported than was previously thought. And Leveson (1968), in a detailed analysis of this issue unmatched by any since, concludes that the reputed problems of comparability of wages and unincorporated business income are largely confined to agriculture. We are here focusing only on nonagricultural workers in metropolitan areas, so it may not be so inappropriate to take a first look, even if a rather cursory one, at how the self-employed fare relative to their wage and salary counterparts.

The model used has the following specification:

$$\ln Y = \gamma_0 + \gamma_1 S + \gamma_2 X + \gamma_3 X^2 + \gamma_4 M + \gamma_5 L + \gamma_6 I_{75} + \gamma_7 I_{70} + \gamma_8 I_{65} \\ + \gamma_9 I_p + \gamma_{10} F + \gamma_{11} N + \gamma_{12} H + \gamma_{13} R_1 + \gamma_{14} R_2 + \gamma_{15} R_3 + e_{ij} \qquad (2)$$

where:

Y = weekly earnings, 1979 (annual earnings/weeks worked);
S = individual's years of schooling completed;
X = years of postschool potential work experience (Age − [S+ 6]);
M = 1 if individual married, spouse present, 0 otherwise;
L = work limited by a physical disability, 0 otherwise;
I_{75} = 1 if immigrated to U.S. 1975–79, 0 otherwise;
I_{70} = 1 if immigrated 1970–74, 0 otherwise;
I_{65} = 1 if immigrated 1965–69, 0 otherwise;
I_p = 1 if immigrated prior to 1965, 0 otherwise;
F = 1 if fluent in English, 0 otherwise;
N = vector of 11 dummy variables for individual's industry of current or most recent employment;
H = hours worked in typical week, 1979;
R_1 = 1 if SMSA in Northeast, 0 otherwise;
R_2 = 1 if SMSA in South, 0 otherwise;
R_3 = SMSA in West, 0 otherwise.

Equation (2) was designed to incorporate the factors cited in our earlier discussion as potentially most relevant to the self-employed, yet still be as close as possible to standard wage functions to enhance the comparability of our results with the larger literature. It is first estimated for individuals who were primarily self-employed in 1979. Since the census questionnaire only asks its "class of worker" question for one's 1980 job but the earnings reported are for 1979, reliance on class of worker data may produce misleading results given considerable year-to-year job turnover in this country. But the question on 1979 earnings does specify whether their source is wages and salary (including incorporated business earning) or unincorporated self-employment income. This enables us to identify self-employment in 1979 based on whether a respondent's self-employment income exceeded his wage and salary earnings.

Tables 6.5 and 6.6 report selected coefficient estimates of the earnings function, run first on the self-employed alone. The estimated effects of more schooling are all positive and statistically significant for males, regardless of ethnicity, as well as for

TABLE 6.5. Hourly Earnings Regressions, Self-Employed Males and Females

Independent Variables	Males			Females		
	Anglo	Black	Hispanic	Anglo	Black	Hispanic
Schooling	.042	.045	.031	.053	.007	.021
	(4.01)	(2.60)	(3.12)	(2.22)	(.15)	(1.05)
Experience	.038	.005	.022	−.015	.003	.003
	(3.95)	(.27)	(1.84)	(.74)	(.07)	(.13)
Experience^2	−.0007	−.0001	−.0004	.0004	−.003	−.002
	(3.87)	(.36)	(2.00)	(1.00)	(.38)	(.50)
Married	.225	.059	.105	−.050	.067	−.174
	(3.42)	(2.58)	(1.25)	(.41)	(.31)	(1.26)
Immigrated, 1975–79	−.144	−.242	−.106	.510	−.036	−.112
	(.48)	(.36)	(.66)	(.64)	(.05)	(.37)
Immigrated, 1970–74	.141	.147	.213	.566	.000	−.094
	(.40)	(.41)	(1.74)	(.70)	(.00)	(.41)
Immigrated, 1965–69	.098	.201	.223	.762	−.056	.386
	(.35)	(.60)	(1.75)	(1.33)	(.08)	(1.96)
Immigrated, Pre-1965	.068	−.300	.204	.422	.653	.428
	(.56)	(.90)	(2.12)	(1.80)	(.80)	(2.58)
English Fluency	−.440	−.608	.356	−.189	−.212	.215
	(1.15)	(.62)	(3.70)	(.16)	(.17)	(1.38)
Constant	4.741	4.776	4.491	4.168	5.413	3.871
	(10.99)	(4.58)	(15.92)	(3.23)	(3.03)	(5.84)
R^2	.121	.143	.183	.131	.151	.294
N	1353	674	791	473	152	254

NOTE: In addition to the variables above, four ethnic group dummies are included in the Hispanic regressions (estimates below) and all equations have three regional dummies, industry dummies, and control variables for hours worked/week and health status (dummy set to 1 if disabled). T-ratios are in parentheses. Dependent variable: natural logarithm of annual 1979 self-employment earnings divided by annual weeks worked.

SOURCE: 1980 Census of Populaiton, Public Use Microdata Samples.

white female non-Hispanics. The coefficients for female blacks and Hispanics are small and insignificant. But this is true of most of their coefficients and may be the result of nothing more than the small self-employed samples for these two groups. The only self-employed subgroup for whom we find that additional work experience has a strongly positive effect is non-Hispanic white males. White and black men, but not Hispanics, also receive an earnings advantage from being married.

There is little evidence of a consistent pattern in earnings by immigration cohort, except among Hispanics. The results for both male and female Hispanics show clearly that earlier self-employed immigrants tend to earn significantly more than otherwise similar immigrants resident in the United States 10 years or less. This could well be due to the adjustment difficulties recent migrants experience in the first few years after arrival. One might object that these significantly positive differentials for the pre-1970 cohorts could simply reflect the large component of

TABLE 6.6. Ethnic Differentials in the Likelihood of Self-Employment
and in Self-Employment Earnings, Nonfarm Hispanic Males
and Females, 25–64

Independent Variables	Dep. Var.: Pr(Self-Emp.)		Dep. Var.: Ln(SE Earnings)	
	Males	Females	Males	Females
Mexican	.001	−.008	.044	−.117
	(.10)	(1.51)	(.31)	(.48)
Cuban	.041	.003	.046	.111
	(4.67)	(.45)	(.27)	(.38)
Other Latin Amer.	.020	−.004	.021	−.102
	(2.33)	(.67)	(.13)	(.37)
Other Hispanic	.025	.000	.089	.033
	(3.25)	(.00)	(.60)	(.13)
Puerto Rican	a	a	a	a

NOTE: In addition to the variables above, regressions include all other variables in Tables 6.4
and 6.5. T-ratios in parentheses. a = excluded reference group.

SOURCE: 1980 Census of Population. Public Use Microdata Samples.

higher-income Cubans (many with prior business experience) in these waves. But
the regression does control for Cuban and other national origins, which should
reduce this influence. The ethnic group differentials in Table 6.6 imply that once
one takes into account personal, migration, and industrial characteristics, no particular group has a significant income advantage.

The regression was next run on the larger pooled sample including both the
wage and salary workers and the self-employed. Perhaps the single most interesting

TABLE 6.7. Earnings Differentials Between the Self-Employed, Multiple Jobholders,
and Other Males and Females

Independent Variables	Males			Females		
	Anglo	Black	Hispanic	Anglo	Black	Hispanic
Self-employed, Single Job	−.009	.004	.035	−.213	−.212	−.101
	(.63)	(.13)	(.38)	(8.18)	(3.94)	(2.73)
Self-employed & Part-time Employee	.268	.663	.537	.192	−.431	.102
	(4.18)	(3.79)	(2.77)	(1.44)	(1.19)	(.43)
Employee & Part-time Self-employed	.075	.012	.534	.072	.220	.211
	(2.78)	(.19)	(4.01)	(1.26)	(2.34)	(2.51)

NOTE: In addition to the variables above, the regressions include the full set of variables in Table 6.5. T-ratios are in
parentheses. Dependent variable: natural logarithm of the sum of weekly employment and self-employment earnings.

SOURCE: 1980 Census of Population, Public Use Microdata Samples.

finding is that those whose sole source of labor market income is from self-employment are generally no better off than otherwise similar employees or, in the case of all three groups of women, significantly worse off. Only in the case of Hispanic men do the self-employed have a slight advantage. But multiple jobholders engaged in some self-employment generally do have a significant income advantage over the wage and salary reference group. This comes, of course, at the cost of longer average workweeks and workyears. But recent BLS data show a clear tendency for growing part-time employment, and self-employment appears to be a rising part of that potentially quite important phenomenon.

Firm Size, Sales, and Employment

The census of population data examined thus far can provide only a partial sense of the experiences of the self-employed, since it lacks information on the size, sales performance, and employment levels of their businesses. The principal data source on the characteristics of women-owned and minority-owned firms is the economic censuses conducted every five years by the Census Bureau. These cover individual proprietorships, partnerships, and those corporations filing 1120S tax returns. The findings for 1982 have the advantage of broader industrial coverage and greater detail on ethnicity than previous surveys. It must be borne in mind when interpreting them that these changes have also reduced the degree of comparability with earlier censuses, especially at the local level, for three main reasons: (1) the 1982 surveys were the first to count multiple businesses owned by the same individual as separate firms rather than a single compound firm; (2) whereas previous censuses determined the owner's sex from the first name (typically the husband's) on joint tax returns, this was replaced by the use of matched Social Security data in 1982, thereby adding an estimated 1,794,000 women-owned firms to the total count; and (3) firms were classified into multiple race/ethnicity categories in 1982 if, for example, the owner identified himself as both black and Hispanic, rather than restricting each firm to a single grouping as in the past.[13]

Based on national data adjusted to reduce intercensal comparability problems, the number of women-owned firms jumped by 124 percent between 1972 and 1982, and black and Hispanic firms increased by 81 percent and 113 percent, respectively.[14] By the end of the decade women were estimated to own 2,884,450 businesses, blacks owned 339,239, and Hispanics 248,141.

However, even if we assume these figures were not artificially inflated by the survey modifications, they reveal that all these groups remain substantially underrepresented. Though a majority of the adult population and a near-majority of the labor force today, women own only 24 percent of the 12 million firms in the census universe. These firms are overwhelmingly small sole proprietorships: 92.3 percent, compared with the national average of 84 percent. Only 3.1 percent of womens' businesses are corporations, which account for 30.4 percent of gross receipts. Nine out of 10 have no paid employees. And three out of four are still concentrated in retail trade and service industries (which produce 63.2 percent of sales receipts). The relatively poor performance of these industries throughout much of the seventies may help explain the fact that average real receipts per firm fell by 19.2 percent from 1972 to 1982.

Blacks, though 12 percent of the population, today own only 2.8 percent of all businesses and receive a mere 0.16 percent of business revenues. Less than 5 percent of all black firms are partnerships or corporations. By many measures, these firms' fortunes have faded markedly in recent years. Only 11.4 percent have any paid employees, down from 16.4 percent 10 years before. Aggregate inflation-adjusted sales receipts were actually lower in 1982 than in 1972, and average revenue per firm dropped by 38 percent.

Hispanic-owned firms experienced almost as large (37 percent) a fall in average real revenues. They are likewise similar to blacks in the tiny fraction of partnerships and corporations. But a larger proportion (16 percent) were employer-firms and there was no significant decrease in this figure over the decade. Sharp differences prevailed by ethnicity and nationality. Persons of Mexican origin owned over 57 percent of the Hispanic total and nearly as large a share of paid employment, whereas Puerto Ricans owned only 5.9 percent of the firms, and their employees represented only 2.9 percent of all jobs. The heterogeneous category of other Hispanics, though only 2.3 percent of all Spanish-origin business owners, accounted for nearly 16 percent of these firms' paid employees; two-fifths were employed in a single industry, manufacturing.

Seventy-eight percent of all Hispanic firms are concentrated in only five states (California, Florida, New Mexico, New York, and Texas), making national comparisons with other groups suspect. So in Table 6.8 we present data for New York State on the number of firms, employment, and receipts in 1982, as well as calculations of the inflation-adjusted change in receipts per firm over the previous decade. The results indicate a decline in real receipts for all groups through 1982, though for women this was relatively modest and confined to trade. For blacks and Hispanics, manufacturing stands out as an especially important source of sales progress. For all groups, the number of jobs provided by these firms grew substantially, doubtless providing a valuable, if still modest, aid to chronically high unemployment areas.

Conclusion

This chapter explored some of the key determinants of and consequences from self-employment among women, blacks, and Hispanics. Relying largely on empirical analysis of 1980 census microdata, I found that some potentially important progress has been made in raising the rate of business ownership among these groups, with positive multiplier effects doubtless improving the employment levels in their communities. More recent work on job creation by firm size has raised questions about Birch's (1979) claims that firms of 20 or fewer employees generated two-thirds of all net employment growth between 1969 and 1976. His findings appear highly sensitive to the length of the time period used. A Brookings study of the same data bank, but covering the period 1976–80, found that these small firms (accounting for 76 percent of all businesses) were responsible for only 35 percent of the net new jobs

TABLE 6.8. Women-Owned and Minority-Owned Firms, Receipts and Employment
in New York State, 1982

	Firms (number)	Firms with Employees (%)	Employees Per Firm	Receipts ($million)	1972–82 Changes in Receipts[a]
WOMEN-OWNED FIRMS					
Total	189,675	11.2%	4.9	$8352.5	−3.7%
Construction	3,145	31.2	4.5	376.5	104.5
Manufacturing	4,806	24.1	11.3	736.1	70.9
Trans., Utils.	3,691	16.8	4.7	233.0	79.3
Wholesale Trade	5,771	19.4	4.4	1050.4	−14.1
Retail Trade	33,566	21.2	4.2	2193.8	−16.3
Finance, Insur.	14,545	15.1	3.1	776.9	15.5
Services	95,106	7.9	5.6	2483.8	8.6
Other Industries	29,041	2.0	2.1	502.0	8.9
BLACK-OWNED FIRMS					
Total	25,560	8.9%	5.4	$918.6	−52.0%
Construction	1,178	16.3	4.0	60.4	43.8
Manufacturing	320	28.8	14.6	97.8	14.0
Trans. & Utils.	2,225	6.0	3.4	64.6	−28.4
Wholesale Trade	743	11.6	3.8	52.1	−86.6
Retail Trade	4,059	14.1	3.6	228.0	−51.0
Finance, Insur.	856	12.4	6.3	48.3	−21.4
Services	12,554	7.9	6.5	309.6	−35.6
Other Industries	3,627	2.5	1.2	57.8	−39.6
HISPANIC-OWNED FIRMS All Hispanics					
Total	14,477	14.0%	4.3	$1018.3	−41.9%
Construction	845	14.8	5.2	46.6	−41.8
Manufacturing	326	37.7	15.9	105.9	38.5
Trans. & Utils.	1,412	5.7	12.0	83.0	−27.5
Wholesale Trade	532	17.8	5.3	255.0	−27.5
Retail Trade	3,221	19.8	2.9	257.0	−35.4
Finance, Insur.	438	13.2	2.9	22.3	−72.7
Services	5,511	14.9	3.2	185.3	−50.5
Other Industries	2,193	3.7	3.2	63.3	−6.3
Mexicans	634	14.8	4.3	35.0	−61.4
Puerto Ricans	5,089	13.4	3.1	276.3	−57.5
Cubans	2,109	15.1	5.1	134.8	−45.9
Other Latin Amer.	4,913	12.0	3.2	208.7	−38.5

[a]Calculated in constant 1967 dollars, using CPI deflator.

SOURCES: U.S. Bureau of the Census (1975b; 1975c; 1986c; 1986d).

created.[15] Nonetheless, this is a significant contribution and may be especially important in providing young workers with their first training opportunities. Schiller (1983) has estimated that firms of this size make two-fifths of initial youth hires. The 30,000 or more young workers (net) who leave them each year for larger firms represent an estimated $200–$300 million investment by small business and a significant savings in corporate training costs.

At the same time, the relatively stagnant share of self-employment in all groups and the low average earnings of the full-time self-employed suggest that this cannot at present be a major force in countering current trends of rising inequality. Though other research has found evidence supporting the efficacy of government loan and set-aside programs, particularly for higher-skilled members of disadvantaged groups, it is hard to see how anything other than broad improvement in the prospects for stable, skilled jobs and rising real earnings for the 9 out of 10 workers employed by others can have a substantial impact.

NOTES

1. All estimates from Lebergott (1964).

2. See Ray (1975); Fain (1980); and Eugene Becker (1984).

3. For example, see Birch (1979).

4. Drucker (1985).

5. On the Labor Department redefinition of the self-employed to exclude incorporated business owners, see Stein (1967).

6. For research on black self-employment, see Bates (1973); Bearse (1984); Bradford and Osborne (1976), and Stevens (1984).

7. See, for example, Light (1972) and Bonacich and Modell (1980).

8. Portes and Bach (1985).

9. See the discussion in chapters 1 and 3.

10. See, for example, Jones (1986) and Scott (1986).

11. See, for example, the evidence on this in Bates (1973) and Presidential Task Force (1978).

12. See the work on various migrant groups by Fagen, Brody, and O'Leary (1968): Foner (1987); Light (1972); and Portes and Bach (1985).

13. U.S. Bureau of the Census (1986f): p. v.

14. These and all subsequent figures in this section are from calculations using data from U.S. Bureau of the Census (1975b; 1975c; 1986c; and 1986d).

15. Armington (1983).

7

The Educational Crisis of Hispanic Youth

The erosion of U.S. global economic strength and of the average family's standard of living over the past two decades has focused new attention on the problems of our educational system. With publication of the highly critical government report *A Nation At Risk* in 1983, the view became widespread that these problems had reached crisis proportions. Twenty-three million adults are functionally illiterate, as are 13 percent of 17-year-olds; among minority teenagers the figure may be as high as 40 percent.[1] In a 1989 follow-up study, the U.S. Department of Education found that, by some key measures, these problems had worsened over time. In particular, the Hispanic high school dropout rate had risen to 35.7 percent—almost triple that of white youth and more than double that of blacks.

In the summer of 1987, the New York Telephone Company found that of the 22,880 New York City applicants tested on basic verbal and numeric skills for entry-level jobs so far that year, 84 percent had failed. That same year, 45 percent of applicants failed examinations (set at the eighth grade level of knowledge) to be new tellers at a major New York bank, compared with only 30 percent five years earlier. One bank official observed:

> They don't understand what a bank teller does or what a bank does. We can't teach them how to read and do arithmetic over the course of a couple of weeks, when they should have been learning that over the course of the last couple of years.[2]

As the center of gravity in the economy continues to shift from manufacturing to services the mismatch between job requirements and job-seekers' skills threatens to become increasingly costly. Not only will economic growth be hindered by skill shortages, but a significant fraction of youth will be faced with long-term joblessness and poverty.

The educational difficulties confronting Hispanics are especially severe. They have the highest school dropout rates and the lowest average educational attainment of any minority group. The important consequences of this for their low income levels and high unemployment have been demonstrated in the empirical analyses of earlier chapters. This chapter begins by reviewing recent evidence on the magnitude of the schooling gap between whites, blacks, and Hispanics. Then I explore a number of the principal explanatory factors responsible for the higher dropout rates of minorities. Finally, logit regression techniques are applied to 1980 census micro-data to estimate two models, one explaining interpersonal differences in the probability of high school enrollment and the other differences in high school graduation propensities.

Educational Attainment Differentials

Over two decades after new antidiscrimination laws and expanded federal school funding raised hopes of rapidly narrowing educational inequality, black and Hispanic Americans are still substantially less well educated on average than whites. Among those 25 years of age and older, 70 percent of whites are high school graduates, compared with only 51 percent of blacks and 44 percent of Hispanics (Table 7.1).

The larger proportion of youth in the minority population could bias their schooling figures downward. But enrollment breakdowns by specific age levels in Table 7.2 show that minorities have consistently lower enrollment rates between ages 16 and 24. In fact, Hispanics are less likely to be enrolled than either whites or blacks at every age, starting with ages 3 to 4 when only one-fourth are in school, compared with nearly one-third of whites and two-fifths of blacks.

Time-series data demonstrate how persistent this pattern has been. Estimates of high school dropout rates from the U.S. Department of Education show that in 1975, 14.7 percent of whites 18–19 years old were dropouts, 25.4 percent of blacks, and 30.1 percent of Hispanics (Table 7.3). In the milder recession of 1980 the black rate fell 4 points, but the Hispanic rate jumped to 39 percent. By 1985, three years into a cyclical upturn, all rates were lower, but the black dropout rate was still 25 percent above the white rate and Hispanics were more than twice as likely to drop out as were whites. Across the period 1974 to 1985, high school completion rates of youth ages 18–19 and of those 20–24 exhibited a persistent pattern: Hispanic rates fell well below blacks, and blacks below whites (Figures 7.1 and 7.2).

It is thus not surprising that blacks and Hispanics are also far less likely to obtain a college education. By the time of the 1980 census, one in three whites aged 25 or over had completed at least a year of college, but only 22 percent of blacks and 19.6 percent of Hispanics had (Table 7.1). And whites had a rate of graduation from four-year institutions of higher education more than twice that of minorities.

Far less expected has been the troubling tendency for the gap between white and minority college enrollment rates to widen in recent years, threatening to reverse the improvements of the 1960s. Among all youth ages 18–24, the proportion enrolled

TABLE 7.1. Educational Attainment of Persons 25 and Over by Race
and Type of Spanish Origin, 1980

Years of School Completed	White	Black	All Hispanic	Mexican	Puerto Rican	Cuban	Other Hispanic
Median	12.5	12.0	10.8	9.6	10.5	12.2	12.3
12 or More (%)	69.6	51.2	44.0	37.6	40.1	55.3	57.4
13 or More (%)	33.5	21.9	19.6	15.3	13.2	30.2	28.5
16 or More (%)	17.4	8.4	7.6	4.9	5.6	16.2	12.4

SOURCE: U.S. Bureau of the Census (1984b).

in college peaked at 27 percent of whites, 23 percent of blacks, and 20 percent of Hispanics in 1976 (Table 7.4 and Figure 7.3). The fraction of black and Hispanic high school graduates entering college (33.5 and 35.8 percent, respectively) that year actually exceeded the white level. However, by 1985, only 20 percent of black and 17 percent of Spanish-origin youth were in college, compared with 29 percent of whites. And, while over 34 percent of white high school graduates entered college, this was true of only 26 to 27 percent of minorities. The result has been a growing underrepresentation of minorities in higher education: while blacks were 13.7 percent and Hispanics 8.2 percent of the nation's 18–24-year-olds by 1985, they accounted for only 9.7 and 5.0 percent, respectively, of all college students in that age group. In fact, even these figures understate the actual inequality in college education, since minorities who do go on to college are far less likely to attend the highest quality four-year institutions: 43 percent of black and 54 percent of Hispanic college students were enrolled in junior or community colleges in 1984, compared with only 36 percent of white students.[3]

Determinants of Enrollment

The task of accounting for interpersonal differences in educational attainment has been a central component in the now-standard human capital model. Becker's (1964) basic approach, as is well known, was to view the individual utility-

TABLE 7.2. School Enrollment Rates by Age, Race, and Type of Spanish Origin, 1980

Age	White	Black	All Hispanic	Mexican	Puerto Rican	Cuban	Other Hispanic
				(% of age group)			
3–4	32.4	38.8	26.0	24.0	24.9	42.4	32.2
5–6	86.2	87.2	84.6	83.3	86.3	91.5	87.3
7–15	98.9	97.7	97.5	97.2	97.9	98.1	97.9
16–17	89.3	87.9	80.2	78.0	78.7	89.1	85.6
18–19	53.1	51.7	43.8	39.2	41.8	65.1	52.9
20–21	33.6	28.4	23.5	18.9	21.7	44.8	33.6
22–24	17.4	15.8	14.6	11.6	13.1	28.5	21.6

SOURCE: U.S. Bureau of the Census (1984b).

TABLE 7.3.　High School Dropout[a] Rates of Persons Ages 14–34
by Race, Spanish Origin, and Sex, 1975–85

Year, race, ethnicity, and sex	Age Groups						
	14–34	*14–15*	*16–17*	*18–19*	*20–21*	*22–24*	*25–29*
1975							
White	12.8	1.7	8.4	14.7	14.8	12.6	14.0
Male	12.1	1.4	7.3	13.7	14.5	12.6	13.2
Female	13.5	1.9	9.6	15.6	15.0	12.7	14.7
Black	23.4	2.6	10.2	25.4	28.7	27.8	27.9
Male	21.9	2.4	9.7	27.7	30.4	25.9	25.5
Female	24.7	2.8	10.7	23.4	27.3	29.2	29.9
Hispanic	33.0	4.0	13.2	30.1	31.6	41.7	42.9
Male	29.9	1.9	11.1	26.3	30.2	40.0	40.6
Female	35.7	6.2	15.5	33.5	32.7	43.2	44.8
1980							
White	12.1	1.7	9.2	14.9	14.5	13.9	12.7
Male	12.4	1.2	9.3	16.1	15.6	15.4	12.7
Female	11.8	2.1	9.2	13.8	13.4	12.6	12.7
Black	18.8	2.0	6.9	21.2	24.8	24.0	22.6
Male	19.0	1.5	7.2	22.7	31.3	24.9	22.1
Female	18.7	2.5	6.6	19.8	19.6	23.3	22.9
Hispanic	35.2	5.7	16.5	39.0	41.6	40.6	40.9
Male	35.6	3.3	18.1	43.1	41.4	42.9	40.1
Female	34.9	7.9	15.0	34.6	41.9	38.6	41.7
1985							
White	11.5	1.8	7.1	13.8	13.4	13.3	13.6
Male	11.8	1.6	6.7	16.3	14.2	14.2	14.0
Female	11.1	2.0	7.6	11.3	12.7	12.5	13.3
Black	15.5	2.1	6.5	17.3	17.7	17.8	17.5
Male	15.6	1.8	7.6	17.7	20.5	18.4	17.0
Female	15.4	2.4	5.4	16.9	15.3	17.4	18.0
Hispanic	31.4	3.6	14.5	30.6	27.9	33.9	39.1
Male	32.1	3.2	10.1	42.2	33.5	33.9	37.6
Female	30.8	4.0	19.2	19.9	22.8	33.8	40.6

[a]Dropouts are persons not enrolled in school and not high school graduates in the survey month (October). Persons who received GED credentials are counted as graduates. From CPS samples of civilian noninstitutional population.

SOURCE: U.S. Department of Education (1987).

maximizer as deciding on the optimal volume of self-investments in schooling through a comparison of the rate of return from additional schooling with the subjective rate of time preference and/or the rate available on alternative investments. The main emphasis was thus placed on the demand side, with demand the product of the expected returns from each schooling level and the individual probability of reaching this level. This in turn contributed importantly to a theory of earnings differences that stressed the role of labor supply, since an individual's accumulation of human capital like schooling was viewed as determining her marginal productivity, which was the basis for her equilibrium wage.[4]

Since rates of return must be calculated net of educational costs (both direct and

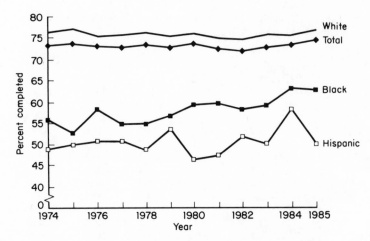

FIGURE 7.1. High school completion rates of persons ages 18–19, by race and Spanish origin, 1974–1985. Source: U.S. Department of Education (1987).

indirect opportunity costs), this approach does in fact implicitly assign a potentially significant role to factors influencing the supply of educational opportunities.[5] The influence of the level of direct costs (school tuition and fees, less any financial aid) may have become increasingly important of late, at least with respect to the rate of return on college. For in every single year in the 1980s, the average cost of a year of college has increased at a faster rate than inflation or average family incomes. By the 1986–87 school year, the annual cost of tuition, room, and board had climbed to $11,870 at the average private university—and to over $17,000 in the Ivy League. By that standard, public universities (average 1986–87 cost: $4,370) and two-year colleges ($3,160) might seem a bargain. But the average costs of all types of

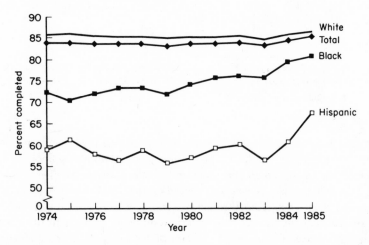

FIGURE 7.2. High school completion rates of persons ages 20–24, by race and Spanish origin, 1974–1985. Source: Same as Figure 7.1.

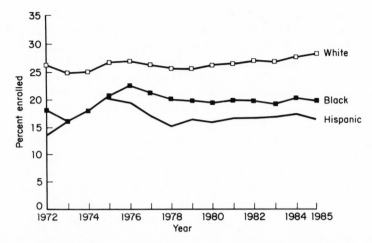

FIGURE 7.3. College enrollment rates of persons ages 18–24, by race and Spanish origin, 1972–1985. Source: Same as Figure 7.1.

postsecondary institutions have increased far faster than either family incomes or government financial assistance. Between the 1980–81 and the 1986–87 school years, the average cost of a year's study at private universities, public universities, and two-year colleges jumped 80.8 percent, 61.2 percent, and 56.4 percent, respectively. Over the same period, the median income level of all American families rose only 40.1 percent. Blacks' average family income grew more slowly (38.9 percent) and Hispanics' income slower still (35.9 percent).[6]

TABLE 7.4. College Enrollment Rates of Whites, Blacks, and Hispanics, and Hispanic Share of Total College Enrollment, 1973–85

| Year | Persons 18–24 Years Old Enrolled in College, as % of Age Group | | | Hispanics, Ages 18–24, Enrolled in College, as % of All College Students 18–24 |
	White	Black	Hispanic	
1973	24.98	15.99	16.03	3.40
1974	25.24	17.87	18.06	4.31
1975	26.94	20.70	20.40	4.25
1976	27.15	22.59	19.92	4.30
1977	26.50	21.29	17.22	3.88
1978	25.70	20.10	15.19	3.63
1979	25.61	19.83	16.65	4.18
1980	26.42	19.35	16.06	4.36
1981	25.78	19.85	16.67	4.51
1982	27.24	19.81	16.84	4.39
1983	27.04	19.17	17.23	4.67
1984	27.95	20.35	17.94	4.77
1985	28.72	19.75	16.88	4.98

SOURCE: U.S. Bureau of the Census (1974–87).

At the same time, federal need-based grants for college students have been sharply scaled back. The average Pell Grant was cut from $643 (constant 1973 dollars) in the 1975–76 school year to $472 ten years later. Supplementary Educational Opportunity Grants, adjusted for inflation, were likewise reduced over the decade from an average of $441 to $252. From 1980 to 1987, the total volume of federal grants was increased only 3.6 percent, which means it fell substantially in real terms. Work-study funds changed a negligible 0.3 percent. Low-income students were thus increasingly forced to rely on loans. The total volume of Federal Guaranteed loans rose 45.7 percent (in current dollars) during the 1980s. But even on these riskless loans backed by the U.S. government, banks were charging 8 percent interest by 1987. The cuts in federal grants posed a serious obstacle for those low-income families faced with the prospect of incurring tens of thousands of dollars of new indebtedness to put a single child through four years of college.[7]

The bulk of social science research on educational attainment has tended to place far more weight on socioeconomic background factors than does the human capital approach. Family income, parents' education, and family structure have generally been found to have effects that rank among the strongest of all measurable variables.[8] The higher family income, of course, the larger the amount and the higher the quality of the schooling that can be afforded for one's children. More-affluent families are also better able to provide good housing, nutrition, health care, and early childhood education, all of which may enhance those physical and mental abilities most useful for successful schooling. Children from such families are also less likely than the offspring of low-income parents to be compelled to drop out of school to take a job in support of the family during hard times.

Higher-income persons are also, on average, better educated. Insofar as children adopt the tastes and aspirations of their parents, the offspring of the well-educated may themselves seek a comparable or superior education. If so, they enjoy the advantage over others of ready access to informed guidance from relatives who have already navigated the course.

Family structure is widely viewed as influential, first, because the absence of one or both parents may reduce the attention, encouragement, and emotional security afforded the children. It is also likely, particularly in female-headed, single-parent households, that financial insecurity will reduce the funds needed for additional schooling and/or require the children to drop out of school in favor of employment. Finally, those teenagers who are forming their own families can be expected to have high dropout propensities the more they feel pressured to establish financial and residential independence from their parents. An early pregnancy will make continued schooling still more difficult for young women. They face not only increased economic demands but often high school policies that require pregnant students to leave school. Even when this is not formally required, the widespread lack of affordable day care as well as pressure from parents, peers, or the child's father often drive young mothers from school. And, for some teenagers, low expectations about their prospects for realizing substantial future socioeconomic gains from more schooling may contribute to a preference for pregnancy over school.[9]

There is less agreement in the literature about the effects of other factors. A prime example is the state of the economy, particularly the local labor market. A worsening of economic conditions can be said to have both income and price effects on school enrollment. The former refer to the impact of a decline in family income levels, which will reduce the demand for normal goods, including education. The price effect works in the opposite direction, since higher unemployment and lower wage offers cut the opportunity cost of attending school. The net impact thus depends on the relative strength of each effect, which requires empirical analysis.[10]

In order to investigate the heterogeneous Spanish-origin population, it is necessary to consider also the possible influences of ethnicity, immigration, and language problems. Nearly three-tenths of all persons of Spanish origin were born outside the continental United States, and 31 percent of these have been in the country less than five years.[11] The large fraction of first- and second-generation immigrants is reflected in the fact that, in response to a 1980 census question, only one in five Hispanics said English was their sole language and only three in five were very fluent in English. While Puerto Ricans are U.S. citizens, not immigrants, about half were born on the island, 48 percent report that they are not very fluent in English, and two-fifths of the latter speak English "poorly or not at all."

Settlement in a new country can involve considerable transitional difficulties, which may disrupt the schooling of children. The necessity to locate housing and employment soon after arrival may require all family members to devote their time to these pressing matters, thereby reducing enrollment rates. The above average fractions of low-skilled workers in recent migrant waves from Mexico and Puerto Rico are likely to experience persistently lower family incomes and higher unemployment rates, putting pressure on teenagers to drop out of school to find jobs. It is also to be expected that the lower average quality of schooling in Mexico and Puerto Rico, particularly during recent years of economic crisis and public spending cutbacks in both countries, may put foreign-born students at a disadvantage on entering U.S. schools.[12]

All of these problems are magnified for most Hispanic migrants by their lack of fluency in English. Not only are students confronted with a different curriculum, school system, educational standards, and cultural norms, but their progress and adjustment are likely to be slowed considerably by language problems. Alicea and Mathis (1975) found, from a major survey project on Puerto Rican school-age youth, that command of English was a strong predictor of high school dropout rates. Since research (such as that of McManus, Gould, and Welch [1983]) on Hispanic American workers has found evidence of a sizable negative impact of language problems on earnings levels, youth from Spanish-speaking households may also be more vulnerable to the pressures of low family income discussed earlier. Unfortunately, local and federal programs of bilingual education are still highly controversial and only cover about one in five Hispanic public elementary and secondary students.[13]

As shown in Figure 7.4, the high school dropout rates of immigrants are above average for Anglo youth as well as for Hispanics, though the latter average far higher rates—exceeding 40 percent for Mexican and Puerto Rican migrants. The difficulties associated with immigration and lack of fluency in English may also help explain why, even after controlling for family income level, Hispanic youth have consistently higher dropout rates than Anglos (Figure 7.5).

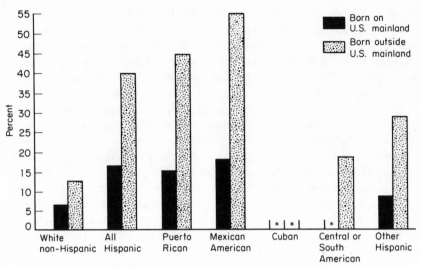

*Percentage not shown where estimate is less than 20,000 persons.

FIGURE 7.4. High school dropout rates of persons ages 14–30, by type of Spanish origin and country of birth, 1976. Source: U.S. Department of Education (1980).

Foreign birth and limited command of English are clearly not the only important determinants of educational attainment, since the Cuban population has the largest share of recent immigrants to the United States and the highest rate of Spanish retention, yet also has school enrollment and completion rates similar to white non-Hispanics (Tables 7.1, 7.2). In sharp contrast, fewer than half of Mexicans and Puerto Ricans complete high school, and only 5–6 percent are college graduates. As

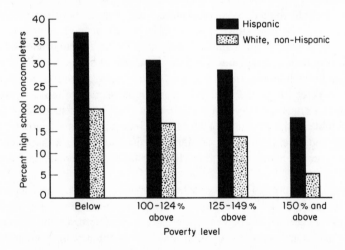

FIGURE 7.5. High school dropout rates of persons ages 14–30, by family poverty level and Spanish origin, 1976. Source: Same as Figure 7.4.

we saw in chapter 2, efforts to account for Cubans' relative success have stressed such factors as the unusually large amount of financial and employment assistance provided the first waves of migrants, the familiarity with the U.S. educational system and job market of the many middle- and upper-class emigres, and the capital stock the latter brought with them. But this research also draws attention to the importance of investigating the effects of labor market structure on immigrants' economic progress.

With a median family income of $14,712 in 1979 the average Hispanic was at a level one-third lower than the white non-Hispanic median ($21,014).[14] This is reflected in the fact that 23.5 percent of Hispanic families were below the official poverty line income, compared with only 8.9 percent of Anglos. And their families were twice as likely as white non-Hispanics to be stretching their income over five or more members and to be female-headed, without a husband present. The two largest groups—Mexicans and Puerto Ricans—are also, on average, the poorest. In fact, Puerto Ricans' median family income was only $10,734, less than half that of white non-Hispanics and almost $2,000 below the black average, and 36.3 percent were below the poverty line compared with 30 percent of black families. Especially high poverty rates are experienced by female-headed families with children, and such families represent 28.5 percent of all Puerto Rican families and 25.6 percent of all black families, but only 5.8 percent of all white non-Hispanic families. And in contrast to the low Cuban unemployment rate (nearly identical to Anglos' 5.7 percent in 1980), Mexican and Puerto Rican joblessness is one and one-half to twice as high.

The focus on school enrollment thus far in this section should not be interpreted to mean it is the only important gauge of educational attainment. No single indicator of economic performance is universally accepted by educators and policymakers. One of the most comprehensive measures is the reading proficiency test developed for the congressionally mandated National Assessment of Education Progress (NAEP) and conducted annually with a national sample of students. The results for 1974–75 and 1983–84 are presented in Table 7.5, for three age groups subdivided by race and Spanish origin. At every age level, whites rank higher in reading proficiency than blacks or Hispanics. For example, among 13-year-olds in the 1980s, two-thirds of whites were reading at the intermediate level, but only 35 percent of blacks and 39 percent of Hispanics. Cross-year comparisons offer encouraging evidence of progress: the percentage of minority 13-year-olds at the intermediate level rose 10 percentage points between the mid-seventies and the mid-eighties. But the gap dividing whites from minorities is still quite wide.

The same is true in terms of another measure of educational performance: school delay, the practice of students being held back in school. As estimates from the 1976 Survey of Income and Education show clearly, Hispanics are much more likely than white non-Hispanics of similar age, family income, and English fluency to be enrolled two or more years below the expected grade level (Figures 7.6, 7.7). School delay is undoubtedly a most discouraging experience, more so the older one gets, which may be a cause of school leaving. Thus some studies have included it as an independent variable in regression analyses of enrollment.[15] But as Figures 7.6 and 7.7 reveal, school delay is worse for white non-Hispanics, as well as for

TABLE 7.5. Elementary and Secondary Students At or Above Reading
Proficiency Levels by Race, Spanish Origin, and Age
(%)

Year, Race, Ethnicity, and Age	Reading Proficiency[a]			
	Rudimentary	Basic	Intermediate	Adept
1974–75				
9-year-olds	93.3	61.7	14.0	0.7
White	95.9	68.4	16.6	0.8
Black	81.5	32.0	1.9	0.0
Hispanic	82.3	33.5	3.2	0.0
13-year-olds	99.6	92.8	57.5	9.7
White	100.0	96.2	64.3	11.5
Black	98.0	75.3	23.9	1.5
Hispanic	98.2	81.4	29.8	1.3
17-year-olds	100.0	97.5	82.0	36.1
White	100.0	99.1	87.5	40.6
Black	100.0	86.0	45.0	7.1
Hispanic	100.0	92.4	56.5	12.9
1983–84				
9-year-olds	93.9	64.2	18.1	1.0
White	96.4	71.1	22.0	1.2
Black	83.6	39.3	4.5	0.1
Hispanic	88.2	43.8	4.7	0.0
13-year-olds	99.8	94.5	60.3	11.3
White	99.9	96.5	66.9	13.6
Black	99.4	87.1	35.3	2.3
Hispanic	100.0	88.3	39.4	1.7
17-year-olds	100.0	98.6	83.6	39.2
White	100.0	99.2	88.9	45.1
Black	100.0	96.5	65.8	15.5
Hispanic	100.0	96.8	69.1	19.9

[a]"Rudimentary" = able to follow brief written directions and select phrases to describe
pictures; "Basic" = able to understand combined ideas and make references based on short
uncomplicated passages about specific or sequentially related information; "Intermediate" =
able to search for specific information, interrelate ideas, and make generalizations about
materials; "Adept" = able to find, understand, summarize, and explain relatively complicated
literary and informational material.

SOURCE: U.S. Department of Education (1987).

Hispanics, the lower their family income and familiarity with English. Thus many
of the same factors may not only help account for minorities' low enrollment rates
but also for their below average achievement scores in school.

Finally, it is impossible to investigate the educational differences between
whites and minorities without considering the possible role of discrimination. The
question of what effect school and teacher characteristics have on educational outcomes has long been hotly contested, particularly after the much-publicized research project led by James Coleman (1966) suggested that the answer was negligible. However, as Hanushek's (1986) survey shows, more recent studies following a

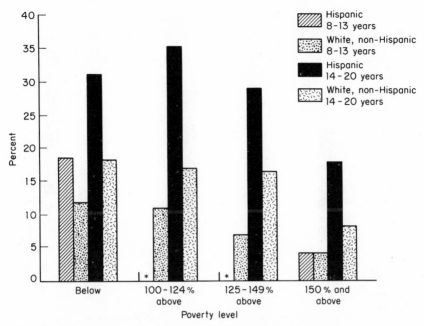

*Percentage not shown where estimate is less than 20,000 persons.

FIGURE 7.6. Percentage enrolled two or more years below expected grade level, by age and poverty level, 1976. Source: Same as Figure 7.4.

wide variety of research paths have produced evidence to the contrary. For example, classroom studies of teacher–student communication patterns have demonstrated the prevalence of biased forms of interaction with minority students, which appear to have long-lasting adverse effects on their confidence, class performance, and educational aspirations. Research for the U.S. Commission on Civil Rights (1973) found that teachers directed praise and encouragement to Anglo students 36 percent more often than to their Mexican American classmates, and were 40 percent more likely to build on the spoken contributions of white non-Hispanics. Similar findings for Puerto Rican students are reported by Duran (1983) and the U.S. Commission on Civil Rights (1976).

Limited evidence also now exists that more racially integrated classrooms tend to have positive effects for both black (Patchen, et al., 1980) and Hispanic students (Mahard, 1978; Duran, 1983). In fact, Coleman's (1982) more recent study of a special nationwide longitudinal survey of high school sophomores and seniors also supports this view. When relevant family background characteristics were held constant, white, black, and Hispanic students in the generally less-segregated private schools attained higher cognitive outcomes than their counterparts in public schools.

Such findings make it all the more troubling to learn, from Orfield's (1987) intensive analysis of 1968–84 U.S. Education Department data, that since 1972 the national level of segregation of blacks in predominantly minority schools has not

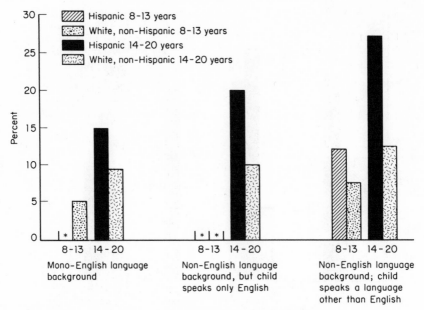

*Percentage not shown where estimate is less than 20,000 persons.

FIGURE 7.7. Percentage enrolled two or more years below expected grade level, by age and language, 1976. Source: Same as Figure 7.4.

changed and that the segregation of Hispanics has actually increased. Between 1968 and 1972 the percentage of black students in predominantly minority schools (i.e., where the majority of the student body were minorities) was cut from 76.6 percent to 63.6 percent (Figure 7.8). Much of this integration was the result of court orders and busing programs. But by 1984, 63.5 percent of blacks were still segregated in such schools. Only 55 percent of Hispanics were in predominantly minority schools in 1968, but this had increased to 61 percent by 1976 and had jumped another 10 percentage points by 1984. In New York—the most segregated of all states, according to the study—the percentage of Hispanics in "intensely segregated" schools (90 percent or more minority students) has risen from 56.8 percent in 1980 to 59.1 percent in 1984. The findings disaggregated by national-origin group reveal (as studies such as Massey and Bitterman [1985] have shown in other ways) that Puerto Ricans experience the worst segregation of all Hispanics.

Regression Analysis of Dropout Behavior

The empirical analysis that follows focuses on two questions: (1) What factors determine the probability of teenagers (ages 16–17) dropping out of school? (2) What factors determine the probability of teenagers (ages 16–19) graduating from high school? I do not here test a model of college attendance. While the differences in the fractions of whites and minorities entering college are large and growing, we

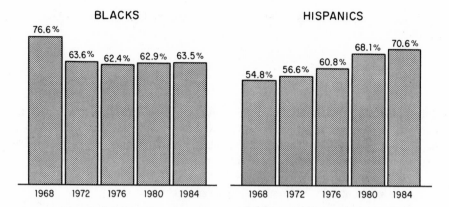

FIGURE 7.8. Percentage of black and Hispanic students enrolled in predominantly minority public elementary and secondary schools, 1968–1984. Source: Orfield (1987).

saw in Table 7.4 that this is largely attributable to the lower high school completion rates of minorities. The rate of college entrance by minority high school graduates has been quite close to that of white graduates, though it began to decline in the 1980s.

Data and Model Specification

The principal data source is the Public Use Microdata Sample of the 1980 Census of Population. Information on Hispanics was drawn from the large 1/100 sample, while the sampling proportion was 1/1000 of Anglos.[16] The study sample was restricted to males and females ages 16–19 who lived in one of the 79 SMSAs with populations over 500,000 in 1980 and who reported all relevant personal information.

Two models are estimated. First, the probability of current enrollment is estimated for a subsample of youths ages 16–17. Then I attempt to predict the probability of completion of high school with a second model, using data on all youths 16–19 years of age, except those currently enrolled in high school. Application of ordinary least squares techniques when the dependent variable is dichotomous (e.g., Enrolled, Not enrolled) has a couple of well-known estimation problems: heteroscedasticity and biased predicted values that may lie outside the (0, 1) interval.[17] Instead I estimate a logit enrollment model of the following form:

$$Pr(E = 1) = \frac{1}{1 + e^{-z}} \tag{1}$$

where E is a dichotomous variable set equal to 1 if the individual is enrolled, 0 otherwise; and

$$Z = \alpha + \beta_i X_i$$

By manipulating the terms in (1) and taking natural logs of both sides of the equation:

$$\ln \frac{Pr(E = 1)}{1 - Pr(E = 1)} = Z = \alpha + \beta_i X_i \qquad (2)$$

That is, the log of the odds that each individual is enrolled is a function of the independent variables represented by X. Based on the theoretical considerations in the previous section, the following explanatory variables are used, in both the enrollment and the high school completion regressions:

Age = age of individual respondent in years, 1980;

Immigrated 1975–79 = 1 if respondent foreign born and immigrated to the U.S. during the period 1975–1979, 0 otherwise;

Immigrated Pre-1975 = 1 if respondent foreign born and immigrated to the U.S. sometime before 1975, 0 otherwise;

English Spoken At Home = 1 if only English is spoken in the respondent's home, 0 otherwise;

Family Below Poverty Line = 1 if total family income in 1979 (or unrelated individual income) was below the 1979 poverty level set by the Census Bureau, 0 otherwise;

Married = 1 if respondent now married (not separated), 0 otherwise;

Children = total number of children ever born to female respondent;

Weeks Unemployed Last Year = total number of weeks in 1979 that the respondent was unemployed, available for and seeking work;

South = 1 if respondent now resident in a southern state, 0 otherwise;

Rate of Return to High School = local posttax rate of return to completion of 12 years of school, in percent;

Rate of Return to College = local posttax rate of return to starting college (completion of 13 or more years), in percent;

Educ. Expenditures Per Pupil = Average real educational expenditures, per pupil-hour of attendance, in respondent's state;

Mexican = 1 if respondent of Mexican origin, 0 otherwise;

Cuban = 1 if respondent of Cuban origin, 0 otherwise;

Other Latin American = 1 if respondent of Latin American origin (other than Mexican or Cuban), 0 otherwise;

Other Hispanic = 1 if respondent of Spanish origin (but not Latin American or Puerto Rican), 0 otherwise.

Three variables in particular require some additional explanation, as they are not contained in the raw census microdata but rather had to be constructed. The Rate of Return to High School Completion in each SMSA was calculated by equating the present value of the posttax benefits to the present value of the costs and solving for the internal rate of return. Separate values were computed for males and females, and for white non-Hispanics and Hispanics, to take into account the differential returns to schooling for these groups revealed by previous studies. The benefits were estimated for each sex/national-origin group for five age levels (18–24, 25–34, 35–44, 45–54, and 55–64) as the difference between the mean posttax earnings of persons in an SMSA who completed four years of high school and the posttax earnings of others in that SMSA who completed one to three years of high school. The opportunity cost of finishing high school was the mean posttax earnings of persons in each sex/national-origin group of each SMSA who were 18 to 24 years old and had only 1 to 3 years of high school. The earnings figures were calculated directly from the census microdata and adjusted for federal and state income taxes (from U.S. Bureau of the Census, 1981) based on current marital status.

The Rate of Return to Starting College was also calculated separately at the SMSA level by sex and ethnicity. The benefits used to compute the internal rate of return were estimated for four age levels (25–34, 35–44, 45–54, and 55–64) as the difference between the posttax mean earnings of persons having one or more years of college and the posttax mean earnings of persons who completed only high school. The costs were estimated as the sum of both opportunity costs and direct costs. Opportunity costs were estimated as the posttax earnings of otherwise comparable persons ages 18–24 who had completed only high school. Direct costs were estimated in a manner similar to Mattila's (1982) methodology: for each state the annual average amount of student financial aid per full-time student was subtracted from the annual average cost of tuition and fees per full-time student.[18]

As a very rough proxy for school quality, Educational Expenditures Per Pupil were drawn from state-level data on the average annual spending on public elementary and secondary day schools per pupil-hour of attendance. The data are available in U.S. Department of Education (1981).

Estimation Results

Mean values of all regression variables are presented in Table 7.6. Among 16–17-year-old youth in major metropolitan areas, 9 out of 10 white non-Hispanics were enrolled in school in the 1980 census week, but only about 8 out of 10 Hispanics. The disparity in graduation rates from high school is far larger: while 72 percent of

TABLE 7.6. Means of Selected Explanatory Factors of Enrollment, Youths Ages 16–17 and 18–19, 1980

	Males, 16–17		Females, 16–17		Males, 18–19		Females, 18–19	
	Anglo	Hispanic	Anglo	Hispanic	Anglo	Hispanic	Anglo	Hispanic
Enrolled in School	.923	.816	.904	.801	.459	.462	.431	.459
Immigrated 1975–79	.004	.112	.003	.100	.004	.087	.006	.073
Immigrated pre-1975	.010	.169	.013	.183	.019	.207	.014	.202
English Spoken at Home	.962	.304	.950	.260	.957	.324	.951	.325
Below Poverty Line	.062	.245	.065	.259	.066	.139	.107	.171
Married	.007	.013	.029	.075	.044	.050	.136	.115
Weeks Unemployed Last Year	1.92	2.18	1.32	1.45	2.80	3.73	2.59	3.06

SOURCE: 1980 Census Public Use Microdata Samples. Sample members in SMSAs of populations >500,000.

Anglo males and 74 percent of females ages 16–19 completed high school, this was true of only 42 percent of Hispanic males and 49 percent of Hispanic females. Less than 3 percent of non-Hispanics were foreign born, compared with one-third of Hispanic females and nearly two-fifths of Hispanic males. In only one-fourth of Hispanic families is English the sole language. And Hispanic families are more than twice as likely to have incomes below the poverty line as white non-Hispanics.

The logit coefficient estimates of the enrollment model and the high school completion model are in Appendix Tables 7A.1 and 7A.2, respectively. Since logit coefficients are not directly interpretable in the same manner as OLS coefficients, simulations were conducted to estimate the marginal contribution of each explanatory variable to the probabilities of enrollment and of graduation. The simulations were performed under two different conditions: first, for an individual assigned the average values of the independent variables characteristic of white non-Hispanics; second, for the individual assigned the mean characteristics of Puerto Ricans (i.e., the dummy variables for the other national-origin groups were set to 0).

The simulation results for the enrollment model are shown in Table 7.7. In brief, the results reveal consistently negative and significant effects on the enrollment probabilities of both Anglos and Hispanics, males and females of four factors: age, low family income, marriage, and unemployment last year. Early pregnancy also has a significantly negative effect for Hispanics and non-Hispanics alike in the female regressions. These results lend support to previous research findings that family background and marital responsibilities are important factors increasing high school dropout rates. The negative sign on the lagged unemployment variable suggests that enrollment tends to be procyclical, since longer spells of joblessness are generated in loose labor markets. It would seem that the income effect of cyclical contractions on enrollment outweighs the price effect here. The estimated coefficients of the two immigration variables are also negative and highly significant for Hispanic youth, but not for non-Hispanics. Immigration within the last five years is associated with a much stronger negative effect on enrollment than arrival over five years ago. This is consistent with the view expressed before that the adjustment difficulties of the immediate postmigration period may disrupt the continuity of teenagers' schooling. This finding is of some consequence for explaining Hispanics' higher dropout rates, since over half of the foreign-born teenagers were in the most recent entry cohort.

In no case were the rate of return to schooling variables found to have a statistically significant impact and the signs of the coefficients were negative as often as positive. Some caution is needed before interpreting this finding as counterevidence to human capital arguments about the central importance of such rates. It may be that the limited variability in inter-SMSA rates in the cross-section is behind these weak estimates.

Likewise, the insignificant coefficient estimates of per-pupil educational expenditures may tell us more about the limited nature of interstate differences in such expenditures than about the actual importance of interschool differences in resources and instructional quality. Were SMSA-level data available for this variable the estimates might be improved. But there is still another problem: as Linda Edwards (1975) notes in explaining her similar findings for this variable in nonwhite enroll-

TABLE 7.7. Predicted Probabilities of Enrollment and Effects
of Personal and Economic Factors, Persons Ages 16–17, 1980

	Males		Females	
	Anglo	*Hispanic*	*Anglo*	*Hispanic*
ANGLO CHARACTERISTICS				
Predicted Probability	.9435	.8488	.9933	.9777
Age	−.0356**	−.0987**	−.0052**	−.0132**
Immigrated, 1975–79	.1468	−.2730**	−.0072	−.0385**
Immigrated, Pre-1975	.0210	−.0841**	−.0069	−.0096**
English Spoken at Home	.0438*	−.0242	−.0028	.0026
Income < Poverty Level	−.0800**	−.0658**	−.0098**	−.0169**
Married	−.1370**	−.2282**	−.0200**	−.0491**
Children			−.0146**	−.0282**
Weeks Unemployed	−.0028**	−.0044**	−.0004**	−.0028*
South	−.0040	−.0226	−.0005	.0049
Rate of Return, H.S.	−.0021	.0004	−.00001	.0003
Rate of Return, College	−.0004	−.0023	−.0001	.0003
Educ. Expenditures	.0007	.0058	.0001	.0003
DISADVANTAGED HISPANIC CHARACTERISTICS				
Predicted Probability	.6616	.0634	.0883	.0904
Age	−.1500**	−.0457**	−.0633**	−.0499**
Immigrated, 1975–79	.6175	−.1263**	−.0877	−.1452**
Immigrated, Pre-1975	.0882	−.0389**	−.0833	−.0363**
English Spoken at Home	.1845*	−.0112	−.0343	.0096
Income < Poverty Level	−.3361**	−.0305**	−.1188**	−.0638**
Married	−.5764**	−.1056**	−.2424**	−.1854**
Children			−.1761**	−.1064**
Weeks Unemployed	−.0116**	−.0020**	−.0045**	−.0014*
South	−.0168	−.0104	−.0064	.0186
Rate of Return, H.S.	−.0087	.0002	−.0001	.0011
Rate of Return, College	−.0018	−.0011	−.0018	.0011
Educ. Expenditures	.0029	.0027	.0017	.0011

NOTE: *p < .05; **p < .01. Calculations based on mean values of continuous variables and modal values of categorical variables in Table 7.6 and logit coefficients from Table 7A.1. "Disadvantaged Hispanics" are recent married migrants in poor families.

ment regressions, no race-specific (much less ethnic-specific) expenditure measures are published. Given the high degree of school segregation of minorities and the lower average expenditures per-pupil characteristic of predominantly minority schools, this is a nontrivial problem here. If errors in measurement of the Educational Expenditures variable are not constant but random, this could result in an even greater downward bias in the coefficient estimates.

The coefficient estimates for the high school completion model (Table 7.8) bear great similarity to those of the enrollment model. Poverty-level family incomes, marriage, early pregnancy, and higher unemployment all exert highly significant negative effects on the probability of graduation for Hispanics and non-Hispanics

TABLE 7.8. Predicted Probabilities of High School Completion and Effects
of Personal and Economic Factors, Persons Ages 16–19, 1980

	Males		Females	
	Anglo	Hispanic	Anglo	Hispanic
ANGLO CHARACTERISTICS				
Predicted Probability	.7681	.5178	.9567	.9331
Age	.1934**	.2115**	.0406**	.0579**
Immigrated, 1975–79	.0044	−.3720**	−.0176	−.0796**
Immigrated, Pre-1975	−.0265	−.0826*	−.0466*	−.0262*
English Spoken at Home	−.0337	.0786*	−.0198	.0294**
Income < Poverty Level	−.1274**	−.1356**	−.0256**	−.0490**
Married	−.1538**	−.2861**	−.0272**	−.0550**
Children			−.0582**	−.0758**
Weeks Unemployed	−.0087**	−.0055**	−.0012**	−.0009*
South	−.0109	.0377	−.0052	−.0092
Rate of Return, H.S.	−.0053	−.0090	−.00004	−.0005
Rate of Return, College	.0009	.0010	.0003	.0001
Educ. Expenditures	.0057*	.0030	.0014*	.0005
DISADVANTAGED HISPANIC CHARACTERISTICS				
Predicted Probability	.4007	.0285	.5691	.1039
Age	.2608**	.0234**	.2401**	.0864**
Immigrated, 1975–79	.0060	−.0412**	−.1044	−.1187**
Immigrated, Pre-1975	−.0358	−.0092*	−.2761*	−.0390*
English Spoken at Home	−.0454	.0087*	−.1172	.0438**
Income < Poverty Level	−.1717**	−.0150**	−.1515**	−.0731**
Married	−.2060**	−.0317**	−.1611**	−.0827**
Children			−.3443**	−.1130**
Weeks Unemployed	−.0118**	−.0006**	−.0071**	−.0014*
South	−.0146	.0042	−.0309	−.0137
Rate of Return, H.S.	−.0072	−.0010	−.0002	−.0007
Rate of Return, College	.0012	.0001	.0017	.0001
Educ. Expenditures	.0077	.0003	.0083*	−.0007

NOTE: *p < .05; **p < .01. Calculations based on mean values of continuous variables and modal values of categorical variables in Table 7.6, and logit coefficients from Table 7A.2. "Disadvantaged Hispanics" are recent married migrants in poor families.

alike. And among Hispanics the foreign born are significantly less likely to graduate, particularly if they are recent immigrants. Unlike the enrollment findings, however, the home language variable has statistically significant implications for Hispanics here. Youth from families in which only English is spoken are more likely to complete high school than those from Spanish-speaking households.

Finally, a fairly consistent result emerges from comparing the predicted probabilities of enrollment and of graduation when the assigned characteristics are alternately those of white non-Hispanics and Hispanics. For example, in the enrollment simulations (Table 7.7) the Anglo male regressions and Anglo characteristics produce a predicted enrollment probability of 94 percent, compared with the prediction of only 76 percent enrollment in the Hispanic coefficients-characteristics case. Once we assign Hispanics the same average characteristics as non-Hispanics, there is a significant improvement in their enrollment probability to 81 percent. But the remaining gap is clearly still very large. The same partial reduction in the male Anglo–Hispanic gap emerges from the graduation simulations in Table 7.8. For women, however, it appears that Hispanics with the same characteristics as non-Hispanics can be expected to have much more similar probabilities of staying in school and graduating.

Conclusion

Recent years have witnessed growing concern in the United States over the persistence of wide educational inequalities between whites and minority groups. Hispanics are still today far less likely than other Americans to complete high school or to attend college. In fact, the Hispanic dropout rate is now twice that of blacks and almost three times that of white youth. But relatively little is known about the schooling problems of Spanish-origin youth.

After tracing recent time-series trends in educational achievement, this chapter discussed the principal explanatory factors that have been proposed in the literature. Two models were then developed to gauge the relative importance to high school enrollment and graduation probabilities of human capital, family background, and labor market factors. The empirical analysis was conducted separately for males and females, subdivided by Spanish origin. The models were tested on a large 1980 census microdata bank using maximum likelihood logit regression techniques.

The principal results are that, first, low probabilities of high school enrollment and graduation appear to be most strongly affected by low parental income, high youth employment, early marriage and/or pregnancy, and (at least among Hispanic youth) recent immigration. Next, the findings did not suggest that internal rates of return to schooling play a significant role in accounting for differences in dropout or graduation rates, at least in the cross-section. Finally, simulation experiments suggested that Anglo–Hispanic differences in measured characteristics explain only a limited portion of the sizable schooling differences among males. This points to the great complexity of the many interrelated factors behind schooling differentials and the need for improved modeling and data sets to try to better account for some of the most potentially important, such as school quality, student performance, and discrimination.

Appendix

TABLE 7A.1. Logit Estimates of School Enrollment Equations,
Anglos and Hispanics, Ages 16–17, 1980

Independent Variables	Males		Females	
	Anglo	Hispanic	Anglo	Hispanic
Age	−.670	−.769	−.786	−.607
	(3.628)	(6.318)	(4.178)	(4.750)
Immigrated, 1975–79	2.758	−2.127	−1.089	−1.766
	(1.359)	(11.388)	(0.870)	(8.350)
Immigrated, pre-1975	.394	−.655	−1.035	−.441
	(0.418)	(3.448)	(1.520)	(2.216)
English Spoken at Home	.824	−.189	−.426	.117
	(1.989)	(0.946)	(0.866)	(0.704)
Income < Poverty Level	−1.501	−.513	−1.476	−.775
	(5.488)	(3.794)	(5.260)	(5.613)
Married	−2.574	−1.778	−3.011	−2.254
	(3.730)	(4.197)	(6.969)	(9.810)
Children			−2.187	−1.294
			(3.808)	(6.780)
Weeks Unemployed Last Year	−.052	−.034	−.056	−.017
	(5.823)	(5.415)	(4.854)	(2.025)
South	−.075	−.176	−.080	.226
	(0.311)	(0.946)	(0.327)	(1.027)
Rate of Return, High School	−.039	.003	−.001	.040
	(1.516)	(0.107)	(1.232)	(1.990)
Rate of Return, College	−.008	−.018	−.022	.013
	(0.206)	(0.819)	(0.698)	(0.504)
Educ. Expenditures Per Pupil	.013	.045	.021	.013
	(0.794)	(2.523)	(1.205)	(0.744)
Mexican		.492		−.063
		(2.228)		(0.267)
Cuban		1.315		1.170
		(3.816)		(3.105)
Other Latin Amer.		1.716		1.393
		(5.583)		(4.394)
Other Hispanic		.510		.479
		(1.870)		(1.570)
Constant	13.144	13.518	18.087	13.247
	(4.153)	(6.417)	(5.594)	(5.995)
−2 X Log Likelihood	747.17	1733.25	703.04	1554.42
N of Cases	1521	2105	1430	2075

NOTE: Dependent Variable: Probability individual, age 16–17, enrolled in school. Asymptotic T-ratios are in parentheses. Among Hispanics, Puerto Ricans are the excluded reference group.

SOURCE: 1980 Census Public Use Microdata Samples. Sample members in SMSAs of populations >500,000.

TABLE 7A.2. Logit Estimates of High School Completion Equations,
Anglos and Hispanics, Ages 16–19, 1980

Independent Variables	Males		Females	
	Anglo	Hispanic	Anglo	Hispanic
Age	1.086	.847	.979	.928
	(11.197)	(12.770)	(10.632)	(14.248)
Immigrated, 1975–79	.025	−1.490	−.426	−1.275
	(0.028)	(8.638)	(0.492)	(6.976)
Immigrated, Pre-1975	−.149	−.331	−1.126	−.419
	(0.261)	(2.009)	(2.144)	(2.490)
English Spoken at Home	−.189	.315	−.478	.471
	(0.490)	(2.308)	(1.228)	(3.328)
Income < Poverty Level	−.715	−.543	−.618	−.785
	(3.123)	(4.107)	(3.013)	(6.165)
Married	−.858	−1.146	−.657	−.881
	(2.809)	(5.871)	(3.273)	(6.024)
Children			−1.404	−1.214
			(6.967)	(10.072)
Weeks Unemployed	−.049	−.022	−.029	−.015
	(6.352)	(4.131)	(3.295)	(2.500)
South	−.061	.151	−.126	−.147
	(0.308)	(0.938)	(0.633)	(0.780)
Rate of Return, High School	−.030	−.036	−.001	−.008
	(1.386)	(1.643)	(1.354)	(0.431)
Rate of Return, College	.005	.004	.007	.001
	(0.189)	(0.215)	(0.311)	(0.024)
Educ. Expenditures Per Pupil	.032	.012	.034	−.008
	(2.269)	(0.776)	(2.301)	(0.520)
Mexican		.284		−.174
		(1.475)		(0.909)
Cuban		1.325		.947
		(4.512)		(3.213)
Other Latin Amer.		1.434		1.039
		(5.618)		(4.074)
Other Hispanic		.889		.330
		(3.643)		(1.357)
Constant	−19.037	−15.840	−15.214	−14.616
	(10.314)	(12.204)	(8.770)	(11.547)
−2 X Log Likelihood	1152.33	2152.41	1106.89	2041.27
N of Cases	1157	1939	1199	2021

NOTE: Asymptotic T-ratios are in parentheses. Dependent Variable: Probability of high school completion among persons ages 16–19. Among Hispanics, Puerto Ricans are the excluded reference group.

SOURCE: 1980 Census Public Use Microdata Samples. Sample members in SMSAs of populations >500,000.

NOTES

1. The report, commissioned by the U.S. Department of Education, concluded that: "If an unfriendly foreign power had attempted to impose on America the mediocre educational performance that exists today, we might well have viewed it as an act of war. As it stands, we have allowed this to happen to ourselves. We have even squandered the gains in student achievement made in the wake of the Sputnik challenge. Moreover, we have dismantled essential support systems which helped make these gains possible." National Commission on Excellence in Education (1983; p. 5).

2. Quote and test results from Neuffer (1987).

3. U.S. Department of Education (1987).

4. For a recent survey of research on educational production functions and earnings functions, see Rosen (1977).

5. Becker himself assigned a far more explicit role to cost factors than most others of the human capital school, at least in one instance. His Woytinsky Lecture (added to the second edition of *Human Capital* in 1975) sketched a more complete supply-demand framework in which the optimal volume of investment in schooling was said to be that at which the marginal rate of return from the last increment was just equal to its marginal financing cost.

6. Educational cost data are from U.S. Department of Education (1987) and family income data are from U.S. Bureau of the Census (1987b).

7. For data on federal aid to higher education see U.S. Department of Education (1987).

8. See, for example: Blau and Duncan (1967); Hill and Stafford (1977); Mare (1980); and Masters (1969).

9. See the empirical findings in Waite and Moore (1978).

10. See, for example, Linda Edwards (1976).

11. 1980 census figures, presented in Table 2.2.

12. See Osborne (1976), Quintero (1972), and U.S. Department of Commerce (1979).

13. 1980 estimate, from U.S. Bureau of the Census (1987b). For research findings on bilingual education, see Duran (1983); Fishman and Keller (1982); and Von Maltitz (1975).

14. See U.S. Bureau of the Census (1984b) for this and the following set of 1980 statistics on average characteristics of non-Hispanic whites and of Hispanic ethnic groups in this section.

15. See, for example, Fligstein and Fernandez (1985).

16. For details on census variables and sample design, see U.S. Bureau of the Census (1983b).

17. For a discussion of the properties of logit, see Amemiya (1981).

18. U.S. Department of Education (1979a, 1979b).

8

Does Immigration Harm
Native Workers?

Few subjects have sparked more heated public debate in recent years than Hispanic immigration to the United States. At the heart of the debate are two key questions. First, do immigrants impose added burdens on native taxpayers by their use of income transfer programs and social services? And second, do they depress the earnings and employment prospects of indigenous workers by competing with them for jobs? These questions have been asked frequently throughout American history. The most intense period of controversy and research was during the peak years of immigration at the turn of the century. But the ethnocentric national origins quota system imposed by Congress in 1921 and 1924 caused a sharp reduction in annual inflows, as well as a marked decline in academic interest. Thereafter, economic analysis of migration was largely confined to internal redistributions of population from the South to the North and from farm to city. The research on international migration that continued was almost exclusively concerned with sociocultural assimilation and refugees.

The dramatic shifts in the volume and composition of immigrant admissions after abolition of the quota system in 1965 changed all of this. The foreign-born population jumped from 9.6 million in 1970 to 14 million by the time of the 1980 census—the largest intercensal increase in half a century. The new immigrants have increasingly been from Asia and Central and South America. Between the 1950s and the 1970s, the share of all immigrants from Asia rose sixfold to 36 percent and the Latin American percentage nearly doubled to 40 percent. In the same period, the fraction from Europe declined from three-fifths to less than one-fifth. The Latin American share is commonly thought to have grown far larger than these admissions figures indicate, owing to the high and rapidly rising volume of illegal entrants said to be arriving from Mexico and a handful of other countries. Authoritative estimates of their number have ranged all the way from 4 to 25 million.

By the late seventies, concern about the "illegal alien problem" and its possible relationship to the chronic stagflation gripping the economy prompted a lengthy series of congressional hearings and a two-year study by the Select Commission on Immigration and Refugee Policy. These inquiries revealed the paucity of systematic up-to-date evidence on the economic consequences of the post-1965 inflows, thereby helping to generate a new and ongoing wave of research by economists in the 1980s.

In what follows, I both discuss the principal findings from these new studies and report the results of my own analysis of Hispanic immigration's effects on the public assistance system and on native workers' earnings and unemployment.

The Magnitude of Migration

In order to assess the economic consequences of immigration it is first necessary to have an accurate sense of its volume and characteristics. Severe data limitations and the politically charged nature of the issue have often combined to create misleading impressions about the size of the immigrant population (particularly its undocumented component) and its relative importance to national population and labor force growth.

In each decade of the postwar period, the average number of legal immigrants arriving annually has risen, from 251,500 in the 1950s to 332,200 in the sixties, 449,300 in the seventies, and nearly 600,000 in the 1980s. This is part of the reason that the share of new immigrants in net U.S. population growth has increased, from only 11 percent in the fifties to 19.1 percent in the 1970s. While a substantial contribution, this is still only half as large as the share accounted for by new foreign admissions at the turn of the century. In two out of three years from 1900 to 1914, immigration exceeded 800,000 annually, and in six of these years it was more than 1 million. In contrast to this period, recent increases in immigration's contribution to population growth are far more the result of low indigenous fertility than historically high levels of immigration. The slowing of native growth rates assures that racial minorities and immigrants will account for a rising fraction of the population in the foreseeable future. But even assuming no increase in the total fertility rate above its very low level (1.8 births per woman), net immigration of 500,000 in every year from 1980 to 2030 would raise the foreign-born share of the overall population to less than 12 percent.[1]

By international standards, the fraction of immigrants in the U.S. population in 1970 (4.7 percent) was far below that of such countries as Australia, Canada, France, Sweden, and Switzerland. In the latter country, about one-sixth of the total population and one-fourth of the Swiss labor force were immigrants throughout most of the late sixties and the seventies. Despite efforts to induce migrant workers to return home from 1974 on, increased entry by other family members over the decade kept the foreign-born fraction of the European population well above the U.S. figure (6.2 percent by 1980). Although some of these countries experienced relatively slower economic growth and higher unemployment rates during the seventies, others generally performed much better than the United States. These circumstances suggest that, rather than presuming some simple, determinate relationship between immigration and various economic indicators, it is essential to take into account the specific historical and institutional features of each country's labor market to understand its particular experience with immigration.

One problem in making historical and intercountry comparisons is that the published figures on legal admissions will be an unreliable indicator of total immigration the greater the number of illegal entrants. The now common perception that the number of undocumented aliens is large and rapidly growing appears to have begun to gain currency in the mid-1970s. Throughout most of the previous two decades, illegal immigration was not a prominent issue. This was due in part to the *bracero* agreement with Mexico, which, from 1942 to its expiration in 1964, provided a legal structure for satisfying the demands of southwestern growers for seasonal farm labor. In addition, the INS's widely publicized Operation Wetback in 1954 succeeded in deporting over 1 million people and intimidated thousands more to leave voluntarily. In the following decade, the number of aliens apprehended fell to an average of only 92,800 per year and the "illegal immigration problem" faded from the public consciousness.[2]

However, by the mid-1970s the robust economy of the late sixties had given way to the highest unemployment levels recorded up to that time in the postwar period. Into the national debate on the causes of this economic decline stepped Leonard Chapman, INS commissioner in the second Nixon administration, with the dramatic claim that at least 1 million jobs had been stolen from native-born workers by undocumented foreigners. In well-publicized testimony before a series of congressional committees, Chapman asserted that an ongoing "silent invasion" had brought from 6 to as many as 12 million illegal residents into the country by 1974. As evidence he pointed to the steady increases in the number of annual INS apprehensions, despite little or no expansion in the border patrol. Indeed, the number of apprehensions did jump sevenfold from 1965 to 1975 and those captured were said by border agents to represent only one-third to one-half of the total illegal influx.

But as the apprehension figures rose (to over 1 million by 1977), so also did the skepticism of economists and demographers about their value as an indicator of the size or composition of the undocumented population. This population is composed of two main groups: persons entering without inspection (known as "EWIs") and those others arriving with illicit documents or overstaying the terms of their admission. The heavy concentration of INS personnel along the southern border has unquestionably led to an undercount of visa abusers and an overstatement of the Mexican share of the undocumented total. Independent research suggests that the former, most arriving by ship or plane, may now be a substantial fraction of the total and are more likely to be non-Mexican and female than those crossing the land border.[3]

The INS arrest data are an equally unreliable gauge of the volume of illegal entry, not only because they inevitably reflect fluctuations in agency staffing and patrolling, but because they are inflated by multiple counts of repeat offenders. Since it is by now well established that many Mexican migrants are sojourners, frequently crossing the border on a seasonal or even daily basis, the degree of bias from multiple counting is probably severe.

The highly speculative nature of the INS figures was fully recognized by the Select Commission on Immigration and Refugee Policy, established by Congress in 1978 to conduct a comprehensive, three-year evaluation of immigration data and policies. Its review of both the INS estimates and the handful of existing studies by private researchers and the Mexican government concluded:

> There are currently no reliable estimates of the number of illegal residents in the country or of the net volume of immigration to the United States in any recent past period. Even if we disregard the more conjectural of the estimates of illegal residents . . . , we cannot confidently accept the results of the analytic and empirical studies. They characteristically depend on broad untested assumptions and are subject to other major limitations.[4]

Nevertheless, as time and budget constraints prevented the commission from undertaking its own data collection and estimation, it was forced to rely on the same questionable studies to make an "educated inference" that the number of illegal residents in the late 1970s was between 3.5 and 6 million.

Since then, however, the early conjectural figures have given way to far smaller estimates. In 1983, Census Bureau demographers employed a residual methodology to calculate the number of the undocumented enumerated in the 1980 census.[5] The number of aliens legally resident in the country at the census date (estimated largely from annual alien I-53 registration records) was subtracted from the total number of aliens in the census (adjusted for overstatement of native-born status and naturalization). Their conclusion: about 2.057 million of the 7.44 million aliens counted in the census were undocumented.

Of course, our uncertainty about how many were actually counted requires viewing this figure as a lower bound on the illegal population. But the Census Bureau's intensive efforts, in both the design and field stages of the 1980 census, to locate previously undercounted minorities and aliens appear to have achieved an unprecedented expansion in coverage. Follow-up studies have found that few housing units were missed and that undercoverage of the resident population was on the order of only 1 percent.[6] Even if the highest undercount rate found to date (one-sixth, for black males in their thirties) was assumed to hold for undocumented aliens as well, it would increase their estimated number to only 2.4 million—far below the typical guesstimates long accepted as authoritative.[7]

Of all undocumented migrants counted in 1980, 1.13 million (55 percent of the total) were from Mexico. This is consistent with Bean, King, and Passel's estimate of the number of Mexicans "missing" from the 1980 Mexican census. The rest of Central America and the Caribbean accounted for another 324,000, Asia for 213,000, and Europe for 150,000.[8]

With the enactment of the 1986 Immigration and Reform Act, the numbers debate entered a new phase. In addition to its penalties for employers knowingly hiring the undocumented, it offered legal status to qualified aliens who applied for amnesty. The details of the act were discussed in chapter 2. By the end of the amnesty period a total of 3 million had applied for legalization. Given the likelihood of additional illegal entry as the Mexican economic crisis worsened in the early 1980s, this number does not seem inconsistent with the census-based estimate for 1980.

Will IRCA succeed in stemming further illegal inflows? The INS points to the 42 percent drop in apprehended aliens between 1986 and 1988 as evidence that the law has been effective in reducing American firms' demand for undocumented workers and lowered the incentive for these workers to attempt illegal entry. Critics have contended that the reduced apprehensions could simply reflect the diversion of INS staff to drug enforcement activities and the increase in the numbers of formerly illegal migrants who are now able to cross the border legally since being amnestied. To test these counterclaims, Bean, White, and Espenshade (1989) used multivariate analysis to estimate the number of monthly apprehensions likely to have occurred in 1987 and 1988 in the absence of IRCA. Controlling for such variables as the distribution of INS resources, Mexican population growth and relative economic conditions, and seasonal factors, they estimated that IRCA was associated with a net reduction in apprehensions of 35 percent. The authors view this reduction as a significant impact, but they are also well aware of the limitations of the INS apprehensions series as an indicator of the true volume of illegal entry.

Other insights on IRCA's initial effects are emerging from survey research on potential migrants in Mexico and on employers in the United States. Based on information from a large interview sample in west-central Mexico in 1988–89, Cornelius (1990a) found both widespread knowledge of IRCA and a widespread conviction that jobs were still attainable across the border. Since the law went into effect, bogus documents (e.g., U.S. "green cards" and Social Security cards) had proliferated and fallen in price (to an average of about $50). The large proportion of interviewees with networks of friends and relatives already in the United States indicated that they could rely on getting prearranged jobs with or without genuine work papers. The survey also produced evidence of two developments with poten- tially quite important consequences in the future. First, earlier migrants whose status was legalized in the amnesty program appeared to be turning away from the pattern of frequent shuttle movements back and forth to their hometowns in favor of long-term settlement in the United States. As a result, there also appears to be a new wave of first-time illegal in-migration by women and children attempting to join the male family members who have obtained legal status.

In another field study undertaken by the Center for U.S.–Mexican Studies (University of California, San Diego) in three southern California counties from May 1987 to June 1988, employer interviews were conducted at a sample of 105 nonagricultural firms (Cornelius, 1990b). The firms were selected from the original universe of enterprises in which at least 25 percent of production jobs had been held by Mexicans in 1983–84 (the first phase of the study). These firms had become "immigrant dependent" for a variety of reasons. One group consisted of companies set up by Mexican immigrants or second-generation Mexican Americans who fol- lowed a policy of "hire your own" and often largely served Mexican customers. Another category relied on immigrants for special skills in short supply among native workers. For example, the California shoe and leather industry has long depended on luring skilled workers away from their jobs in the Mexican shoe firms clustered in Guadalajara and Leon. Another group of firms rely on immigrants for low-skilled jobs widely unappealing to natives in such industries as hotels, building maintenance, and poultry processing.

Regardless of industry, 95 percent of the employers said they were routinely requiring job applicants to show them the documents required by IRCA. But there was little evidence that the law was altering their demand for immigrant labor. Only 7 percent anticipated that they would have to scale back their operations because of the law, and most did not feel the need for strategies (e.g., subcontracting or shifting work abroad) to circumvent IRCA. There was neither a pattern of mass layoffs nor any significant surge in job quits by the undocumented. In fact, from interviews with undocumented workers at the firms surveyed, the researchers found that only 15 percent contemplated quitting because of the new law.

Impacts on the Public Transfer System

Though it appears likely that the number of aliens illegally resident in the United States is much smaller than earlier thought, there are still grounds for concern about their potential economic impact. Nearly half of the undocumented in 1980 were concentrated in a single state, California, and seven out of eight were concentrated in only 10 states.[9] Over 45 percent were in the most recent entry cohort (1975–80), thought by the labor substitution school to pose the greatest employment threat to native-born workers. In fact, undocumented migrants from Spanish-speaking nations accounted for 53.7 percent of all immigrants (legal and illegal) who arrived in the years 1975–80.

Any population's degree of reliance on government income-support programs is inversely related to nontransfer family income levels. Nontransfer incomes are dominated by labor earnings, particularly at low income levels. Native–immigrant differences in labor market outcomes thereby explain the bulk of their differences in program participation. How then do the native and the foreign born compare in their earnings patterns?

Comparative Earnings Patterns

This question dominated the initial research by economists during the first few years of the profession's revived interest in immigration in the late 1970s. In a series of influential papers, Chiswick (1978, 1980) made extensive use of 1970 census data to compare the annual earnings of native- and foreign-born adult men resident in the United States. Individual wages in 1969 were regressed on such variables as educational attainment, years of work experience, and marital status, as well as a set of dummy variables indicating whether the individual was foreign born and, if so, the period of immigration. From the estimated coefficients, wage differentials were predicted according to duration of U.S. residence. Chiswick reported that, among white males, foreign-born workers in the United States under five years earned 10 percent less than comparable native-born workers. But after about 13 years, the foreign born attained the native level and, by their twentieth year in this country, received 6 percent higher wages. Likewise, within separate black, Mexican, and Filipino male subsamples, the "overtaking point" of native by immigrant earnings was said to occur after about 10 to 15 years of entry.

Rather different results emerged from studies of wage differences among women. DeFreitas (1979) and Long (1980) both found, from regression analyses of 1970 census microdata, that most groups of female immigrants tended to begin employment in the United States at somewhat higher earnings levels than otherwise similar native-born women. However, due to immigrants' slower rate of wage growth with more experience, the differential narrows over time.

Subsequent research exploited the greater detail on year of immigration, fluency in English, and foreign schooling contained in the 1976 Survey of Income and Education (SIE), which only became available to most researchers in the early 1980s. Reimers's (1985) analysis of real 1975 wages confirmed the pattern of overtaking by foreign-born men, but only over a time period nearly twice as long as that found in the studies of 1969 wages. Black and other Hispanic migrants exhibited a more erratic pattern, with the newest arrivals actually earning more than comparable natives. Among females, at least one immigrant cohort among non-Hispanic whites and blacks and Hispanics was found to have higher wages than otherwise similar native women. A pattern of rising wage levels with increased duration of U.S. residence was identified, but the rate of progress seemed far less consistent than in the earlier studies. Among white non-Hispanic and Cuban women, the highest immigrant wages were for those who had only entered the country within the last five years.

How can these earnings patterns be explained? According to Chiswick: "the theoretical analysis of the economic progress of immigrants is based on two key concepts—the international transferability of skills acquired in the country of origin and the self-selection of immigrants" (1980, p. 6). Skill transferability is expected to be greatest for those from advanced economies, especially those with English as the native tongue, and for those migrating for economic reasons rather than for family or refugee motives. To the extent that the skills acquired in foreign schools and jobs are country-specific, the lower will be the partial effects of schooling and work experience on earnings in the United States, and the lower will be immigrant earnings relative to the native born during the first few years after arrival. If employers have difficulty evaluating foreign credentials and regard migrants as more transient individuals, they will be less likely to risk giving them firm-specific training. Hence, the initial entry period will be characterized by primarily general training, thereby steepening the wage profile. The ability of some immigrants to overcome early obstacles and ultimately overtake the earnings level of comparable natives is attributed to the generally higher motivation and, perhaps, ability of immigrants. Carliner (1980) has developed this argument at length, claiming that migrants reveal by their willingness to move that they place lower value on family and social ties and higher value on the economic returns expected by migration. If they are thus more motivated to succeed economically than others in the sending country, they may also be more motivated than nonmigrants in the host country and this could be reflected in their higher earnings.

These explanations have been criticized for focusing too narrowly on the individual migrant, exaggerating the role of personal attributes like motivation. The difficulties of skill transference, particularly from the Third World, are not denied. In fact, while human capital theorists have only inferred these difficulties from their regression estimates, most of what is actually known about skill transference comes from sociological case studies, such as Senior and Manley's (1955) work on return migrants in Jamaica, Wright's (1968) surveys of British firms in the Midlands, and Moncarz's (1973) survey of occupational mobility among Cuban-trained professionals in Miami. But, in contrast to human capital theory, researchers taking a more structural view emphasize the economic advantages afforded most migrants by the support networks that characterize chain migration.[10]

The relative earnings growth of the foreign born can, of course, change over time as the state of the economy and the composition of the immigrant work force changes. Borjas (1985) made use of newly available 1980 census microdata to compare specific immigrant cohorts in 1970 and 1980. He concluded that, contrary to the earlier results based on the 1970 census cross-section, the wage growth of individual migrant cohorts during the seventies did not significantly exceed that of the native born. He interprets this as evidence that more recent entrants tend to have lower worker "quality" than earlier cohorts, perhaps due to the 1965 changes in admissions criteria. But Chiswick (1986) studied the same two census data sets, together with the 1976 SIE, using a somewhat different methodology, and concluded that there was little change in the earnings profiles of foreign-born whites compared to the earlier period and some improvement for those of Asian immigrants. This issue will no doubt require more than just these two exploratory studies before it can be resolved.

Whatever the effects of the post-1965 policy of allocating more places for family reunification, the amendments also reserved 10 percent or more of admissions for persons with skills needed in the United States and erased long-standing barriers to Asian immigration. The result was an enormous influx of professionals and others with above average education from China, India, Korea, and elsewhere. As the census tabulations in Table 8.1 show, three-fourths of Asians arriving in the 1970s had completed high school by 1980—compared with only one-half of all earlier immigrants and two-thirds of all Americans—Asians have a rate of college graduation more than double the national average, and they are 50 percent more likely to have professional specialty occupations.

However, the skill distribution of recent immigrants is bimodal, with the large population from Mexico characterized by low levels of educational attainment, fluency in English, and professional or managerial employment. If there was in fact some increase in undocumented immigration from the mid-1960s on, this increase may be thought to have played a role in depressing these averages during the seventies. But what little reliable survey data exist on illegal entrants from Mexico reveal that two-thirds are from towns or cities, 9 out of 10 have been employed over a year at the time of emigration, and the majority had been in nonfarm occupations.[11] As the research on Central and South American migrants reviewed in chapter 2 has indicated, persons from most other Spanish-speaking countries appear to be far more urban and well educated than those from Mexico. It is thus unsurpris-

TABLE 8.1. Selected Social and Economic Characteristics
by Nativity, Immigration Year, and Source Country, 1980

			Immigrants, 1970–80		
	Total	Immigrants Pre-1970	Total	Asia	Mexico
Population (thsnds.)	226,545	8,520	5,560	1,763	1,270
Age (median)	30.0	52.9	26.8	27.9	23.6
Years of School Completed[a]					
12 or more (%)	66.5	51.5	56.9	74.5	17.0
16 or more (%)	16.2	13.2	22.2	37.4	2.7
Language Other Than English Spoken at Home (%)	11.0	61.7	83.7	92.3	98.5
Speak English Well/Very Well	81.7	77.8	59.6	74.0	38.5
Labor Force Status[b]					
% in Labor Force	62.0	51.3	64.4	60.6	69.1
% Unemployed	6.5	6.5	8.1	6.2	10.3
Mean Duration of Unemp. (Wks)	14.1	15.0	14.0	13.4	14.4
Occupational Distribution[c]					
Professional	12.3	12.8	10.8	18.0	1.4
Managerial	10.4	10.6	6.9	9.7	1.6
Technical, Sales	30.3	26.9	21.0	28.2	7.4
Crafts	12.9	13.6	11.8	8.5	14.7
Opertvs., Labor	18.3	18.7	27.3	17.4	44.0
Services	12.9	14.8	18.1	17.1	17.6
Farm Workers	2.9	2.6	4.1	1.1	13.3
Family Income (1979 $median)	19,917	18,959	15,244	17,861	11,782
% Families Below Poverty Line, 1979	9.6	8.7	20.7	19.2	28.2
Persons per Family (mean)	3.3	3.3	3.8	3.8	4.4
% of Families Female-headed	13.9	14.2	11.6	9.1	9.7

[a]Persons 25 years old and over.

[b]Persons 16 years old and over in civilian population.

[c]Employees in occupation as % of all employees, ages 16 and over.

SOURCE: U.S. Bureau of the Census (1984b): Table 255.

ing that immigrants in the United States are increasingly urban: 88 percent of Hispanics in the 1980 census lived in a metropolitan area and about three out of four undocumented Mexicans in the North–Houston (1976) sample held nonfarm jobs.

Nevertheless, recent immigrants had average family income of only $15,244 in 1979, over $3,600 below the national median, and a poverty rate (20.7 percent) twice the national level. Just over 18 percent of recent South American migrant families, 20.5 percent of Cubans, 28.2 percent of Mexicans, and 36.1 percent of Dominicans were poor.[12] The average rate (19.2 percent) among Asian migrants was considerably inflated by the special refugee program admitting massive numbers of Indochinese, 37 percent of whom were counted below the poverty line shortly after their entry. By contrast, less than 7 percent of recent entrants from India and the Philippines were poor, well below the national rate.

Empirical Analysis of Program Participation

The foregoing discussion of past research on immigrant earnings indicates the importance of distinguishing between different year of arrival cohorts in any study of native–migrant differentials. But expectations about how immigrant status is related to usage of transfer benefit programs in the United States remain far from unambiguous. Insofar as higher earnings lower dependence on transfers, earlier immigrants would seem less likely to use transfer programs than more recent entrants. The below average incomes and above average poverty rates of the 1970s cohort (Table 8.1) would imply, all else the same, greater need to rely on such programs. On the other hand, recent immigrants have an average age half that of pre-1970 migrants and higher labor force participation rates, and are likely to have acquired far less job experience or information about how to acquire transfer payments. The longer they are in the country, the more they obtain sufficient work history and information needed to qualify for such payments. If these factors dominate, a positive relation between duration of U.S. residence and use of transfers is to be expected.

Data

Given the ambiguous effects of immigration, empirical analysis is needed to determine the relative strength of these underlying factors. Surprisingly little previous research exists on this issue, perhaps, in part, because government agencies do not typically differentiate by nativity of beneficiaries in their records. The 1980 Census of Population does contain specific information on each family's dollar volume of "public assistance" income received in 1979, which consists of the following: Aid to Families with Dependent Children (AFDC), General Assistance, Old Age Assistance, Aid to the Blind, and Aid to the Permanently and Totally Disabled. Because of the relatively small size of the Hispanic population, information on it was drawn from the large 1/100 Public Use Census Microdata tape file, while the sampling proportions were 1/200 of non-Hispanic blacks and 1/1000 of Anglos. The study sample was restricted to families with a householder at least 16 years old who lived in one of the 79 SMSAs with populations over 500,000 and who reported all relevant personal and income information. Individuals, regardless of race, are classified as "Hispanic" according to Census Bureau criteria based on their self-reported ancestry, birthplace, national origin, and language.[13]

Incidence of Transfer Usage

The proportions of public assistance recipients among families led by native- and foreign-born individuals in 1979 are presented in Table 8.2. A consistent pattern

TABLE 8.2. Incidence of Public Assistance Recipiency and Dollar Value of Public Assistance Payments[a] by Nativity, Year of Immigration, Race, and Spanish Origin of Family Head

		Foreign Born		
	Native Born	Total	Immigrated 1975–79	Immigrated Pre-1975
% of Families Receiving Public Assistance, 1979				
White Non-Hispanic	3.18	1.91	4.26	1.66
Black Non-Hispanic	19.84	8.52	5.15	9.60
Hispanic	11.28	6.70	4.51	7.35
Mean Dollar Value of Public Assistance Payments of Families Receiving Payments				
White Non-Hispanic	2531	3021	3325	2940
Black Non-Hispanic	2704	3006	3108	2989
Hispanic	2911	2910	2826	2924

[a]Public Assistance consists of Aid to Families with Dependent Children, Old Age Assistance, General Assistance, Aid to the Blind, and Aid to the Permanently and Totally Disabled, 1979.

SOURCE: 1980 Census Public Use Microdata Samples.

emerges from the calculations: among whites, blacks, and Hispanics alike, native families use public assistance programs at a rate about twice that of immigrant families. While the incidence of participation by foreign-born blacks (8.5 percent) and Hispanics (6.7 percent) is higher than that of native-born non-Hispanic whites (3.2 percent), this appears to reflect more the disadvantaged status of these minority groups rather than any special problems of immigrants. Among both blacks and Hispanics, families settled in the United States before 1975 had higher program participation than those immigrating from 1975 on, but the reverse was true among white immigrants.

To better compare native- and foreign-born usage of benefits, one must take into account the differences between them in their characteristics that may become confounded with the independent influence of immigration. Toward this end, ordinary least squares regressions were estimated in which the dependent variable was a dichotomous index of receipt of any public assistance in 1979 (= 1 if received any benefits, 0 otherwise) and the explanatory variables were as follows: Age (in years), and a series of dummy variables (in each case set equal to 1 if the specified characteristic currently applied, 0 otherwise): Family Head Married; Residence in a southern state; Foreign born, immigrated 1975–79; Foreign born, immigrated 1970–74; Foreign born, immigrated 1965–69; Foreign born, immigrated 1960–64; Foreign born, immigrated before 1960; Family with no children; Family with one child; Family with two children.[14] Inclusion of all these variables in the regressions means that the reference group is the subset of families headed by native-born, unmarried women, living outside the South, with more than two children.

TABLE 8.3. Regression Estimates of Differences in the Incidence of Public Aid Recipiency between Native and Immigrant Families, 1979[a]

Explanatory Variables	White Non-Hispanics		Black Non-Hispanics		Hispanics	
Age	-.0012**	-.0015**	-.0022**	-.0035**	-.0012**	-.0020**
	(11.63)	(13.60)	(10.61)	(16.41)	(7.53)	(11.61)
Married	-.1306	-.1285	-.2650	-.2660	-.2356	-.2377
	(1.20)	(0.75)	(1.63)	(0.83)	(0.17)	(0.62)
Southern State	-.0180**	-.0173**	-.0792**	-.0802**	-.0396**	-.0371**
	(6.44)	(6.20)	(14.61)	(14.94)	(9.30)	(8.72)
Immigrant, 1975–79	.0135	.0166	-.1254**	-.1242**	-.0608**	-.0583**
	(0.78)	(0.97)	(5.19)	(5.19)	(10.02)	(9.64)
Immigrant, 1970–74	-.0012	.0001**	-.1109**	-.1108**	-.0366**	-.0367**
	(0.07)	(0.01)	(4.93)	(4.97)	(6.30)	(6.34)
Immigrant, 1965–69	-.0140	-.0128	-.1111**	-.1149**	-.0188**	-.0153*
	(0.92)	(0.85)	(4.74)	(4.95)	(3.03)	(2.47)
Immigrant, 1960–64	.0055	.0054	-.0284	-.0386	-.0151*	-.0109
	(0.38)	(0.36)	(0.66)	(0.91)	(2.12)	(1.53)

	(1)	(2)	(3)	(4)	(5)	(6)
Immigrant, Pre-1960	−.0120 (1.64)	−.0114 (1.57)	−.0348 (1.11)	−.0329 (1.06)	−.0175* (2.40)	−.0157* (2.15)
No Children in Family		−.0323** (7.65)		−.0844** (8.18)		−.0528** (7.86)
1 Child in Family		−.0182** (4.86)		−.1289** (19.47)		−.0601** (11.62)
2 Children in Family		−.0190** (5.99)		−.0824** (12.24)		−.0204** (4.25)
Constant	.1955** (34.72)	.2195*** (34.07)	.4394** (50.73)	.5525*** (53.60)	.3388** (46.69)	.3926** (45.46)
R^2	.0807	.0844	.1381	.1550	.1385	.1450
Mean of Dependt. Var.	.0311	.0311	.1930	.1930	.0892	.0892
N	16,988	16,988	20,249	20,249	20,397	20,397

*p < .05; **p < .01.

[a]Absolute values of T-ratios in parentheses. Dependent variable: Probability that individual received public assistance income in 1979.

SOURCE: 1980 Census Public Use Microdata.

The regression results in Table 8.3 reveal that, among otherwise comparable Hispanic families, immigrants are significantly less likely to receive any public assistance benefits than native-born Hispanics. The most recent migrant cohorts have the lowest incidence of program participation, relative to natives, while nativity differences diminish the longer a cohort has been in this country. Even those who immigrated before 1960 are significantly less likely to receive transfers than the native born. Likewise, among black families, all immigrant cohorts that arrived since the mid-1960s have rates of program participation that are significantly below those of indigenous blacks. There is no statistically significant difference between native blacks and pre-1965 cohorts. Among white non-Hispanics there is no significant difference between natives and immigrants in the likelihood of receiving transfers.

Public Assistance Levels

The study sample was next restricted to the subsample of families receiving a nonzero value of public assistance income in 1979. The sample means in Table 8.2 indicate that among white non-Hispanic aid recipients, the average dollar value of transfers received by immigrant families that year was about 19 percent above the native level. Relative to natives, the immigrant level was about $800 higher for the most recent cohort, but was only half that for earlier entrants. Among blacks, immigrant transfer recipients also had a higher average benefit level than natives, though the differential (11 percent) was smaller than that found for whites. In contrast, the average transfer level of foreign-born Hispanics was identical to that of native aid recipients. And the most recently arrived migrants averaged $100 less than earlier cohorts.

The parameter estimates from regressions of the dollar value of transfers on the same set of independent variables used in the incidence equations are presented in Table 8.4. The results indicate that regardless of the racial or national-origin group, there are generally no statistically significant differences between the native and the foreign born in the amount of public assistance received. Among non-Hispanic whites, the 1965–69 cohort of white immigrants appear to have received a higher level of transfers in 1979 than indigenous whites. The unusually large size of the coefficient estimate suggests this anomalous result could be attributable to a few outlying cases. No other group of immigrants received a different volume of transfers than native families.

Other Government Transfers

Since the preceding analysis was limited to AFDC and several other forms of public assistance, it could give a biased image of overall native–migrant differences in program participation. The 1976 Survey of Income and Education, though not as large or as recent as the 1980 census data set, contains information on both public assistance and on the main social insurance benefits: unemployment insurance, veterans' benefits, workmen's compensation, and Social Security. Blau (1984) found that if one looked only at average levels of the sum of public assistance and social insurance transfers in the subset of families receiving some government aid, the SIE data indicated that immigrants received benefits 52 percent above the native level in male-headed families, and 13 percent higher in female-headed families. But her regression analysis revealed that virtually all of this difference in simple averages was due to the fact that the immigrant sample had a larger fraction of older individuals. After controlling for a few age-related variables in regressions run separately on male-headed and female-headed families, she found that immigrant families were significantly *less* likely than comparable natives to be recipients of either public assistance or social insurance. And, among those already receiving some form of benefits, the total expected amount of transfer payments to natives and immigrants was nearly identical in male-headed families, while in female-headed families immigrants received 8 percent lower payments than comparable natives.

In a RAND research project on foreign-born Mexicans in California, McCarthy and Valdez (1986) estimated that fewer than 5 percent of Mexican immigrants in California in 1980 received any form of public assistance, compared with a state-wide average of 12 percent. In all but one of the social services examined, Mexicans were contributing more to public revenues than to service usage costs. The exception was education where, like all the state's low-income groups, foreign-born Mexicans were unable to cover the full $2,900 annual cost for each public school student. But, as the authors point out, subsidized education has long been accepted in this and most other industrialized countries as a necessary public investment. By making it readily available to successive waves of immigrants, governments can both speed their sociocultural integration and help meet future manpower needs. Half of the 3 million new jobs expected in California by 1995 are projected to be in white-collar professional and high-level service fields. Rapid improvement in educational skills is essential to prepare the large supply of Mexican immigrants to help meet the growing demand for skilled workers.

Undocumented Aliens

To the extent that government surveys like the SIE undercount the elusive undocumented population, the previous estimates may be biased measures of immigrants' program participation. In the North–Houston (1976) interviews with 793 undocumented aliens, respondents were asked a series of questions about program participation while in the United States. Only 0.5 percent said they had, over the last five years, received any AFDC payments, 1.3 percent received some food stamps, 3.9 percent collected one or more weeks of unemployment insurance, 1.4 percent participated in government-funded job training programs, and 3.7 percent had children in American schools. About one in four also reported visits to clinics or hospitals, but 83 percent of such persons indicated that either they, their hospital insurance, or their employer paid for this health care.

As North and Houston themselves recognized, "the characteristics of the respondents, who were typically young male workers, are not those of a population which is likely to receive income transfer payments."[15] While caution is clearly required in extrapolating from a sample possibly tainted by some selectivity bias to the entire population, it can still provide wholly accurate information about a portion of the population of interest. And since the undocumented are widely thought to be disproportionately young, male, labor force participants, this particular sample may represent a very sizable portion indeed. It includes individuals as young as 16

TABLE 8.4. Regression Estimates of Differences in the Amounts of Public Aid Received by Native and Immigrant Families, 1979[a]

Explanatory Variables	White Non-Hispanics		Black Non-Hispanics		Hispanics	
Age	-.1108*	-.1521*	-.0623**	-.1706**	-.1458**	-.2292**
	(2.08)	(2.65)	(2.70)	(7.12)	(4.03)	(5.96)
Married	-2.1178	-1.8033	-2.6829**	-2.8872**	-4.8885**	-5.0170**
	(1.36)	(1.14)	(3.16)	(3.34)	(4.89)	(4.95)
Southern State	-5.2908**	-5.6204**	-10.0147**	-10.1267**	-12.1290**	-12.0124**
	(2.96)	(3.12)	(15.03)	(15.57)	(9.61)	(9.60)
Immigrant, 1975–79	8.1585	8.3548	4.0622	4.3284	.4968	.9386
	(1.00)	(1.02)	(0.78)	(0.85)	(0.26)	(0.50)
Immigrant, 1970–74	1.0860	1.2837	-.6492	-.2130	-.3716	.0275
	(0.12)	(0.14)	(0.16)	(0.06)	(0.24)	(0.02)
Immigrant, 1965–69	43.1080**	43.2677**	5.6599	4.9412	2.3178	2.5011
	(3.76)	(3.79)	(1.21)	(1.08)	(1.49)	(1.62)
Immigrant, 1960–64	3.8966	3.9045	3.7885	3.3036	2.4045	2.8565
	(0.48)	(0.48)	(0.73)	(0.65)	(1.32)	(1.58)

	(1)	(2)	(3)	(4)	(5)	(6)
Immigrant, Pre-1960	−7.5726	−7.9494	−.5307	−1.1209	2.9252	3.1252
	(1.14)	(1.20)	(0.14)	(0.30)	(1.61)	(1.73)
No Children in Family		−9.7961		−5.8419*		−8.8760*
		(1.75)		(2.20)		(2.40)
1 Child in Family		−4.2062*		−9.8766**		−7.0895**
		(2.28)		(13.66)		(5.99)
2 Children in Family		−.5551		−5.5214**		−3.7677**
		(0.31)		(7.49)		(3.46)
Constant	31.0534**	33.9971**	32.1302**	37.7811**	36.7785**	42.3736**
	(14.25)	(12.50)	(36.68)	(38.50)	(28.01)	(26.17)
R^2	.0458	.0555	.0586	.1029	.0712	.0902
Mean of Dependt. Var.	25.4451	25.4451	27.0998	27.0998	29.1040	29.1040
N	527	527	3,908	3,908	1,819	1,819

*p < .05; **p < .01.

aAbsolute values of T-ratios in parentheses. Dependent variable: Annual family income from public assistance in 1979. Sample restricted to public assistance recipients that year.

SOURCE: 1980 Census Public Use Microdata.

and with as little as two weeks of employment while in the United States. Over 47 percent of the sample were married (including common law unions) and 48 percent had one or more children under the age of 18. Given the wording of the questions on public program usage, a large fraction of the responses were in fact yielding information not only about the largely male sample but about their wives and children as well.

What then explains their relatively infrequent interaction with transfer and service programs? First, since at least the early 1970s when these programs' regulations were tightened, the undocumented have been ineligible for most of them. Fear of detection and deportation has thus probably kept many from attempting to become participants. Next, the intended period of residence is so brief for many that the risk and the red tape of involvement with these programs may seem best avoided. The average duration of U.S. residence was only about two and one-half years with return trips home common during that period. Hence, only 17 percent of respondents had their wives in the United States, and 21.8 percent had their children with them. Mexicans were the least likely to do so: only 11 percent brought their wives and only 9.6 percent their children. Finally, the relative youth (average age: 28.5 years) of the undocumented and the requirement of at least 10 years of covered employment in the United States before one can collect Social Security benefits mean that the Social Security taxes that are invariably withheld from their pay will largely remain transfers from the undocumented to the program's coffers. While it is possible that the minority with sufficiently long duration of American employment could draw Social Security benefits in their old age in Mexico, a study of Social Security Administration data found that the number of beneficiaries in Mexico by 1978 was only 50,126, some of whom were U.S. citizens seeking a warmer, less expensive retirement home.[16]

The small number of studies of this issue have certainly not built anything like a consensus view. For example, Van Arsdol's (1979) survey of undocumented aliens in Los Angeles included a far larger fraction of women than the North–Houston survey. The rates of reported participation in (undefined) "welfare programs" were much higher than in North–Houston: 8.9 percent of men and 18.5 percent of women. However, it seems highly likely that these estimates were biased upward by the way the sample was collected. The researchers questioned individuals who were in contact with an immigrant-serving agency to select their study group. Insofar as persons seeking assistance from such agencies are more likely to be relatively disadvantaged, findings based on their activities will overstate program participation.

Other findings on the undocumented in Los Angeles have emerged from data collected by the L.A. County Department of Public Social Services. The department has local responsibility for AFDC, food stamps, and Medicaid, among other programs. As part of the county's effort to ban the undocumented from public assistance, all applicants are required to present proof of their citizenship or legal alien status. In the 12 months from July 1979 to June 1980, 21,413 alien applicants were found ineligible because of illegal status, either by their refusal to provide documentation or by INS checks. Since an estimated 658,000 undocumented aliens lived in the area that year according to the Census Bureau, the ineligible applicants represent roughly 3.2 percent of the undocumented.[17] This potential rate of service usage is above that found in the earlier North–Houston study, but well below the norm for the overall civilian population.[18] After reviewing this and other studies, North (1983) concluded that there appeared generally to be below average utilization of social service programs by the undocumented, compared with average utilization by legal immigrants and above average utilization by recent refugees.

Net Effect on the Public Treasury

While the evidence reported here suggests that immigrants are typically less likely than native-born persons to receive welfare benefits or other government transfers, it is not by itself sufficient to address the claim of some immigration critics that the foreign born take more in public services than they pay in taxes. This larger issue has been little studied, no doubt in part because it is even more difficult to find any data on taxes that distinguish the taxpayer's nationality than it is to find comparable data on transfer payments. The most detailed and careful effort, to my knowledge, is that of Simon (1989). In addition to using the full set of SIE information on public assistance and social insurance benefits studied by Blau, he also estimates the costs of Medicare, Medicaid, and schooling used by the foreign born. To derive dollar values for Medicare and Medicaid usage, the average annual cost per user in 1975 was assigned to individuals who reported using either service. Likewise, schooling costs were derived by multiplying average annual expenditures per student in public elementary and secondary schools by the reported number of children, ages 5–17, living at home in the SIE samples. Summing all of these costs reveals that, on average, regardless of the year of arrival, immigrants in the country since 1960 received less in all public services in 1975 than did native families—by amounts ranging from $32 to $1,079 per year. Simon then uses SIE data on family earnings to derive estimates of average local, state, and federal tax payments. Comparing immigrants' average taxes to the average value of all the public assistance, social insurance, and schooling they receive, he concludes that immigrants pay more in U.S. taxes than they receive from these public programs in every year following migration until they reach retirement age. If elderly immigrants tend to have levels of Social Security and other services similar to natives, this is unlikely to imply a serious net burden on native taxpayers. After all, in addition to spending their most productive years in the United States contributing to tax revenue, the typical immigrant family's offspring represent a continuing contribution to the public coffers. The taxes paid by the second generation help finance the retirement of the first generation. In fact, the present value of the stream of net tax revenues from immigrants was estimated to benefit native families by amounts ranging (depending on the discount rate applied) from $15,262 to $20,600.

As Simon himself recognizes, such tax and benefit estimates are "tenuous, but crucial," not only because they often require imputing average program costs to specific individual recipients but also because they rely on cross-section data to infer life-cycle patterns. Still, they do not appear unreasonable in light of the ample evidence that most recent cohorts arrive in this country relatively early in their working lives and thus only begin to use the most costly government programs, Social Security and Medicare, after many years of tax payments.

These estimates are also not inconsistent with the available information, skimpy as it may be, on undocumented workers. Although only a minute fraction of the undocumented aliens in the North–Houston survey reported any use of public services, 73.2 percent had federal income taxes withheld by their most recent U.S. employer, 77.3 percent had Social Security taxes withheld, and 44 percent had hospitalization insurance payments withheld. However, while nearly three in four had income taxes withheld, fewer than one in three (31.5 percent) filed an income tax return (North and Houston, 1976). Whether due to language problems with the forms, a fear of revealing one's address, or other factors, this low incidence of filing could well mean that the undocumented were considerably less likely to receive tax refunds than were native-born low-income persons.

Impacts on Domestic Earnings and Unemployment

Even if immigrants do tend to contribute more to U.S. tax revenue than they receive in government benefits and services, it is still possible that they impose a net burden on the indigenous population if they cause lower earnings and higher joblessness among native workers.

Competing Theoretical Views

Economists' disagreements over the labor market effects of immigration have been dominated by three main perspectives: the labor substitution theory, the Marxian hypothesis of the industrial reserve army, and the labor market segmentation model. While sharing a common theoretical emphasis on migration's impacts on the low-wage work force, they can be clearly distinguished both by their analytic frame-works and their principal predictions about the magnitude and time-paths of those impacts.

The Labor Substitution View

In the years 1901–10 a record 9 million people entered the country, prompting a number of the best-known economists of the day to begin applying the still-new neoclassical methodology to the analysis of migrants' impacts on income, productivity, and unemployment. The 42-volume Dillingham Commission report of 1911, alleging that the growing volume of Southern and Eastern Europeans was responsible for deteriorating wage levels and working conditions, drew upon some of this early research and was viewed as key evidence in the successful legislative drive to establish the ethnocentric national-origins quota system in the early twenties.

This view has been echoed periodically over the years by other economists for whom immigrants appear to serve primarily as production substitutes for various components of the indigenous work force. Thus, for example, Reder wrote in an influential article in 1963 (p. 227):

> A greater flow of immigration will injure labor market competitors with immigrants; they are predominantly Negroes, Puerto Ricans, unskilled immigrants presently able to enter the country and native rural-urban migrants (Negro and white). Increased immigration would also lead to labor market substitution of immigrants for categories of workers other than non-skilled males. There is evidence that secondary earners, for example, married women, youths, and aged persons act as an urban labor reserve, responding to varying labor demands much like rural migrants. . . . As many of these job openings are of an unskilled or semi-skilled nature they might well be filled by immigrants.

Most contemporary neoclassical models view the individual migrant as the archetypal rational economic man engaging in utility-maximizing human capital investments. This leads to an analysis of labor market entry and subsequent employment dominated by supply considerations. Thus Chiswick argues that an understanding of immigrants' economic progress requires analysis of only two key concepts: the international portability of skills and the higher propensity of more able and achievement-oriented persons to undertake the risks and expense of long-distance moves. The first few years after arrival are said to be characterized by modification of "country-specific" skills to fit American norms and the acquisition of new skills and labor market information through a process of interfirm and interregional mobility. As a result, new entrants are expected to have relatively high rates of turnover and unemployment.[19]

The implications of this for assessments of immigration's labor market impact are viewed as dependent on labor demand and supply elasticities and on the substitutability of native- and foreign-born production inputs. Of course, complementary as well as substitute inputs figure in neoclassical production theory. But the notion that immigrant and native labor might be largely complementary was always a marginal one in the literature. Though disagreement persisted about the size of the net impact, most prominent neoclassical writers on the subject long held that immigration was responsible for depressing the wages and increasing the unemployment of low-skilled labor.[20] This claim was based on an implicit supply and demand structure of the sort displayed in Figure 8.1(a). An influx of unskilled foreign workers shifts the supply curve from S_n to S_{n+f}. The lower the elasticity of demand, the larger will be the induced reduction in the equilibrium wage (from W^1 to W^2). While the result could be an increase in total employment (like that from L_n^1 to L_{n+f}^2), the higher the supply elasticity of native labor the greater will be their displacement as wages fall. In the diagram, $L_n^1 L_n^2$ previously employed natives either become unemployed or withdraw from the affected labor market. The displacement effect would be intensified by a high degree of substitutability (i.e., positive cross-wage demand elasticities) between the native and foreign born since the availability of less expensive migrants could lower the demand curve for indigenous labor, further dampening their wage and job prospects.

The Marxian Model

The postwar movement of over 30 million people to Western Europe, some from former colonies, many others recruited under contract labor programs, prompted

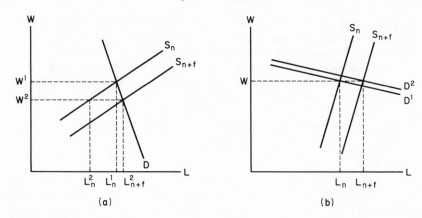

FIGURE 8.1. Alternative wage and employment effects of immigration, under different demand/supply structures.

new interest in Marx's argument that the capitalist accumulation process depended on production of a disposable labor surplus to restrict wage and employment demands. While all unemployed or "partially employed" workers were included, the reserve army was said to have three main forms: (1) the "floating reserve" of experienced adult male laborers displaced from capitalist industries by either a secular industrial decline, the availability of cheaper substitutes (youth, women), or old age; (2) the "stagnant reserve," the "hospital of the active labor-army" filled with paupers and the physically disabled as well as workers made redundant in precapitalist sectors like handicrafts; and (3) the "latent reserve" of potentially exploitable labor that could be drawn upon when labor markets were tight and just as easily expelled once demand slackened; the agrarian populations of the English and Irish countrysides were the classic examples in Marx's day.

In a wide-ranging comparative study, Castles and Kosack argued that Southern European and Third World workers had become the modern equivalents of the nineteenth century's rural migrants: a vast pool of easily recruited labor during boom periods that could be speedily deported under the terms of most *gastarbeiter* contracts when recession threatened. While some foreigners experienced high job turnover in response to interindustry demand shifts at the same time that others held stable though menial positions, both were seen as fulfilling the reserve-army function of increasing employers' bargaining power over the indigenous work force.[21]

Adriana Marshall (1973) also viewed the reserve army construct as consistent with the postwar experience insofar as immigrants were a source of surplus labor supply that could be mobilized as needed, flowing quickly into sectors with rising vacancy rates. But she proposed an alternative to the more traditional model of Castles and Kosack:

> Presentday labour force immigration to the advanced countries has a specific feature, lacking in the migration of a typical latent reserve army of labour; today, most if not all of the migrants from the underdeveloped countries, when under

"control," are directly incorporated into employment and they do not add to the unemployed indigenous workers (especially since restrictions on immigration have been imposed).

This specific difference, however, does not prevent the immigration of labour forces from performing the functions of a latent reserve army: it can provide additional labour to meet, partially or wholly, the requirements of expanding investments at the existing level of wages, and in this way potentially exert a "pressure" on the growth of wages.[22]

Segmented Labor Markets

In striking contrast to the neoclassical image of the unskilled foreigner entering a unified labor market in which he competes directly with the native born, segmentation theory emphasizes the social context of the migration process and contends that recent immigrants tend to hold jobs distinct from and largely complementary to those of the indigenous work force. The typical pattern, according to Piore, is one in which the early waves from developing countries are not the rural unskilled but rather the skilled and semiskilled city dwellers best suited to master the maze of immigration procedures, to afford transportation and living expenses, and to adjust readily to a new industrial setting.[23] These pioneers pave the way for their urban and rural kinsmen by advising them on the optimal timing of the move, facilitating the acquisition of visas, and offering financial assistance. This system of chain migration establishes an institutional structure in ethnic communities of the receiving country that provides newcomers with housing, social contacts, training and employment opportunities, and small business loans.

Migrant networks are attached to the secondary segment of low-wage jobs in the competitive industrial "periphery," from which there is only the most limited upward mobility to the primary sector of oligopolistic "core" industries. The low social status and inferior wage and career opportunities of unskilled work in industries subject to wide seasonal and cyclical fluctuations cause the indigenous population to shun such jobs. Recent immigrants are willing to take them because they typically view their stay as temporary, a means to amass some target level of savings to improve their family's living standard and social status upon return home. Although the instability of secondary sector demand makes migrants more vulnerable to layoffs, the impact of this on their measured incidence and duration of unemployment will be counterbalanced by the willingness of target earners to accept low reservation wages and almost any available vacancies.

By filling the jobs at the base of the social hierarchy, recent migrants function as a complementary rather than substitute labor supply. Ethnic networks channel newcomers into those openings in the community most advantageous to their countrymen's jobs and small businesses. Their employment increases the demand for raw materials, equipment, and intermediary goods produced by native workers. And their ready availability and flexibility facilitate capitalist expansions and absorb the unstable portions of industry demand. However, insofar as immigrants lengthen their stay and shift from temporary to permanent settlement, negative economic consequences become, Piore argues, increasingly likely. Once workers relocate their social identities from origin to destination and are joined by dependents, they become more concerned with job status and security, less willing to accept menial secondary sector jobs, and may begin encroaching on natives' job and wage prospects.

Previous Research Findings

The conventional view that immigration harms native workers seems open to question on at least three points. First, the prediction that supposed migration-induced wage reductions will cause many of the native born to become unemployed or labor force dropouts is based on an implicit assumption of higher elasticities of labor supply than seem warranted by the substantial body of empirical estimates, particularly those for low-wage labor in two decades of negative income tax experiments. Although the range of recent estimates of low-wage labor supply elasticities has been quite wide, especially for females, the most careful studies agree that male labor supply is relatively wage-inelastic.[24] Less is known about the elasticity of demand for low-wage labor, but recent estimates have generally exceeded unity, with some ranging about 1.5.[25] Such findings seem more consistent with demand-supply structures of the sort depicted in Figure 8.1(b) than in Figure 8.1(a). The steeper the supply curves and the flatter the demand curve, the weaker the wage and disemployment effects of immigration on natives. Second, the actual volume of low-skilled migration appears to be far lower than earlier authoritative claims. As noted previously, the most careful demographic estimates to date suggest that the total number of undocumented aliens is probably not much more than the 3 million counted by 1989 in the IRCA amnesty program.

Finally, the theory's supply-side orientation has led it to neglect the fact that besides increasing the number of people looking for jobs, immigration may increase the number of jobs available as well. Immigration-induced shifts of the labor demand curve at destination could result from several possible sources:

1. Consumption Effects—immigration not only increases the number of people available for work, it also increases the number of consumers. Increased consumer spending contributes to an increase in the derived demand for labor.

2. Productivity Effects—immigrants may enhance domestic labor productivity in a number of ways: (a) increasing the variety and quality of occupational and entrepreneurial skills relative to the native work force; (b) bringing physical or money capital from home; (c) insofar as investors perceive immigrants as highly motivated workers likely to enhance the rate of return to capital, Rivera-Batiz (1983) has pointed out that their presence in a particular industry could attract new capital investment; (d) the increased consumer market caused by immigration could generate scale economies, realized through increased specialization and diversification between firms.

3. Direct Job Creation—the rate of self-employment among the foreign born is known to exceed the native level, and it is especially high among some of the Asian nationalities (e.g., Chinese, Indians, and Koreans) who have been among the fastest growing components of recent entry cohorts (Borjas, 1986).

Hence, immigration is likely to cause not only an increase in the supply of workers (a rightward shift of the supply of labor curve in the standard neoclassical model) but an increase in labor demand as well (a rightward shift in the demand for labor curve). Whether the actual supply and demand elasticities and the shifts in each curve result in a net positive, negative, or (as pictured in Figure 8.1[b]) negligible impact on native workers is the key question. But it cannot be settled theoretically; it requires empirical testing.

The Marxian reserve-army view has been questioned recently by Lever-Tracy (1983) as incompatible with the small migrant–nonmigrant unemployment differentials in the two countries she examines (France and Australia) and with the inability of European governments to expel foreign workers in the seventies. Her arguments echo some of the questions raised by Humphries (1983), Power (1983), and Rubery and Tarling (1988) about earlier characterizations of women as a latent reserve. In fact, Castles (1984, p. 35) himself, in a follow-up study to his 1973 book, now looks upon the 1945–73 period as only a phase of mass labor migration, which has been superseded by family reunification and the rise of new ethnic minorities:

> Western Europe has shifted from the strategy of mobilizing an external latent surplus population of unemployed and underemployed workers in underdeveloped areas of Europe and the Third World to that of creating a "floating surplus population" of unemployed and deskilled workers at home.

This transition is more readily understandable in light of research indicating that the backgrounds of the latent reserve at origin are considerably less rural and unskilled than either Castles or neoclassical writers have thought. In addition to the findings in this regard for the United States (see earlier), there is similar evidence for Europe. For example, Suzanne Paine's (1974) research on Turkish migrants in the late sixties and early seventies revealed that the majority interviewed in large national surveys originated in urban centers of the richest, most Westernized regions, and that two out of three of these were experienced skilled or semiskilled workers.

These findings appear to be more consistent with the modified reserve army model developed by Adriana Marshall (1973), based on her empirical research on postwar immigration to the Netherlands. Very little work has as yet been done to test whether immigration to the United States has effects on wage growth of the sort she detected in the Dutch experience. One study of annual wage growth among manual manufacturing workers did find evidence of slower growth in U.S. metropolitan areas with higher concentrations of foreign-born manual workers.[26] However, the magnitude of the estimated impact was relatively small and only achieved statistical significance in the handful of metropolitan areas in which 20 percent or more of manual workers were immigrants.

While segmentation theory has generally given greater stress to demand effects than either neoclassical or Marxian theory, it nonetheless fails to take into account the full range of possible employment adjustments immigrants may undertake as they settle in the United States, which may increase their complementarity with native labor. For example, the theory's most influential exponent, Michael Piore (1979a), has argued that once migrants raise their expectations to those of an advanced economy and relocate their dependents, they become far more status- and security-conscious, less willing to accept menial secondary employment, and more competitive with native job-seekers. But this ignores the possible offsetting benefits of greater demand expansion by long-term migrants compared with their short-term counterparts: the longer they stay, the more likely they are to accumulate the funds and know-how needed to establish new businesses and the larger the share of their income directed to domestic savings and expenditures instead of remittances to relatives abroad. Some survey evidence also shows relatively high rates of union membership among immigrants (including the undocumented) the longer their duration of U.S. residence. Over one-fourth of undocumented workers in the United States two years or more reported union membership in the North–Houston (1976) survey. The theory's other principal shortcoming is that the standard sectoral definitions (originally made in the 1960s to account for ghetto employment problems) omit such major immigrant employers as retail trade and service industries. The obvious problems this creates for econometric research doubtless help explain the dearth of empirical tests of the theory.

A number of both economic and sociological studies on immigrants in New York, Miami, and Los Angeles have detailed the far-reaching impact of ethnic networks on migrants' employment progress.[27] Because so many appear to rely on kinsmen for their first job, the employer–employee relationship in ethnic enclaves often involves a web of obligations, understood to be reciprocal, which seem to result in reduced layoff and quit rates. Colombians and Dominicans in the Fordham survey had jobless rates at or below the citywide average, and the 10.2 percent average annual rate among the undocumented studied by North and Houston (p. 98) was well below that for young labor force entrants nationally.

Detailed industry studies have also revealed the considerable degree to which immigrants are often concentrated in specific job clusters or industry subsectors. For example, in the New York garment trades those remaining production jobs that have not yet been moved to the Sunbelt or abroad are overwhelmingly filled by immigrants, while unskilled and semiskilled natives are largely in the associated fashion, design, and marketing segments of the business.[28] Likewise, foreign-born workers in the restaurant industry are disproportionately concentrated either in immigrant-owned restaurants or in the kitchen staffs of urban restaurants, whereas natives are far more likely to fill waiter and cashier jobs.[29] These findings lend support to claims that migrants and natives are complements in production.

Finally, all three theories ignore the fact that by far the largest source of new migrant workers in American cities is not immigration, but rather native-born workers' internal migration. From 1975 to 1980, over 33 million persons ages 16 and above moved to a different county in the United States—almost 10 times the number of adult immigrants entering the country in the entire decade of the seventies.[30] Nearly 20 percent of adults were intercounty movers (the majority of whom were interstate movers as well) in this five-year span, and they moved disproportionately to many of the same destinations, like New York, Miami, and Los Angeles, that also attract immigrants.[31] It would thus not be surprising if the impact of native in-migrants on destination labor markets was at least as substantial as that of immigrants. Hence, the general failure to control for this confounding effect in past empirical work may well have produced biased estimates of the effect of immigration alone.

The direction of the bias is of course dependent on whether internal migrants are themselves substitutes or complements with the indigenous work force at destination. Greenwood (1973) examined aggregate data for the 1950s and 1960s with a simultaneous model and found that higher in-migration rates had insignificant effects on local rates of income growth, but significantly increased employment growth rates. Greenwood and Hunt's (1984) analysis of 1958–75 Social Security Continuous Work History Survey (CWHS) data on 57 large metropolitan areas estimated that, on average, each net in-migrant is directly responsible for 1.26 jobs at destination.[32] They attributed this to migration-induced shifts in labor demand offsetting migration's impact on labor supply. This seems to be more plausible in light of Bartel's (1979) findings, from three different longitudinal surveys, that only a small minority of intercounty and inter-SMSA migrants moved due to layoffs and that over one-third of migrants were transfers.

Testing the Impact of Migration

Previous econometric studies of migration have generally lacked a research design suitable for comparative tests of the conventional labor substitution, Marxian, and segmentation models.[33] They almost invariably have focused on the aggregate male labor force with little or no attention to sectoral divisions, to the distinction between internal native migrants and immigrants, or to the female labor force. The lack of any research on immigration's effects on working women may be due in part to the stereotypical image of immigrants, particularly the undocumented, as typically young, economically motivated, and male. But one of the least-known facts about the subject is that, for at least the past half-century, the majority of immigrants to the United States have been women. In every single year since 1930, the Immigration and Naturalization Service has counted more female than male entrants (Houston, et al., 1984). This could reflect the chain migration patterns observed in many countries, whereby an initial male vanguard is later joined abroad by wives and children who then come to dominate mature migration flows. But the unusually high female representation in immigration to the United States is doubtless attributable to additional factors, such as the large-scale entry of "war brides" after World War II, Korea, and Vietnam, and the high priority assigned family reunification in official policies dating back to the 1930s.

A General Expositional Model

The key points at issue in this debate can be clarified, and the underpinnings of the upcoming empirical approach made plain, by sketching a simple model. First assume that native-born nonmigrant workers' labor market outcomes, Y^{rn}, (e.g., hourly wages and annual weeks of employment) can be expressed as:

$$Y^{rn} = Y(C,K,D,L) \tag{1}$$

where C is a vector of personal characteristics, K a vector of job and industry characteristics, and D and L indexes of local labor demand and supply, respectively. To investigate the independent effects of migrants, L must be disaggregated:

$$L = (L^r + L^m)$$
$$= (L^{rn} + L^{rf} + L^{mn} + L^{mf}) \qquad (2)$$

The total labor supply of a local labor market consists of long-term residents (L^r), both native born (L^{rn}) and foreign born (L^{rf}), and recent in-migrants (L^m), both native-born migrants from other areas of the United States (L^{mn}) and the foreign born (L^{mf}). It is important to note that nearly all large microdata sets contain information only on the volume of net in-migration to each SMSA. Net migration between any two SMSAs a and b can be expressed as:

$$L^m_{ab} = G_{ab} - G_{ba} \qquad (3)$$

where G represents gross unidirectional migration flows.

Most economic research on geographic and job mobility in the past two decades has assumed that the representative individual or family weighs the expected costs and benefits of mobility in the context of a general investment problem.[34] At the margin, mobility occurs if the probability-weighted earnings gain it yields is in excess of expected direct and indirect costs of geographic migration and job search at destination:

$$[P_b P^o_b (\bar{W}^o_b - W^o_b) - SC_{ab}] > 0 \qquad (4)$$

where p_b is the probability of receiving a job offer from an employer at destination, P^o_b is the probability (conditional on a job offer) of receiving an acceptable wage offer, w^o_b is the minimum acceptable wage, $\bar{w}^o_b$ the average of acceptable wage offers, and SC the mobility costs. If the components of (4) are functions of vectors of personal demographic (R) and labor market characteristics (Z), then:

$$G_{ab} = R_{ab}\delta + Z_b\lambda \qquad (5)$$

$$G_{ba} = R_{ab}\delta' + Z_b\lambda' \qquad (6)$$

Substituting (5)-(6) into (3) yields:

$$L^m_{ab} = (\delta - \delta')R_{ab} + (\lambda - \lambda')Z_b \qquad (7)$$

If personal characteristics have symmetric effects on in-migration and out-migration propensities, then the first right-side term in (7) will tend to zero. This permits net migration to be expressed as a simplified function of labor market factors alone.[35]

Estimation Problems and Procedures

The functional relationship in (7) has potentially serious implications for efforts to produce econometric estimates of the wage and employment effects of the variables in (1). Since destination wage and employment levels are likely to be important components of Z, inclusion of L^m as an explanatory variable in a regression of wages or of weeks worked creates positive correlation between the regressor and the error term. OLS estimates will be biased and inconsistent.

A Three-Equation Model

In order to develop tests free of simultaneity bias and of a form suited to evaluating the major theoretical positions, I estimate the following three-equation system separately for white non-Hispanic ("Anglo"), non-Hispanic black, and Hispanic males and females in low-skill occupations:

$$FB75_j = \alpha_0 + \alpha_1 POP74_j + \alpha_2 INC74_j + \alpha_3 WELF74_j \\ + \alpha_4 UN74_j + \alpha_5 SUNBELT_j + \alpha_{6j} \tag{8}$$

$$NB75_j = \beta_0 + \beta_1 POP74_j + \beta_2 INC74_j + \beta_3 WELF74_j \\ + \beta_4 UN74_j + \beta_5 SUNBELT_j + \beta_{6j} \tag{9}$$

$$W_{ij} = \gamma_0 + \gamma_1 EDUC_i + \gamma_2 EX_i + \gamma_3 EX_i^2 + \gamma_4 MAR_i + \gamma_5 HEALTH_i \\ + \gamma_6 IND_i + \gamma_7 SOUTH_i + \gamma_8 UNION_j + \gamma_9 UNRATE_j \\ + \gamma_{10} LABFORCE_j \\ + \gamma_{11} FBPRE75_j + \gamma_{12} NB75_j \\ + \gamma_{13} FB75_j + e_{ij} \tag{10}$$

where the i and j subscripts denote the individual and the SMSA of residence, respectively; all variables are defined in Table 8.5.

In addition to regressions on the natural log of native workers' hourly wages (WAGE), a full set of employment regressions are estimated with the dependent variable (WEEKS) measuring the log of annual weeks worked by native employees. The specifications of the wage and the employment models were designed both to facilitate tests of the hypotheses discussed above and to maximize the comparability of the findings with those of other studies in the internal and international migration literature.[36] In regressions on male subsamples, *LABFORCE* is measured as the size of the total male labor force in each metropolitan area; *NB75* as the number of native-born male in-migrants to each SMSA entering from 1975 on; *FB75* as the number of foreign-born male Hispanic labor force participants who arrived from 1975 on; and *FBPRE75* as the stock of male Hispanic immigrants in the local labor force who moved into that SMSA before 1975. In the regressions on indigenous female workers, these values are replaced by the numbers of women in each category. Note that by including *LABFORCE* in all regressions, we insure that the migrant supply coefficients measure migrants' wage and employment impacts independent of variations in the size of each area's labor market.[37]

Equations (8) and (9) use 1974 values of a set of metropolitan characteristics now standard in the geographic mobility literature as predictors of the inter-SMSA distributions of 1975–79 native- and foreign-born migrants. More populous metropolitan areas (*POP74*) are thought generally to offer a wider array of employment and self-employment opportunities, and these were nowhere more promising in the 1970s than in the South and Southwest, hence the *SUNBELT* regional dummy. The probable benefits of in-migration are still greater the higher per capita income

TABLE 8.5. Definitions of Variables, Immigration Impact Regressions

Endogenous Variables	
W	Alternately, the hourly wage rate and the annual weeks worked in 1979 of natives, in natural logarithmic form
FB75	Number of recent (immigrated 1975–79) Hispanic male (female) immigrants in the local labor force in 1979
NB75	Number of recent (arrived 1975–79) native-born male (female) migrants in the local labor force in 1979
Explanatory Variables	
CHILD	Number of children ever born to individual
EDUC	Years of school completed, entered as a spline with the break at 12 years
EX	Years of estimated postschool work experience (Age − EDUC − 6), entered as a quadratic (EX^2 = years of experience squared)
FBPRE75	Number of earlier (immigrated before 1975) Hispanic male (female) immigrants in the local labor force
HEALTH	1 if have a disability that limits work, 0 otherwise
INC74	Median per capita income in SMSA, 1974
IND	Vector of 10 industry dummy variables
LABFORCE	Total size of SMSA labor force (by sex)
MAR	1 if married, spouse present, 0 otherwise
POP74	Total population of SMSA, 1974
SOUTH	1 if resident in southern state, 0 otherwise
SUNBELT	1 if state in South or Southwest, 0 otherwise
UNION	Percent of SMSA's production workers who are union members
UN74	Annual unemployment rate in SMSA, 1974
UNRATE	Annual local unemployment rate of Anglo males in white-collar occupations
WELF74	Average monthly government welfare (AFDC) benefits per family in SMSA, 1974
Additional Regressors in Hispanic Equations	
CUBAN	1 if individual of Cuban origin, 0 otherwise
MEXICAN	1 if individual of Mexican origin, 0 otherwise
NONWHITE	1 if individual nonwhite, 0 otherwise
OTHRLATN	1 if individual of other Central or South American origin, 0 otherwise
OTHRSPAN	1 if individual of other Spanish-origin group, 0 otherwise

(*INC*74). On the other hand, the higher local jobless rates (*UN*74) and the lower available public assistance (*WELF*74), the greater the disincentive to risk job search in a new area. Since the principal urban destinations of newly arrived foreigners also tend to attract disproportionate shares of natives moving from other parts of the United States, substitution of the instrumental variables *FB*75 and *NB*75 into equation (10) both permits a disentangling of their separate effects and insures independence of the regressors from e_{ij}.[38] The important fact (discussed in the last section) that the majority of the 1975–80 Hispanic migrant cohort appear to have been illegal entrants enables us to interpret *FB*75 as a proxy for the volume of recent undocumented migration.

In addition to the individual supply characteristics of schooling, work experience, marital status, and health (*EDUC, EX, MSP, HEALTH*), the female regressions also include a fertility variable (total number of children born) to control for the effects of childcare responsibilities on the duration and continuity of women's work experience. A vector of industry dummies are included to capture differences in job environment and (insofar as capital–labor ratios vary by industry) in capital stock. The local rate of unionization among production workers controls for intermetropolitan discrepancies in worker bargaining power. The state of demand in the local labor market is proxied by a regional dummy and by the SMSA unemployment rate for Anglos in white-collar occupations (so defined to minimize collinearity with the migration variables). To take into account the racial and national-origin (and associated locational) heterogeneity of Hispanics, their regressions also include dummy variables for nonwhites, Mexicans, Cubans, other Latin Americans, and other Spanish origin (with Puerto Ricans as the omitted benchmark). The three overidentified equations are estimated by two-stage least squares.

A wide variety of classification schemes have been used in the dual labor market literature to identify segment boundaries. Some of the earliest and most prominent economists working in this tradition have relied on the industrial divisions derived from Oster's factor analysis of 83 three-digit industries using over two dozen characteristics (including layoff rates, hours worked, unionization, labor productivity, and market concentration).[39] Gordon has recently combined industrial and occupational information to define a three-tiered primary sector.[40] However, both the Oster and Gordon methodologies have the limitation, for our purposes, of excluding retail trade and service industries—two of the most important employers of immigrants. Hence, the strategy adopted in this chapter is to test migration's impacts on natives classified in several different ways: (1) all low-skilled workers, defined by employment in operative, fabrication, laborer, food preparation and service, and cleaning and building occupations (based on the standard 1980 census three-digit categories); (2) low-skilled workers in Oster's peripheral industries; (3) low-skilled workers in "immigrant-intensive" industries, defined as those in which the proportion of foreign-born males (females) exceeds their share of the male (female) labor force nationwide; and (4) secondary sector workers as defined by Gordon's occupational and industrial criteria.[41]

Data

The principal data source is the Public Use Microdata Sample of the 1980 Census of Population. As in the study of transfer usage above, the 1/100 sample of Hispanics is used together with a 1/200 sample of non-Hispanic blacks and a 1/1000 sample of white non-Hispanics.[42] The study sample was restricted to nonstudents ages 16–64 who lived in SMSAs with populations over 500,000 and who reported all relevant personal and employment information. Puerto Ricans born on the island were included among the foreign born because, though U.S. citizens, their migration experience is most similar to that of immigrants from other Spanish-speaking developing countries.[43]

Econometric Results

The percentage distributions in Table 8.6 reveal that immigrants are substantially more likely to be in low-skill occupations than are native non-Hispanic whites.

TABLE 8.6. Sector and Skill Distributions of Anglos, Blacks, and Hispanics
by Sex and Nativity[a]

Sector and Skill Group	Anglos			Blacks			Hispanics		
	NB	FB	FB75	NB	FB	FB75	NB	FB	FB75
MALES									
All Industries	100	100	100	100	100	100	100	100	100
Low Skilled	21.5	25.0	32.7	45.9	35.5	37.3	39.5	50.5	59.7
Core	13.5	12.7	13.1	15.8	10.4	11.3	13.6	11.4	9.4
Low Skilled	4.5	5.0	5.9	10.2	4.5	4.5	6.8	6.4	7.0
Periphery	21.8	23.5	23.5	24.4	24.5	24.9	29.2	35.6	40.4
Low Skilled	9.7	8.7	14.4	15.8	13.9	13.0	15.6	20.7	23.5
Immigrant-Intensive	33.6	60.8	60.8	37.1	53.4	50.8	37.5	60.0	64.9
Low Skilled	8.7	15.7	20.3	20.2	22.1	22.6	17.3	33.4	42.4
FEMALES									
All Industries	100	100	100	100	100	100	100	100	100
Low Skilled	16.1	24.8	31.9	27.3	12.2	4.2	28.4	47.3	53.4
Core	7.4	6.1	7.2	9.4	4.8	4.2	10.1	11.6	9.9
Low Skilled	2.3	2.6	5.8	4.3	0.7	0.0	5.5	7.1	6.1
Periphery	11.0	16.0	14.5	10.3	8.8	16.7	15.6	30.2	35.9
Low Skilled	3.8	10.2	7.2	6.4	2.7	4.2	9.1	22.9	29.8
Immigrant-Intensive	44.4	52.7	55.1	48.4	68.7	62.5	49.5	73.7	86.3
Low Skilled	10.9	19.1	23.2	18.6	11.6	4.2	20.1	41.0	48.1

[a]NOTE: NB = Native Born; FB = All Foreign Born; FB75 = Foreign Born, immigrated in period 1975–79. For definitions of Core, Periphery and Immigrant Intensive industrial sectors and of low-skilled occupations, see text. Note that each entry represents, for a given sex, race, ethnicity, and nationality, the percentage of all labor force participants ages 16–64, in the cited sector/skill grouping. Columns do not sum to 100 because these groups are not exhaustive.
SOURCE: 1980 Census Public Use Microdata Samples.

Within each racial/ethnic group only black migrants have an advantage (perhaps due to their more skilled work backgrounds at home) over their native counterparts. Consistent with segmentation theory, migrants tend to be underrepresented in core industries and, while only one-third of native Anglo men in the core are low skilled (.045/.135), this is true of 43 percent of black and 56 percent of male Hispanic migrants. Hispanics are also more concentrated in peripheral industries, where over 30 percent of foreign-born Hispanic women and 36 percent of male migrants work, three-fifths of them in the bottom skill layer. At the same time, there is little nationality difference among Anglos and blacks in the fraction in the periphery and for most population groups that sector does not account for a majority of the low skilled.

However, this appears to say more about the limited applicability of a classification scheme developed with 1970 data and excluding trade and service industries than it does about the extent to which immigrants are in segmented markets today. This becomes clear once industries are classified by the proportion of the work force that is foreign born. Of the 101 three-digit "immigrant-intensive" industries with above average fractions of migrants, 37 overlap with Oster's peripheral category of 62 industries, some of which (e.g., apparel, leather, furniture, taxis) are quite important employers of immigrants. But half of the two dozen industries with over

TABLE 8.7. Selected Employment Characteristics of Anglos, Blacks, and Hispanics by Sex, Nativity, and Sector[a]

Sector and Skill Group	Anglos			Blacks			Hispanics		
	NB	FB	FB75	NB	FB	FB75	NB	FB	FB75
MALES									
All Industries									
Wage Rate ($)	9.59	10.71	9.71	8.64	7.70	7.09	8.00	7.06	5.64
Weeks Worked	41.62	47.00	42.64	42.39	42.90	40.37	44.96	44.37	40.71
Unemp. > 1 Wk	15.26	14.93	18.95	26.18	23.94	30.51	23.57	22.20	29.53
Unemp. > 15 Wks	5.08	4.40	5.88	12.48	9.01	11.30	8.32	6.99	9.10
Ages 16–24	15.74	7.18	16.34	18.81	11.83	16.95	27.52	20.58	41.64
≥ 12 yrs educ	46.98	43.82	50.33	27.39	31.83	30.51	27.50	19.28	12.62
Periphery, Low Skilled									
Wage Rate ($)	8.13	8.18	7.69	8.29	6.64	5.88	7.65	6.51	5.10
Weeks Worked	43.43	45.95	47.77	43.31	44.16	43.77	42.58	44.34	41.54
Unemp. > 1 Wk	28.20	24.18	13.64	29.65	25.25	17.39	29.78	25.52	33.11
Unemp. > 15 Wks	10.96	7.69	4.54	13.57	8.08	4.35	12.08	7.61	9.15
Immigrant Intensive									
Low Skilled									
Wage Rate	6.52	7.00	6.27	7.16	7.46	4.63	7.90	5.58	4.40
Weeks Worked	40.67	41.85	43.51	40.30	43.07	40.39	40.67	44.27	42.96
Unemp. > 1 Wk	25.92	17.07	6.45	29.90	24.20	35.00	29.81	23.00	28.02
Unemp. > 15 Wks	9.38	3.05	3.23	14.70	8.92	15.00	11.54	7.07	7.93
FEMALES									
All Industries									
Wage Rate ($)	6.15	6.12	5.48	6.55	6.37	6.39	5.13	4.86	3.73
Weeks Worked	41.97	42.22	36.65	41.86	44.71	40.21	39.51	40.47	38.15
Unemp. > 1 Wk	16.38	16.35	17.39	20.86	16.33	25.00	22.78	23.71	25.95
Unemp. > 15 Wks	4.16	5.65	2.90	7.88	4.08	0.00	8.46	8.22	8.40
Ages 16–24	20.62	8.71	17.39	18.60	8.16	20.83	33.15	19.19	34.35
≥ 12 yrs educ	85.08	74.00	72.46	71.23	70.70	62.50	63.98	41.61	23.66
Periphery, Low Skilled									
Wage Rate ($)	4.80	4.89	3.76	5.60	2.45	2.51	5.00	4.08	3.85
Weeks Worked	40.98	41.45	40.00	40.20	36.48	16.00	36.60	39.61	39.33
Unemp. > 1 Wk	28.28	27.59	0.00	33.51	25.00	0.00	28.36	29.58	25.64
Unemp. > 15 Wks	7.90	12.64	0.00	13.30	0.00	0.00	10.45	11.28	7.69
Immigrant Intensive									
Low Skilled									
Wage Rate	5.18	5.20	4.26	5.62	4.67	2.51	4.33	4.30	3.95
Weeks Worked	38.18	39.72	36.06	39.46	45.23	16.00	37.50	39.10	37.57
Unemp. > 1 Wk	27.14	23.46	25.00	25.41	5.88	0.00	23.81	29.13	25.40
Unemp. > 15 Wks	8.23	9.26	6.25	10.50	0.00	0.00	6.80	11.02	6.35

[a]Mean wage rate and weeks worked calculated from samples restricted to wage and salary workers ages 16–64 who reported nonzero earnings, hours, and weeks worked in 1979. Entries for unemployment incidence, age group, and educational attainment are percentages of labor force participants, ages 16–64.

SOURCE: 1980 Census Public Use Microdata Samples.

TABLE 8.8. Estimated Wage Effects of Hispanic Immigration on Native-Born Low-Skilled Workers, 16–64[a]

Independent Variables	Males			Females		
	Anglos	Blacks	Hispanics	Anglos	Blacks	Hispanics
EDUC	.0486** (8.24)	.0376** (6.30)	.0455** (7.22)	.0302** (3.40)	.0114 (1.65)	.0133* (2.03)
EDUC > 12	-.0335** (2.64)	.0166 (1.02)	-.0024 (0.12)	.0088 (0.53)	-.0014 (0.07)	.0461 (1.76)
EX	.0269** (9.52)	.0198** (6.54)	.0238** (6.36)	.0144** (4.17)	.0178** (5.17)	.0137** (3.35)
EX^2	-.0003** (5.91)	-.0002** (3.18)	-.0002** (3.19)	-.0002** (2.67)	-.0002** (3.44)	-.0002 (1.84)
MAR	.1890** (8.12)	.2235** (9.53)	.1743** (5.52)	-.0132 (0.53)	.0534* (2.22)	-.0220 (0.72)
HEALTH	-.2511** (6.72)	-.1150** (2.67)	-.0664 (1.04)	.0252 (0.48)	-.0217 (0.44)	-.0969 (1.33)
SOUTH	-.0334 (1.07)	.0021 (0.05)	-.0514 (1.02)	-.0434 (1.08)	-.1279** (2.85)	.0040 (0.07)
UNION	.0048** (4.04)	.0067** (4.45)	.0106** (6.10)	.0041** (3.07)	.0031* (2.23)	.0095** (4.56)

	(1)	(2)	(3)	(4)	(5)	(6)
UNRATE	-.0844	-.2799	-0.722	-.5121	-.2543	-.2618
	(0.26)	(0.63)	(0.12)	(1.39)	(0.56)	(0.41)
LABFORCE	.0005	-.0003	-.0005	-.0024**	-.0018*	-.0028**
	(0.92)	(0.52)	(0.74)	(3.05)	(2.56)	(3.36)
Hispanic Immigrants Pre-1975	-.0488**	-.0003	-.0265	.0373	.0500*	-.0132
	(3.18)	(0.03)	(1.34)	(0.93)	(2.43)	(0.34)
1975–79 Native Migrants	.0073	.0238	.0192	.0566**	.0604**	.0337*
	(0.62)	(1.83)	(1.39)	(3.46)	(3.95)	(2.08)
1975–79 Hispanic Immigrants	.9610**	-.2200	.4777	-.1239	-.1939**	.0544
	(2.59)	(0.80)	(1.05)	(1.02)	(2.74)	(0.52)
CHILD	—	—	—	-.0092	-.0098	.0017
				(1.14)	(1.75)	(0.21)
CONSTANT	.8310**	.7230**	.4861**	.9823**	1.2114**	.9189**
	(8.24)	(6.46)	(3.83)	(7.56)	(9.59)	(5.49)
R^2	.1896	.1096	.1305	.1024	.0609	.0823
N	4264	6193	3194	2284	3438	1780

*p < .05; **p < .01.

[a]T-ratios in parentheses. All equations estimated by 2-Stage Least Squares with the natural log of 1979 hourly wages as dependent variable. Ten industry dummies and, in the Hispanic regressions, 5 race/ethnic dummy variables are also included in each equation. See text for definitions of variables and low-skilled occupations. Native-born migrant, Hispanic immigrant, and total labor force counts in 100s. Samples restricted to nonstudent civilian wage and salary workers reporting positive labor earnings, hours, and weeks worked in 1979.

one-fifth of their workers foreign born (twice the national average) are not included in the periphery, largely due to the omission of such trades and services as hotels, bakeries, and dressmaking. The degree of immigrant segmentation is evident in Table 8.6: one-half of foreign-born black men and Anglo women, three-fifths of male Anglo and Hispanic migrants, and over two-thirds of female black and Hispanic immigrants are concentrated in that sector. In contrast, less than two-fifths of male and under one-half of female natives work in such firms. The sector accounts for over 60 percent of all low-skilled male immigrants and over three-fourths of low-skilled foreign women.

With the majority of Hispanic migrants at the bottom of the occupational ladder it may not be surprising to see in Table 8.7 that their mean hourly earnings are far below the native Anglo average. The above average proportion under 25 and their below average rate of high school completion are commonly cited contributing factors. And foreign-born Hispanics and blacks are subject to the same discriminatory forces as their native counterparts (whose wages are also far below those of Anglos). But when we control for age, their sectoral concentrations and earnings disadvantages are just as strong among men 25 to 44. Wages in immigrant industries are below average for all groups and also tend to fall below the peripheral level.

Low wages appear to be the tradeoff involved for immigrants in securing year-round employment. Although, in the aggregate, the 1975–79 cohort has jobless rates slightly above average, this is almost entirely due to their concentration in unstable sectors. Among the low skilled in peripheral and immigrant industries, the unemployment differentials are much smaller. Recent migrants are less prone to long-term (over 14 weeks) joblessness and they work the same—and in some cases more—weeks per year than natives. An oft-cited source of downward bias in foreign workers' unemployment figures is the presumed reticence of many, especially those lacking proper papers, to register for government jobless benefits. By using retrospective information self-reported by the individuals themselves instead of aggregate data on registered unemployment we avoid this problem. But it could also be argued that by relying on data for a single, nonrecession year, any tendency for migrants to suffer disproportionately in cyclical downswings will not be captured. The dearth of time-series or panel data on immigrants in the United States makes this proposition difficult to test. However, we saw in chapter 4 that analysis of the duration and frequency of jobless spells in 1975—the year of the worst postwar recession up to that point—revealed little significant difference between the native and foreign born; in fact, regression analysis of pooled samples (with a standard set of controls for personal and labor-market factors) suggested that recent Hispanic immigrants had a lower incidence of unemployment than otherwise comparable native Hispanics. The evidence thus appears to run counter to both the neoclassical and the Marxian images of high-turnover migrants.

Two-stage least squares estimates of the wage equation for native-born low-skilled males and females are presented in Table 8.8. To permit evaluations of the separate effects of recent native as well as foreign in-migration to each SMSA the regressions were run on natives residing in the same SMSA in 1980 as in 1975. The estimated coefficients of the personal characteristics are fairly conventional: additional schooling and work experience have highly significant positive effects, whereas health disabilities exert the expected negative influence. Postsecondary schooling is, however, unrewarded by steeper earnings profiles in the lowest job strata. The fact that married men are significantly higher paid than others may be taken as evidence that the greater job attachment of men with family obligations is of value to secondary-sector employers, contrary to the claims of some of the earliest segmentation studies. Among working women, however, once differences in family size (*CHILD*) are controlled for, only black wives (spouse present) have a small wage advantage over unmarried blacks.

Of the other control variables the only one with consistently significant coefficients is the proportion of local workers in unions. The positive union wage effect would no doubt have been found even more pronounced were we able to include a variable for the respondent's own union membership (unavailable in the census).

To interpret the coefficients of the migration variables one must take into account, for each sex separately, the increase in total labor force size that accompanies increased numbers of native or foreign-born newcomers. That is, from equation (10):

$$\frac{\partial W}{\partial FB75} = \gamma_{10} + \gamma_{13}$$

The net effect of the 1975–79 cohort is thus the sum of the coefficients of the local labor force plus the migration cohort. For all low-skilled native men the results indicate that there are no significant negative effects on their wage levels from recent Hispanic immigration. In fact, such migration has a significantly positive influence on Anglo male earnings. Coupled with the negative coefficient on the long-term migrant stock variable (*FBPRE75*) in the Anglo regression this seems to lend support to Piore's view, though its magnitude (−.0005) is extremely small.

The only persons whose wages appear to have been somewhat adversely affected by illegal migration since the mid-seventies are black women. An increase in the number of recent Hispanic migrants by 1,000 is associated with 1.9 percent lower hourly earnings. With an average of 5,010 such migrants per SMSA, 1,000 more represent a 19.96 percent increase. Hence, the labor supply cross-elasticity, evaluated at the mean, is about −.095. However, this effect is not only relatively small but is also transitory: a larger number of settled (pre-1975) migrants have a significantly positive impact on black women's wages.

One possible criticism of these results could be that the proximity of our low-skilled sample to the legal minimum wage sharply reduces the downward flexibility of wages. If so, the negative effects of immigration are more likely to be felt— particularly among the lowest paid minorities—through decreased employment. Table 8.9 presents regressions of the log of total weeks worked in 1979 on an identical set of explanatory variables. For no racial/ethnic group, male or female, is there a discernible negative effect of illegal immigration on employment. In fact, most of the estimated coefficients are positive.

The results thus far are for all unskilled and semiskilled native-born workers across the full range of industries. One possible reason for the weak migration effects could be that large migrant flows into particular metropolitan areas displace natives into the industrial periphery of nonunion firms with inferior working conditions. If so, it is possible that any negative effects on this subset are masked by

TABLE 8.9. Estimated Employment Effects of Hispanic Immigration on Native-Born Low-Skilled Workers, 16–64[a]

Independent Variables	Males			Females		
	Anglos	Blacks	Hispanics	Anglos	Blacks	Hispanics
EDUC	.0216**	.0178**	.0162**	.0373**	.0286**	.0345**
	(4.88)	(4.67)	(3.74)	(4.40)	(4.66)	(4.64)
EDUC > 12	.0115	.0077	.0231	.0155	.0030	.0187
	(1.20)	(0.75)	(1.63)	(0.83)	(0.17)	(0.62)
EX	.0191**	.0242**	.0208**	.0281**	.0387**	.0411**
	(9.02)	(12.47)	(8.10)	(7.20)	(12.64)	(8.95)
EX^2	-.0003**	-.0003**	-.0003**	-.0003**	-.0005**	-.0005**
	(6.90)	(7.40)	(5.69)	(3.32)	(7.13)	(5.15)
MAR	.1061**	.1034**	.1642**	-.0916**	.0324	-.0881*
	(6.06)	(6.89)	(7.56)	(3.22)	(1.51)	(2.52)
HEALTH	-.2908**	-.3876**	-.2729**	-.3764**	-.2448**	-.2093**
	(10.35)	(14.05)	(6.23)	(6.55)	(5.60)	(2.60)
SOUTH	-.0075	.0458	.0831*	.0234	.0954*	.1038
	(0.32)	(1.75)	(2.39)	(0.51)	(2.38)	(1.64)
UNION	-.0016	-.0011	-.0005	.0006	.0001	.0005
	(1.85)	(1.11)	(0.46)	(0.41)	(0.79)	(0.20)

	(1)	(2)	(3)	(4)	(5)	(6)
UNRATE	-.3131	-.0683	-.3156	-.0360	.3343	-.0415
	(1.27)	(0.24)	(0.77)	(0.08)	(0.82)	(0.06)
LABFORCE	.0002	-.0003	.0002	-.0007	.0003	.0006
	(0.66)	(0.75)	(0.37)	(0.83)	(0.50)	(0.66)
Hispanic Immigrants Pre-1975	-.0024	.0076	-.0192	-.0184	-.0264	-.0242
	(0.20)	(1.14)	(1.41)	(0.41)	(1.42)	(0.54)
1975–79 Native Migrants	.0003	.0029	-.0011	.0079	-.0128	-.0203
	(0.03)	(0.34)	(0.12)	(0.43)	(0.93)	(1.10)
1975–79 Hispanic Immigrants	-.0224	-.1502	.4314	.0674	.0924	.0626
	(0.08)	(0.85)	(1.38)	(0.49)	(1.45)	(0.52)
CHILD	—	—	—	-.0396**	-.0205**	-.0390**
				(4.38)	(4.13)	(4.41)
CONSTANT	3.3236**	3.2036**	3.2028**	3.0027**	2.7480**	2.7381**
	(43.83)	(44.68)	(36.73)	(20.39)	(24.40)	(14.42)
R^2	.1017	.1265	.1178	.1196	.1244	.1199
N	4264	6193	3194	2284	3438	1780

*p < .05; **p < .01.

[a]T-ratios in parentheses. All equations estimated by 2-Stage Least Squares with the natural log of 1979 weeks worked as dependent variable. Ten industry dummies and, in the Hispanic regressions, 5 race/ethnic dummy variables are also included in each equation. See text for definitions of variables and low-skilled occupations. Native-born migrant, Hispanic immigrant, and total labor force counts in 100s. Samples restricted to nonstudent civilian wage and salary workers reporting positive weeks worked in 1979.

offsetting effects in the core industries included in our full sample. To evaluate this possibility, a similar set of wage and employment regressions were run on that native-born male subset whose last main industry of employment was in the periphery (as defined by Oster). The analysis was also conducted on those in the broader "immigrant-intensive" sector. The estimates in Tables 8.10 and 8.11 reveal that among Anglo and Hispanic males and among all working women there is no evidence of significant migration effects. But recent immigrants do appear to exert a highly significant depressant effect on the number of weeks worked by black men in the periphery. An increase in the number arriving in the last five years by 1,000 is associated with 5.6 percent fewer weeks worked by indigenous blacks. This effect is, however, not only confined to the periphery but also transitory, diminished over time by the significantly positive impact of larger populations of settled Hispanics.

The positive and statistically significant influence of immigration since the mid-seventies on Anglo males (in both Tables 8.8 and 8.10) is consistent with Chiswick's "rather unexpected" finding that among the full sample of native whites in 1970, recent immigration has a positive wage effect but long-term immigration a (small) negative effect—a result that is, he admits, "unexplained" by his labor-substitution model.[44] It is, however, quite understandable once immigration is viewed as a sequential process by which newcomers are integrated into ethnic job clusters on arrival in such a way as to minimize competition with their countrymen, though some may initially take jobs that might otherwise go to the other principal occupants of unskilled inner-city labor markets: native-born blacks. Over time, as migrants progress out of the most menial jobs and disperse from the immigrant enclave, competition with blacks declines as it potentially increases with low-wage native whites. While the common neoclassical expectation that recent immigrants will have adverse effects on natives finds some support in the regression results for blacks, the low magnitude of these coefficients and, most striking of all, the absence of any significant effects on native Hispanics (presumed to be the closest substitutes for Hispanic migrants) run directly counter to traditional theory.

Conclusion

The U.S. economy has increasingly come to depend on Third World nations for latent labor reserves that can be readily tapped in expansionary periods. This chapter has shown that migrant workers today are disproportionately concentrated in low-wage jobs in a distinct set of industries. But it has also found that, contrary to most Marxian as well as neoclassical models, recent immigrants do not typically constitute a high-turnover labor pool with unemployment above that of similar natives. Rather, just as rural migrants of an earlier era made the transition from a latent to a floating reserve fully assimilated into the industrial labor force, so also have immigrants ceased to be merely a short-term employment buffer that can be forced about to suit business needs.

This chapter investigated the two most contentious issues in current debates on the economic consequences of immigration for the United States. First, are the foreign-born more likely than native families to make use of government transfers and services? After reviewing research on the volume of legal and illegal immigra-

TABLE 8.10. Estimated Wage Effects of Hispanic Immigration on Native-Born Low-Skilled Males in Peripheral and Immigrant-Intensive Industries[a]

Independent Variables	Anglos		Blacks		Hispanics	
	Periphery	Imm. Ind.	Periphery	Imm. Ind.	Periphery	Imm. Ind.
LABFORCE	−.0001	.0004	.0009	−.0005	−.0010	−.0017
	(0.12)	(0.72)	(0.98)	(0.94)	(0.87)	(1.71)
Hispanic Immigrants Pre-1975	−.0638**	−.0494**	−.0012	−.0062	−.0215	−.0217
	(2.81)	(2.86)	(0.08)	(0.55)	(0.63)	(0.76)
1975–79 Native Migrants	.0335	.0038	.0001	.0288*	.0324	.0400
	(1.87)	(0.30)	(0.01)	(2.46)	(1.42)	(1.85)
1975–79 Hispanic Immigrants	1.3023*	1.0596*	−.3543	−.1338	.2851	.4002
	(2.33)	(2.56)	(0.83)	(0.46)	(0.36)	(0.62)

*p < .05; **p < .01.

[a]T-ratios in parentheses. Full regressions include all other variables in wage equations, Table 8.8. See text for definitions of periphery and immigrant-intensive industries (Imm. Ind.). Native-born migrant, Hispanic immigrant, and total labor force counts in 100s.

tion and on the initial impact of the 1986 IRCA provisions, recent findings on the comparability of the earnings patterns of migrant and native workers were evaluated. Empirical analysis of nationality differences in the incidence and level of public assistance recipiency was then undertaken, employing 1980 census microdata on families subdivided by race and Spanish origin. The principal results are that immigrant families appear to be generally less likely to receive public assistance than comparable natives, and, among those who are recipients, there is little significant native–immigrant difference in the average dollar value of benefits.

TABLE 8.11. Estimated Employment Effects of Hispanic Immigration on Native-Born Low-Skilled Males in Peripheral and Immigrant-Intensive Industries[a]

Independent Variables	Anglos		Blacks		Hispanics	
	Periphery	Imm. Ind.	Periphery	Imm. Ind.	Periphery	Imm. Ind.
LABFORCE	−.0002	.0001	−.0002	−.0002	−.0012	.0010
	(0.20)	(0.25)	(0.20)	(0.51)	(0.30)	(1.00)
Hispanic Immigrants Pre-1975	−.0193	−.0005	.0210*	.0028	−.0217	.0343
	(1.14)	(0.04)	(2.02)	(0.38)	(0.20)	(1.70)
1975–79 Native Migrants	.0034	.0001	.0134	.0009	.0472	−.0058
	(0.25)	(0.01)	(1.05)	(0.10)	(1.38)	(0.38)
1975–79 Hispanic Immigrants	.4837	−.0321	−.5628*	−.0313	−.0349	.6698
	(1.16)	(0.10)	(2.06)	(0.17)	(0.44)	(1.45)

*p < .05; **p < .01.

[a]T-ratios in parentheses. Full regressions include all other variables in employment equations, Table 8.9. See text for definitions of periphery and immigrant-intensive industries (Imm. Ind.). Native-born migrant, Hispanic immigrant, and total labor force counts in 100s.

The second issue examined is whether increased immigration lowers the earnings or the employment levels of the native born. The major theoretical positions on the matter—neoclassical factor substitution theory, the Marxian reserve army model, and the dual labor market view—were first discussed in the light of research findings on the American and the European experiences with postwar immigration. Multiequation regression analysis was conducted on labor force participants in major metropolitan areas, using 1980 census data. While the empirical analysis raises questions about some aspects of the segmentation model as applied to immigration, the findings are far more consistent with it than with theories emphasizing migrant–native substitutability over complementarity.

The results indicate that increased immigration from Spanish-speaking countries has not significantly affected the wages or employment of native-born Hispanics. Recent undocumented migration does reduce black women's wages and black men's employment somewhat, and larger concentrations of settled immigrants are associated with lower white non-Hispanic wage levels, but the estimated magnitudes of these effects are not large.

This does not of course imply that the imposition of even relatively small economic costs on the most disadvantaged social groups should not be cause for concern. But much-improved employment and training programs to speed the upward mobility of natives out of the worst-paid jobs, stepped-up enforcement of labor standards for minimum wages and working conditions, and greater access to collective bargaining for both the native and migrant unskilled could produce much more positive long-term effects than drastic cuts in immigration.

Nor should these results be taken to imply that far larger volumes of immigration than those of the recent past would necessarily have similarly low costs. Attempts to extrapolate much beyond the range of available data are usually as misleading as they are difficult. It is certainly conceivable that, should the government decide one day to increase admissions to some multiple of present levels, the absorptive capacities of New York, Los Angeles, Miami and other magnet labor markets could be severely strained. Given the high economic stakes involved, the most sensible policy would surely be to only undertake any future expansion in a cautious, incremental manner and with federal funds set aside to assist any localities that are affected adversely.

A strong case can also be made for redesigning entry criteria to better serve domestic manpower needs as well as traditional humanitarian concerns. The 1990 immigration reforms took a very small step in that direction by doubling the number of "green cards" reserved for skilled workers (from 54,000 to 140,000 per year). But the fact that most of these will be given to the relatives of the skilled workers, coupled with the increase in the overall number of visas to 700,000, means that such workers will still represent less than 10 percent of annual admissions. A substantial increase in this share of the overall visa total could help reduce what job competition there may be in the near future between newcomers and indigenous workers. Of course, the greater availability of skilled migrants must not be allowed to detract in any way from the critical task of expanding educational and training programs for low-income Americans.

Since the one point of agreement of all economic studies of immigration is that it increases the rate of return on capital, there are also strong grounds for more generous income redistribution programs—particularly in the wake of a decade of such regressive fiscal policy. Short of such efforts, perhaps the most promising development in the near future is the decline in the supply of new native labor force entrants brought on by falling birth rates and the aging of the baby-boom cohort. Should this continue at the rate currently forecast, it is likely that the domestic costs of immigration will become still smaller and the benefits more pronounced.

NOTES

1. Bouvier (1983).
2. These and other alien arrest figures are from the INS *Annual Reports* for various years.
3. See North and Houston (1976), ch. 4.
4. Siegel, Passel, and Robinson (1981).
5. Warren and Passel (1987).
6. See U.S. Bureau of the Census (1982a).
7. After a two-year evaluation of these and all earlier estimates, the Panel on Immigration Statistics of the National Academy of Sciences recently concluded that national immigration policy "has been made in a data vacuum." Relying largely on the Warren–Passel census findings, it argued for a range of from 2 to no more than 4 million as the most plausible estimate of the number of undocumented residents in 1980. See National Research Council (1985).
8. Bean, King, and Passell (1983).
9. Passel and Woodrow (1984). New York had the second largest state total with 234,000, followed by Texas (186,000), Illinois (135,000), and Florida (80,000).
10. See, for example, Bach and Schraml (1982) and the papers discussed therein.
11. See North and Houston (1976): p. 65 and Table V-5.
12. U.S. Bureau of the Census (1984c): Table 255).
13. See U.S. Bureau of the Census (1982a) for a discussion of the errors discovered in early 1980 census counts based solely on answers to the Spanish-origin question, and their recommended matrix of characteristics to establish Hispanic ethnicity.
14. Linear probability models of this kind have well-known shortcomings, in particular heteroscedasticity and predicted values that are unbounded by the 0-1 interval. They are used here in place of logit or probit techniques because the latter require much higher computer expenses and typically produce roughly similar coefficient estimates.
15. North and Houston (1976): p. 142.
16. See North (1980).
17. For the Census Bureau estimates of the undocumented by metropolitan area, see Passel (1985).
18. A study of the undocumented in Orange County, California found similarly low rates of program usage. See Sullivan (1978).
19. Chiswick (1981).
20. See, for example, Briggs (1984); Fogel (1980); Greenwood (1979); and George Johnson (1980). In his introduction to an immigration symposium, Fogel (1980) refers to this position as the "orthodox economic" or "conventional" theory.
21. See Castles and Kosack (1973).
22. Adriana Marshall (1973): p. 17.

23. Piore (1979a), ch. 5.

24. See the findings surveyed in Mark Killingsworth (1983).

25. See, for example, Coterill (1975).

26. DeFreitas and Marshall (1984).

27. See, for example, Bailey (1985); Light (1972); Portes and Bach (1985); and Waldinger (1986).

28. See Waldinger (1986). This is, of course, one reason for the strong opposition to restrictive immigration laws by the New York local of the International Ladies' Garment Workers' Union.

29. See the survey by Bailey (1985).

30. Author's calculations from U.S. Bureau of the Census (1984b: U.S. Summary): Table 259; and Houston (1984): Table 2.

31. The simple correlation coefficient between the number of 1975–79 native-born migrants in each major SMSA and the number of 1975–79 Hispanic immigrants in the same SMSAs is 0.62. Source: Author's calculations from 1980 Census Public Use Microdata Samples.

32. Muth's (1971) study of a 1960 cross-section found a similar positive effect on employment growth. Chiswick (1981) reports a significant negative effect of recent internal migrants on native Anglo males' 1969 wages (but not on their employment). However, unlike these other studies Chiswick used OLS rather than simultaneous estimation methods, thereby increasing the possibility of biased coefficients and making comparisons with the Greenwood and Muth results difficult.

33. See the excellent surveys of recent immigration research by Bean, Telles, and Lowell (1987); Borjas and Tienda (1987); Greenwood and McDowell (1986); and U.S. Dept. of Labor (1989).

34. See, for example, Bowles (1970) and the survey by Greenwood (1985).

35. Note that labor market variables (like income and unemployment at destination j) which have different coefficient signs in (5) and (6) will have their effects amplified in (7).

36. See in particular the close relatives to this model in the wage and employment equations in Chiswick (1981) and King, Lowell, and Bean (1986).

37. Tests of other specifications with the migration variables redefined as the percentage of migrants in each SMSA yielded similar results. For example, see DeFreitas (1988a).

38. A variety of alternative specifications were tested, including single-equation models and redefined migration variables (e.g., percentage of local labor force foreign born instead of the migrant stock variable, and inclusion of immigrants of all nationalities rather than only those with Hispanic origins), without qualitative changes in the results.

39. See Oster (1979); Gordon, Edwards, and Reich (1982); and Reich (1984).

40. Gordon (1984). See Ryan (1981) on the classificatory issue.

41. The distributional and regression results for the Gordon classification were nearly identical to the low-skilled periphery findings, and are not presented here. Complete results, together with a list of the specific industries and occupations in each of the four categories, are in a statistical appendix available from the author on request. I am grateful to David Gordon and Gerald Oster for providing me the detailed industrial and occupational codes used in constructing their respective sectoral groupings.

42. For details on census variables and sample design, see U.S. Bureau of the Census (1983a).

43. Population, income, and AFDC data for 1974 were taken from U.S. Bureau of the Census (1983a), 1974 unemployment rates from U.S. Department of Labor (1978), and union membership estimates from Freeman and Medoff (1979).

44. Chiswick (1981): p. 76.

9

Epilogue

At the beginning of the postwar era in the United States, the mid-century census reported that only 2.6 million Americans were of Spanish origin. By almost any measure, they were a severely disadvantaged minority. Only 15.5 percent had completed high school by 1950 and over one-third of their families lived below the poverty line. The Hispanic male unemployment rate was 12 percent, the female rate 10 percent—at a time when the national average was only 5.3 percent. Of those able to find work, 7 out of 10 were in unskilled or semiskilled operative occupations. The earnings of Hispanic men averaged $1,700 per year ($8,114 in 1987 dollars), some 41 percent lower than what the average non-Hispanic white earned.

Over the course of the past four decades the Spanish-origin population expanded by nearly 700 percent, passing the 20 million mark in 1989. From a mere 1.7 percent of the nation, it has grown to over 9 percent. With this growth has come some impressive progress in economic status. The fraction with a high school diploma has risen to one-half. The poverty rate and unemployment rate have both fallen markedly. And Hispanic income and labor earnings have improved. For example, the average annual earnings of Hispanic males registered a 67.6 percent increase in inflation-adjusted dollars to $13,599 by 1987.

This book has studied the earnings, employment, and unemployment of the Hispanic labor force, investigating their postwar patterns and the impact upon them of education, immigration, discrimination, structural shifts in the economy, and other forces. The empirical analysis, both cross-sectional and time-series, has produced many and various findings not easily summarized. The principal conclusions are presented at the end of each chapter.

Perhaps it would be useful at this point to highlight the main unifying themes. First, while important gains have clearly been made in the postwar years, the average income and employment gaps between Hispanics and non-Hispanics have remained persistently large. In fact, the findings here reveal that after a burst of improvement in the 1960s, ethnic inequality has actually increased substantially in recent years. From 1973 to 1987 the standard of living of families of Spanish origin dropped an average of 9 percent and their poverty rate jumped from 20 percent to over 25 percent—three times higher than the white rate. The average income of Hispanic males, while higher than in 1950, was 12 percent lower than its 1973 level. Hispanic unemployment has been chronically one and one-half times the national average. But even among males with full-time, year-round jobs, the average ratio of Hispanic to white income has fallen from 67 percent in 1975 to 63 percent a dozen years later.

A second theme stressed in each chapter is that significant economic differences exist among the various national-origin groupings. At one extreme, Cubans have unemployment and poverty rates almost as low as those of white non-Hispanics. At the other extreme, Puerto Ricans average unemployment rates twice as high as Cubans and have the highest poverty rate of any racial or ethnic group in the country, including Native-American Indians.

The issue that has sparked most of the growing public awareness about Hispanics is immigration. The rising fraction of recent immigrants from Spanish-speaking countries has caused a highly charged public dialogue, fanned by the decline in the U.S. standard of living since the mid-seventies and by often-inflated claims about the size and impact of the undocumented alien population. Another principal theme of this book is that immigration has important, but complex effects, both with respect to the migrants' own experiences in the American labor market and to their impact on the indigenous population. Three out of 10 Hispanics ages 15 and over are immigrants, and about another 40 to 45 percent are the children of immigrants. Almost all working-age Puerto Ricans and Cubans now in the United States are either first- or second-generation immigrants. The book's empirical results suggest that the limited English-language abilities and below average schooling of many of these individuals have undeniable importance for their income and employment prospects. At the same time, contrary to a long-held view that Third World emigrants are mainly drawn from the rural unemployed surplus, many of those from Spanish-speaking nations are increasingly from the middle-income strata of towns and cities. They are, on average, better educated than their countrymen and have experience in jobs demanding above average levels of skill. They also tend to have a surprising degree of familiarity with the U.S. labor market and a support network of friends and relatives to assist their integration into the destination labor market. The stronger these support networks are, the smaller the economic disadvantage of immigrants' lack of fluency in English or educational credentials appears to be.

The findings presented here also contradict the conventional wisdom on the impact of immigration on the American economy. Increases in the numbers of Hispanic immigrants, whether documented or undocumented, do not appear to have any significant negative effects on either the wage levels or the unemployment of native-born workers. The empirical results suggest that the relatively small magnitude of immigration and its positive effects on the demand for goods and for labor in the United States outweigh whatever adverse impacts that might be associated with it. Furthermore, immigrants are even less likely to compete with natives for public transfers than they are to compete for jobs. They have a lower average incidence of participation in government income-support programs, and may well pay substantially more in taxes than they receive from the public treasury.

Hispanic immigration seems destined to become an ever-more sensitive and important issue in coming years. This is most clearly the case with respect to the largest source country, Mexico. All indications suggest that the socioeconomic integration of the U.S. Southwest with Mexico will continue, if not accelerate in the near future. Mexico has never been of more crucial economic importance to the United States. It is now the country's third largest trading partner, behind only Canada and Japan. Two-thirds of its imports are purchased from U.S. firms. Seventy percent of the foreign investments in Mexico are owned by Americans. Now the third largest petroleum producer in the world (behind only the Soviet Union and Saudi Arabia), Mexico accounts for over one-fifth of all American crude oil imports—by far the largest amount of any single country.

But the 1980s brought the worst depression in Mexico since the 1930s. By 1987, the foreign debt had exploded to $103 billion. Thanks to a relatively high (though declining) birth rate, it has become the eleventh most populous nation on earth. The World Bank forecasts that its population will jump from the 1985 level of 79 million to 110 million by the year 2000. In the same period its labor force will grow about 3 percent per year, nearly four times faster than the growth of the American labor force. But with domestic underemployment currently estimated at close to half the labor force and deep structural problems plaguing the economy, the pressure for more migration seems inevitable. How the United States responds to that pressure will have significant implications for the future of both countries' economies.

The continuing severity of Hispanic educational problems and their importance to the employment patterns we have examined constitute the fourth broad theme of this study. While it has long been known from past research that educational attainment differences help explain part of black–white and male–female wage gaps, the far larger distance between the average schooling levels of Hispanics and non-Hispanics has been shown to play a much larger role in widening their earnings gap. In part their lower schooling can be attributed to all the difficulties associated with language and cultural adjustment problems experienced by the large number of migrants from Spanish-speaking countries. But this does not explain the below average educations acquired by the more than two-thirds of Hispanics who are not immigrants.

We have seen that the average Hispanic child is likely to begin life confronting far more obstacles than most others. Two out of five children of Spanish origin lived in poverty in the late 1980s. Hispanic three- and four-year-olds are much less likely to be enrolled in preschool programs than either whites or blacks. Hispanic teenagers are far more likely to be high school dropouts than either whites or blacks. The research findings reported in chapter 7 demonstrate the considerable impact that low family income and high unemployment have on their high school dropout rates. They also show that the past decade saw a marked deterioration in the college enrollment gains registered in the 1970s. In addition to the families' economic conditions, the sharp cuts in federal scholarship grants over the past decade appear to account for much of this worrisome pattern.

The fifth main theme of the book is that the dominant theoretical approaches that economists have long relied on to account for inequality are alone insufficient to explain the conditions of Hispanics. Orthodox neoclassical theory has been constructed on the assumption that product and labor markets are usually quite competitive and full employment the norm. It places primary emphasis on the decisions of self-interested individuals, each of whom is assumed to select the amounts of schooling, skill training, and other human capital investments that will generate a desired career earnings profile. Based on a decision calculus akin to that of business investment, the individual is viewed as continuing to spend time and money on such activities until their expected net rates of return are no higher than average alternative market rates. Observed differentials in earnings between individuals or groups are thus largely attributed to the differential investment levels they have chosen for themselves.

A large number of the findings presented here attest to the strong influence that inadequate schooling, limited or unsuitable U.S. work experience, and weak English language skills have on many workers' employment prospects. Among individuals of similar age, education, English fluency, and other work-related characteristics, Hispanic wages and unemployment rates are much closer to non-Hispanics' than is true in the overall labor force. However, in such comparisons most Hispanics are still at a sizable disadvantage. The narrowing of educational and other productivity differentials between Hispanics and others over time has not been matched by the narrowing of differences in their labor market positions implied by orthodox theory.

A heterogeneous group of alternative theories has emerged since the 1960s to complement or challenge the neoclassical view. Insofar as common elements can be identified, all tend to accord far greater weight to the effects of family and class background, racial and ethnic discrimination, government policies, and structural forces in the labor market. In contrast to the conventional assumption that workers' supply choices are mainly responsible for their economic fates, nonorthodox theories contend that many are severely constrained in the choices available to them. Whereas the dominant model deemphasizes discrimination as a short-term problem steadily being eliminated by competitive market forces, these critics argue that it remains deeply entrenched in the key social and economic institutions and powerfully influences both the educational and other preemployment activities of most women, blacks, and Hispanics and their experiences at work. According to the most influential alternative perspective, the American labor market is segmented into a sector of relatively secure, good-paying, often unionized jobs offering skill training and promotional ladders, and a secondary sector of largely unstable, low-skilled, dead-end jobs. It is to the latter that discriminatory forces tend to channel disproportionate numbers of minorities and women. Thus the focus is shifted to the labor demand behavior of employers, the labor supply activities of labor unions, and the impacts of government on both demand and supply.

In studying the Spanish-origin labor force we have seen that neither the conventional nor the existing alternative models of labor economics are fully satisfactory guides. For example, much of the nonorthodox literature can be faulted for underestimating the importance of individual initiative and effort, even in the most disadvantaged circumstances. This not only weakens one's interpretation of many research findings but also it can make it difficult to move from research to the design of feasible policy reforms. In ours, as in nearly all advanced economies, public opinion polls regularly show that widespread support of antipoverty programs goes hand in hand with a popular insistence that all families make a good faith effort to work themselves up the economic ladder. Other research problems stem from the industrial composition of the labor market divisions emphasized by the segmentation literature. We have seen that substantial modification of traditional segment boundaries are required if this perspective is to be usefully applied to Hispanic workers today.

Nevertheless, in trying to make sense of these diverse findings, one is drawn back time and again to the influences of broader structural forces over which individuals have little control. The disproportionately large number of Hispanics in the unskilled and semiskilled work force have borne along with similar non-Hispanic workers the sharp drop in stable job opportunities, the weakening of union protections, and the fall in real wages common to manufacturing and other industries since the 1960s. It is possible that the trend toward worsening economic inequality will prove to be a short-term phenomenon. Insofar as youth can adjust their schooling and occupational decisions to the ongoing rise in wage premia for skilled workers, economists expect that the increased supply of such workers may ultimately narrow the relative earnings gaps. The same outcome could result if there is sufficient tightening of the low-skill labor market as the baby bust's restraining effect on labor force growth is felt in coming years.

However, it is difficult to be sanguine about the economic position of Hispanic workers in the near future. International economic competition seems likely to go on intensifying, which could further depress the wage and employment prospects of the less skilled in vulnerable industries. And there are few signs on the horizon of a reversal of the secular decline in stable, relatively well-paid manufacturing jobs and in unionization. Aggressive public policies to markedly increase access to affordable schooling, language instruction, and job training, to relocate and retrain mature workers, to stimulate job creation, and to eradicate racial and ethnic discrimination could make an enormous difference. Whether we shall have a strong enough national commitment to marshal the necessary resources for the sweeping changes required cannot be predicted. But it can be said with certainty that as the Hispanic share of the American labor force grows ever larger in coming years, so too will the human, social, and economic costs of inaction.

Bibliography

Abraham, Katherine G. "Structural/Frictional vs. Deficient Demand Unemployment: Some New Evidence." *American Economic Review,* vol. 83 (September 1983): 708–24.

Acuna, Rodolfo. *Occupied America: A History of Chicanos.* New York: Harper & Row, 1981.

Akerlof, George A., and Main, Brian G. "Unemployment Spells and Unemployment Experience." *American Economic Review,* vol. 70 (December 1980): 885–89.

Akerlof, George A., and Yellen, Janet L., eds. *Efficiency Wage Models of the Labor Market.* Cambridge: Cambridge University Press, 1986.

Alicea, V., and Mathis, J. *Determinants of Educational Attainment Among Puerto Rican Youth in the U.S.* Washington, D.C.: Universidad Boricua, 1975.

Altonji, Joseph G., and Ashenfelter, Orley. "Wage Movements and the Labor Market Equilibrium Hypothesis." *Economica,* vol. 47 (August 1980): 217–45.

Amemiya, Takeshi. "Qualitative Response Models: A Survey." *Journal of Economic Literature,* vol. 19 (December 1981): 1483–1536.

Armington, Catherine. "Further Examination of Sources of Recent Employment Growth: Analysis of USEEM Data for 1976 to 1980." Research monograph, Brookings Institution, 1983.

Arrow, Kenneth. "Some Mathematical Models of Race Discrimination in the Labor Market." In Pascal, Anthony, ed. *Racial Discrimination in Economic Life.* Lexington, MA: D.C. Heath, 1972.

Ashenfelter, Orley. "Changes in Labor Market Discrimination Over Time." *Journal of Human Resources,* vol. 5, no. 4 (Fall 1970): 403–29.

Aspe, Pedro, and Beristain, Javier. "The Distribution of Education and Health Opportunities and Services." In Aspe, Pedro, and Sigmund, Paul, eds. *The Political Economy of Income Distribution in Mexico.* New York: Holmes and Meier, 1984.

Azariadis, Costas. "Implicit Contracts and Underemployment Equilibria." *Journal of Political Economy,* vol. 83 (December 1975): 1182–1202.

Azicri, Max. "The Politics of Exile." *Cuban Studies,* vol. 11 (July 1981): 55–74.

Bach, Robert L. "Mexican Immigration and the American State." *International Migration Review,* vol. 12, no. 4 (Winter 1978): 536–58.

Bach, Robert L., Bach, Jennifer, and Triplett, Timothy. "The 'Flotilla Entrants.' " *Cuban Studies*, vol. 11 (1981/82): 29–48.

Bach, Robert L., and Schraml, Lisa A. "Migration, Crisis and Theoretical Conflict." *International Migration Review*, vol. 16, no. 2 (Summer 1982): 320–41.

Bailey, Thomas. "A Case Study of Immigrants in the Restaurant Industry." *Industrial Relations*, vol. 24 (January 1985): 205–21.

Baily, Martin N. "Wages and Employment Under Uncertain Demand." *Review of Economic Studies*, vol. 41 (January 1974): 37–50.

Bane, Mary Jo. "Household Composition and Poverty." In Danziger, S. H., and Weinberg, D.H., eds. *Fighting Poverty: What Works and What Doesn't*. Cambridge: Harvard University Press, 1986.

Bane, Mary Jo, and Ellwood, David. *The Impact of AFDC on Family Structure and Living Arrangements*. Washington, D.C.: Office of Planning and Evaluation, U.S. Department of Health and Human Services, 1984.

Barkin, David. "Mexico's Albatross: the U.S. Economy." *Latin American Perspectives*, vol. 2 (Summer 1975): 64–80.

Barrera, Mario. *Race and Class in the Southwest*. South Bend, IN: Notre Dame University Press, 1980.

Barron, J.M., Bishop, J., and Dunkelberg, W.C. "Employers Search: The Interviewing and Hiring of New Employees." *Review of Economics and Statistics*, vol. 67 (February 1985): 43–52.

Bartel, Ann P. "The Migration Decision: What Role Does Job Mobility Play?" *American Economic Review*, vol. 69 (December 1979): 775–86.

Bates, Timothy M. *Black Capitalism: A Quantitative Analysis*. New York: Praeger Publishers, 1973.

———. "Profitability in Traditional and Emerging Lines of Black Business Enterprise." *Journal of Urban Economics*, vol. 32 (April 1978): 155–59.

Bean, Frank, King, Alan, and Passel, Jeffrey. "The Number of Illegal Immigrants of Mexican Origin in the United States." *Demography*, vol. 20 (February 1983): 99–109.

Bean, Frank, Telles, Edward, and Lowell, B.L. "Undocumented Migration to the United States: Perceptions and Evidence." *Population and Development Review*, vol. 13, no. 4 (December 1987): 671–90.

Bean, Frank, and Tienda, Marta. *The Hispanic Population of the United States*. New York: Russell Sage Foundation, 1987.

Bean, Frank, White, Michael J., and Espenshade, Thomas J. "The U.S. Immigration Reform and Control Act and Undocumented Migration to the United States." Program for Research on Immigration Policy Paper PRIP-UI-5, The Urban Institute, July 1989.

Bearse, Peter J. "An Econometric Analysis of Black Entrepreneurship." *Review of Black Political Economy*, vol. 12 (Spring 1984): 111–134.

Becker, Eugene. "Self-Employed Workers: An Update to 1983." *Monthly Labor Review*, vol. 107 (July 1984): 14–18.

Becker, Gary. *The Economics of Discrimination*. Chicago: University of Chicago Press, 1957.

———. *Human Capital*. New York: Columbia University Press, 1964.

Bell, Linda A., and Freeman, Richard B. "The Facts About Rising Industrial Wage Dispersion in the U.S." *Industrial Relations Research Association, Proceedings*, no. 39 (1987): 331–37.

Beller, Andrea. "The Impact of Equal Opportunity Laws on the Male/Female Earnings Differential." In Lloyd, Cynthia, ed. *Women in the Labor Market*. New York: Columbia University Press, 1979.

Betsey, Charles, and Dunson, Bruce. "Federal Minimum Wage Laws and the Employment of Minority Youth." *American Economic Review, Proceedings,* vol. 71 (May 1981): 379–84.

Bills, Mark J. "Real Wages over the Business Cycle: Evidence from Panel Data." *Journal of Political Economy,* vol. 93 (August 1985): 666–89.

Birch, David L. *The Job Generation Process.* Cambridge: MIT Press, 1979.

Bishop, Katherine. "California Says Law on Aliens Fuels Job Bias." *New York Times,* January 12, 1990.

Blackburn, McKinley L., Bloom, David E., and Freeman, Richard B. "The Declining Economic Position of Less-Skilled American Males." Brookings Economics Discussion Papers, The Brookings Institution, November 1989.

Blanchard, Olivier, and Summers, Lawrence. "Beyond the Natural Rate Hypothesis." *American Economic Review,* vol. 78 (May 1988): 182–87.

Blank, Rebecca, and Blinder, Alan. "Macroeconomics, Income Distribution, and Poverty." In Danziger, S.H., and Weinberg, D.H., eds. *Fighting Poverty: What Works and What Doesn't.* Cambridge: Harvard University Press, 1986.

Blau, Francine. "The Use of Transfer Payments by Immigrants." *Industrial and Labor Relations Review,* vol. 37 (January 1984): 222–39.

Blau, Francine, and Kahn, Lawrence. "Causes and Consequences of Layoffs." *Economic Inquiry,* vol. 19 (April 1981a): 270–86.

———. "Race and Sex Differences in Quits by Young Workers." *Industrial and Labor Relations Review,* vol. 34 (July 1981b): 563–77.

Blau, Francine, and Ferber, Marianne A. "Discrimination: Empirical Evidence from the United States." *American Economic Review,* vol. 77 (May 1987): 316–20.

Blau, Peter, and Duncan, O.D. *The American Occupational Structure.* New York: John Wiley and Sons, 1967.

Bluestone, Barry, and Harrison, Bennett. *The Deindustrialization of America: Plant Closings, Community Abandonment, and the Dismantling of Basic Industry.* New York: Basic Books, 1982.

———. "The Growth of Low-Wage Employment: 1963–86." *American Economic Review,* vol. 78 (May 1988): 124–28.

Bonacich, Edna, and Modell, John. *The Economic Basis of Ethic Solidarity.* Berkeley: University of California Press, 1980.

Borjas, George J. "The Substitutability of Black, White and Hispanic Labor." *Economic Inquiry,* vol. 21 (January 1983): 93–106.

———. "Assimilation, Changes in Cohort Quality, and the Earnings of Immigrants." *Journal of Labor Economics,* vol. 3 (October 1985): 463–89.

———. "The Self-Employment Experience of Immigrants." *Journal of Human Resources,* vol. 21 (Fall 1986): 485–506.

Borjas, George J., and Tienda, Marta. "The Economic Consequences of Immigration." *Science,* vol. 235 (February 1987): 645–51.

Bosanquet, Nicholas. "'Structuralism' and Structural Unemployment." *British Journal of Industrial Relations,* vol. 17 (November 1979): 299–313.

Bouvier, Leon F. "U.S. Immigration: Effects on Population Growth and Structure." In Kritz, Mary M., ed. *U.S. Immigration and Refugee Policy.* Lexington, MA: D. C. Heath and Co., 1983.

Bowles, Samuel. "Migration as Investment: Empirical Tests of the Human Investment Approach to Geographic Migration." *Review of Economics and Statistics,* vol. 52 (November 1970): 356–62.

Bowles, Samuel, Gordon, David M., and Weisskopf, Thomas F. *Beyond the Wasteland.* Garden City, NY: Doubleday, 1983.

Boyer, Robert. "La Flexibilité du Travail: Des Formes Contrastées, Des Effets Mal Connus." *Travail et Société/Cahiers Économiques de Bruxelles,* vol. 12 (January 1987): 107–29.

Bradford, William D., and Osborne, Alfred E. "The Entrepreneurship Decision and Black Economic Development." *American Economic Review,* vol. 66 (May 1976): 316–19.

Bray, D.B. "La agricultura de exportación, la formación de clases y migración en la Republica Dominicana." *Ciencia y Sociedad* (Santo Domingo), vol. 10 (April/June 1985): 217–36.

———. "The Dominican Exodus: Origins, Problems, Solutions." In Levine, B.B., ed. *The Caribbean Exodus.* New York: Praeger Publishers, 1987.

Briggs, Vernon. *Immigration Policy and the American Labor Force.* Baltimore: Johns Hopkins University Press, 1984.

Brown, Charles, Gilroy, Curtis, and Kohen, Andrew. "The Effect of the Minimum Wage on Employment and Unemployment." *Journal of Economic Literature,* vol. 20 (June 1982): 487–528.

Brown, Clair, and Pechman, Joseph, eds. *Gender in the Workplace.* Washington, D.C.: Brookings Institution, 1987.

Buchele, Robert. "Jobs and Workers: A Labor Market Segmentation Perspective on the Work Experience of Middle-Aged Men." Ph.D. dissertation, Harvard University, 1975.

Bulow, Jeremy I., and Summers, Lawrence. "A Theory of Dual Labor Markets with Application to Industrial Policy, Discrimination, and Keynesian Unemployment." *Journal of Labor Economics,* vol. 4 (July 1986): 376–414.

Burtless, Gary. "Why Is Insured Unemployment So Low?" *Brookings Papers on Economic Activity,* no. 1 (1983): 225–49.

———. "Earnings Inequality over the Business and Demographic Cycles." Brookings Economics Discussion Papers, The Brookings Institution, July 1989.

Bustamente, Jorge A. *Mexican Migration to the United States.* Cambridge: MIT Press, 1978.

Butler, Richard, and Heckman, James. "The Government's Impact on the Labor Market Status of Black Americans: A Critical Review." In Hausman, Leonard, et al., eds. *Equal Rights and Industrial Relations.* Madison: Industrial Relations Research Association, 1977.

Cain, Glen G. "The Economic Analysis of Labor Market Discrimination: A Survey." In Ashenfelter, Orley, and Layard, Richard, eds. *Handbook of Labor Economics.* Amsterdam: North-Holland Press, 1987.

Carliner, Geoffrey. "Female Labor Force Participation Rates for Nine Ethnic Groups." *Journal of Human Resources,* vol. 16 (Fall 1981): 286–93.

———. "Wages, Earnings, and Hours of First, Second, and Third Generation American Males." *Economic Inquiry,* vol. 18 (January 1980): 87–102.

Casal, Lourdes, and Hernandez, Andres. "Cubans in the U.S.: A Survey of the Literature." *Cuban Studies,* vol. 5 (July 1975): 1–24.

Castles, Stephen. *Here for Good: Western Europe's New Ethnic Minorities.* London: Pluto Press, 1984.

Castles, Stephen, and Kosack, Godula. *Immigrant Workers and Class Structure in Western Europe.* London: Oxford University Press, 1973.

Centro de Estudios Puertorriquenos [CENEP], City University of New York. *Labor Migration Under Capitalism: The Puerto Rican Experience.* New York: Monthly Review Press, 1979.

Chaney, E. M. "Colombian Migration to the United States (Part 2)." In *The Dynamics of International Migration*. Washington, D.C.: Smithsonian Institution, 1976.

Cherry, Robert. *Discrimination: Its Economic Impact on Blacks, Women, and Jews*. Lexington, MA: Lexington Books, 1989.

Chick, Victoria. *Macroeconomics After Keynes*. Cambridge: MIT Press, 1983.

Chiswick, Barry. "The Effects of Americanization on the Earnings of Foreign-Born Men." *Journal of Political Economy*, vol. 86 (October 1978): 897–921.

———. *An Analysis of the Economic Progress and Impact of Immigrants*. Washington, D.C.: National Technical Information Service, 1980.

———. "The Effects of Immigration on Earnings and Employment in the U.S." Report to International Bureau of Labor Affairs, U.S. Dept. of Labor, 1981.

———. "The Employment of Immigrants in the U.S." In Fellner, William, ed., *Contemporary Economic Problems*. Washington, D.C.: American Enterprise Institute, 1982.

———. "Is the New Immigration Less Skilled than the Old?" *Journal of Labor Economics*, vol. 4 (April 1986): 168–92.

Clark, Kim, and Summers, Lawrence. "Labor Market Dynamics and Unemployment." *Brookings Papers on Economic Activity*, no. 3 (1979): 3–60.

———. "Demographic Differences in Cyclical Employment Variation." *Journal of Human Resources*, vol. 16 (Winter 1981): 61–79.

Clark, Victor S. "Mexican Labor in the United States." *Bulletin of the U.S. Department of Labor*, No. 78. Washington, D.C.: U.S. Dept. of Labor, 1908.

Cockcroft, James. *Mexico*. New York: Monthly Review Press, 1983.

———. *Outlaws in the Promised Land: Mexican Immigrant Workers and America's Future*. New York: Grove Press, 1986.

Cohen, Malcolm, and Gruber, William. "Variability by Skill in Cyclical Unemployment." *Monthly Labor Review*, vol. 93 (August 1970): 8–11.

Coleman, James S., et al. *Equality of Educational Opportunity*. Washington, D.C.: U.S. Department of Health, Education, and Welfare, 1966.

Coleman, James S., Hoffer, Thomas, and Kilgore, Sally. *High School Achievement: Public, Catholic, and Private Schools Compared*. New York: Basic Books, 1982.

Coleman, Thomas S. "Essays on Aggregate Labor Market Business Cycle Fluctuations." Ph.D. dissertation, University of Chicago, 1984.

Cooney, Rosemary. "Intercity Variations in Puerto Rican Labor Force Participation." *Journal of Human Resources*, vol. 14 (Spring 1979): 222–35.

Cornelius, Wayne A. "Mexican Migration to the United States: Causes, Consequences, and U.S. Responses." Working Paper. Center for International Studies, MIT, 1978.

———. "Impacts of the 1986 U.S. Immigration Law on Emigration from Rural Mexican Sending Communities." In Bean, Frank D., Edmonston, Barry, and Passel, Jeffrey, eds. *Undocumented Migration to the United States: IRCA and the Experience of the 1980s*. Washington, D.C.: The Urban Institute Press, 1990a.

———. "Determinants of Employer Demand for Mexican Labor in the California Economy." In Cornelius, Wayne, ed. *The Changing Role of Mexican Labor in the U.S. Economy: Sectoral Perspectives*. San Diego: Center for U.S.-Mexican Studies, 1990b.

Corwin, Arthur. "Early Mexican Labor Migration." In Corwin, Arthur, ed. *Immigrants— and Immigrants: Perspectives on Mexican Migration to the United States*. Westport, CT: Greenwood Press, 1978.

Corwin, Arthur, and Cardoso, Lawrence A. "Vamos Al Norte: Causes of Mass Mexican Migration to the United States." In Corwin, Arthur, ed. *Immigrants—and Immi-*

grants: Perspectives on Mexican Migration to the United States. Westport, CT: Greenwood Press, 1978.

Cotterill, Phillip. "The Elasticity of Demand for Low-wage Labor." *Southern Economic Journal,* vol. 41 (January 1975): 520–25.

Council of Economic Advisers. *Economic Report of the President and the Economic Situation and Outlook: Hearings.* Washington, D.C.: Government Printing Office (GPO), 1961.

Cripps, T. F., and Tarling, R. J. "An Analysis of the Duration of Male Unemployment in Great Britain, 1932–73." *Economic Journal,* vol. 84 (June 1974): 289–316.

Danziger, S.H., and Gottschalk, P. "The Poverty of *Losing Ground.*" *Challenge,* vol. 28 (May/June 1985): 32–40.

———. "Do Rising Tides Lift All Boats? The Impact of Secular and Cyclical Changes in Poverty." *American Economic Review,* vol. 76 (May 1986): 405–10.

Danziger, S.H., Haveman, R.H., and Plotnick, R.D. "Antipoverty Policy: Effects on the Poor and the Nonpoor." In Danziger, S.H., and Weinberg, D.H., eds. *Fighting Poverty: What Works and What Doesn't.* Cambridge: Harvard University Press, 1986.

Darity, William A., and Myers, Samuel L., Jr. "Changes in Black-White Income Inequality, 1968–78: A Decade of Progress?" *Review of Black Political Economy,* vol. 10 (Summer 1980): 354–80.

———. "Changes in Black Family Structure: Implications for Welfare Dependency." *American Economic Review, Proceedings,* vol. 77 (May 1983): 59–64.

Darity, William A., and Horn, B.L. "Involuntary Unemployment Reconsidered." *Southern Economic Journal,* vol. 49 (January 1983): 717–33.

DeFreitas, Gregory. "The Earnings of Immigrants in the American Labor Market." Ph.D. dissertation, Columbia University, 1979.

———. "Ethnic Differentials in Unemployment among Hispanic Americans." In Borjas, George, and Tienda, Marta, eds. *Hispanics in the US Economy.* New York: Academic Press, 1985.

———. "A Time-Series Analysis of Hispanic Unemployment." *Journal of Human Resources,* vol. 21 (Winter 1986): 24–43.

———. "Labor Force Competition and the Black-White Wage Gap." *Review of Black Political Economy,* vol. 16 (Winter 1988a): 103–13.

———. "Hispanic Immigration and Labor Market Segmentation." *Industrial Relations,* vol. 27 (Spring 1988b): 195–214.

DeFreitas, Gregory, and Marshall, Adriana. "Immigration and Wage Growth in U.S. Manufacturing in the 1970s." *Industrial Relations Research Association Proceedings,* no. 36 (1984): 148–56.

Dickens, William, and Lang, Kevin. "The Reemergence of Segmented Labor Market Theory." *American Economic Review,* vol. 78 (May 1988): 129–34.

Dietz, James L. *Economic History of Puerto Rico.* Princeton: Princeton University Press, 1986.

Disney, Richard. "Recurrent Spells and the Concentration of Unemployment in Great Britain." *Economic Journal,* vol. 89 (March 1979): 109–19.

Doeringer, Peter, and Piore, Michael. *Internal Labor Markets and Manpower Analysis.* Lexington, MA: D.C. Heath, 1971.

———. "Unemployment and the Dual Labor Market." *The Public Interest,* no. 38 (Winter 1975): 66–79.

Dooley, Martin D., and Gottschalk, Peter. "Earnings Inequality among Males in the United

States: Trends and the Effects of Labor Force Growth." *Journal of Political Economy*, vol. 92 (February 1984): 59–89.

Driehuis, W. *An Analysis of the Impact of Demand and Cost Factors on Employment in the Netherlands*. Research Memorandum No. 7604, Dept. of Economics, University of Amsterdam, 1976.

Drucker, Peter F. *Innovation and Entrepreneurship*. New York: Harper & Row, 1985.

Duran, Richard P. *Hispanics' Education and Background: Predictors of College Achievement*. New York: College Entrance Examination Board, 1983.

Eatwell, John. "Theories of Value, Output and Employment." In Eatwell, John, and Milgate, Murray, eds. *Keynes's Economics and the Theory of Value and Distribution*. New York: Oxford University Press, 1983.

Edwards, Linda N. "The Economics of Schooling Decisions: Teenage Enrollment Rates." *Journal of Human Resources*, vol. 10 (Spring 1975): 155–73.

———. "School Retention of Teenagers over the Business Cycle." *Journal of Human Resources*, vol. 11 (Spring 1976): 200–208.

Edwards, Richard C. "The Social Relations of Production in the Firm and Labor Market Structure." In Edwards, Richard C., Reich, Michael, and Gordon, David M., eds. *Labor Market Segmentation*. Lexington, MA: D.C. Heath and Co., 1975.

———. *Contested Terrain*. New York: Basic Books, 1979.

Ellwood, David T., and Summers, Lawrence H. "Poverty in America: Is Welfare the Answer or the Problem?" In Danziger, S.H., and Weinberg, D.H., eds. *Fighting Poverty: What Works and What Doesn't*. Cambridge: Harvard University Press, 1986.

England, Paula. "The Failure of Human Capital Theory to Explain Occupational Sex Segregation." *Journal of Human Resources*, vol. 17 (Spring 1982): 358–70.

Evans, David S., and Leighton, Linda S. "Some Empirical Aspects of Entrepreneurship." *American Economic Review*, vol. 79 (June 1989): 519–35.

Evans, John S., and James, Dilmus D. "Conditions of Employment and Income Distribution in Mexico as Incentives for Mexican Migration to the U.S." *International Migration Review*, vol. 13 (Spring 1979): 4–24.

Exter, Thomas. "How Many Hispanics?" *American Demographics*, vol. 9 (May 1987): 36–38.

Fagen, Richard R., Brody, Richard A., and O'Leary, Thomas J. *Cubans in Exile: Disaffection and the Revolution*. Palo Alto: Stanford University Press, 1968.

Fain, T. Scott. "Self-employed Americans: Their Number has Increased." *Monthly Labor Review*, vol. 103 (November 1980): 3–8.

Feldstein, Martin. *Lowering the Permanent Rate of Unemployment*. Washington, D.C.: GPO, 1973.

Fishman, Joshua A., and Keller, Gary D., eds. *Bilingual Education for Hispanic Students in the U.S.* New York: Columbia University, Teachers' College Press, 1982.

Fitzpatrick, Joseph. *Puerto Rican Americans: The Meaning of Migration to the Mainland*. Englewood Cliffs, NJ: Prentice-Hall, 1971.

Flaim, Paul O. "New Data on Union Members and their Earnings," *Monthly Labor Review*, vol. 32 (January 1985): 13–14.

Flanagan, Robert. "Discrimination Theory, Labor Turnover and Racial Unemployment Differentials." *Journal of Human Resources*, vol. 13 (Winter 1978): 187–206.

Fligstein, Neil, and Fernandez, Roberto. "The Causes of School Transitions for Hispanics, Whites, and Blacks." In Borjas, George, and Tienda, Marta, eds. *Hispanics in the U.S. Economy*. New York: Academic Press, 1985.

Fogel, Walter. "United States Immigration Policy and Unsanctioned Migrants." *Industrial and Labor Relations Review*, vol. 33 (April 1980): 295–311.

Foner, Nancy, ed. *New Immigrants in New York*. New York: Columbia University Press, 1987.

Freeman, Richard. "The Changing Labor Market for Black Americans, 1948–72." *Brookings Papers on Economic Activity*, no. 1 (1973): 67–120.

———. "Evaluating the European View that the United States Has No Unemployment Problem." *American Economic Review*, vol. 78 (May 1988): 294–99.

———. "Inequality and Tight Labor Markets." Paper presented at American Economic Association Convention, December 1989.

Freeman, Richard, and Medoff, James. "New Estimates of Private Sector Unionism in the United States." *Industrial and Labor Relations Review*, vol. 32 (January 1979): 143–74.

———. *What Do Unions Do?* (New York: Basic Books, 1984).

Friedman, Milton. "The Role of Monetary Policy." *American Economic Review*, vol. 58 (March 1968): 1–12.

Fuchs, Victor. "Self-employment and Labor Force Participation of Older Males." *Journal of Human Resources*, vol. 17 (Fall 1982): 339–57.

Fullerton Jr., Howard N. "New Labor Force Projections Spanning 1988 to 2000." *Monthly Labor Review*, vol. 112 (November 1989): 3–12.

Galarza, Ernesto. *Merchants of Labor*. Santa Barbara, CA: McNally and Loftin, 1964.

Gilman, Harry. "The White/Non-White Unemployment Differential." In Perlman, Mark, ed. *Human Resources and the Urban Economy*. Washington, D.C.: Resources for the Future, 1963: 75–113.

———. "Economic Discrimination and Unemployment." *American Economic Review*, vol. 55 (December 1965): 1077–96.

Gilpatrick, Edward G. *Structural Unemployment and Aggregate Demand*. Baltimore: The Johns Hopkins University Press, 1966.

Gilroy, Curtis. "Black and White Unemployment: The Dynamics of the Differential." *Monthly Labor Review*, vol. 97 (February 1974): 38–47.

Glazer, Nathan, and Moynihan, Daniel P. *Beyond the Melting Pot*. Cambridge: MIT Press, 1970.

Gordon, David M. "Segmentation By the Numbers." Unpublished paper, New School for Social Research, 1984.

———. "The Un-Natural Rate of Unemployment: An Econometric Critique of the NAIRU Hypothesis." *American Economics Review*, vol. 78 (May 1988): 117–23.

Gordon, David M., Edwards, Richard, and Reich, Michael. *Segmented Work, Divided Workers*. Cambridge: Cambridge University Press, 1982.

Gordon, Robert J. "Wage Gaps and Output Gaps: Is There A Common Story for All of Europe?" NBER Working Paper, No. 2454, 1987.

Grasmuck, Sherri. "Consequences of Dominican Out-Migration for National Development: The Case of Santiago." In Sanderson, Steven, ed. *Americans in the New International Division of Labor*. New York: Holmes and Meier, 1984.

Gray, Lois S. "The Jobs Puerto Ricans Hold in New York City." *Monthly Labor Review*, vol. 98 (October 1975): 12–16.

Greenwood, Michael. "Urban Economic Growth and Migration: Their Interaction." *Environment and Planning*, vol. 5 (January 1973): 91–112.

———. "The Economic Consequences of Immigration for the United States." In *Interagency Task Force on Immigration Policy: Companion Report*. Washington, D.C.: Departments of Justice, Labor and State, 1979.

———. "Human Migration: Theory, Models, and Empirical Studies." *Journal of Regional Science*, vol. 25 (November 1985): 521–44.

Greenwood, Michael, and Hunt, Gary. "Migration and Interregional Employment Redistribution in the U.S." *American Economic Review,* vol. 74 (December 1984): 957–69.

Greenwood, Michael, and McDowell, John. "The Factor Market Consequences of U.S. Immigration." *Journal of Economic Literature,* vol. 24 (December 1986): 1738–72.

Grenier, Giles. "the Effects of Language Characteristics on the Wages of Hispanic-American Males." *Journal of Human Resources,* vol. 19, no. 1 (Winter 1984): 35–52.

Gurak, Douglas, and Kritz, Mary. "Kinship Networks and the Settlement Process: Dominican and Colombian Immigrants in New York City," Unpublished paper, Hispanic Research Center, Fordham University, 1983.

———. "New York Hispanics: A Demographic Overview." In Acosta-Belen, Edna, and Sjostrom, Barbara J., eds. *The Hispanic Experience in the United States.* New York: Praeger, 1988.

Gwartney, James D., and Long, James E. "The Relative Earnings of Blacks and Other Minorities." *Industrial and Labor Relations Review,* vol. 31 (April 1978): 336–46.

Hall, Robert E. "Why is the Unemployment Rate So High at Full Employment?" *Brookings Papers on Economic Activity,* no. 3 (1970): 369–402.

Hamermesh, Daniel. *Jobless Pay and the Economy.* Baltimore: The Johns Hopkins University Press, 1977.

Hanushek, Eric A. "The Economics of Schooling: Production and Efficiency in Public Schools." *Journal of Economic Literature,* vol. 24 (September 1986): 1141–77.

Harrison, Bennett, and Bluestone, Barry. *The Great U-Turn: Corporate Restructuring and the Polarizing of America.* New York: Basic Books, 1988.

Heckman, James J. "Sample Selection Bias as a Specification Error." *Econometrica,* vol. 47 (January 1979): 153–61.

Hill, C. Russell, and Stafford, Frank P. "Family Background and Lifetime Earnings." In Juster, F.T., ed. *The Distribution of Economic Well-Being.* Cambridge, MA: Ballinger Press, 1977.

Hoffman, Abraham. "Repatriation During the Great Depression: A Reappraisal." In Corwin, Arthur, ed. *Immigrants—and Immigrants: Perspectives on Mexican Labor in the United States.* Westport, CT: Greenwood Press, 1978.

Holzer, Harry J. "Search Method Use by Unemployed Youth." *Journal of Labor Economics,* vol. 6 (January 1988): 1–20.

Horvath, Francis. "Job Tenure of Workers in January 1981." *Monthly Labor Review,* vol. 105 (September 1982): 34–36.

Houston, Marion F., et al. "The Female Predominance of Immigration to the United States." *International Migration Review,* vol. 18 (Winter 1984): 908–63.

Howe, Marvine. "Immigration Laws Linked to Job Bias." *New York Times,* February 26, 1990.

Howe, Wayne J. "Education and Demographics: How Do They Affect Unemployment Rates?" *Monthly Labor Review,* vol. 111 (January 1988): 3–9.

Humphries, Jane. "The Emancipation of Women in the 1970s: From the Latent to the Floating." *Capital and Class,* no. 20 (Summer 1983): 6–28.

Jackman, R. "Search Behavior of Unemployed Men in Britain and the United States." Working Paper No. 550, Centre for Labour Economics, London School of Economics, 1985.

Johnson, D.L., ed. *Intermediate Classes: Historical Studies of Class Formation on the Periphery.* London: Sage Publications, 1983.

Johnson, George E. "The Labor Market Effects of Immigration." *Industrial and Labor Relations Review,* vol. 33 (April 1980): 331–41.

Jones, Edward W. "Black Managers: The Dream Deferred." *Harvard Business Review*, vol. 64 (May/June 1986): 84–93.

Juhn, Chinhui, Murphy, Kevin M., and Pierce, Brooks. "Wage Inequality and the Rise in Returns to Skill." Paper presented at American Economic Association Convention, December 1989.

Kaitz, Hyman. 'Experience of the Past: the National Minimum." In *Youth Unemployment and Minin 'um Wages*. Bulletin 1657. Washington, D.C.: Bureau of Labor Statistics, 1970.

Kasarda, John D. ' Irban Change and Minority Opportunities." In Peterson, P.E., ed. *The New Urban Reality*. Washington, D.C.: Brookings Institution, 1985.

Keynes, John Maynard. "Relative Movements of Real Wages and Output," *Economic Journal*, vol. 49 (1939): 34–51.

———. *The General Theory of Employment, Interest and Money*. London: Macmillan, 1973a.

———. *The General Theory and After, Part II: Defense and Development*, vol. 14. In Moggridge, Donald, ed. *The Collected Writings of John Maynard Keynes*. London: Macmillan, 1973b.

Killingsworth, Charles. Statement before the U.S. Senate, Committee on Labor and Public Welfare. In *The Nation's Manpower Revolution*. Washington, D.C.: GPO, 1963.

———. "The Fall and Rise of the Idea of Structural Unemployment." *Industrial Relations Research Association, Proceedings* (August 1978): 1–16.

Killingsworth, Charles, and King, C. "Tax Cuts and Employment Policy." In Taggart, Robert, ed. *Job Creation: What Works?* Salt Lake City: Olympus Publishing Co., 1977.

Killingsworth, Mark. *Labor Supply*. Cambridge: Cambridge University Press, 1983.

King, Allan G., Lowell, B. Lindsay, and Bean, Frank D. "The Effects of Hispanic Immigrants on the Earnings of Native Hispanic Americans." *Social Science Quarterly*, vol. 67 (1986): 672–89.

Klundert, Van de. "Introduction to Special Issue on Unemployment." *De Economist*, no. 1/2 (1976).

Kniesner, Thomas J., and Goldsmith, Arthur H. "A Survey of Alternative Models of the Aggregate U.S. Labor Market." *Journal of Economic Literature*, vol. 25 (September 1987): 1241–80.

Kossoudji, Sherrie. "English Language Ability and the Labor Market Opportunities of Hispanic and East Asian Men." *Journal of Labor Economics*, vol. 6, no. 2 (April 1988): 205–28.

Krashevski, Richard S. "What is So Natural About High Unemployment?" *American Economic Review*, vol. 78 (May 1988): 289–93.

Kregel, Jan A. "Constraints on the Expansion of Output and Employment: Real or Monetary." *Journal of Post Keynesian Economics*, vol. 7 (Winter 1984–85): 139–52.

Kutscher, Ronald, and Personick, Valerie. "Deindustrialization and the Shift to Services." *Monthly Labor Review*, vol. 109 (June 1986): 3–13.

Larson, Eric, and Sullivan, Teresa. "'Conventional Numbers' in Immigration Research: The Case of the Missing Dominicans." *International Migration Review*, vol. 21 (Winter 1987): 1474–97.

Lazear, Edward P. "The Narrowing of Black-White Wage Differentials is Illusory." *American Economic Review*, vol. 69 (September 1979): 553–64.

Lebergott, Stanley. *Manpower in Economic Growth*. New York: McGraw-Hill, 1964.

Leibowitz, Arnold H. *Federal Recognition of the Rights of Minority Language Groups*. Rosslyn, VA: National Clearinghouse for Bilingual Education, 1982.

Leonard, Jonathan S. "The Impact of Affirmative Action on Employment." *Journal of Labor Economics*, vol. 2 (October 1984): 439–63.

———. "The Effect of Unions on the Employment of Blacks, Hispanics, and Women." *Industrial and Labor Relations Review*, vol. 39 (October 1985): 115–32.

Lever-Tracy, Constance. "Immigrant Workers and Postwar Capitalism: In Reserve or Core Troops on the Front Line?" *Politics and Society*, vol. 12 (1983): 127–57.

Leveson, Irving. "Nonfarm Self-employment in the United States." Ph.D. dissertation, Columbia University, 1968.

Levy, Frank, and Michel, Richard. "An Economic Bust for the Baby Boom." *Challenge*, vol. 29 (March/April 1986): 33–40.

Levy, M.B., and Wadycki, W. "The Influence of Family and Friends on Geographic Labor Mobility: An International Comparison." *Review of Economics and Statistics*, vol. 55 (May 1973): 198–203.

Light, Ivan. *Ethnic Enterprise in America*. Berkeley: University of California Press, 1972.

Lillard, Lee, Smith, James P., and Welch, Finis. "What Do We Really Know About Wages? The Importance of Nonreporting and Census Imputation." *Journal of Political Economy*, vol. 94 (June 1986): 489–506.

Lippman, Steven, and McCall, John. "The Economics of Job Search: A Survey." *Economic Inquiry*, vol. 14 (June 1976): 155–89.

Lipsey, R.G. "Structural and Deficient Demand Unemployment Reconsidered." In Ross, A.M., ed. *Employment Policy and the Labor Market*. Berkeley: University of California Press, 1965.

Lloyd, Cynthia, and Niemi, Beth. *The Economics of Sex Differentials*. New York: Columbia University Press, 1979.

Long, James E. "The Effect of Americanization on Earnings: Some Evidence for Women." *Journal of Political Economy*, vol. 88 (June 1980): 620–29.

Lucas, Robert E. *Studies in Business Cycle Theory*. Cambridge: MIT Press, 1981.

Mahard, R.E. *The Influence of High School Racial Composition on The Academic Achievement and College Attendance of Hispanics*. Santa Monica: The Rand Corporation, 1978.

Mare, Robert D. "Social Background and School Continuation Decisions." *Journal of the American Statistical Association*, vol. 75 (June 1980): 295–305.

Marsden, David. *The End of Economic Man? Custom and Competition in Labour Markets*. Brighton: Wheatsheaf Books, 1986.

Marshall, Adriana. *The Import of Labour*. Rotterdam: Rotterdam University Press, 1973.

———. "Immigration in a Surplus-Worker Labor Market: The Case of New York." *Occasional Paper*, Center for Latin American and Caribbean Studies, New York University, 1983.

———. "Immigration, Labor Demand, and the Working Class." *Politics and Society*, vol. 13 (1984): 425–53.

Marshall, Ray. "The Economics of Discrimination: A Survey." *Journal of Economic Literature*, vol. 12 (September 1974): 849–71.

Massey, Douglas S., and Bitterman, Brooks. "Explaining the Paradox of Puerto Rican Segregation." *Social Forces*, vol. 64 (December 1985): 306–31.

Masters, Stanley H. "The Effects of Family Income on Children's Education: Some Findings on Inequality of Opportunity." *Journal of Human Resources*, vol. 4 (Spring 1969): 158–75.

Matilla, J.P. "Job Quitting and Frictional Unemployment." *American Economic Review*, vol. 64 (March 1974): 235–39.

———. "Determinants of Male School Enrollments: A Time-Series Analysis." *Review of Economics and Statistics,* vol. 64 (May 1982): 242–51.

McCarthy, Kevin F., and Valdez, R. Burciaga. *Current and Future Effects of Mexican Immigration in California.* Santa Monica: Rand Corp., 1986.

McMahon, P.J., and Tschetter, J.H. "The Declining Middle Class." *Monthly Labor Review,* vol. 109 (September 1986): 22–27.

McManus, Walter, Gould, William, and Welch, Finis. "Earnings of Hispanic Men: The Role of English Language Proficiency." *Journal of Labor Economics,* vol. 1, no. 2 (April 1983): 101–30.

McWilliams, Carey. *North From Mexico.* New York: Greenwood Press, 1968.

Mellor, Earl, and Stamas, George. "Usual Weekly Earnings: Another Look at Intergroup Differences and Basic Trends." *Monthly Labor Review,* vol. 105 (April 1982): 15–24.

Milgate, Murray. "Keynes on the 'Classical' Theory of Interest." In Eatwell, John, and Milgate, Murray, eds. *Keynes's Economics and the Theory of Value and Distribution.* New York: Oxford University Press, 1983.

Mills, C. Wright, Senior, Clarence, and Goldsen, Rose. *Puerto Rican Journey.* New York: Harper & Row, 1950.

Mincer, Jacob. "Comment: The White-Non-White Unemployment Differential." In Perlman, Mark, ed. *Human Resources and the Urban Economy.* Washington, D.C.: Resources for the Future, 1963.

Mincer, Jacob, and Leighton, Linda. "Labor Turnover and Youth Unemployment." In Freeman, Richard, and Wise, David, eds. *The Youth Labor Market Problem.* Chicago: University of Chicago Press, 1982.

Mincer, Jacob, and Jovanovic, Boyan. "Labor Mobility and Wages." In Rosen, Sherwin, ed. *Studies in Labor Markets.* New York: National Bureau of Economic Research, 1981.

Moncarz, Raul. "A Model of Professional Adaptation of Refugees: The Cuban Case in the U.S.: 1959–70." *International Migration,* vol. 11 (1973): 46–57.

Murray, Charles. *Losing Ground: American Social Policy: 1950–80.* New York: Basic Books, 1984.

Muth, Richard F. "Migration: Chicken or Egg?" *Southern Economic Journal,* vol. 37 (January 1971): 295–306.

Nardone, Thomas J. "Part-time Workers: Who Are They?" *Monthly Labor Review,* vol. 109 (February 1986): 13–19.

National Commission for Employment Policy. *Hispanics and Jobs: Barriers to Progress.* Washington, D.C.: National Commission for Employment Policy, 1982.

National Commission on Excellence in Education. *A Nation at Risk: The Imperative for Educational Reform.* Washington, D.C.: GPO, 1983.

National Research Council. *Immigration Statistics: A Story of Neglect.* Washington, D.C.: National Academy Press, 1985.

Neuffer, Elizabeth. "Poor Skills Cited in New York Entry-Level Applicants." *New York Times,* July 4, 1987.

Newman, Morris. "A Profile of Hispanics in the U.S. Work Force." *Monthly Labor Review,* vol. 101 (December 1978): 3–13.

North, David. *Immigration and Income Transfer Policies in the U.S.: An Analysis of a Nonrelationship.* Washington, D.C.: New Transcentury Foundation, 1980.

———. "The Impact of Legal, Illegal, and Refugee Migrations on U.S. Social Service Programs." In Kritz, Mary M., ed. *U.S. Immigration and Refugee Policy.* Lexington, MA: D.C. Heath and Co., 1983.

North, David, and Houston, Marian. *The Characteristics and Role of Illegal Aliens in the U.S. Labor Market.* Washington, D.C.: Linton and Co., 1976.

O'Neill, June. "The Trends in the Male-Female Wage Gap in the United States." *Journal of Labor Economics,* vol. 3 (January 1985 Supp.): S91–S116.

Orfield, Gary. "School Segregation in the 1980's." University of Chicago, School of Education, 1987.

Organization for Economic Cooperation and Development (OECD). *Employment Outlook.* Paris: OECD, 1984.

———. *Flexibility in the Labour Market: The Current Debate.* Paris: OECD, 1986.

Orshansky, Mollie, ed. *The Measure of Poverty: Technical Papers,* Vol. I. Washington, D.C.: GPO, 1974.

Ortiz, Vilma. "Changes in the Characteristics of Puerto Rican Migrants from 1955 to 1980." *International Migration Review,* vol. 20 (Fall 1986): 612–28.

Osberg, Lars. *Economic Inequality in the United States.* Armonk, NY: M.E. Sharpe, 1984.

Osborne, T.N. *Higher Education in Mexico: History, Growth and Problems in a Dichotomized Economy.* El Paso: Texas Western Press, 1976.

Oster, Gerald. "A Factor Analytic Test of the Dual Economy." *Review of Economics and Statistics,* vol. 61 (February 1979): 33–59.

Paine, Suzanne. *Exporting Workers,* Cambridge: Cambridge University Press, 1974.

Parsons, Donald. "Models of Labor Market Turnover: A Theoretical and Empirical Survey." In Ehrenberg, Ronald, ed. *Research in Labor Economics.* Greenwich, CT: JAI Press, 1977.

Passel, Jeffrey S. "Estimates of Undocumented Aliens in the 1980 Census for SMSAs." Memorandum, Population Division, U.S. Bureau of the Census, 1985.

Passel, Jeffrey S., and Woodrow, Karen. "Geographic Distribution of Undocumented Immigrants: Estimates of Undocumented Aliens Counted in the 1980 Census by State." *International Migration Review,* vol. 18 (Fall 1984): 642–71.

———. "Change in the Undocumented Alien Population in the United States: 1979–83." *International Migration Review,* vol. 21 (Winter 1987): 1304–34.

Patchen, Martin, Hoffman, G., and Brown, W. "Academic Performance of Black High School Students under Different Conditions of Contact with White Peers." *Sociology of Education,* vol. 53 (January 1980): 33–51.

Pedraza-Bailey, Sylvia. "Cubans and Mexicans in the United States: The Functions of Political and Economic Migration. *Cuban Studies,* vol. 11 (July 1981): 79–98.

Piore, Michael. "Notes for a Theory of Labor Market Stratification." In Reich, M., Gordon, D.M., and Edwards, R.C., eds. *Labor Market Segmentation.* Lexington, MA: D.C. Heath and Co., 1975.

———. *Birds of Passage: Migrant Labor and Industrial Societies.* Cambridge: Cambridge University Press, 1979a.

———. "Introduction." In Piore, M., ed. *Unemployment and Inflation.* White Plains: M.E. Sharpe, 1979b.

Podgursky, Michael. "Sources of Secular Increases in the Unemployment Rate, 1969–82." *Monthly Labor Review,* vol. 107 (July 1984): 19–25.

Poitras, Guy. "Through the Revolving Door: Central American Manpower in the United States." *Inter-American Economic Affairs,* vol. 36 (Spring 1983): 63–78.

Portes, Alejandro, and Bach, Robert. *Latin Journey: Cuban and Mexican Immigrants in the United States.* Berkeley: University of California Press, 1985.

Power, Marilyn. "From Home Production to Wage Labor: Women as a Reserve Army of Labor." *Review of Radical Political Economics,* vol. 15 (Spring 1983): 71–91.

Presidential Task Force on Women Business Owners. *The Bottom Line: Unequal Enterprise in America*. Washington, D.C.: GPO, 1978.

Prieto, Yolanda. "Cuban Women in the U.S. Labor Force." *Cuban Studies*, vol. 17 (1987): 73–91.

Quintero, Angel G. *Educacion y Cambio Social en Puerto Rico*. Santiago: Universidad de Puerto Rico, 1972.

Ray, Robert N. "A Report on Self-Employed Americans in 1973." *Monthly Labor Review*, vol. 98 (January 1975): 49–54.

Reder, Melvin W. "The Economic Consequences of Increased Immigration." *Review of Economics and Statistics*, vol. 45 (August 1963): 221–30.

Reich, Michael. *Racial Inequality: A Political-Economic Analysis*. Princeton: Princeton University Press, 1981.

————. "Segmented Labour: Time-series Hypotheses and Evidence." *Cambridge Journal of Economics*, vol. 8 (March 1984): 63–81.

————. "Postwar Racial Income Differences: Trends and Theories." In Magnum, Garth, and Philips, Peter, eds. *Three Worlds of Labor Economics*. Armonk, NY: M.E. Sharpe, 1988.

Reich, Michael, Gordon, D. M., and Edwards, R. C. "A Theory of Labor Market Segmentation." *American Economic Review*, vol. 63 (May 1973): 359–65.

Reimers, Cordelia. "Labor Market Discrimination Against Hispanic and Black Men." *Review of Economics and Statistics*, vol. 65 (November 1983): 570–79.

————. "The Wage Structure of Hispanic Men: Implications for Policy." *Social Science Quarterly*, vol. 65, no. 2 (June 1984): 401–16.

————. "A Comparative Analysis of the Wages of Hispanic, Black, and Non-Hispanic Whites." In Borjas, George, and Tienda, Marta, eds. *Hispanics in the U.S. Economy*. New York: Academic Press, 1985: 27–76.

Rima, Ingrid H. "Involuntary Unemployment and the Respecified Labor Supply Curve." *Journal of Post Keynesian Economics*, vol. 6 (Summer 1984): 540–50.

Rivera-Batiz, Francisco. "Trade Theory, Distribution of Income, and Immigration." *American Economic Review*, vol. 73 (May 1983): 183–87.

————. "English Language Proficiency and the Wages of Immigrants in the U.S." Dept. of Economics, Rutgers University, New Brunswick, NJ, May 1989.

Rodriguez, Nestor P. "Undocumented Central Americans in Houston: Diverse Populations." *International Migration Review*, vol. 21 (Spring 1987): 4–26.

Rogg, Eleanor. *The Assimilation of Cuban Exiles*. New York: Aberdeen Press, 1974.

Rogler, Lloyd H., Cooney, Rosemary Santana, and Ortiz, Vilma. "Intergenerational Change in Ethnic Identity in the Puerto Rican Family." *International Migration Review*, vol. 14 (Summer 1980): 193–214.

Rones, Philip. "Recent Recessions Swell Ranks of the Long-Term Unemployed." *Monthly Labor Review*, vol. 107 (February 1984): 25–29.

Rosen, Sherwin. "Human Capital: Survey of Empirical Research." In Ehrenberg, Ronald, ed. *Research in Labor Economics*. Greenwich, CT: JAI Press, 1977.

————. "Implicit Contracts: A Survey." *Journal of Economic Literature*, vol. 23 (September 1985): 1144–75.

Rosenberg, Samuel. "The Dual Labor Market: Its Existence and Consequences." Ph.D. dissertation, University of California, Berkeley, 1975.

————. "The Marxian Reserve Army and the Dual Labor Market." *Politics and Society*, vol. 7 (1977): 221–28.

————. "A Survey of Empirical Work on Labor Market Segmentation." *Occasional Paper*. Berkeley: Institute of Industrial Relations, 1979.

————. "Restructuring the Labor Force: The Role of Government Policies." In Cherry, Robert, et al., eds. *The Imperiled Economy, Vol. II.* New York: URPE, 1988.

Rosenfeld, Carl. "Job Search of the Unemployed." *Monthly Labor Review*, vol. 100 (November 1977): 39–42.

Rubery, Jill, and Tarling, Roger. "Women's Employment in Declining Britain." In Rubery, Jill, ed. *Women and Recession.* London: Routledge and Kegan Paul, 1988.

Ryan, Paul. "Segmentation, Duality, and the Internal Labor Market." In Wilkinson, Frank, ed. *The Dynamics of Labor Market Segmentation.* Cambridge: Cambridge University Press, 1981.

Safa, Helen. "Female Employment in the Puerto Rican Working Class." In Nash, June, and Safa, Helen, ed. *Women and Change in Latin America.* South Hadley, MA: Bergin and Garvey Publishers, 1985.

————. "Migration and Identity: A Comparison of Puerto Rican and Cuban Migrants in the United States." In Acosta-Belen, Edna, and Sjostrom, Barbara R., eds. *The Hispanic Experience in the United States.* New York: Praeger, 1988.

St. Marie, Stephen, and Bednarzik, Robert. "Employment and Unemployment During 1975." *Monthly Labor Review*, vol. 99 (February 1976): 11–20.

Samora, Julian. *Los Mojados: The Wetback Story.* South Bend, IN: University of Notre Dame Press, 1971.

Sassen-Koob, Saskia. "The New Labor Demand in Global Cities." In Smith, M.P., ed. *Cities in Transformation.* Beverly Hills, CA: Sage Publications, 1984.

Schiller, Bradley R. "Corporate Kidnap of the Small Business Employee." *The Public Interest*, no. 72 (Summer 1983): 72–87.

Scott, Carole E. "Why More Women are becoming Entrepreneurs." *Journal of Small Business Management*, vol. 24 (October 1986): 37–44.

Senior, C., and Manley, D. *A Report on Jamaican Migration to Great Britain.* Kingston, Jamaica: Government Publications, 1955.

Shank, Susan E. "Preferred Hours of Work and Corresponding Earnings." *Monthly Labor Review*, vol. 109 (November 1986): 40–44.

Shapiro, David. "Wage Differentials Among Black, Hispanic, and White Young Men." *Industrial and Labor Relations Review*, vol. 37 (July 1984): 570–81.

Shulman, Steven. "Racial Inequality and White Employment: An Interpretation and Test of the Bargaining Power Hypothesis." *Review of Black Political Economy*, vol. 18 (Winter 1990): 5–20.

Siegel, J., Passel, J., and Robinson, J. "Preliminary Review of Existing Studies of the Number of Illegal Residents in the United States." In *U.S. Immigration Policy and the National Interest*, Appendix E. Washington, D.C.: Select Commission on Immigration Policy, 1981.

Simon, Julian L. *The Economic Consequences of Immigration.* New York: Blackwell, 1989.

Smith, David J. *Racial Disadvantage in Britain.* Harmondsworth: Penguin Books, 1977.

Smith, James, and Welch, Finis. "Black-White Male Wage Ratios: 1960–70." *American Economic Review*, vol. 67 (June 1977): 323–39.

————. *Closing the Gap: Forty Years of Economic Progress for Blacks.* Santa Monica, CA: Rand Corp, 1986.

————. "Black Economic Progress After Myrdal." *Journal of Economic Literature*, vol. 27 (June 1989): 519–64.

Smith, Sharon P. *Equal Pay in the Public Sector: Fact or Fantasy?* Princeton: Princeton University Press, 1977.

Solow, Robert M. "What Happened to Full Employment?" *Quarterly Review of Economics and Business*, vol. 13 (Summer 1973): 7–20.

Sowell, Thomas. "Three Black Histories." In Sowell, T., ed. *Essays and Data on American Ethnic Groups*. Washington, D.C.: Urban Institute, 1978.

———. *Ethnic America: A History*. New York: Basic Books, 1981.

Stein, Robert L. "New Definitions for Employment and Unemployment." *Employment and Earnings* (February 1967): 3–27.

Stephenson, Stanley P. "The Economics of Youth Job Search Behavior." *Review of Economics and Statistics*, vol. 58 (February 1976): 104–12.

Stevens, Richard L. "Measuring Minority Business Formation and Failure." *Review of Black Political Economy*, vol. 12 (Spring 1984): 71–84.

Stinson, John F. "Moonlighting by Women Jumped to Record Highs." *Monthly Labor Review*, vol. 109 (November 1986): 22–25.

Sullivan, Maggie. "The Economic Impact of Undocumented Immigrants: The Orange County Report." *Migration World*, vol. 6 (April 1978): 7–9.

Summers, Lawrence. "Why Is The Unemployment Rate So Very High Near Full Employment?" *Brookings Papers on Economic Activity*, no. 2 (1986): 339–83.

———. "Relative Wages, Efficiency Wages, and Keynesian Unemployment." *American Economic Review*, vol. 78 (May 1988): 383–88.

Taylor, Milton. *Industrial Tax Exemption in Puerto Rico*. Madison: University of Wisconsin Press, 1957.

Tienda, Marta, et al. *Hispanic Origin Workers in the U.S. Labor Market: Comparative Analyses of Employment and Earnings*. Washington, D.C.: National Technical Information Service, 1981.

Tienda, Marta, and Diaz, William A. "Puerto Rican's Special Problems." *New York Times*, August 28, 1987.

Ugalde, Antonio, Bean, Frank D., and Cardenas, Gilbert. "International Migration from the Dominican Republic: Findings from a National Survey." *International Migration Review*, vol. 13 (Summer 1979): 235–54.

U.S. Bureau of the Census. *U.S. Census of Population 1950*. Vol. II, *Characteristics of the Population*, Part 1 (U.S. Summary and Part 53 (Puerto Rico). Washington, D.C.: GPO, 1953.

———. *U.S. Census of Population 1960*. Vol. I, *Characteristics of the Population*, Parts 1 and 53. Washington, D.C.: GPO, 1964.

———. *Public Use Samples of Basic Records from the 1970 Census: Descriptive and Technical Information*. Washington, D.C.: GPO, 1972.

———. *U.S. Census of Population 1970*. Vol. I, *Characteristics of the Population*, Parts 1 and 53. Washington, D.C.: GPO, 1973a.

———. *Technical Documentation for the 1960 Public Use Sample*. Ann Arbor: Inter-University Consortium for Political and Social Research, 1973b.

———. *1970 Census of Population*. Subject Reports, *Occupational Characteristics*, PC(2)-7A. Washington, D.C.: GPO, 1973c.

———. *1970 Census of Population*. Subject Reports, *Industrial Characteristics*, PC(2)-7B. Washington, D.C.: GPO, 1973d.

———. *1970 Census of Population*. Subject Reports, *National Origin and Language*, PC(2)-1A. Washington, D.C.: GPO, 1973e.

———. *1970 Census of Population*. Subject Reports, *Persons of Spanish Origin*, PC(2)-1C. Washington, D.C.: GPO, 1973f.

———. *1970 Census of Population*. Subject Reports, *Puerto Ricans in the United States*, PC(2)-1E. Washington, D.C.: GPO, 1973g.

———. *Current Population Reports: School Enrollment—Social and Economic Characteristics of Students*, Series P-20. Washington, D.C.: GPO, 1974–87.

————. *Historical Statistics of the United States: Colonial Times to 1970*, Part 1. Washington, D.C.: GPO, 1975a.

————. *Survey of Minority-Owned Business Enterprises, 1972* (Blacks and Hispanics). Washington, D.C.: GPO, 1975b.

————. *Survey of Women-Owned Business Enterprises, 1972*. Washington, D.C.: GPO, 1975c.

————. *Current Population Reports: Money Income and Poverty Status of Families and Persons in the United States*, Series P-60, Washington, D.C.: GPO, 1975–88.

————. *Current Population Reports: Persons of Spanish Origin in the United States, March 1975*, Series P-20. Washington, D.C.: GPO, 1976.

————. *Technical Documentation of the 1976 Survey of Income and Education*. Washington, D.C.: GPO, 1977a.

————. *County and City Data Book*. Washington, D.C.: GPO, 1977b.

————. *Persons of Spanish Origin By State: Supplementary Report*. Washington, D.C.: GPO, 1982a.

————. *1980 Census of Housing, Detailed Housing Characteristics*, HC80-1 (state volumes). Washington, D.C.: GPO, 1982b.

————. *Statistical Abstract of the United States 1983*. Washington, D.C.: GPO, 1983a.

————. *1980 Census of Population: Public-Use Microdata Samples, Technical Documentation*. Washington, D.C.: GPO, 1983b.

————. *1980 Census of Population, General Population Characteristics*. U.S. Summary, PC80-1-B1. Washington, D.C.: GPO, 1983c.

————. *1950 Census of Population: Public-Use Microdata Sample, Technical Documentation*. Washington, D.C.: GPO, 1984a.

————. *1980 Census of Population, General Social and Economic Characteristics*. Washington, D.C.: GPO, 1984b.

————. *1980 Census, Detailed Population Characteristics*. Washington, D.C.: GPO, 1984c.

————. *Current Population Reports: Projections of the Hispanic Population: 1983–2080*, Series P-25. Washington, D.C.: GPO, 1986a.

————. *Estimates of Poverty Including the Value of Noncash Benefits*. Technical Paper 56. Washington, D.C.: GPO, 1986b.

————. *Survey of Minority-Owned Business Enterprises, 1982* (Blacks and Hispanics). Washington, D.C.: GPO, 1986c.

————. *Survey of Women-Owned Business Enterprises, 1982*. Washington, D.C.: GPO, 1986d.

————. *Statistical Abstract of the United States 1987*. Washington, D.C.: GPO, 1987.

————. *Current Population Reports: Money Income and Poverty Status in the United States, March 1987*, Series P-20. Washington, D.C.: GPO, 1988.

————. *Current Population Reports: The Hispanic Population in the United States, March 1988*, Series P-20. Washington, D.C.: GPO, 1989a.

————. *Current Population Reports: The Black Population in the United States, March 1988*, Series P-20. Washington, D.C.: GPO, 1989b.

U.S. Commission on Civil Rights. *Teachers and Students: Differences in Teacher Interaction with Mexican American and Anglo Students*. Washington, D.C.: GPO, 1973.

————. *Puerto Ricans in the Continental U.S.: An Uncertain Future*. Washington, D.C.: GPO, 1976.

————. *Unemployment and Underemployment Among Blacks, Hispanics, and Women*. Washington, D.C.: GPO, 1982.

U.S. Department of Commerce. *Economic Study of Puerto Rico*, 2 vols. Washington, D.C.: GPO, 1979.

————. *Women and Business Ownership: An Annotated Bibliography.* Washington, D.C.: GPO, 1986.

U.S. Department of Education, National Center for Educational Statistics. *Digest of Educational Statistics.* Washington, D.C.: GPO, 1979a.

————. *Financial Statistics of Institutions of Higher Education.* Washington, D.C.: GPO, 1979b.

————. *The Condition of Education for Hispanic Americans.* Washington, D.C.: GPO, 1980.

————. *Statistics of Public Elementary and Secondary Day Schools.* Washington, D.C.: GPO, 1981.

————. *The Condition of Education, 1987.* Washington, D.C.: GPO, 1987.

U.S. Department of Labor. *Employment and Training Report of the President: 1978.* Washington, D.C.: GPO, 1978.

U.S. Department of Labor, Bureau of International Labor Affairs. *The Effects of Immigration on the U.S. Economy and Labor Market.* Washington, D.C.: U.S. Dept. of Labor, 1989.

U.S. Department of Labor, Bureau of Labor Statistics. *Employment and Earnings.* Washington, D.C.: GPO, 1973–88.

————. *Educational Attainment of Workers—Some Trends from 1973.* Special Labor Force Report 225, Washington, D.C.: GPO, 1979.

————. *Labor Force Statistics Derived from the Current Population Survey: A Databook,* Bulletin 2096. Washington, D.C.: GPO, 1982.

————. *Educational Attainment of Workers, March 1981.* Bulletin 2159. Washington, D.C.: GPO, 1983.

————. *Employment, Hours, and Earnings: States and Areas, 1939–1982,* Bulletin 1370-17. Washington, D.C.: GPO, 1984.

————. *Handbook of Labor Statistics 1985,* Bulletin 2217. Washington, D.C.: GPO, 1985.

————. *Displaced Workers 1981–86,* Bulletin 2289. Washington, D.C.: GPO, 1987.

————. *Projections 2000,* Bulletin 2302. Washington, D.C.: GPO, 1988a.

————. Middle Atlantic Regional Office. *Mid-Year Report.* New York: U.S. Bureau of Labor Statistics, 1988b.

U.S. Department of Labor, Employment Standards Administration. *Minimum Wages and Maximum Hours Standards Under the FLSA.* Washington, D.C.: GPO, 1983.

U.S. General Accounting Office. *Central American Refugees: Regional Conditions and Prospects and Potential Impact on the United States.* Report to the Congress of the U.S. by the Controller General of the U.S. Washington, D.C.: GPO, 1984.

————. *Immigration Reform, Employer Sanctions, and the Question of Discrimination.* Washington, D.C.: GPO, 1990.

U.S. Immigration and Naturalization Service. *Statistical Yearbook of the Immigration and Naturalization Service, 1987.* Washington, D.C.: GPO, 1988.

————. *Immigration Statistics: Fiscal Year 1988 (Advance Report).* Washington, D.C.: GPO, 1989a.

————. *Provisional Legalization Application Statistics.* Washington, D.C.: INS Office of Plans and Analysis, 1989b.

U.S. President. *The State of Small Business, 1984.* Washington, D.C.: GPO, 1985.

Urrea Giraldo, Fernando. "Life Strategies and the Labor Market: Colombians in New York City in the 1970s." *Occasional Paper,* No. 34, Center for Latin American and Caribbean Studies, New York University, 1982.

Van Arsdol, M.D., et al. *Non-apprehended and Apprehended Undocumented Residents in the Los Angeles Labor Market.* Los Angeles: University of Southern California Press, 1979.

Viscusi, W.K. "Sex Differences in Worker Quitting." *Review of Economics and Statistics,* vol. 62 (August 1980): 388–98.

Von Maltitz, F.W. *Living and Learning in Two Languages: Bilingual-Bicultural Education in the United States.* New York: McGraw-Hill, 1975.

Wachter, Michael, and Kim, Choongsoo. "Time Series Changes in Youth Joblessness." In Freeman, Richard, and Wise, David, eds. *The Youth Labor Market Problem.* Chicago: University of Chicago Press, 1982.

Waite, Linda, and Moore, Kristin. "The Impact of an Early First Birth on Young Women's Educational Attainment." *Social Forces,* vol. 56 (March 1978): 845–65.

Waldinger, Roger. *Through the Eye of the Needle: Immigrant Enterprise in New York's Garment Trades.* New York: New York University Press, 1986.

Wallis, Kenneth. "Seasonal Adjustment and Relations Between Variables." *Journal of the American Statistical Association,* vol. 69 (March 1974): 18–31.

Walsh, Kenneth. *Long-Term Unemployment: An International Perspective.* London: Macmillan, 1987.

Warren, Robert, and Passel, Jeffrey. "A Count of the Uncountable: Estimates of Undocumented Aliens Counted in the 1980 Census." *Demography,* vol. 24 (August 1987): 375–93.

Weeks, John. *The Economies of Central America.* New York: Holmes and Meier, 1985.

Weisskoff, Richard. *Factories and Food Stamps: The Puerto Rican Model of Development.* Baltimore: The Johns Hopkins University Press, 1986.

Weisskoff, Richard, and Wolff, Edward. "Development and Trade Dependence: The Case of Puerto Rico." *Review of Economics and Statistics,* vol. 57 (November 1975): 470–77.

Wilson, William J. *The Truly Disadvantaged: The Inner City, the Underclass, and Public Policy.* Chicago: University of Chicago Press, 1987.

World Bank. *Colombia: Economic Development and Policy Under Changing Conditions.* Washington, D.C.: World Bank, 1984.

———. *World Development Report 1987.* New York: Oxford University Press, 1987.

Wright, Peter L. *The Coloured Worker in British Industry.* London: Oxford University Press, 1968.

Zarnowitz, Victor. "Recent Work on Business Cycles in Historical Perspective: A Review of Theories and Evidence." *Journal of Economic Literature,* vol. 23 (June 1985): 523–80.

Index